10/04

Digital Photography Bible

Desktop Edition

Dan Simon

WILEY

Wiley Publishing, Inc.

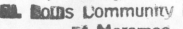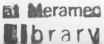

Digital Photography Bible, Desktop Edition

Published by
Wiley Publishing, Inc.
10475 Crosspoint Boulevard
Indianapolis, IN 46256
www.wiley.com

Copyright © 2004 by Wiley Publishing, Inc., Indianapolis, Indiana

Published simultaneously in Canada

ISBN: 0-7645-6875-2

Manufactured in the United States of America

10 9 8 7 6 5 4 3 2 1

For general information on our other products and services or to obtain technical support, please contact our Customer Care Department within the U.S. at (800) 762-2974, outside the U.S. at (317) 572-3993 or fax (317) 572-4002.

Wiley also publishes its books in a variety of electronic formats. Some content that appears in print may not be available in electronic books.

Library of Congress Control Number: 2004103147

Trademarks: Wiley, the Wiley Publishing logo and related trade dress are trademarks or registered trademarks of John Wiley & Sons, Inc. and/or its affiliates, in the United States and other countries, and may not be used without written permission. All other trademarks are the property of their respective owners. Wiley Publishing, Inc., is not associated with any product or vendor mentioned in this book.

About the Author

Dan Simon is a contributing author for *Digital Photography All-in-One Desk Reference For Dummies* (Wiley). He is also a regular contributor to the *Growing Edge* and *Pennsylvania* magazines.

Dan has more than 25 years experience as a journalist and photographer. He began his career as a Navy journalist with assignments aboard several ships, and in Norfolk, VA, Dededo, Guam, and McMurdo Station, Antarctica.

After leaving the service in 1990, Dan worked as a river guide and photographer on Pennsylvania's Lehigh River. During the past 10 years, he's worked as a writer and photographer for several Pennsylvania and New Jersey newspapers, including the *Wilkes-Barre Times Leader* (Hazelton edition) and *Allentown Morning Call*.

His writing and photography have appeared in numerous books, magazines, web sites, and newspapers, including: *The New York Times;* ESPN; *National Geographic Reference Atlas of North American Birds*, Fifth Edition; *Mid-Atlantic Real Estate Journal; Baltimore Daily Record; Tri-State Real Estate Journal; Corridor Real Estate Journal; All Hands* magazine; *Army Times; Gloucester County Times; White Haven Journal Herald; Butler Eagle;* www.greenworks.tv; and http://www.drexel.edu/doj/gallery.asp

Dan is currently working on a master's degree in communications from Drexel University (Philadelphia, PA). Dan holds a bachelor's degree in general studies (design arts) from Drexel and an associate's in computer graphic arts from Gloucester County College (Sewell, NJ). He is also a graduate of the military's Defense Information School (Information Specialist Journalist and Broadcaster and Intermediate Photojournalism).

Credits

Acquisitions Editor
Debra Williams Cauley

Development Editors
Brian Herrmann
Jodi Jensen

Production Editor
Gabrielle Nabi

Technical Editors
Dave Evans
Lisa Simon

Copy Editor
TechBooks Production Services

Editorial Manager
Mary Beth Wakefield

**Vice President & Executive
Group Publisher**
Richard Swadley

**Vice President and Executive
Publisher**
Bob Ipsen

Vice President and Publisher
Joseph B. Wikert

Executive Editorial Director
Mary Bednarek

Project Coordinator
Erin Smith

Permissions Editor
Laura Moss

Media Development Specialist
Kit Malone

Proofreading and Indexing
TechBooks Production Services

Cover Illustration
Anthony Bunyan

Interior Design
Lissa Auciello-Brogan

I usually refer to her as the "Old Battleaxe" and joke that she dragged me to the altar kicking and screaming. The truth is, I can't think of anyone or anything more important to me than my wife, Lisa.

I tease her about being my faithful assistant, but I love her more than anything else in the world.

Thank you, Lisa, for being my wife.

Preface

In 1975, I met my first computer. Well, it wasn't exactly a computer: it was a dumb terminal connected to a computer at the local college. I was one of about a half dozen students at my high school introduced to this desk-sized apparatus in the school basement. Little did I know I was looking at a piece of world-changing technology. At the time, the contraption seemed like one of those interesting but not terribly useful gizmos high school science teachers were fond of getting us to try and learn. You couldn't do much with it, just plug in some simple code to do basic mathematical operations. Since I could already multiply 10 by 100 in my head, I wasn't really sure what the fuss was all about. In the two-and-a-half decades since, I've watched an almost magical transformation. Computers have gone from room-filling multimillion-dollar leviathans to tiny chips that can fit on your fingertip.

The revolution from mainframe to home computer, led by people such as Bill Gates and Steve Jobs, has made the home PC as ubiquitous as the toaster. Even more amazing has been the revolution in digital photography. I bought my first home computer in 1980, a scant five years after that first meeting in the basement of my high school, but I didn't meet my first digital camera until the mid-1990s—an early digital single lens reflex (DSLR) camera with the breathtakingly low price of $14,000 (without lenses). Just a few years later, in 2000, I was able to buy my own digital camera for less than $600. Now, four years after that, a camera with the same capabilities (and a quarter of the size) can be had for less than $150, and it makes better pictures to boot. A DSLR far superior to the one I tested in 1995 can now be had for less than $1000. Looking back, the relatively swift transition from bulky view cameras and their assorted paraphernalia to today's point-and-shoot camera has been truly astonishing.

The speed at which the current change is happening is almost frightening, for it means that photographers constantly have to adapt to new technology. What stops this transition from being completely terrifying is the payoff in increased capability. Yes, photographers have to work harder to keep abreast of changes in equipment, but at least you're rewarded with superior performance. Although film photography diehards bemoan the impact that digital has had on the medium, the reality is that digital photography has rekindled interest in photography for many people. Even better, in the hands of dedicated users, the technology provides incredible potential for learning and improvement. The ability to review an image immediately after its creation while there is time to analyze it and improve upon it is immensely valuable. This alone is worth the price of admission.

Who Should Read This Book?

Digital photography is for everybody. Although this book is geared for beginners and intermediates, there's information here that can help advanced amateurs and working pros considering the switch from film to digital photography.

When you get right down to it, digital photography is still *photography*. Whereas the process used to be divided between shooting and processing in the wet darkroom, it's now a question of shooting and processing in the digital darkroom.

There are some differences in making pictures with a digital camera and making them with a film camera, but the real sea change in photography has occurred in the processing end of the equation. This is in part because while lots of people make pictures, a much smaller number have ever processed their film. The advent of the digital process has made image processing possible (or necessary) for many people who would never have entered a conventional darkroom.

What Hardware and Software Do You Need?

It's difficult to provide such a list for this type of book. If you're a hobbyist who just wants to take better pictures and plans on letting your camera do all the processing, you don't need much at all. A basic computer with a way to move images from your camera to the computer, in addition to a CD-burner for making file backups, is more than enough.

On the other hand, if you're a working pro or advanced amateur looking to move into digital photography and take advantage of all that the digital darkroom has to offer, your requirements are greater. A little later in this section, I provide Adobe's requirements for its latest version of PhotoShop (PhotoShop CS). If you're thinking about getting into digital in a big way, meeting these requirements would be a good way to start.

More than anything else, you need a camera. Beyond that, it would be nice if your computer had some kind of image-editing software (such as Photoshop or Photoshop Elements) and cataloging software (such as ACDsee or iView).

As long as your computer was purchased in the last two or three years, you should have more than enough processing power to manipulate and manage digital files. When in doubt, adding RAM (more computer memory) provides a low-cost alternative to buying a new machine. Any home computer with 128MB of RAM or more is in decent shape to start.

If you want to use the latest version of PhotoShop (PhotoShop CS), Adobe says your system should meet the requirements described in the following sections.

Macintosh

+ PowerPC G3, G4, or G5 processor
+ Mac OS X v.10.2.4, 10.2.5, 10.2.6, or 10.2.7
+ 192MB of RAM (256MB recommended)
+ 320MB of available hard drive space
+ Color monitor with 16-bit color or greater video card
+ 1,024 x 768 or greater monitor resolution
+ CD-ROM drive

Windows

+ Intel Pentium III or 4 processor
+ Microsoft Windows 2000 with Service Pack 3 or Windows XP
+ 192MB of RAM (256MB recommended)
+ 280MB of available hard-disk space
+ Color monitor with 16-bit color or greater video card
+ 1,024 x 768 or greater monitor resolution
+ CD-ROM drive
+ Internet or phone connection required for product activation

Certainly, if you meet these requirements, you are more than ready for anything in this book. If you're planning to work with a less demanding image editing program, or if you just don't expect to process many images, a less powerful or older machine should work just fine.

How This Book Is Organized

This book is divided into different parts. Like most instructional books, this one starts out with simple concepts and then moves to the more advanced. While every effort has been made to be as comprehensive as possible, I realize many readers aren't looking to become professional photographers—they just want to do a better job of making the images they consider important. I've tried to organize things in a way this type of person will find useful. Here is what you'll find in the various parts of the book:

+ **Part I, "Laying the Foundation—Basic Digital Photography."** This part covers (no surprise here) the basics. It's designed to help someone making his or her first foray into digital photography. Here you find information to help you understand the features digital cameras offer and what you need to know to either buy and operate a digital camera.

✦ **Part II, "Taking the Next Step—Photographs That Wow!"** This part is all about becoming a better photographer. Here I cover the methods photographers use to make images people want to look at. The information in this part helps you take better pictures no matter how simple or sophisticated your equipment. It's a roadmap to good photography.

✦ **Part III, "Tackling Different Photographic Subjects."** This part focuses on shooting various subjects, such as people, sports, or the outdoors. Here I share techniques that can help you get better shots, regardless of what you are shooting. I have done all these types of photography for many years, and I try to share the things I've learned during that time. If your goal is to grow as a photographer, trying new forms of photography is a good way to stretch your abilities and learn new tricks.

✦ **Part IV, "Doing Your Own Image Processing."** This part is your entry into the digital darkroom. You learn the techniques pros use to optimize their photos and correct image imperfections. This part is a primer on how to use your computer to make your pictures better. It examines color correcting, spotting and image repair, and how to sharpen a photo and fix exposure problems. Part IV also introduces the idea of masking and selecting areas of a photograph so you can apply an effect to just that one spot. This part also lays out a step-by-step image management process. This digital road map provides a clear path for how to handle your images from the time you create them until you safely back them up.

✦ **Part V, "Photography for Professionals in Other Fields."** I wrote this part to help people who have to take pictures on the job, even though they may not have any kind of photographic training. Since many professions require their practitioners to take pictures, I wanted to provide you with some detailed advice on how to make the best of your photographic opportunities. In Part V, I provide basic checklists to make sure you show up with all the gear you need. This part also provides information on gear that can help you make better photos while keeping your shoots simple and inexpensive.

✦ **Part VI, "Digital Photography Projects."** The chapters in this part fill in a few remaining holes in this book's coverage. This part covers techniques and topics not handled in the preceding sections, such as dealing with reflections, photographing fireworks, and other creative endeavors.

✦ **Appendixes.** You can find some valuable additional information in the four appendixes that appear in this book. Find digital photography definitions and techniques; a listing of some handy tools, gadgets, and gizmos; plus information about new features that two popular image editing programs—Adobe's PhotoShop and PhotoShop Elements—have added to their latest upgrades.

Navigating This Book

I've used some tools to help make this book easier to navigate and, hopefully, easier to read. The following list explains what each of these special elements means so that you can choose the ones you want to stop and read along the way:

 Provides a trick I've relied on as a solution for a particular photographic problem.

 I use this icon when I want to call your attention to an important idea or observation.

 Some techniques or situations present hazards the photographer needs to be aware of. The Caution icon gives you information to help you decide whether getting a photo is worth the risks involved.

 This icon refers you to another section of the book that contains pertinent or more detailed information about the subject at hand. Keeps you from having to read through information that I've already covered elsewhere.

 This icon points you to the book's companion web site (www.wiley .com/compbooks/simon) for additional information and goodies. This web site offers full-color versions of the grayscale photos that appear in the book, links to manufacturers' web sites, and offerings or freebies such as PhotoShop actions or downloadable checklists.

Sidebar

These gray boxes indicate that I'm off on a tangent, but one that is instructive. Sidebars frequently provide insight into how you can actually use a technique; or they show an alternative method or comment in more detail on a potential problem.

The Companion Web Site

My goal is to make this book's companion web site a valuable resource for you. To meet this goal, I've provided color versions of all the photos appearing in this book, links to web sites I feel are valuable, downloadable materials such as checklists, and extra information I wanted to include in the book but couldn't because space considerations prevented it. Please remember that my copyright still applies to the images provided on the web site. Feel free to download these images to experiment with; just remember that they are not available to sell or give away.

Feel free to download my images from the web site and run them through the same processing steps I describe in the digital darkroom section. When applicable, I provide before and after versions of the images so you can see what I started with and what I ended up with.

Further Information

The web is a gold mine of valuable information and advice, and manufacturer and software developer web sites are often excellent places to start when searching for the latest online advice. Adobe maintains a very useful PhotoShop web site you can access from the Help menu of the program itself. This site contains tutorials and links to user forums. It's a good place to turn for detailed information on the program.

You can also contact me via e-mail at dgsimagery@hotmail.com.

I make an effort to answer all e-mail I receive. Give me some time, and I'll try to get back to you.

Acknowledgments

Writing a book is more of a collaboration than people actually know. While one person may do the bulk of the writing, it takes a team of people to see a book from idea to fruition. I've been blessed with a truly outstanding team of people to help me with this project.

First and foremost, I'm grateful to my agent Margot Maley. Margot has been described as "the best agent in the world," and she certainly has been for me.

I'd also like to offer special thanks to my friends at Wiley Publishing. Debra Williams Cauley helped guide me through the shaping and planning stages of this project. Her wisdom and experience have helped produce a work fitted for the needs of today's digital photographers.

I'd also like to thank Jodi Jensen, who has been a real joy to work with. Jodi has borne the demanding task of dealing with the fairly regular stream of questions, comments, and harebrained ideas I sometimes came up with. Through it all, she has been patient, enthusiastic, supportive, and cheerful. In addition, I'm grateful to development editor Brian Herrmann. His efforts have done much to make this book tighter and easier to read.

I further benefited from the help of two talented technical editors: my friend and colleague, David Evans, and my faithful assistant, Lisa Simon. These two have been constantly looking over my shoulder, at least figuratively, to help make sure this book was as accurate as possible.

Several organizations provided access and assistance for both research and photography for this work. The Hawk Mountain Sanctuary, Kempton, PA; Longwood Gardens Kennett Square, PA; Greenworks.tv/Greentreks.tv; and Norwegian Cruise Lines, Miami, FL; have all been enthusiastic, cooperative, and accessible.

Certain companies and software makers have been kind enough to provide me with evaluation copies of their software or loan me their product to make this book as comprehensive as possible. One of these companies, iView Multimedia, has been kind enough to offer a discount on their software for readers of this book. I use their product myself and have no problem recommending it.

I'd also like to thank LowePro, Kaidan, SmartTrax, Extensis, the Digital Imaging Factory and ACD Systems.

On a personal basis, I'd like to thank two hard-working people at the U.S. Veteran's Administration, Louis Namm and Dennis Best, for the help they've given me over the years. They're just a couple of the many terrific people I've encountered at the VA.

And finally, for each of us there is that one person who started us down the path that led to works such as this. For me, that person has been my friend, mentor, and colleague, Sherry London, who has my heartfelt thanks for her part in helping me realize a lifelong dream.

Contents at a Glance

Contents

●●●

Part I: Laying the Foundation—Basic Digital Photography   1

Part II: Taking the Next Step—Photographs That Wow!   43

Chapter 4: Creating Magic with the Right Lens 45

Chapter 5: Going to Extremes: Aperture and Shutter Speed Magic 59

Chapter 6: Expanding Your Horizons: Panoramic and Bad Weather Photography 77

Part III: Tackling Different Photographic Subjects   103

Part IV: Doing Your Own Image Processing   247

Chapter 14: Introduction to the Digital Darkroom 249

Chapter 15: Image Processing 259

Chapter 16: Setting Up a Workflow 287

Chapter 17: Image Management and Archiving 303

Part V: Photography for Professionals in Other Fields   321

Chapter 18: Getting It Together: Help for the Occasional Photographer 323

Chapter 23: Digital Photography for Research and Documentation

Laying the Foundation— Basic Digital Photography

We all need to start somewhere.

For many of us, that means buying our first digital camera and learning how to use it.

The chapters in this part of the book introduce you to the basics. Here's where you can find advice on how to determine what is the best camera for you and also learn what features are important and which ones aren't.

In Chapter 3, you also learn some of the fundamentals to better picture-making.

What You Need to Know to Get Started

Digital cameras are *sexy!* Digital cameras are *exciting!* Digital cameras are *fun!*

If you're one of the many people who has responded to the promises made about digital photography, you may have found yourself lured into considering the purchase of a digital camera. Let's face it, it's nice to be able to take as many pictures as you want for free, and even better, to be able to see those pictures immediately after you press the shutter release.

Yet, for many people, these promises of pure ease and simplicity are left unfulfilled. After they bring their high-tech camera home, they find things are more complicated than they thought. What looks and sounds so easy and fun in the camera ads turns out to be more complicated than it first appeared.

My intention in this first chapter is to help bring the fun and excitement back to your digital camera purchase by giving you some tips on choosing the best camera for your needs.

The Advantages of Digital Photography

Digital photography offers many advantages over film. For one, you can take as many pictures as you want without the burden of buying and processing film. In addition, most digital cameras offer a built-in LCD screen that allows you to view an image right after you've tripped the shutter.

These factors alone make digital photography a wonderful tool for better photography. You can fire off a shot, review it on the LCD screen, and decide whether you should try to take the shot again.

Digital images also offer the advantage of perfect reproducibility. You can make as many perfect duplicates of your images as you want without trouble. This makes sharing photos much easier. You can e-mail pictures to friends, or you can upload them to online photo printers and send folks the URL to the online photo album. That way, they can order whatever prints they want.

Getting a Handle on Digital Camera Choices

Digital cameras have introduced a new wrinkle to the equipment upgrade issue: The lure of this attractive new technology causes you to want to go out and buy new gear. But this same technology is changing so quickly that it forces you to face a much faster obsolescence path than you ever witnessed in the past.

The first digital cameras on the market offered minimal resolution (640 x 480 = 640K), rapidly replaced by higher resolution (1068 x 768 = 1.4 megapixels), replaced by still higher (1600 x 1200 = 2.1 megapixels), and so on. The current high-end crop of digital cameras hits about 6 megapixels for point-and-shoot cameras and more than 10 megapixels for digital single lens reflex (DSLR) cameras. So digital camera buyers, much like computer buyers, have become conditioned to upgrading their machines every couple of years.

Even though you may be tempted to upgrade more frequently, you also get increasingly more bang for your buck as the price-to-power comparison becomes more pronounced. The 2.1 megapixel camera that cost $1,000 when it was first introduced is replaced six months later by a 3.4 megapixel camera at half the original price. Plus, this newer model corrects some flaws in the previous version and tacks on some extra features, such as the capability to record audio or video. So suddenly, that expensive camera is a much more attractive (and affordable) purchase.

The fundamental question, then, for most prospective camera buyers is "How do I figure out which camera is right for me?" The following sections try to answer this question.

Camera Basics—What's Important?

Auto-focus, built-in flash, video, megapixels, built-in MP3 player, PDA, built-in cell phone, TV remote, remote control garage door opener—okay, I'm kidding about the garage door opener (I think). But digital cameras come with so many features these days that it's enough to make your head swim. How do you ever decide which features are important and which aren't?

Answering this question properly, more than anything else, will determine how happy you are with your digital camera. All too often, buyers go for the fully loaded "does everything" camera and find that it's too complicated to use and doesn't make it very easy to do any one thing—including taking pictures—well.

So the first step in figuring out what kind of camera you should buy is to determine your photographic needs. The following list can help you make this determination:

✦ **Output:** What kind of output are you looking for? Most people prefer 4 x 6 prints. If it's been more than a year since you last had a picture blown up to an 8 x 10 or larger, guess what? You're normal. The average person takes a bunch of pictures, gets 4 x 6 prints, and puts them in a photo album designed to hold 4 x 6 prints.

✦ **Resolution:** If you fall into the *normal* category, a camera capable of creating 2 to 3 megapixel images will meet your needs just fine. In fact, it will give you some quality to spare, just in case you do decide you want to get an enlargement made.

 See Chapter 15 for some advice on how you can stretch those pixels even further.

✦ **Hype:** So why all the hype about 4, 5, and 6 megapixel cameras? Well, it helps manufacturers sell cameras, for one thing. And there are some people who really do want to make big prints. If your budget allows for the extra money, buying a higher resolution camera can offer you practical advantages over one with the minimum requirements. On the other hand, if your budget is tight, save a few bucks and skimp a little on resolution. It's okay, you can spare it.

If you are one of the few who expect to regularly produce quality enlargements, then by all means look toward the higher resolution cameras.

Decisions, Decisions: Point-and-Shoot versus DSLR

As prices drop on DSLRs, more and more people are choosing them over their point-and-shoot counterparts. How big an advantage are interchangeable lenses, and are there any other advantages to using a DSLR over a point-and-shoot camera? The following sections compare the two so that you can make the right decision for your situation.

Point-and-shoot cameras

Most people find that a good point-and-shoot does an adequate job. Certainly, if taking pictures at a gathering or an event isn't your first priority, a small, versatile point-and-shoot digital camera may provide all the photographic capability you need.

Even sophisticated amateurs can find high-end point-and-shoot digital cameras, such as the Canon G series and the Nikon Coolpix, that are capable of delivering professional quality images and giant enlargements. Many of these cameras also accept add-on lenses to extend their wide-angle and telephoto range and have powerful accessory flash units available.

These cameras pack a lot of photographic power into small, lightweight packages that are easy to carry and use. This can be a real boon for older photographers. The weight of a heavy camera bag and the stress of handholding a big lens and camera combination can aggravate joint pains and afflictions such as Carpal Tunnel Syndrome.

DSLR cameras

As terrific as point-and-shoot cameras are, they still don't provide the versatility and control available in a good interchangeable lens DSLR.

Through their use of interchangeable lenses, DSLRs provide you with a huge range of options. Most camera manufacturers offer not only a variety of focal lengths, but also provide multiple choices for the most popular lens types. Third-party lens makers such as Sigma, Tamron, and Tokina provide even more options with their lens lines.

With the many lens choices offered by DSLR manufacturers, you can tailor your camera bag to meet the needs of a particular shoot. If your passion is close-up photography, you can choose from close focusing and macro lenses, as well as a whole range of other tools, such as extension tubes, bellows, and add-on close-up lenses (not to be confused with filters, even though they look like filters). All these tools mean that you can take your photography beyond the norm, one of the secrets to producing memorable images.

Figure 1-1 shows an example of a photograph I took using my DSLR and some special tools. I was out photographing the flowers in a springtime display at a botanical garden. Wanting to try something different, I brought out a 400mm telephoto lens (normally used for sports and wildlife photography) and a set of extension tubes.

 Don't forget, you can see each figure in full color on this book's web site at www.wiley.com/compbooks/simon.

By using an extreme telephoto as a close-up lens (made possible by the extension tubes), I was able to create an entirely different look for these daffodils. Such an image would have been impossible for most point-and-shoot cameras, but a DSLR handled the challenge fairly easily.

You can read more about lens choices in Chapter 4 and extension tubes in Chapter 5.

Figure 1-1: Close-ups are usually made with modest focal lengths. As this picture shows, you can make a striking close-up image with a long telephoto lens.
© 2004 Dan Simon

The downside to going the DSLR route includes higher costs and carrying more weight when you're out shooting. Still, if photography is your primary reason for leaving the house, it's hard to beat a good DSLR system.

 Project: **Choosing a digital camera**

Choosing the right digital camera can be a challenge. All too often, camera buyers obsess more over what brand to choose than what features they need. The first step is to think about how you plan to use your camera. For most people, a general-purpose camera will do quite nicely. There are, however, some uses that cry out for more specialized equipment. To help you determine what type of camera best fits your photography needs, work through the following steps:

1. Consider the kind of photography you will use the camera for most of the time. The following list explains some of the types of photography you may want to consider:

   • **Sports photography:** Taking photographs of sporting events requires long focal lengths, fast shutter speeds, and high-speed motor drives, if possible. Although you can create memorable

Continued

Project *(continued)*

action photos without a fast motor drive (five frames-per-second or better), it does make your job more difficult. The Fujifilm FinePix S5000 Z has a 5fps motor drive and 370mm focal length at the long end of its zoom.

- **Nature photography:** Photographing birds in flight and animals in their native surroundings are a couple of the most difficult photographic challenges. Wildlife pros rely on top-of-the-line cameras and lenses costing thousands of dollars. If you're planning to do this kind of photography as a hobby, and you're on a more limited budget, look for a camera with a longer zoom range (preferably greater than 300mm with the capability to accept add-on lenses). Keep in mind, another option popular with amateur wildlife photographers is something known as *digiscoping*. Digiscoping involves mating a camera and spotting scope to greatly boost the reach of the camera lens. Cameras such as the Kodak DX6490 and Canon PowerShot S1 IS offer such capabilities.

   To find out more about digiscoping, see Appendix B.

- **Underwater photography:** Specialized underwater digital cameras are available for the scuba or snorkeling enthusiast. These cameras are either built to be watertight or come with their own custom housings. It's frequently more economical to buy a digital camera specifically designed for underwater photography (such as the Sony DSC-U60) than it is to buy a camera and underwater housing separately. One thing to watch out for is the distressingly low maximum resolutions (1.3 megapixels) some of these cameras offer. Such a low maximum resolution means you can put a lot of images on a memory card, which is no small thing since changing memory cards under water isn't really an option. Unfortunately, it also means that you won't be able to do much in the way of enlargements if you just happen to capture the Loch Ness monster swimming by while on her Caribbean vacation. Even using some of the pixel-stretching options I discuss in later chapters, it's doubtful that you'll ever be able to do any better than an 8 x 10 or maybe an 11 x 14 print.

   You can find more information about pixel-stretching options in Chapter 15.

- **Architectural photography:** It's possible to use a point-and-shoot digital camera for basic architectural photography provided that you can finish the process in the digital darkroom with an image-editing program such as Adobe Photoshop or Photoshop Elements. These programs can be used to manipulate and correct images in all sorts of ways. Keep in mind, however, that photographing skyscrapers on crowded city blocks calls for very wide-angle lenses. Even more important, the lens needs to be wide enough to provide the necessary extra space around the building in order to correct the *keystone* effect. This effect makes the building look like it's falling away from you when you tilt the camera up to fit the entire structure in the image. DSLRs that accept special tilt/shift lenses to control this problem can offer better results than you can achieve with a point-and-shoot camera.

 To find out more about the keystone effect, see Chapters 15 and 19.

2. Think about what, if any, extra features you want your digital camera to have. If you're not planning to engage in any of the specialized uses mentioned in Step 1, then it's just a matter of looking for a basic camera. Although manufacturers hype extra features such as the camera's capability to record video or serve as an MP3 player, you're better off focusing on whether the camera is easy to operate and can take the kind of pictures you want it to. Even if the camera can record video, how good is the quality, and how likely is it that you will ever do anything with that video? Using your camera to play MP3s ties up memory capacity, drains batteries, and is all too frequently a more complicated process than the average person wants to be bothered with.

3. Determine some of the other requirements you have for your digital camera. Here are some of the most important items to consider:

   • **Lens choice:** Point-and-shoot digital cameras come with a built-in lens, so once you buy the camera, you're pretty much stuck with that optic. Low-end cameras may have only a fixed focal length lens or a basic 3-to-1 zoom, which means that the longest telephoto setting is three times the focal length of the widest wide-angle setting.

      Two terms you'll see when looking at digital camera optics are *optical* and *digital* zooms. The optical zoom is the actual physical zoom range of the lens and is what you should really be concerned with. Digital zooms are nothing more than in-camera *cropping* (cutting out unnecessary portions of the image) followed by some interpolation (educated guesses by the camera's software) to increase the image resolution to what you were originally supposed to be getting.

   • **Memory:** Choosing a camera based on the kind of memory it uses isn't a bad idea. When you figure that you might change cameras every two or three years, amassing a collection of

Continued

Project *(continued)*

memory cards that you can't use in your next camera isn't the best decision. Compact Flash cards are the most popular and least expensive, so picking a camera that uses this type of memory is worth considering.

 Caution Some types of memory cards, such as Smart Media cards, require the camera to provide the card controller. If you buy a card that has a larger capacity than your camera is aware of, you have to send the camera back to the manufacturer for a firmware upgrade in order for the camera to recognize your media.

• **Buffer:** A buffer is a form of temporary parking for images that haven't yet been written to your memory card. Without a memory buffer, the camera has to finish writing the image to the memory card before you can take another photo. If you're using a camera with a decent size buffer, you can take multiple shots (important if you're using a motor drive function and shooting a sequence) before the camera has to stop shooting to write data. Buffer capacity is particularly important if you're using a camera that relies on mini-CDs as its memory because the CD writing process can be relatively slow.

• **Batteries:** Does the camera use a convenient type of battery, such as AA or AAA, or are you required to buy the camera maker's proprietary battery, which is usually a lot more expensive? DSLRs frequently rely on specialized batteries that only the manufacturer makes, although third-party equivalents are sometimes available that are cheaper and offer more power.

• **LCD screen:** Low-end cameras frequently come without an LCD screen (see Figure 1-2) for reviewing photos. Although this lack of screen makes for a very inexpensive camera, it eliminates one of the most powerful tools a digital camera has to offer—the capability to review an image immediately after you've created it. It's hard to overestimate how valuable this feature is for improving your photographs. Save money somewhere else—this is one feature you really have to have.

4. Using the criteria presented in the preceding steps, you should be narrowing down your requirements and getting a handle on the features you really need in a digital camera. Next, you need to be sure that your home computer can handle its end of the process. Theoretically, it's possible to own a digital camera without owning a home computer. You can just pull your memory card out of the camera and take it to many of the photo processing centers or home printers that can make prints directly from the media.

Figure 1-2: LCD viewers give you a vital tool for improving your photography.

© *2004 Dan Simon*

Still, that approach limits the benefits of digital photography. Using your home computer to manage your digital images makes the full power of the digital process possible. Your home computer lets you edit, manage, and manipulate your images in a way never possible with film. When considering specific computer requirements, keep in mind that if you're a hobbyist, you generally aren't manipulating files quite as large or as complex as those handled by a professional photographer, so your system requirements aren't as great. Here are some things to consider as you evaluate whether your home computer is up to the digital processing task:

- **RAM:** Photo editing programs such as Photoshop benefit from lots of RAM. The good news is that computer memory is very cheap these days; so maximizing out your home computer's

Continued

Project *(continued)*

RAM (if necessary) won't break the bank. A home system with 256MB of RAM should work for most people, but even less RAM can do the trick, just not as quickly.

- **Hard drive space:** Image files start adding up after a while, and having enough hard drive space to manage them can make life easier. Because both internal and external hard drives have gotten pretty cheap, it's not that difficult to add another hard drive if your system needs one. If you're an amateur just getting started in digital photography, an extra 10 or 20 gigabytes (GB) of hard drive space will meet your needs for a year or two.

- **CD/CDRW/DVD:** You need some kind of removable storage medium for sharing images and for making backup copies of your precious files. Of the three types, don't use CDRW for backup purposes because they usually aren't as dependable as the other two. CDs and the various flavors of DVD can offer dependable storage if properly cared for. They need to be kept in a fairly cool environment away from exposure to the sun. Never leave a CD lying out in sunlight for extended periods of time. Try to buy good quality CDs rather than the cheapest media you can find. There's some debate over the life span of home-burned CDs (which use a different process than commercially made ones), but 10 years is a reasonable expectation. Make more than one backup copy of important images. That's a big advantage of digital imaging, you can make as many perfect copies of a photo as you like!

- **Card readers:** You can transfer images from your camera to your computer (a process known as *capturing*) in several ways. One of the easiest is through a card reader that plugs into your machine via either a USB port (version 1 or 2.0) or a Firewire (also known as IEEE 1384 and iLink) connection. If you're using an older machine, you may also have a serial or parallel port option. A card reader reads the images off your memory card.

  If you don't anticipate capturing a lot of images at any one time, USB version 1 works just fine for digital photography. Serial and parallel ports can also be serviceable if you can find the right adapters or an older card reader to work with these ports. Far and away the best and fastest choices, however, are FireWire and USB 2.0 (USB 2.0 has to go through a USB 2.0 port without any earlier USB 1 devices tied in), particularly if you have a lot of data to move.

  Are card readers the best option? I think so. They're inexpensive, many are compatible with several different types of media so that they should work with your next camera, and they save you and your camera from the hassle of trying to use the camera as a transfer device (usually needing some kind of software). A similar device—the PCMCIA card adapter—can be used to capture images into your laptop computer. This is also a good option provided you have a laptop computer that can use these adapters.

- **Miscellaneous accessories:** There are lots of other nice gadgets you can add to your computer to help with digital photo processing, such as a pressure sensitive pen and drawing tablet and a bigger or extra monitor, but these things aren't vital. Odds are, if you purchased a home computer in the past year or two, it's more than capable of handling digital photography without you having to buy more RAM, hard drive space, or other gear.

Don't be sidetracked by all the extra features and handy gadgets that are available for digital cameras. The most important considerations when choosing the right digital camera are your budget and what you're going to do with the images. As heretical as it sounds, I'm going to tell you *not* to obsess over which manufacturer you choose unless you're buying a DSLR.

The truth is, any of the big name camera makers produce a number of high-quality cameras capable of making great photographs. It's all about finding a camera that's easy for you to understand, feels good in your hands, and has the basic features you need. The story is a bit different, of course, if you're considering an interchangeable lens camera. Then, your purchase decision involves a bit more of a commitment. Once you start buying lenses and accessories, it becomes harder to switch to a different line later. So be sure to take the time you need upfront to determine whether a point-and-click or DSLR camera is right for you!

Summary

Making the move to digital isn't really that hard. It's just understanding what you need a camera to do. Today's cameras are smaller, lighter, and more powerful than many of their film predecessors. Best of all, they free you from the cost of film and processing.

This chapter looked at the basics of choosing a digital camera and tried to help you understand the features that make a camera useful. The bottom line is to choose a camera that is easy to work with and gives you the options you need to shoot the kind of photos you most often want to take. Sometimes people obsess too much about what brand of camera to buy. Relax. Look for one that feels right and will help you make good digital pictures.

Basic Camera Operation

After you bring your brand new digital camera home, it's time to set it up for photography. The process is a bit different than it is for film cameras that don't require quite as much tweaking as digital cameras do.

It's important to understand how to prepare your digital camera because setting certain controls improperly is the electronic equivalent of forgetting to put film in the camera or accidentally loading the wrong film.

In this chapter, I help you get things set up correctly so that you can begin taking memorable pictures right from the start.

Prepping the Camera

Fortunately, the list of adjustments you have to make to your new camera is relatively manageable. Although this chapter goes into detail about lots of possibilities, after you've selected some favorites, you won't have to worry about them again.

Batteries

Gone are the days when a camera could function without any battery power at all. Not only do cameras require power to drive zoom lenses, auto-focus, and auto-exposure, but those LCD screens suck up juice, too. All digital cameras require some form of power supply, most commonly AA batteries. Because these cameras tend to drain batteries quickly, I always recommend taking along a supply of rechargeable batteries instead of regular ones.

Rechargeable batteries come in several forms, each with its own strengths and weaknesses. An Internet search for *digital camera batteries* provides a long list of battery suppliers and options. The simplest and easiest answer is to go with a set of rechargeable nickel-cadmium batteries (Ni-Cads), but there are other viable battery options.

Here's a rundown on your battery options. Keep in mind that battery longevity is based on how many pictures you take and how much time you spend reviewing images on your camera's LCD screen. In other words, your mileage may vary. Heavy users may need multiple sets of batteries to get them through the day (recharging them at night), whereas casual photographers who only fire off a few frames a day might go a couple of days between battery charges.

✦ **Ni-Cads:** An inexpensive and easy solution to digital camera battery concerns. Two sets of Ni-Cads plus a back-up set of alkaline AAs will usually get the hobbyist photographer through a family outing, event, or vacation day.

✦ **Nickel-Metal-Hydride Batteries:** Another form of rechargeable AA battery. Nickel-metal-hydride batteries cost a little more than Ni-Cads, but they aren't subject to the memory effect Ni-Cads sometimes suffer. The *memory effect* happens when you repeatedly recharge a Ni-Cad battery before it's fully discharged. After a while, the battery drops its maximum capacity to the levels you've been recharging them at.

✦ **Li-Ions:** Lithium-ion batteries constitute another form of rechargeable power supply. Not found in AA or AAA form, this technology is frequently used in proprietary battery designs. Li-Ion batteries generally store more power with less storage loss when idle than the other two types but are more expensive to manufacture. Li-Ion batteries don't have a problem with the memory effect either.

Your shooting habits will determine how much battery power you need. If you're going to spend a lot of time reviewing images on the LCD or showing pictures to your friends every time you trip the shutter, plan on carrying extra batteries or a larger power pack.

Although today's batteries pack plenty of power, sometimes a layer of corrosion can build up on both camera and battery contacts. It can be a good habit to carry a pencil with a full eraser, which you can use to clean off those contacts when a set of "good" batteries stops working.

Another power option is a portable battery pack. These tend to provide more power than AAs and also last longer, but they are bulkier than regular batteries. A portable battery pack is a nice option, however, if you take a lot of pictures. These units range from small packs costing about $40 for ones capable of powering a point-and-shoot digital camera, to large units costing $300 or more that can simultaneously power a pro digital SLR and portable flash unit.

Memory

Some manufacturers offer memory cards that are capable of receiving data from your camera faster than others. (Kind of like a 16x CD-ROM versus a

4x CD-ROM.) Depending on your particular camera model, this high-speed memory may be an option for you. Is fast memory particularly important? Maybe, maybe not. First off, many cameras (including some very high end pro models) simply don't process data fast enough to take advantage of anything faster than 4x or 6x memory. If your camera falls into this category, then worrying about high-speed memory is unnecessary.

High-speed memory is also not necessary if your camera doesn't offer a high-speed motor drive function.

So how much memory should you buy for that new digital camera? This is a fiendishly difficult question to answer. Unlike film, where you can just pick up an extra roll or two as needed for special occasions, digital memory costs more and sits around a lot. What may be more than enough capacity for a birthday party or day trip, clearly won't suffice for a two-week vacation. Fortunately, you can purchase additional memory in the form of a memory card, as shown in Figure 2-1.

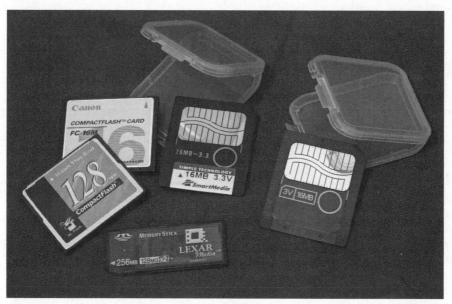

Figure 2-1: Memory cards come in many different types, including compact flash cards, smart media cards, and memory sticks.
© *2004 Dan Simon*

Pros and serious hobbyists generally get around this problem by bringing along a laptop computer or portable hard drive such as those offered by Sima, Nixvue, Mindstor, and others. Certainly a laptop computer is an ideal answer because you not only get storage space to relieve your memory cards, you can also view and edit photos while on vacation.

The challenge is greatest for the family photographer who just wants to take some nice vacation photos without having to turn photography into a project that distracts from the fun. Unfortunately, there's not a lot of good advice for this person. If you have a laptop computer, consider bringing it with you on vacation. This does provide the added advantage of letting you get a good look at your pictures at the end of the day. When possible, I suggest spacing out memory purchases over as long a time as possible rather than buying a full collection of cards all at once. Because memory prices over the long term keep moving downward, this approach can reduce the overall cost of memory. Waiting until just before your vacation to add capacity will at least save you a little money. Of course, this isn't much help if you just bought a camera to take on the vacation you're taking next week.

One other option that is becoming more common is the photo processing kiosks that offer a CD-ROM archive disc. These machines are becoming more common in department stores and tourist centers, so they may be an option depending on how remote a vacation you're planning. Most of these machines accept the most commonly used types of memory (compact flash, smart media, memory stick, and xd memory), and cost about the same as photographic reprints. To use one, simply insert your memory card into the appropriate receptacle and follow the directions on the kiosk. Some of these machines even make an archive CD-ROM for you (at extra cost of course).

Camera Settings

Your digital camera has a number of internal settings that help determine your overall image specifications. Some of these you only have to set once and then can forget about; others you have to consider every time you pick up the camera.

Quality settings

One of the first things to consider when rigging your new camera is making sure its resolution is set to the quality level you want to use. Unlike film cameras, your digital camera gives you a choice of several quality settings ranging from 640 x 480 all the way up to the camera's maximum setting. That maximum may be 1600 x 1200 for a 2.1 megapixel camera to 2160 x 1440 for a 3.4 megapixel camera or even more for higher resolution cameras such as the Kodak DCS SLR/n that creates a whopping 13.8MB file and a 4536 x 3024 pixel image.

Remembering to check your camera's resolution setting before using it is one of the most important habits you can develop. Few things are more disappointing than taking a bunch of photos during a once-in-a-lifetime vacation and then finding out you shot them at your camera's lowest resolution setting instead of its highest. Some cameras default to a specific menu of settings each time the camera is turned back on, so even though you may have set it to your preferences the last time you used it, it's not set that way now.

There is the temptation when you're on vacation to dial down the camera's resolution setting in order to stretch your memory—shooting as many pictures as your memory device can hold. It's not a bad idea as long as you're still shooting at a high enough quality setting to get the size prints you want once you get back home. The problem with this approach is that it leaves you in a bind if you get a great photo and don't have enough resolution to get a bigger print.

Why Is Resolution Important?

The higher the file resolution, the larger the print you can make. If you've ever seen a digital image with jaggy, pixelated edges, the file was printed too big for its file size. Generally, a 1 megapixel image makes an acceptable 4 x 6 or 5 x 7 photo. A 2 megapixel file can be printed effectively at 8 x 10 and maybe even 11 x 14. The size of your print depends largely on the printer you're using and how well the image is set up in an image editing program. The bar is shifting on print quality too. As printer and sensor technologies improve, it becomes possible to make bigger prints from smaller files.

A good general rule is to aim for a 1600 x 1200 resolution image, which equates to a 2.1 megapixel file. This setting gives you more than enough resolution for a high-quality (rather than an "acceptable") 4 x 6 print. Thanks to improved printing technology and better match-ups between digital files and photographic printers, a 2.1 megapixel file can even produce a good 8 x 10 print.

Even if you don't plan on making prints, I always recommend choosing a resolution setting that enables you to make good quality prints. Never mind that you may only want to use the images for your web site or for presentations.

I suggest this for two reasons. First, you never know when you're going to get a remarkable or memorable image. If this happens while you're shooting at a low-resolution setting, there's not much you can do to get that lost resolution back. Second, a higher resolution gives you the chance to crop your image as needed while still retaining enough image quality for effective use.

White balance

Ever wonder why certain film is labeled as *daylight* film? This designation is used to differentiate between films created for daylight lighting, Tungsten (studio) lighting, or infrared lighting. Film comes with various light ratings because different types of light have different color *casts* that can affect the quality of your photos. A classic example is the heavy green cast film prints suffer from when pictures are taken under florescent lighting.

Just because photography has gone digital, it doesn't mean that problems from different types of light have been solved. It just means that the digital photographer has more control over these lighting situations than his film counterpart.

The easy way to handle various lighting situations is to make sure your camera's white balance (WB) setting is on auto, and just forget about it. Most digital camera's auto white balance features do a good enough job of choosing the right setting.

Sometimes though, the *right* setting isn't the best setting. There's no rule that says that just because it's sunny out, your white balance has to be set for sunlight. You can experiment with white balance settings to create different colorcasts that may be more in tune with the image you want to create. When in doubt, take two pictures: one at the indicated setting and one with the experimental one.

Here's one example. Because heavy shade has a lot of blue light, digital camera white balance settings for shade will add some red to neutralize that blue light. Setting your white balance to shade for a picture taken under direct sun will produce a "warmer" image because of that red.

ISO

Next, consider your choice of ISO settings. ISO (International Organization for Standards) is a measure of how sensitive your film or recording sensor is to light. One of the great advantages of digital cameras is that you can change the ISO settings on the fly. Back in the days when film ruled, if your lighting conditions changed, you had to change your film to match. Digital cameras enable you to change ISO settings to adapt to both changing lighting conditions and also to respond to different shooting situations. Most point-and-shoot digital cameras offer ISO settings of 100, 200, and 400, with each increase doubling the sensor's sensitivity to light. Many DSLRs offer even more choices and a greater range of sensitivities.

Light sensitivity doesn't come for free. As you change ISO settings to compensate for falling light levels, *noise* becomes more of an issue. Noise is a problem caused by individual pixels within the camera's sensor misfiring as their sensitivity is boosted. *This problem shows up as individual pixels in the image being the wrong color.* Noise becomes most apparent in shadow areas where, instead of a solid black, you find individual red, yellow, and green pixels mixed in with the black ones (see Figure 2-2).

Generally, you want to choose the lowest ISO setting that gives you a workable combination of lens opening and shutter speed for the kinds of photos you want to make. Remember, changes in ISO setting affect the overall exposure needed to expose an image properly. Your lens opening and shutter speed are part of that equation, so changing ISO affects those settings too.

Choosing the Exposure Setting

Properly exposed photos are the result of the right combination of shutter speed and lens opening (aperture). Most cameras give you a series of choices for settings that achieve different exposure goals. These choices range from ones in which the camera does everything for you, all the way down to full manual control by the user.

Figure 2-2: This image was created using a very high ISO setting (1600). The camera produced a very noisy image, as you can tell by the color degradation in the dark background.
© *2004 Dan Simon*

Here are some of the modes you may have available, along with an example of text that may appear on the camera to identify the mode:

✦ **Manual mode:** You control both shutter speed and aperture. This mode gives you complete control over the image-making process, but you have to keep a close eye on changing light conditions.

✦ **Program mode:** The camera makes all the choices for you. Most cameras follow an algorithm designed to create the best chance of an acceptable image. Because the major cause of rejected photos is the perception of poor focus, program mode algorithms place a priority on getting the camera's shutter speed fast enough to prevent blur from camera shake. Indeed, even in this day and age of high-speed auto-focus, many apparently out-of-focus images are actually blurred from camera shake and not out-of-focus from poor focusing technique. As light levels increase, the algorithm chooses faster and faster shutter speeds until it reaches a speed that avoids blur from camera shake. The program then starts closing down the lens opening, which increases the area of sharpness throughout the image. Program mode is a nice, easy way of ensuring acceptable pictures. If you just want to grab a photo and go back to having fun, this is the right mode for you.

✦ **Tv** **Shutter Priority mode:** This mode lets the user pick the shutter speed and then the camera chooses the appropriate lens opening for proper exposure. There are a couple of ways to use this mode. One way is to use it to set a minimum shutter speed necessary to freeze action. The other is to set the camera to the slowest shutter speed necessary to prevent camera shake so that the camera stops the lens down to the smallest opening possible. This creates the maximum depth of field (depth of sharp focus) possible for the lighting conditions under which you're working.

✦ **Av** **Aperture Priority mode (AV):** This mode is the reverse of the previous mode. Here the user chooses the lens setting and the camera sets the shutter speed. Aperture Priority is useful for stopping action because the user can set the lens wide open so the camera chooses the fastest possible shutter speed. This mode can also work when you want to have exact control over the range of sharpness throughout the image such as for portraiture or landscape photography.

✦ **A-DEP** **DEP mode:** A mode offered by some cameras. This setting is for situations where you need to keep an exact area in sharp focus. DEP modes call for the user to select the near and distant focus points and then the camera picks an aperture (lens opening) setting that will keep everything within those two points sharp. Although this choice can produce nice results, remember that there's no guarantee the resulting shutter speed will be fast enough to prevent blur from camera shake or stop motion. Using a tripod or setting the camera on a solid surface may be necessary.

Many cameras also offer little icons such as a running person, mountain, flower, and head and shoulders view of a person. As explained in the following list, each of these symbols is a code for a certain type of automated exposure:

✦ **Sports mode:** Represented by the icon of a person running. When you press this button, the camera chooses a shutter speed and aperture combination designed to freeze the motion of fast-moving athletes.

✦ **Landscape mode:** Represented by the mountain icon. Press this button when you're shooting scenic photos, and the camera picks settings that allow for the maximum depth of field. It also produces a sharp overall image without worrying about fast shutter speeds because there is little motion to worry about stopping.

✦ **Portrait mode:** Represented by the head-and-shoulders icon. Press this button to activate the camera's auto mode for portrait photography. This program opens the camera lens to create shallow depth of field and throws distracting backgrounds out of focus.

✦ **Macro mode:** Represented by the flower icon. For close-up photography, press this button to activate the camera's close focusing settings and to close the lens down to create the greatest possible depth of field. This mode should also turn on the camera's LCD screen for use as an electronic viewfinder.

Aiming for Technical Quality

Your goal at this point is to create a technically good photograph. This isn't the same thing as a *good* photo, but it is the first step.

A technically good image is one that's properly exposed, properly focused, and has accurate color. By setting up your new digital camera with some thought, you can put yourself into position to achieve this goal.

Proper exposure

A technically good exposure means your image has a complete tonal range from black to white with discernable detail in the shadow and highlight areas. It's this last requirement that can prove a challenge for digital cameras.

Most people making the switch to a digital camera do so from color negative film. Unfortunately, digital sensors don't handle the degree of contrast that color negative does, so new digital users find themselves confronted with blown-out highlights and blocked-up shadows.

Generally, digital sensors compare more closely to transparency film (slide film) than color negative. Just as with transparency film, it's better to slightly underexpose a digital image in order to save the highlights, rather than try for a properly exposed photo. You can always bring out the shadow detail in the digital darkroom using the information provided later in this book.

 See Chapter 15's explanation of exposure correction techniques as part of image processing for details on bringing out shadow detail in your photos.

Exposure compensation

One camera control that helps you deal with such a situation is the exposure compensation feature. This option lets you dial in a certain amount of compensation depending on your lighting conditions. Because cameras vary, it's impossible to say exactly how to set up a specific camera, but usually this feature is labeled as *Exp. comp.* and provides settings in one-third increments. Manufacturers most commonly provide this feature as a control button, or you can find it by navigating through the LCD menu. Choosing negative compensation cuts exposure (increases shutter speed or aperture) while choosing positive compensation boosts it (reduces shutter speed or lens opening).

Choices

For the casual photographer, setting a camera to be ready on a moment's notice is fairly easy, provided you're familiar with your model's idiosyncrasies. It's important to know whether your camera automatically defaults to its original set-up every time your turn it off or remembers its last settings.

You do want to be familiar enough with your camera to be able to quickly set its ISO settings, exposure automation, and exposure compensation settings.

A generation of newspaper photographers ago, the motto was "F8 and be there." The idea was to set your camera to F8 and pre-focus the lens to its hyper-focal distance (the point where depth of field provides sharp focus from just a few feet all the way through infinity). This way, the photographer was ready to just grab the camera and shoot without having to worry about focusing or setting controls. In fact, under such discipline a photographer of 40 years ago could still get off a shot faster today than someone using a point-and-shoot digital camera or all but the best digital SLRs.

 Project: **Setting up a point-and-shoot camera**

After you attach your camera strap, install the batteries, and load a memory card, it's time to configure the camera's controls.

To set up your point-and-shoot camera, follow these steps.

1. Select an appropriate ISO setting for your anticipated shooting conditions. (100 ISO for most daylight conditions, 200 ISO for very overcast or cloudy lighting, 400 ISO for evening lighting or shooting indoors.)

2. Set an exposure priority. Most of us get comfortable with a particular setting that meets our needs and rely on that. Shutter priority (TV) is a good choice because you can set it for a minimum speed that prevents blur from camera shake. Or you can go with aperture priority (AV) and pick a setting that keeps the lens wide open so you're always sure of the fastest possible shutter speed.

3. Set the exposure compensation. The setting depends on lighting conditions, as follows:

   - **Flat lighting (overcast or cloudy days, subdued indoor lighting):** No compensation required.

   - **High contrast lighting (noonday sun, bright indoor lights):** Use about one full stop of compensation (−1).

   - **Back lighting (where your primary light source is almost directly behind your subject):** Use two stops exposure compensation (+2). Better still, use flash (either accessory or built in) to help balance the light between foreground and background. (If you use this approach, dial down the exposure compensation to +1 if your back light is very powerful (i.e., the sun) or turn it off completely if it is some lesser source.

4. Choose motor drive or continuous shooting mode, if available. Many cameras offer a continuous shooting capability. For at least a few, the camera provides this option by dropping your resolution to a lower setting. If your camera does, you may also have to pick a particular

lower setting. There are times when this choice is worth it; just be sure you don't give up too much in the way of resolution. If your camera provides this capability without lowering resolution, consider whether you have enough memory to use this feature. The way you change this setting varies from camera to camera. Usually, it's a user-controlled setting on DSLRs and a menu function with point-and-shoot cameras.

Having a continuous shooting capability is handy for many types of photography, including sports and action. It's also nice for dealing with fast-moving subjects such as pets and children.

Simple, But Useful, Accessories

It's hard to buy just a camera. There's usually at least a couple of items you want to use with it, plus there's the stuff you have to carry, such as extra batteries and lens tissue.

Although it would be fun to write about all the useful photographic accessories the marketplace offers, this is only a 500-page book and it is supposed to provide information about making your photography better and more enjoyable, not necessarily more expensive.

The next few pages are limited to some basic accessories that will help most photographers. Those wishing for more detailed information about the many items, can have some fun by visiting eBay and checking out the many categories of photographic accessories offered there. It's not that I don't enjoy writing about them—Lord knows, I love talking about this stuff—but it's easy to get carried away with this topic.

 This book's companion web site contains additional information on gear, plus links to manufacturer's web sites.

Camera bags

Once you start talking about accessories, it's wise to consider something to put them in. Because even a basic point-and-shoot camera in the hands of the most casual photographer needs extra batteries, lens cleaning cloth and possibly extra memory cards, some kind of carrying bag is a good idea. Still, there's nothing wrong with a handbag, fanny pack or belt pouch for those taking a minimalist approach.

There are tons of good camera bags on the market. Lowepro, Tamrac, Tenba, Billingham, and Domke are just a few companies that make great camera bags, but there are plenty of others. There's enough choice that someone searching for just a simple camera bag may be a bit overwhelmed by all the different styles and options out there. Choices include shoulder bags, fanny packs, backpacks, suitcase style bags, chest pouches, modular systems and bags that swing around to your front when you need a piece of gear and then return to hanging off your back when you don't need access. Oh yeah, you can even get a camera vest that looks sort of like a fishing vest. These items can be quite handy because they have plenty of pockets for gear and distribute the weight more evenly over your body than an over the shoulder bag. An extra benefit is your teenage kids, and possibly, even your spouse most likely won't want to be seen with you while you're wearing it, providing you the much needed peace and quiet you've been craving.

Picking the right bag is a question of analyzing your needs, leaving a little room to grow and making sure you find something that's rugged enough to survive rough handling and easy enough to use quickly.

If you're the type that carries a lot of equipment and your bag contents vary from assignment to assignment, then consider one of the modular designs such as Lowepro's Street and Field system, which uses a combination of camera bags, webbed belts and harnesses with individual lens and accessory pouches. Such a system lets you configure for a light day with minimal equipment and then add on gear till you're loaded up like a Sherpa on an Everest expedition. Tamrac and Kineses are two other manufacturers who make such modular systems.

Lowepro has also come out with a waterproof camera backpack called the Dryzone (see Figure 2-3). This bag has a watertight main compartment that enables you to keep your gear dry even when in deep water—provided you seal the bag properly!

Figure 2-3: Lowepro's Dryzone camera backpack protects what's most important—your gear!
© 2004 Dan Simon

Try to stay with name-brand bags. Although it's tempting to save a few bucks by buying generic or house brands, usually these aren't as well made or easy to use.

Characteristics of a Good Camera Bag

Here are some key things to look for when shopping for a camera bag:

✦ **Top panel with flap.** Make sure that the flap extends down beyond the main compartment to cover the side of the bag at least an inch or two. This way, if you're caught in a rainstorm, water will be directed down the side of the bag instead of leaking into the main compartment.

✦ **Box stitching with an X.** This is a very strong type of stitching that adds extra reinforcement. You should expect this type of stitching at the important weight-bearing junctures of the bag.

✦ **Shoulder strap that attaches fully to the bag.** Is the shoulder strap merely tacked on where the bag meets the strap or does it extend down the sides and under the bottom of the bag? The latter type is much stronger and safer.

✦ **Appropriate material.** Bags can be made from canvas, nylon, leather, or something you can't quite identify. Good quality nylon can be durable and handle the elements well. Canvas doesn't hold up to abrasion as well as nylon, but it hugs the body better and tends to be softer. Leather is certainly stylish, but it's also expensive and requires more care. If you're not carrying much gear and your camera bag is as much a part of your look as your clothing, then leather can't be beat.

✦ **Padding.** There are a couple of schools of thought when it comes to protecting camera gear. Most bag designers pad the bag everywhere to provide the maximum protection. A few (such as Domke) provide padded compartments for the lenses, but no extra padding for the rest of the bag. Many photojournalists favor this kind of bag because it's lighter and conforms to the body more comfortably (important if you're moving quickly with a camera bag).

Flash units

There are times when available light just isn't enough for a given situation. Even though your camera may already have a built in flash unit, most of these are under-powered and inconveniently located close to the lens.

Red eye, the bane of people photography, is caused by light from your flash traveling at a shallow enough angle from the flash to your subject's eyes and then being reflected back into the camera lens. Pro photographers try to get their flash units up high and positioned at an angle to their subjects. This technique not only provides a more natural looking lighting, but it also reduces the likelihood of red eye. Children are particularly prone to this problem because their eyes contain more pigment than adult eyes.

Using an auxiliary flash with your digital camera means you have to find a way to make the two devices work together. For some cameras this is easy. The manufacturer has already considered the problem and included a hot shoe mount plus designed an accessory flash for use with your specific camera. It's not unusual to find this option available in many mid-level cameras on up. DSLRs certainly provide this feature.

Camera makers frequently don't bother with this option for low-end cameras under the theory that people who are buying the cheapest cameras aren't interested in spending extra dollars on accessories. It's tough to fault them for this philosophy; they are in business to make money, after all. Still, adding a flash unit can do a lot to improve your photography for a relatively modest increase in cost.

If your digital camera doesn't offer a dedicated flash unit, you still have some options. One choice is a line of flash unit by Digi-Slave. These are slaved flash units designed specifically for digital cameras. *Slaved* flashes are units triggered by other flash units firing (one reason why smart wedding photographers now use wireless setups instead of photoelectric ones). Although there are lots of photo slave adapters available, those designed for film cameras won't work properly on digital point-and-shoots because they tend to rely on a pre-flash to get information for certain settings. If you try to use a regular slaved flash unit on a digital camera, the flash fires before the shutter opens and its light is wasted.

Some digital cameras do offer what's known as a "PC" connection (not the same as the PC connection that hooks your camera up to your personal computer). This is an electronic connection between a camera and flash unit that surmounts this problem. PC connections are actually provided so these cameras can be used with studio lighting setups, but many older flashes (such as the venerable Vivitar 283 and 285 models) can be fired the same way. Fewer and fewer point-and-shoot digital cameras offer this feature, however, so don't be surprised if your camera doesn't.

If you're going to go this route, consider using a flash bracket with you camera. A flash bracket provides a good solid grip for your camera and flash combination and also provides a way for you to lift your flash high enough off the camera to eliminate red-eye and create a more pleasing style of lighting. The flash bracket is also handy with a Digi-Slave style flash unit.

Tripods, monopods, and other stabilizers

Numerous customer satisfaction surveys have shown that the most common reason photographic prints are rejected by one-hour photo customers is because they're out of focus. Ironically, what's often blamed as a focusing mistake is actually blur from camera shake.

As cameras get smaller and lighter, it becomes increasingly more difficult to hold them steady while you trip the shutter. When you add in the effects of poor technique (such as jabbing the shutter release instead of squeezing it) it's not surprising that blurred pictures are the result.

Let's face it. Some people are steadier than others. What might be an acceptably fast shutter speed for one photographer to avoid blur from camera shake, might not be enough for another. Almost every camera these days is programmed to emit a warning beep when your shutter speed is too slow to handhold, but this feature is activated by the shutter speed setting and not a sensor that evaluates the camera's actual physical vibration.

You can't always rely on available light, and flash frequently isn't enough (no, the camera's built-in flash won't light the Grand Canyon or a football stadium), so photographers frequently have to turn to other tools to get sharp pictures.

Tripods

Professional photographers obsess about tripods. Sure, there are lots of times tripods aren't practical, but whenever the situation allows for their use, they will make a picture better. A good tripod will make for a sharper image and give you the option of maximizing your depth of field. This is important for landscape and scenic photography and absolutely vital for close-up work where shifting your body back and forth an inch two is enough to throw your image in and out-of-focus.

Professional landscape, scenic, and architectural photographers always use some form of camera support for their images unless it's absolutely impossible (see Figure 2-4). Tripods don't work on the deck of a heaving ship, for instance.

Figure 2-4: Tripods make all the difference for nature and scenic photographers trying to capture the beauty of the great outdoors.
© 2004 Dan Simon

A good, massive tripod can hold a camera steady enough to permit the five and 10 second exposures needed for great depth of field at low ISO settings (or with fine grain film). Pros also use long exposure techniques to blur moving or make moving cars invisible (the vehicles don't stay in the scene long enough to register).

There are several things to consider when looking for a good tripod:

✦ **Camera weight:** Just like people, cameras vary greatly in how much they weigh. A tripod that works just fine supporting a point-and-shoot digital camera is likely not to have the rigidity necessary to hold a pro-level DSLR with a heavy lens.

✦ **Tripod material:** Tripods come in several different types of construction. Most are machined from aluminum, but some (the more expensive kind) are made from carbon fiber composites. Both types of tripod can be good if made properly, but the carbon fiber tripods are a bit lighter than their aluminum counterparts. This can be an important consideration if you do a lot of photography in the back country. It's still possible to find wooden tripods, which do provide great strength when properly made, but these monsters tend to be big and heavy. More often than not, they're used by large format film photographers rather than digital shooters.

✦ **Tripod sections:** Most tripods are built to be collapsible so that they take up less room when not in use. Although more sections can mean a smaller tripod when fully collapsed, they also mean more potential failure points and a tripod that won't be quite as solid as the same model with fewer sections. (Many manufacturers offer the same basic design in three- and four-section models.)

✦ **Tripod heads:** Tripods generally come in two parts, the *legs* (usually with a center column that can extend upward), and the *head*, where the camera mounts. Cheaper versions usually come with a basic head of some type, whereas better ones are usually sold as two distinct units because more serious photographers have their own preferences. There are all sorts of heads available, so try to check out a variety of them to see which style you find most comfortable. For many photographers, the ball head is a favorite because you can adjust it many ways while only having to turn one knob. It's a quick and reliable device for repositioning your camera.

✦ **Extension posts:** These come standard with most tripods but there are some things to look for when considering a new unit. Does the extension post have a camera mounting screw on the bottom so you can mount your camera for low-angle shots? Is it removable so you can replace it with a shorter or longer post? Can it take a hook on the bottom so you can hang a camera bag or weight from it to make the tripod steadier?

Monopods

A monopod is a kind of tripod lite. The device is a single (frequently collapsible) support that provides some steadiness for a camera. More often, photographers use monopods to help support the weight of heavy telephoto lenses.

Although a good, solid tripod can support a camera for very long exposures (seconds, minutes, even hours if properly managed), a monopod probably buys you an f-stop or two of steadiness at best, and that's only if your technique is good. A variant of the monopod is the hiking stick with a built in lens screw hidden under a screw-off cap. These rigs are perhaps an f-stop better than nothing. Still, a good solid wall, rock or boulder, will provide an even better support.

Although using a monopod is not especially difficult, it does take a little thought. Here's a technique to help you:

1. Position the bottom of the monopod so that it is braced against your left foot. Your foreleg below the knee should also brace against the monopod to help hold it steady.

2. Brace the back of the camera against your forehead, making sure that your own balance is comfortable.

3. Use your left hand as a brace underneath the camera lens (if possible), tucking your left elbow against your chest. Part of your wrist or forearm should also help hold the monopod taut.

Other supports

Many other types of camera supports are available, ranging from bean bags to mini table top tripods, to clamps, to suction mounted devices that mount the camera on a window or sheet of glass.

Some of these devices work very well. Others are little more than gimmicks. Although it's hard to provide useful general advice for such a wide range of options, here's one thing to consider. Many of these devices are simply too small to properly support a camera for a long exposure. If you're considering one of these items, be careful to find one sturdy enough for your gear.

Summary

In this chapter I introduced you to your digital camera's basic functions, controls, and settings. Additionally, I covered some important accessories and gear. Remember, start out small and inexpensive, and figure out what you need and what you don't.

In the next chapter, I build on the skills you learned here, showing you how to compose interesting photographs and manipulate your camera so that you get the results you want.

Taking Interesting Photographs

People buy books like this one in part because they're dissatisfied with the pictures they take and hope to find some tips or tricks to make them better photographers or because they're new to digital technology. One of the simplest tricks—and a major trade secret of professional photographers—is to take lots and lots of pictures. In 2002, for example, I shot more than 50,000 images, a not especially noteworthy number for a working pro.

When you also consider that professionals carefully review their images and ask themselves how they could have made them better, you start to understand why their images may look a little bit different than yours. The great thing about a digital camera is that it enables you to take lots of photos without the cost of buying a ton of film. Fortunately, it's possible to improve your technique without firing off 50,000 shots a year, but that doesn't mean that you shouldn't begin shooting. You won't turn into a pro overnight, but shooting more images and working to improve the quality of those images will eventually make you a better photographer.

Photographers rely on a variety of artistic tools and rules to create interesting images. In this chapter, I examine some of those rules.

The Rule of Thirds

Some people argue that photography isn't an art, but there's more to taking a good photograph than just pointing the camera at an interesting scene and tripping the shutter release.

Composition is about arranging the elements of a scene to convey information simply or to evoke a mood or emotion. The principles behind such arrangements aren't new; in fact they date back to the artists of the Italian Renaissance and to the ancient Greeks and Romans before them.

Fortunately, you don't have to be an art history expert to learn the principles of effective composition. Instead, just remember that all too often, the mistake novice photographers make is in trying to crowd too much into a scene. Effective composition is more often about refining an image to its most basic element and then making that element leap to the forefront of the photograph.

Over time, some basic rules of composition have been developed to help make it easier for artists to learn the secrets of effective composition, which I examine in this chapter. You can see one example in Figure 3-1.

Figure 3-1: Carefully placed, the model's silhouette draws the viewer's eye toward the glow of an Atlantic City casino.
© 2004 Dan Simon

 Don't forget, you can see each figure in full color on this book's web site at www.wiley.com/compbooks/simon.

One of the most basic compositional tools is the *rule of thirds*, which divides a photograph into equal thirds horizontally and vertically, creating intersections that are key points for positioning important elements in your photograph.

The rule of thirds helps you figure out where to place moving subjects to give them room to move within the image without falling off the edge of the frame. Following this rule also helps you avoid common mistakes, such as placing the horizon line in the exact center of the photograph.

In Figure 3-2 the subjects are moving from right to left. If you place them in the center of the picture, you haven't left them enough room to travel through the image because the mind tends to visualize continuation of motion. Odds are that you've also left empty space behind one of the subjects, which serves no purpose. Placing the runner at the vertical third at the right end of the photo fills space effectively and gives the runner room to move through the picture.

Check out Figure 3-2 to see what I mean.

Figure 3-2: Using the rule of thirds helps you arrange elements within an image.
© 2004 Dan Simon

Rules, however, are made to be broken. One interesting way to break the rule of thirds is to position your subject so she is moving out of the frame. Although this is normally a compositional no-no, positioning your subject in such a way creates tension with the viewer and makes the image look a little different. It's important to make it clear that your subject is leaving something. It can be your teenaged daughter leaving a room (or a conversation), but it's important that there be a reason for the movement. By adding emotional content to your composition, your photos take on a more professional quality and rise above the pack.

Framing

Framing is a simple but effective technique that directs the eye to an image's center of interest. Your subject becomes much more obvious if you find a naturally occurring frame within your scene. As such, your frame can be anything that surrounds your subject much the way a picture frame does, except now, you're looking for frame-like shapes as they occur within the scene. Figure 3-3 illustrates how a frame can be something concrete, such as the archway surrounding Bethlehem Steel's furnaces, or how it can be more abstract, such as tree branches around a building.

Figure 3-3: (Left) This arched window pulls the eye right into the image's subject matter, the furnaces at Bethlehem Steel. (Right) Tree branches and foreground bushes can create frames that draw the eye into your main subject.
© 2004 Dan Simon

The human mind has a tendency to fill in gaps, which photographers can use to great advantage. It's often better to suggest a frame rather than explicitly show one.

Leading Lines

Leading lines are lines in the image that lead the eye in a certain direction. They are a powerful tool for directing the eye through a photograph. In addition, certain types of lines can create a mood or feeling. If you place a line in a photo, the eye is drawn to it and tends to follow the course that the line takes.

The eye's tendency to follow lines is a useful photographic tool. In Figure 3-4, notice how the lines seem to point to the two men walking toward the camera.

I shot Figure 3-4 for a magazine cover. Because I needed to leave room for the magazine layout artist to include the sub-heads on the sides of the page and the magazine's flag at the top, I had to find a way to pull the viewer's eye into the picture and direct it on the two men in the photo. Leading lines let me do that.

Figure 3-4: The greenhouse frame overhead and the tanks on the greenhouse floor create lines that move the eye deeper into the image.
© 2004 Dan Simon

Leading lines come in two basic types, straight and curved:

✦ **Straight lines** can be vertical, horizontal or diagonal. Besides showing direction, straight lines can also portray certain feelings. Straight vertical lines convey strength. On the other hand, straight horizontal lines convey a sense of solidness and tranquility. Diagonal lines create tension and movement.

✦ **Curved lines** lend themselves to the more graceful emotions. One type of curve—the S-curve—denotes both grace and femininity. If you're taking a woman's portrait, an S-curve is a very flattering look (see the left side of Figure 3-5).

Figure 3-5 illustrates different ways to use straight and curved lines in your photographs.

Figure 3-5: (Right) Curved lines, such as the sweep of these reeds, can add grace to landscape photos. Here, the curve also leads the eye through the frame and towards the lighthouse at the other edge of the photo. (Left) The model's head tilts left (from your point of view), whereas her upper body angles slightly to the right and her lower body angles the opposite way to counterbalance her weight.
© 2004 Dan Simon

Horizontal versus Vertical

Turning your camera on its side to compose a vertical shot is one of the simplest compositional changes a photographer can make, yet it's also one of the most overlooked.

Buildings, people, trees, mountains, and many other things in our lives are vertically oriented, yet the vast majority of all photos printed at one-hour photo processors are horizontally oriented.

This isn't a new phenomenon. One of the first photography books I ever read (more than 30 years ago) identified this exact pitfall.

Vertical orientation accomplishes a couple of things. First, because most images are created horizontally, it makes your pictures look different. Second, it allows you to use space more effectively. All too often, in an effort to make a vertical subject fit into a horizontal image, you are forced to zoom out drastically to make it fit. If you turn the camera vertically, you could fill the frame with the subject.

Playing the Angles

Sometimes photographers develop bad habits. One of the most common is the tendency to take photos from whatever position you're in. Most of the time, this means taking pictures at eye level while standing up. You can vary this orientation by taking pictures at eye level while sitting down.

Changing your perspective can really give your images some much-needed variety. Here are some different perspectives you can work with:

✦ **High-angle:** Also known as bird's-eye view, high-angle shots provide detail and perspective completely different from what you normally see. The enterprising photographer has many opportunities to exploit the high-angle perspective. You can stand on a chair or climb a ladder (think about using this idea for a shot of the kids gathered around the Christmas tree opening their presents), or you can take advantage of opportunities to shoot from pedestrian walkways, the tops of buildings, or second-story windows. You can even hold the camera above your head and point it downward. You can always check your LCD screen and delete the shot if it didn't work and try again.

✦ **Low-angle:** Also known as bug's-eye view, this is another oft-ignored camera angle. Low-angle shots are particularly good for photographing children and pets, but not many photographers think to shoot from this perspective. Shooting low-angle shots is really quite simple. You can get down on all fours, lie prone, crouch, or squat. For those photographers with less than athletic knees, one option is to set your zoom lens to a wide angle setting and reach down with the camera to take the photo. Then check your LCD finder to see if the shot worked or not. Cameras that offer a swiveling LCD display can be very handy for taking low-angle shots because you can position the LCD viewer so you can compose your image while holding the camera low.

 Don't be afraid to experiment with different angles. Reach up or down with your camera and trip the shutter to see what works. Thanks to your LCD finder, you can just review an image and decide whether it's a keeper or not.

Figure 3-6 illustrates what a low-angle shot looks like.

The easy way to shoot the photo shown in Figure 3-6 would have been to tilt the camera down towards the dog from a standing position. Instead, I got down on my knees and held the camera almost at ground level so the angle is up towards the dog. Because this perspective is so different from most of the images people make, it stands out. Plus, you get to see what's really important about the dog—his expression. I'd have lost that sense of eagerness if I'd made this shot from above.

Choosing a lower than normal angle can help you create an image with which viewers can empathize. Taking a low-angle photo of a child hidden among a forest of adults gives viewers insight into the child's world and can bring back childhood memories of being lost in the crowd.

Shooting from ground level and pointing the camera straight up can also lead to some interesting images, although judging exposure properly in these conditions can be dicey (hint: turn your flash on). See Figure 3-7 for a good example of this technique.

Figure 3-6: Low-angle shots not only look different from typical snapshots, they also preserve what's important to the shot—in this case, the dog's anxious expression.

© *2004 Dan Simon*

Figure 3-7: I used a wide-angle lens held low underneath these lilies to create this image. Even though the camera was pointed towards a bright sky, its metering system was able to find an exposure that produced a well-lit photo. Notice the translucent petals. Backlighting (putting the main light source behind the subject) flower petals can produce this effect.

© *2004 Dan Simon*

Figure 3-8: A bird's eye view provides a striking look at the multi-deck atrium on the NCL Sun. At the same time, this high-angle viewpoint captures the hustle and bustle of the first day of a cruise.
© 2004 Dan Simon

Summary

Creating pleasing photographic compositions can be easy, yet exasperatingly difficult at the same time: It may require photographers to do things differently from how they're used to doing them. The tools covered in this chapter provide you with some simple ways to create more interesting compositions. As usual, dealing with a mass of new information can be a bit overwhelming. If that's the case, remember, the idea isn't to use all of these tools in one photo but rather to find the right approach for the image you're making.

Go ahead and play with the rules and techniques presented in this chapter. Pick one and see if you can make a series of images following its principles. Then pick the best of the bunch. You might be pleasantly surprised!

Taking the Next Step– Photographs That Wow!

❖ ❖ ❖ ❖

Nuts and bolts.

This part gives you the *advanced basics*, if I can use that contradiction in terms. These chapters tell you how to use your basic tools in ways the average person doesn't.

These chapters show you how to get the most out of your equipment.

❖ ❖ ❖ ❖

Creating Magic with the Right Lens

C H A P T E R

Professional photographers carry and use lots of different lenses. My own lens collection ranges from an 8mm fisheye all the way up to a 170–500mm zoom, not to mention that I have several tele-converters to increase the range if need be.

Good quality point-and-shoot digital cameras have also begun to offer impressive optics. A couple of years ago, a 3-to-1 zoom was about the best you could expect to get without breaking the bank. (The phrase *3-to-1 zoom* by the way, means the longest end of the lens' range is three times the focal length of its widest setting. A common example would be a 35 to 105mm zoom.)

Now it's not unusual to see reasonably priced (sub $500) point-and-shoot digital cameras offering zooms in the range of 10 to 1. That's pretty impressive when you consider there's only a handful of interchangeable lenses that do that.

Yet even with all that optical firepower, lens use is woefully unimpressive. All too often, zoom lenses are nothing more than a gimmick that saves the lazy photographer the trouble of taking a few steps back or a few steps forward. Zoom in, zoom out, never once does anybody ask if maybe there's a better way to use their lens.

The truth is, there is.

Each focal length has its own characteristic and its own use. More often than not lens choice should be determined by what the lens's personality can do for you rather than answering the question: "Can I save a few steps by using a different focal length?" This chapter helps answer this question so that you can decide which lens will give you the best result in each situation.

Understanding Focal Length Options

Whether you're working with the latest and greatest digital SLR or a basic point-and-shoot digital camera, using focal lengths effectively can make your images much more exciting. It's true that the lowest end digital cameras may not even offer a choice; however, you can still find add-on adapter lenses to lengthen or widen your optical reach.

In simplest terms, focal lengths fall into three categories:

✦ **Normal:** Once upon a time, SLRs came with something known as a *normal* lens. The idea was that the optic came reasonably close to simulating the field of view normally captured by the human eye. This normal focal length became the mid-point lens that other lens families were referenced against. Generally, the term *normal* (sometimes called *medium range*) refers to focal lengths ranging from about 35mm to 85mm (in their 35mm camera equivalents). Most basic 3-to-1 zooms include this range and extend out to 105 mm, which is usually considered a short telephoto focal length.

Explaining 35mm Equivalents and the Multiplier Effect

Your entry into the world of digital photography introduces you to a phrase you'll see pretty often: *in their 35mm equivalents*. Unlike a piece of 35mm film, whose size remains constant in every 35mm camera, digital camera sensors vary greatly in size from camera to camera. With only a few exceptions, these sensors are smaller in size than a piece of 35mm film, so lenses that are designed to work at a specific focal length with the 35mm format actually change their effective focal length depending on the sensor they're coupled with.

For example, the Canon EOS D30 has a sensor that's smaller than the 35mm piece of film. Lenses mounted on this camera receive a 1.6x multiplier effect as a result. Say you're using a 200mm f2.8 lens on your Canon film body and then switch the lens to your D30 digital body. Thanks to the smaller sensor, the lens *effectively* becomes a 320mm f2.8 lens (1.6 x 200 = 320mm), which is referred to as the *multiplier effect*.

The same principle applies to point-and-shoot digital cameras, whose lenses are designed to work with the smaller sensors these cameras have. You frequently see two descriptions of the zoom range. The first is the actual zoom range and the second is the 35mm equivalent, because many camera buyers are used to using the 35mm format and use it as a frame of reference.

✦ **Wide-angle:** To one side of the normal focal lengths are lens that offer a greater field of view, commonly referred to as *wide-angle* lenses. This lens family contains several subcategories including super-wide (14mm to 18mm), extremely wide (19mm to 20mm), very wide (24mm to 28mm), and wide (28mm to 35mm). There's another category made up of extreme optics known as *fisheye* lenses. These can provide all the way up to a 180-degree field of view, but can also produce incredible distortion along the way. (Fisheye lenses are named as such because their front element bulges out of the lens much the way a fish's eye bulges out of its body.) Figure 4-1 shows the view through a fisheye lens.

Figure 4-1: A fisheye lens provides a tremendous field of view.
© *2004 Dan Simon*

✦ **Telephoto lenses:** Optics on this type of lens—on the long side of the normal focal lengths—are designed to extend the reach of the camera. Telephotos range from as short as 85mm all the way out to 800mm super telephotos and sometimes longer. There are probably a dozen point-and-shoot digital cameras that offer zoom lenses with telephoto capability of greater than 300mm. Keep in mind that you can also add a tele-extender adapter to increase the range of the lens. DSLR users have even more choices, including *mirror* lenses that use internal mirrors to magnify the image (at some loss of quality, no auto-focus, and a fixed, unchangeable aperture). Mirror lenses are cheaper than regular optics and can be lots of fun to play with, but generally they don't provide the optical quality of a good, name brand lens. One manufacturer, Kenko, even offers an extreme tele-extender with an 8x multiplier effect for point-and-shoot digital cameras.

 Visit this book's companion web site for more information on point-and-shoot digital cameras with extreme focal lengths. You'll also find a link to an equipment maker who offers a variety of point-and-shoot adapters designed to increase focal length.

Working with wide-angle focal lengths

Wide-angle lenses come in a variety of ranges and styles. At the most extreme end of this lens family is the fisheye lens, which is also available in front-mounting adapters for point-and-shoot cameras. Fisheye optics can provide extreme fields of view but also extreme distortion. At the other end, you find the modest wide-angle focal lengths that are a good choice for landscapes, groups and other compositions requiring a little extra room. Wide-angle lenses generally come in 20mm to 35mm focal lengths.)

Sometimes you have no choice. You need to go wide just to fit things in. If you find yourself in this predicament, here are some things to consider:

✦ **Most of the distortion from a wide-angle focal length happens at the edges of the frame.** Keep the most important elements of your composition toward the center of the image (still keeping in mind the rule of thirds).

 I discuss the rule of thirds in depth in Chapter 3.

✦ **Straight lines suffer most from wide-angle views.** The wider the lens, the worse this becomes, so try to minimize straight lines in a wide-angle photo if possible. If you can't, then expect straight lines to curve as they get toward the edges of the image. It is possible to correct these curving lines using software such as Photoshop.

 You can find more information about correcting the distortion created by wide-angle lenses near the end of Chapter 15.

✦ **People's faces can become very distorted (the fun house mirror effect).** This is one problem you can't fix in Photoshop. Either keep people from the very edge of the frame, or pose the relatives you don't like at the edges. (And to my brother David: Look, it wasn't intentional, I just had to put everybody else closer to the center because of height issues, I swear!)

✦ **Wide-angle distortion becomes extremely pronounced if you tilt the camera up or down, especially with buildings.** This produces something known as the *keystone effect* because Pennsylvanians are particularly prone to this kind of mistake. (No, I'm just kidding, *keystoning* describes the way a building seems to fall away from the viewer when the camera is pointed up to fit a building completely in the picture. Always try to keep the camera as level as possible when photographing buildings to avoid both keystoning and supposedly straight lines that are curving. If you can get a few floors up in another building so that you're closer to halfway up the height of the structure you're photographing, it's easier to keep your camera level.

 Visit this book's companion web site for more information on keystoning and to view the color versions of all photographs.

Using wide-angle lenses creatively

Wide-angle focal lengths can do so much more than just fit more stuff into an image. These are very popular lenses for street photojournalists because they create a sense of intimacy between the viewer and people photographed.

Used effectively, wide-angle lenses can also help you catch people unaware. Although that's an easy thing to abuse, it can also lead to some incredibly natural looking photos. I personally hate posed photographs. It's much more important to me to show the reality of an event or gathering. Wide-angle lenses help me do that.

 When shooting candid shots with a wide-angle lens, remember not to violate anyone's privacy. If you're shooting for personal use, you have more leeway in terms of the shots you can get. Working pros, however, must follow stricter guidelines.

Wide-angle views also help create separation between your subject and a cluttered background. Just as telephoto lenses compress apparent foreground to background distance, wide-angle lenses expand it. This can be a wonderful tool for giving your subject primacy, while still keeping enough information in the background to be useful, without being distracting (see Figure 4-2).

Figure 4-2: An extreme wide-angle lens made this flower prominent while de-emphasizing the background.
© *2004 Dan Simon*

I once created an environmental portrait of a high school football player in which I posed him on the sidelines. His teammates were on the field in a huddle, and I wanted to include them in the shot. By choosing a wide-angle lens (a 20mm extreme wide-angle), I was able to make my subject fill up a large amount of the frame, while putting enough distance between him and his teammates. The entire football team was reduced enough in size to fit the small space over the athlete's shoulder. They were part of the image, but not a distraction.

Working with telephoto lenses

Telephoto lenses are tremendously popular, and with good reason. Whether you're trying to photograph your kids on the athletic fields, attempting to catch a bird in flight, or want to document activities that are just a little too far away, these lenses help us get closer to the action.

Just like their wide-angle counterparts, telephoto focal lengths have their own strengths and weaknesses:

✦ **Reach:** Brings you closer to the action

✦ **Magnification:** Makes little objects bigger. This means longer focal lengths can be very effective close-up and macro lenses. Ever try photographing a spider with a short macro lens? Two points to consider:

1. *Squish!* (Trust me, cleaning a crushed spider off the front of a lens element is not good for your gear.)

2. You have to get a lot closer to a creepy-crawly than any normal person would like. If you use a telephoto for macro photography, you can keep a nice, safe distance away from the critters.

 I discuss macro photography in greater detail in Chapter 5.

✦ **Portraiture:** Remember how wide-angle lenses elongate and distort facial features? Telephoto lenses do just the opposite. These optics tend to flatten facial features and make them look much more appealing, as shown in Figure 4-3.

✦ **Tracking problems:** On the downside, because long focal lengths have such a narrow field of view, it can be difficult following a fast-moving subject with a telephoto lens.

✦ **Vibration:** Telephoto lenses not only magnify your subject, they also magnify every little shake and shudder. This means you need to use substantially faster shutter speeds than you do with wide-angle lenses.

✦ **Minimal depth of field:** This is both a plus and a minus because there are times when having shallow depth of field is good. (I'll explain in a couple of paragraphs.) On the other hand, because these lenses provide so little depth of field, focus needs to be perfect. If the focus adjustment is off by just a foot or two, your subject will be unacceptably out of focus.

✦ **Cost:** Point-and-shoot digital cameras with longer focal lengths are actually quite reasonably priced, but they still cost more than those with less powerful optics. DSLR users on the other hand can easily spend more on just a decent telephoto lens than on a good point-and-shoot digital camera with long range. Professional telephoto lenses cost thousands of dollars. (Don't tell my wife. I told her they were on sale.)

Figure 4-3: I used a 300mm telephoto for this portrait of Gina.

© 2004 Dan Simon

Generally you can find point-and-shoot digital cameras with telephoto ranges of 300mm to 380mm for less than $500. An inexpensive 400mm f5.6 third party lens (from manufacturers like Sigma, Tamron, and Tokina) can be found for about $300. A professional quality 300mm f2.8 lens (by Canon) may run more than $4,500 brand new.

Using telephoto lenses creatively

Long focal lengths are an invaluable tool in the photographer's bag. As noted earlier, these lenses can be very useful for macro and portrait photography. One of their strongest benefits is that they're wonderful tools for isolating your subject.

Experienced photographers turn to longer focal lengths for a variety of creative uses:

✦ **Selective focus:** Set your camera to its largest possible lens opening and fastest shutter speed, and then focus on your subject. With the lens wide open on a longer focal length (200mm or longer), depth of field is extremely shallow. If you're framing your subject tightly (say a head shot, or head and shoulders composition), your subject will be in focus and the background will be a blur.

✦ **Compression:** Telephoto lenses compress the apparent distance between foreground and background objects, so these focal lengths can be used to make objects appear closer to each other than they really are.

✦ **Isolation:** Telephoto lenses are wonderful for picking out a tiny slice of a large (and frequently cluttered) scene, as shown in Figure 4-4. (I show you an example of this technique shortly in my discussion of the pier and the pilings in the section "Using Focal Lengths for Artistic Effect.")

Figure 4-4: I used a telephoto lens to create an almost abstract view of this Flamingo.

© 2004 Dan Simon

Figure 4-4 pulls all these attributes together in one image. I was photographing animals at a local zoo whenI came to the flamingos. A crowd had gathered, and lots of people were photographing the flock. We were tripping all over each other.

I decided to back up a bit and pulled out a 170–500 zoom lens, which I used to isolate one flamingo from the crowd, zooming in until I'd created an almost abstract view of a bird we're all used to seeing photographed in a very different manner. This view becomes even more abstract because of the power of the lens to compress elements of an image and make them less three-dimensional. Finally, because I was shooting with the lens wide open and comparatively close to my subject, the background is rendered completely out of focus.

Digiscoping—The poor man's answer to a super telephoto lens

The average photographer either can't afford or isn't interested in buying a professional quality, super telephoto lens. Most photographers just get by with whatever options fit their wallet. How many people actually need extremely long focal lengths for everyday photography?

Well, it turns out that there's at least one group of people that doesn't necessarily fall into the category of avid photographers but that wants to be able to take photos of small objects a long way off: bird watchers.

Many "birders" have a passionate interest in the hobby and see photography as a way to provide a record of a particular sighting. It may be difficult, however, for these folks to justify the purchase of a $4,000 or $5,000 lens when they've already invested a bundle on high-quality binoculars or spotting scopes.

Well, one day a birder tried positioning his point-and-shoot digital camera to shoot through his spotting scope to photograph a bird in the next county. And hey, it worked!

The results didn't match what you could get from even a lower quality telephoto lens. But they were encouraging enough that the same inventive types who gave us pine cones smeared with peanut butter as do-it-yourself bird feeders have gotten better and better at making their cameras and bird-viewing optics work together. The result is known as *digiscoping*, which the birding community decided sounds a lot better than *sticking a point-and-shoot digicam up next to a spotting scope*.

The process of mating camera and binocular or scope has become more refined. Top practitioners get some amazing images these days, at least of birds at rest.

Many individuals have machined adapters to hold the camera in position and make it easier to swing out of the way when they need to refocus the spotting scope. This technique has grown in popularity so that at least one company now manufactures these adapters.

 You can find out more about setting up your camera for digiscoping, as well as links to other digiscoping information, in Appendix B on this book's companion web site at www.wiley.com/compbooks/simon.

Thinking Outside the Box with Focal Lengths

Lens choice becomes a key part of the creative process once you start to understand the way each focal length can be used. Because each type of focal length produces a specific sort of effect, it's possible to make your lens choice a prime factor in the way a photograph looks.

This is where that old saying "the camera doesn't lie" really gets shown to be misleading. You can photograph the same subject with two different lenses and create two very different photographs.

One day the postman arrived and brought me two very special bundles of joy: a 300mm f4 telephoto and a 14mm f2.8 extreme wide-angle lens.

Of course, the first thing any sensible photographer does when acquiring new equipment is play with it. (What? You think I'm any different than you?). Needless to say, I needed something to photograph. Spotting our Maine Coon cat, Smudger, resting on his kitty condo (his wonderfully soft fur provides a great lens test), I put both lenses to work. Figure 4-5 shows the results of my experimentation.

Figure 4-5: Two views of our cat, Smudger. Left: Shot with a 14mm wide-angle lens. Right: Shot with a 300mm telephoto lens.
© 2004 Dan Simon

At the time of the photo, Smudger was only about an inch or two from the front lens element. Cats have a tendency to want to sniff the front of the lens. Anticipate this, get the shot, and then back off before you end up cleaning nose prints off your brand new lens.

I shot the image on the right from a safe distance a few minutes later with the 300mm telephoto lens. Even though it's the same cat (no make-up, no tricks with the hair brush), the images and the moods the two photos evoke are remarkably different.

I knew before I made these photos that I would get the results I did. This is simply because any telephoto lens compresses facial features in a flattering sort of way and any wide-angle lens (particularly the extreme versions) distorts facial features, especially when used close to your subject.

Using focal lengths creatively

Now that you're aware that lens choice makes a difference in how a subject can look in a photograph, here's how to use that knowledge to your advantage.

Telephoto lenses compress things. Wide-angle lenses expand them. Place two people side by side but about 10 feet apart from front to back. If you photograph them with a 200mm telephoto lens, for example, the subjects look like they're much closer together. If you photograph them with a 20mm wide-angle lens, on the other hand, they appear as if they're much farther apart.

Telephoto lenses

Telephoto lenses are a good choice for portraiture because their ability to compress elements of a composition flattens facial features making people look more attractive.

Telephoto lenses also provide less depth of field, making it easier to blur the background completely out of focus and to isolate your subject from a distracting background. (This trick works better with DSLR lenses than point-and-shoot telephoto lenses because DSLR lenses are so physically small that their tiny lens openings produce greater depth of field.)

Wide-angle lenses

It's difficult to produce pleasing traditional style portraits with a wide-angle lens because of the type of distortion created by these optics. Because you need to get very close to your subject to fill the frame, the parts of the face toward the edges of the frame become distorted in a most unflattering manner.

Of course, for certain family members, this can be the perfect way to photograph them. I have a couple of nephews who are pretty goofy. Photographing them up close with an extreme wide-angle lens as they mug for the camera captures their personalities perfectly.

Using focal lengths for artistic effect

Sometimes a given focal length can be used strictly for its artistic effect. Each category of lens—fisheye, wide-angle, normal, telephoto, and super telephoto— plus all the zoom lens variations, has its own meaningful characteristics.

Telephoto lenses tend to compress elements of a scene, making them look closer together than they really are. Because these lenses magnify and isolate, they can be wonderful tools for making reality look a little bit different.

Red Bank Nation Battlefield is located in the little town of National Park, N.J. Site of a Revolutionary War fort that defended the Delaware River and located across from Philadelphia, the battlefield is an interesting local site for photographers and other artists. People like to stop by here to enjoy the beautiful sunsets, watch ships and boats navigate the river, and sometimes catch a glimpse of local wildlife such as the occasional Great Egret fishing along the riverbank or the Canadian Geese flying overhead.

While working the park one evening, I began photographing an observation pier at the water's edge. I thought the combination of pier, pilings, water, and late-day light had some interesting possibilities. Taking advantage of the light from a beautiful sunset, I started exploring the compositional possibilities of the scene. Figure 4-6 shows one of my first images, made with a 28mm wide-angle lens.

Figure 4-6: Pier on the Delaware River shot with a 28mm wide-angle lens.
© 2004 Dan Simon

Although I liked this image, I knew I needed to keep exploring. One habit that good photographers develop is to mine a scene to its fullest. It's often a mistake to create only one composition, even if you do come up with a great shot. There's frequently more than one interesting image to be found in a scene like this. You just have to take some time to study your surroundings and consider the possibilities that different focal lengths might offer.

The process of creating winning photos involves walking around a scene and considering it from different angles and directions. It also means trying different focal lengths, both from the same distance, and also from other distances in order to take advantage of various lens characteristics.

In the case of the pier, I was drawn to the two pilings in the water. Switching from wide-angle to telephoto, I framed a tightly composed image of just the two pilings with a 300mm telephoto lens (a focal length increasingly available in point-and-shoot digital cameras these days or achievable by using an add-on tele-extender). My camera was mounted on a tripod. Shooting with my camera set to 400 ISO, I chose a shutter speed of 1/90th of a second and an aperture of f2.8, giving the fastest possible shutter speed under the conditions. This tight composition of two pilings in the Delaware River makes the objects look closer together than they really are due to the telephoto lens's ability to compress foreground depth. This same characteristic also made the ripples in the water seem closer. The result is shown in Figure 4-7. Although this image is certainly different from others I shot that day, I wasn't that happy with it. I decided to try something different.

Figure 4-7: Pilings in the water shot with a 300mm telephoto lens at 1/90th of a second.
© 2004 Dan Simon

Choosing the fastest possible shutter speed with a long telephoto lens helps reduce the likelihood of blur from camera shake. Because I was using a tripod, I had the luxury of picking very slow shutter speeds. (Keep in mind, tripods aren't magic. Shooting with a tripod still requires excellent technique.) I decided to try a shot with a very small aperture and very slow shutter speed to see how that would turn out.

 See Chapter 6 for more detailed information about proper tripod technique.

For my next attempt, I set my camera controls to a shutter speed of one full second, stopping down my lens to f19 and leaving my ISO settings unchanged. By shooting at a slower shutter speed, I was able to create an image that is rather impressionistic in effect. Because the shutter was held open so long (a second is a very long time in photographic terms), the movement of the water blurred and became indistinct, as did the shadow from the pilings. Although you can't tell it from this grayscale image, the water picked up the blues and reds from the sunset adding some nice color as well. Figure 4-8 shows the result.

 You can see a color version of this image later in the book in the special color insert section. And don't forget that the full-color versions of all the photographs in this book can be viewed on this book's companion web site at www.wiley.com/compbooks/simon.

I felt that this last image was much more interesting than the earlier shots, and I decided that I was satisfied with this particular element of the waterfront. I was working during a period of rapidly changing light, so it was important to work quickly and move from composition to composition.

Figure 4-8: Pilings in the water, shot at a shutter speed of one full second.
© *2004 Dan Simon*

Back when photographers had to worry about film costs and processing expenses, it was normal to be conservative while taking photos. Digital cameras make it a lot easier to try extra shots because there's no added cost. You can take advantage of this by making an effort to create the same photo several times trying different focal lengths each time.

Experiment. As you do, you'll learn more and more about what a focal length does and how you can make it work for you.

Summary

Lens choice is one of the basic elements of photographic composition. Modern optics are amazingly versatile and capable. They can do so much more than zoom in close or back out wide; they can become an important tool in your creative arsenal. You don't have to spend thousands of dollars on a lens for it to have a huge impact on the quality of your photographs.

Going to Extremes: Aperture and Shutter Speed Magic

Many amateur photographers measure success by properly exposed images.

Stop that!

At some point, proper exposure should be a given and not a goal. Taking the next step as a photographer means it's time to exert more control over the image-making process. After you determine the necessary settings for correct exposure, the next thing to consider is how to manipulate those settings to achieve your photographic vision.

Digital cameras offer photographers great control over the image-making process. Not only can you shift shutter speed and aperture controls as needed, but you can also change ISO settings from image to image. If a shot requires greater depth of field than conditions allow, you can dial up a higher ISO setting and gain an extra f-stop or two. If there's too much depth of field for a desired effect, dial down your ISO setting and lose an f-stop or two.

You should always have some understanding of why you're using a certain aperture or shutter speed combination. It can be as vague as making sure you have a fast enough shutter speed to stop action or a wide enough aperture to throw the background out of focus, but you should still exercise some logic when choosing your settings.

In this chapter, I show you how to get the most out of your camera by manipulating shutter speed and aperture settings.

Getting the Most from Your Camera

Many people think that photography documents reality; but in truth, it only captures incredibly brief moments. How many tasks do you perform in your everyday life that can be measured in **1/30** of a second? Yet **1/30** of a second is considered a *slow* shutter speed in photographic terms.

One of the greatest modern photographers, Henri Cartier Bresson, is best known for expressing the need to capture the *decisive moment*—the split second when action is at its peak and emotion at its most intense. Part of photography's challenge is to recognize the exact moment to create a photograph. This section helps you understand shutter speed and your camera's response so that you can fire off the shot at precisely the right moment.

Documenting that magic moment is in part a function of how long your camera's shutter remains open. Learning to recognize when to favor one extreme over another can lead to dramatic impact in your images.

Speeding up your camera's response time

Before you consider how to use shutter speeds most effectively, you need to know how to make your camera respond to your needs.

Modern cameras (both film and digital) have to accomplish an amazing number of tasks before the shutter fires. They need to take light meter readings, make auto-exposure settings, and lock auto-focus in a split second. In addition, digital cameras often add another step. If you're using a micro-drive as your media (as your "digital film"), you're working with a miniature computer hard drive. Its micro-drive platters (which receive the image data) need to be spun up to the proper operating speed for recording data.

The time necessary for your camera to accomplish all these tasks is known as *shutter lag*. It's the reason why nothing happens when you first press the shutter button. Depending on your camera, there are usually some things you can do to compensate for shutter lag.

Some cameras allow you to press the shutter button halfway down to activate many of the systems just mentioned. If your camera has this functionality, it's wise to develop the habit of pressing the shutter button halfway shortly before you anticipate taking a photo. Be mindful that this technique drains your batteries faster, so be prepared with extra batteries.

Another way to make your camera more responsive is to *pre-focus* it. This trick resulted in sharp images long before the advent of auto-focus, and it still increases the odds of getting an in-focus shot—even with the best auto-focus systems.

Pre-focusing works with almost any type of digital camera. Simply focus the camera on the spot where you anticipate the action will happen. Although this technique may not give you the perfect shot every time, at least you give your camera a head start on focusing. This technique helps your camera lock focus faster. These are the kinds of tricks pros use to get the most out of their gear. I've certainly relied on them for many of my favorite photos.

After you tweak your camera's responsiveness, you're ready to concentrate on getting the shot.

Selecting the right shutter speed

Perhaps it's overkill, but most cameras offer a broad range of shutter speeds, from as much as 30 seconds to as fast as thousandths of a second. Who really needs a 10-second exposure, or **1/2000** of a second, for that matter?

You do.

These extremes make it possible to create images that stand out. Here are some examples of how to use extreme shutter speeds.

Slow shutter speeds:

✦ **Moving water:** Long exposures give moving water a beautiful spun glass texture. Set your camera up on a tripod or stable surface and rig your camera for a five-second exposure or longer. You can choose your lowest ISO setting and use neutral density filters to block light so you can get to the slow shutter speed.

 If you're photographing water in the shade, consider using a warming filter to get rid of some of the excess blue light.

✦ **Fireworks:** A shutter speed measured in seconds can give your camera's sensor time to record several good bursts, creating a spectacular image, as in Figure 5-1.

 Don't forget, you can see each figure in full color on this book's web site at www.wiley.com/compbooks/simon.

✦ **Removing cars and people:** With long exposures, moving objects aren't in the scene long enough to register as part of the image. Before Photoshop, photographers used very long exposures to remove people and moving cars from their images.

✦ **Ribbons of light:** Find a busy roadway and set your camera up on a tripod. Set up for a long exposure and the passing vehicles' headlights and taillights register in the image as ribbons of colored light.

Fast shutter speeds:

✦ **Moving water:** Extremely fast shutter speeds can also create interesting effects when shooting moving water. Here the tiny fraction of a second the shutter remains open can freeze individual water droplets into a crystalline spray, or capture a waterfall as it plunges over a cliff.

Figure 5-1: To achieve spectacular images of fireworks, consider using a long exposure, such as the three-second exposure that produced this image.

© 2004 Dan Simon

✦ **Freezing motion:** Extremely fast shutter speeds stop motion. Often, this doesn't result in a spectacular image, but you can use fast shutter speeds to your advantage. You can freeze an athlete's hair flying through the air or freeze a ball in mid-flight as it approaches an athlete.

Choosing a shutter speed that's fast enough to freeze most of your subject, but still slow enough to blur parts of it (such as hands or feet), is one of the trickiest ways to photograph motion. Still, this kind of shot does much to give a feeling of movement to a photo.

Generally, a shutter speed between **1/60** and **1/90** of a second is a good starting point for attempting a blurred extremities image, but it depends on what subject you're shooting.

A variation of the slow shutter-partial frozen action approach is called *panning*. When shooting a panning shot, you follow your subject with your camera as it moves through a scene. Besides moving your camera, add a slow enough shutter speed (which is dependent on how fast your subject is moving) so the shutter remains open long enough to blur the background. You've just created an image in which your subject is sharp and the background is blurred, giving a sense that your subject is moving rapidly.

Without knowing specifics of the shot, it's hard to quantify what shutter speed you should use, but here are some examples to consider:

✦ **Jogger:** Experiment with shutter speeds ranging from 1/30th to 1/60th of a second.

✦ **Cyclist moving quickly:** Try 1/30th to 1/125th of a second.

✦ **Automobile moving at normal driving speeds:** Try 1/30th to 1/125th of a second.

✦ **Automobile moving at highway speeds:** Try 1/125th to 1/250th of a second.

✦ **Automobile racing:** Try 1/250th to 1/500th of a second.

This isn't the kind of photography where you shoot once and figure you've nailed it. It takes trial and error and a willingness to waste shots (something that's easier to do with a digital camera).

Take some practice swings first. In other words, practice pivoting the camera and your upper body around as you follow your subject. Remember, you're going to have to press the shutter button during your pivot, so you want this motion to be as smooth as possible.

Accept the fact that you might have to take 30 pictures to get one good one with this technique. It can be worth it because that one good shot will be so different than all the other photos you take.

Making your aperture selection work for you

The terms *F-stop* and *aperture* are used interchangeably to describe the same thing: how much the lens opens to let light hit the camera's sensor. This is the second part of the relationship that reads *shutter speed + f-stop = exposure*.

In simple terms, the correct combination of shutter speed and lens opening produces the correct exposure. From a purely technical standpoint, you need a value of X for a proper exposure; if your shutter speed and aperture add up to X, you've got a good exposure.

Achieving proper exposure is a minimal accomplishment for the creative photographer, particularly with today's sophisticated digital cameras. The creative part of the process comes when the photographer decides on a certain combination of shutter speed and aperture that achieves proper exposure and also takes advantage of the nuances the two controls offer. Shutter speeds offer the ability to freeze or blur motion, and f-stops offer the ability to control *depth of field*.

Depth of field is an issue that many novice photographers have trouble grasping. Even though the photograph is a two-dimensional image, the scene depicted within it represents a three-dimensional world. The apparent distance from foreground to background is the image's depth of field. The range of apparent sharpness from foreground to background is determined by the size of the lens opening (the aperture or f-stop). Use a large lens opening, and the range of sharpness is minimal. This is described as "shallow depth of field" because only a small range of foreground to background area will be sharply focused. Use a small lens opening, and the range of apparent sharpness will be much greater.

Keeping the entire image area sharp from foreground to background depends entirely on your choice of aperture setting. The smaller the lens opening, the sharper the photograph's focus is from foreground to background.

Aperture sizes are determined by dividing the focal length of the lens by a particular lens opening. As the lens openings get smaller, the f-stop number increases, hence larger f-stop numbers translate to smaller lens openings.

For example, most high-end lenses offer great light-gathering capabilities. These lenses frequently offer a maximum lens opening of f2.8. As you close down the size of the lens opening (an action referred to as "stopping down") the lens opening gets smaller, whereas its f-stop designation gets larger. A normal sequence goes f2.8, f4, f5.6, f8, f11, f16, f22. Math aficionados will likely recognize this as a logarithmic progression.

Understanding that a larger lens opening results in a shallower depth of field, and a smaller lens opening provides greater depth of field, provides the photographer with a useful set of tools for creative control.

If you want the entire scene sharp from foreground to background, choose a small lens opening (large f-stop number, such as f11 or f16). Figure 5-2 illustrates what I mean.

If you're trying to photograph a subject within a cluttered scene and want to isolate your subject from everything else, go with a large lens opening and focus precisely on your subject to throw the background out of focus.

There are a couple of focusing options that you can use, *zone* and *selective* focusing, and they are described in the following two sections.

Zone focusing

This technique calls for you to choose a fast enough shutter speed to avoid camera shake, while choosing the smallest possible f-stop to maximize depth of field. Then you set the lens focus point to an approximate mid-point distance representing how far away you think your subject might be.

Thanks to the depth of field created from the small lens opening, you'll have a zone both before and behind your focusing point that will be in acceptably sharp focus.

I use zone focusing a lot at parties, proms, and other get-togethers where a lot of people are interacting. Because I'm usually employed to get candid shots, I don't want to tip off my subjects that I'm about to take their photo. Instead, I set my camera up with a fairly wide-angle lens, choose an aperture around f8, and pre-focus my camera to a distance of about five feet so that everything from three feet to 10 feet is in focus. As I walk around, I just point my camera and trip the shutter. This system works much faster than hoping my camera's auto-focus system can acquire a subject and lock focus before people realize I'm trying to take their picture.

Figure 5-2: To achieve maximum depth of field, I used a 1/90 shutter speed and an f9.5 aperture.
© 2004 Dan Simon

 You can find information on a more extreme form of zone focusing using a hyper-focal point in Chapter 11.

Selective focus

Selective focus is a popular technique for portrait photography and it revolves around minimizing depth of field in order to focus the eye on a specific subject.

Several factors are involved in making selective focus work properly:

1. **Pick a longer focal length.** Some lenses have more inherent depth of field than others. Longer lenses, such as telephotos, have much less inherent depth of field than wide-angle lenses.

2. **Set your aperture to its widest possible opening** to reduce depth of field.

3. **Focus as tightly as you can** while still creating an effective composition. The closer your focusing distance, the shorter the area of sharp focus, which maximizes the selective focus effect. Figure 5-3 shows two examples of selective focus.

Figure 5-3: Two images of the same scene reveal how selective focus works: The stop sign is the focusing point of the image on the left, whereas in the image on the right, the focusing point is the large cog in the foreground.
ⓒ *2004 Dan Simon*

Lenses have sweet spots. For most camera lenses, the sweet spot is two f-stops past the maximum aperture. Although it's not a hard and fast rule to try and hit this particular aperture, it's useful to have a reason for deviating from it.

Getting Close to Your Subject

Getting up close to your subject can open up a whole new world of photography. Although true *macro* photography involves photographing very small objects from one-third of their true size to life size, close-up photography isn't quite so far reaching.

Many cameras and lenses offer a close-focusing capability rather than true macro, even though they may be called macro lenses. (Oh gee, a manufacturer stretched the truth a little about their product—what a surprise!).

This close-focusing capability is still valuable, even if it isn't a true macro. Photographers encounter many opportunities to create tight compositions, such as the ones listed here:

✦ **Scrapbook items:** You have many opportunities during a vacation or family event to capture perfect scrapbook details. During a cruise I took with my wife, we received plates of goodies (chocolates, canapes, pate) every afternoon as gifts from the staff, and we'd photograph each plate and its accompanying card. You can also get close-ups of interesting details unique to the environment you're in. For example, if you're on a ship or a train, close-ups of fixtures or machinery can provide interesting details to go with overall views. You can also record such things as place settings or decorations at weddings and birthday parties. Heirloom jewelry and other objects are often displayed at family reunions and these also make good subjects for this kind of photography.

✦ **Signs and markers:** You can use your camera to record the signs and markers that denote historical sights. It's a cheap and easy way to get such information and you can use such images later on as a title slide in a multimedia presentation or a cover image for a photo album about your trip. This also makes your camera a handy note-taking device!

> **Tip** For best results, make sure to level your camera on the same plane as the sign to keep the entire sign in focus.

✦ **Interesting flowers and plants:** Interesting flora is quite often all around you. These plants can be too delicate to move (not to mention that it is often considered unethical or illegal to take the plant with you) so photograph them instead.

> **Tip** Try using a reflector or diffuser to improve lighting when shooting plants, otherwise it's easy to end up with blown out highlights (pure white spots where there should be some detail) or blocked up shadows (too dark shadow areas).

✦ **Family events:** There are many things at family get-togethers you can shoot close up. Photograph place settings and floral arrays at weddings. Take close-ups of party invitations. If circumstances permit, shoot the bride's bouquet or ring bearer's pillow. If you're at a birthday party, close ups of the writing on the cake, shots of the wrapped presents, or photos of the festive decorations always make for nice pictures. In Figure 5-4, I tried to create a tight composition to show the folds and texture of the holiday bow and the snow. I also tried to shoot at the same level as the bow instead of pointing the camera down from a standing position.

✦ **People:** Create a unique portrait by getting in close and showing someone's face. Photographers have a saying: "Ears don't show emotion!" Although this doesn't work for every portrait (it can be very unflattering if you're not careful) sometimes, it can make for a revealing or charming image, as shown in Figure 5-5. This works well with children and can produce wonderful images with the rich life-experienced faces of the elderly, but tends to be brutally honest with those of us who have middle-aged faces.

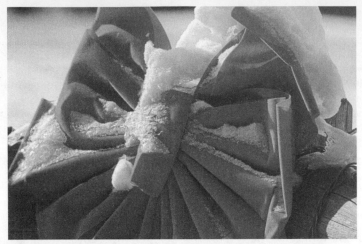

Figure 5-4: Creating a tight composition and shooting at the same level as your subject results in a memorable, unique photo of a holiday present.
© *2004 Dan Simon*

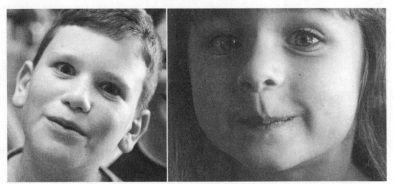

Figure 5-5: (Left) The extreme focal length creates an exaggerated perspective that helps show my nephew, Allan's, over-the-top personality. (Right) By using a telephoto lens, I was able to focus closely and make the most of the young girl's expression and the wonderful content in her eyes. I used a slower shutter speed, so I braced my elbows on a picnic table to help steady the lens.
© *2004 Dan Simon*

Close-up photography tools

You have a number of tools at your disposal that enable you to get close to your subjects. These choices include the following:

✦ **Built-in close focusing capability:** Most point-and-shoot digital cameras offer some sort of close focusing mode. Because these cameras use a rangefinder design, which means that you look through a separate viewfinder aimed in the same direction as the lens, most of these cameras will switch to viewing through their LCD finder for close-up work to provide a more accurate composition. You can get very good results with such arrangements (see the photo of a Monarch butterfly in Figure 5-6. Keep in mind that you have very little depth of field working in your favor when you're doing close-up work. If your body sways back and forth as you focus the camera, there's a good chance your subject will drift in and out of focus. If you have a tripod, this is a good time to use it.

Figure 5-6: When using your camera's close-focusing capabilities, take advantage of natural light, ensure that your camera and your subject are on the same plane, and don't scare your subject away!

© 2004 Dan Simon

Close Focusing Using the LCD Screen

I photographed the Monarch butterfly shown in Figure 5-6 on my front lawn with the close-focusing set up of my point-and-shoot digital camera. Although the

Continued

Continued

camera required me to use the LCD screen for composition, this proved to be an advantage because it was easier to hold the camera, level with the subject. Another advantage was that I could keep my body farther from the butterfly, reducing the possibility that I might scare it off. This was actually a very simple photograph to make. I didn't use any light modifiers or supplemental lighting, no filters or close-up lenses, and did nothing to attract the butterfly except marry a woman who likes to garden. The keys to this image are using the camera's close focussing capability, positioning the camera so that it was level with the butterfly, and choosing a vertical composition to match the shape of the butterfly and the plant it was feeding on.

✦ **Close-up lenses:** These small lenses attach to the front of the built-in camera lens and help magnify an image. Close-up lenses are available either as screw-in adapters (which screw into your lens) or in a rectangular format that slides into an adapter mount, manufactured by companies such as Cokin. These lenses, or *diopters* as they're also known, frequently come in sets of three. Each diopter has its own designation: +1, +2, +3, and so on. You can use diopters singly, or you can combine them for even more magnification. (If you combine diopters, put the strongest one on first.) These can be the least expensive and easiest choice for point-and-shoot camera owners if the camera's close-focusing capability isn't enough.

 If you can get almost, but not quite, close enough to your subject, and generally shoot at less than your camera's highest resolution, set the camera to a higher resolution, take the shot, and crop the image to fill the frame. Or, if you're already at your camera's highest resolution, consider re-sampling the image in Photoshop, a topic I cover in Chapter 15.

✦ **Extension tubes (interchangeable lens SLR cameras only):** Extension tubes mount between your camera and lens and extend the lens away from the film plane or sensor. This changes the lens's focusing characteristics, allowing you to get closer to your subject while still achieving sharp focus. You lose the capability to focus at the far end of the lens's focusing distance, but only while using the extension tube, not permanently. The extension tube also blocks some light, slowing down your shutter speed or requiring a larger aperture. Because you're not adding any glass or resin (as you would with a filter), image quality doesn't suffer.

✦ **Tele-converters:** A tele-converter's main purposes are to multiply the lens's focal length and to increase its telephoto capability. The tele-converter places another piece of glass (usually multiple elements) between the lens and camera sensor, which magnifies the image without increasing the lens's closest focusing distance. Say, you place a 2x tele-converter on a 200mm telephoto lens capable of focusing to a distance of eight feet. With the tele-converter, your 200mm lens becomes a 400mm lens but can still focus to eight feet, doubling the size of your subject in the viewfinder. On the down side, tele-converters cost you light. A 2x tele-converter will cost you two full f-stops of exposure. To counteract the loss of light, you can shoot with a slower shutter speed, open up the lens a couple of f-stops, or add some extra light.

Getting creative with macro photography

Macro photography lets you enter a fascinating new world. Here you can document a wildlife kingdom as varied and interesting as our own (see Figure 5-7). Macro photography also gives you the chance to find the beauty in flowers and all sorts of manmade and natural objects.

Figure 5-7: Forget the birds and the bees, the grasshoppers provide all the action!
© *2004 Dan Simon*

The passports into this tiny world are the macro-capable lens and the tripod.

Note

You can make any lens macro-capable with one or more of the tools, such as extension tubes or diopters, described in the preceding bullet list.

It's hard to overestimate the importance of a good tripod for macro photography. Your depth of field is so shallow in macro photography that any slight body movement will drift your subject in and out of focus. In fact, one popular macro photography accessory is a *focusing rail*, a device that moves the camera back and forth with very fine control because it's easier to move the camera into focus than the lens for this type of photography.

Developing an interest in macro photography also helps you deal with the occasional frustration many photographers feel, namely, "There's nothing to photograph around here!" You may live in the most boring neighborhood in the country, but at your feet is a tiny environment as strange and exotic as any you could ever hope to visit. These miniature kingdoms feature all sorts of neat stuff:

✦ **Insects:** These tiny creatures have long been the stuff of horror and science fiction movies, but why should Hollywood have all the fun? The most challenging part of photographing insects is catching them when they're still enough to photograph, but patience and determination works. Spiders are particularly good subjects because they tend to stay fairly still. Spider webs covered with early morning dew can make for attractive images too, particularly if you experiment with back lighting (putting the sun behind the web) and side lighting, which helps bring out detail. I suppose there's even a potential series on squished bugs, but I'm certainly not recommending that as a theme. See Figure 5-8 for a shot of a busy insect.

Figure 5-8: Insects and flowers are a wonderful subject for macro photography.
© 2004 Dan Simon

✦ **Flowers:** Close-up photography shows the beauty of the entire flower, but you can take more unique shots by diving deeper into the plant. Macro images of the pistil and stamen—or other individual parts of the flower—can lead to an almost abstract image (think Georgia O'Keefe). Backlit flower petals also provide a soft, ethereal splash of color.

✦ **Textures:** Look for patterns and textures in the sand or soil. Small rock or pebble formations lit creatively can form an otherworldly landscape.

✦ **Moving water:** It doesn't matter if it's a rapid on the Colorado River or the tiny current of a garden hose trickling across your lawn, water follows the same laws of physics while it moves.

 Creating your own tiny riverscapes with the help of a garden hose, some rocks, and your imagination is a great way to practice slow shutter speed moving water photography.

Lighting for macro photography

One of the main challenges in macro photography is coming up with enough light to allow the small f-stops necessary to produce a decent amount of depth of field. While setting up the camera on a tripod and using a long exposure works quite nicely for moving water shots, and does just fine for static miniature landscapes, it doesn't do the trick for living creatures or delicate subjects if any kind of breeze occurs. The answer is supplemental lighting, which can be found in many forms.

✦ **Accessory flash:** Portable daylight. These flash units can illuminate a macro subject, but not very well. Good ones tilt down and aim the light at the subject.

✦ **Off-camera flash:** Functions just like accessory flash, but this time you use an off-camera flash adapter (a special adapter your camera maker offers to allow the flash to communicate with the camera while it's used off camera) to position the light close to and directly toward the subject. The most important advantage of off-camera flash is that the light becomes more effective the closer you move the flash to your subject. This technique also lets you vary the direction the light comes from, something that can help bring out detail if you aim the light properly.

 Chapter 7 contains more detailed information about side lighting, a great lighting technique for showing detail.

✦ **Off-camera flash and reflector:** Now you're getting fancy! Combine a side-angled off-camera flash with a reflector pointed toward the side of your subject, and you've got a recipe for professional looking lighting. This combination gives you nice detail from each side and fills in any pronounced shadows. The down side is that you need to hold the flash with one hand, the reflector with another and then press the shutter release button with another. Most macro enthusiasts use an *accessory arm*, a device that mounts to your tripod and holds either the flash or the reflector.

✦ **Ring lights:** A ring light is a small, circular pair of flash tubes that mounts on the front of your lens, and provides even, directional illumination all around your subject. If you have to handhold your camera to do your macro shots, this is the piece of gear to do it with! Ring lights provide a beautiful, even illumination. Better units even let you adjust the power ratio between flash tubes for more elegant macro lighting. Best of all, there are even versions available for point-and-shoot digital cameras. Prices for these useful gadgets range from about $100 for very low-end third-party units, to as much as $500 for pro systems by Canon or Nikon. If you're serious about macro photography, ring lights are worth the investment.

 Project: **Shooting close-ups of flowers with and without lighting improvements**

The following steps walk you through shooting a flower close up without additional lighting:

1. Select the flower you want to photograph. Use a post or twine to hold the stem in place and keep the plant from moving.

2. Set up your camera and tripod to provide a tight composition. You can orient your camera straight down, at a three-quarters view, from the side, or even from underneath depending on how you want to show the flower.

3. Check your background. If it's cluttered or just generally uninteresting, try positioning a piece of black or green cloth behind the plant, but don't let it get too close to the flower. You want enough distance between the plant and your background so that the material is out of focus. Fortunately, because you're doing close-up photography, your depth of field will be very shallow to begin with, and keeping the background out of focus shouldn't be difficult.

4. Check your flower. Look for any debris that you can remove or trim. Remove any insect-damaged petals; do whatever you can to spruce up the flower. This includes lightly spraying the plant with a mister (use water or glycerin) to create some water droplets on the petals. You're creating a plant portrait, not a photojournalistic rendering, so it's okay to make it look its best. If you are creating a photojournalistic rendering, ignore everything you just read. Instead, wait for a morning when there's dew on the plant and shoot early in the day.

5. Focus on the flower's stamen (the male part) and pick a small enough aperture for good depth of field—the smaller the better. Aim for f8, f11, or f16 if possible, but these settings result in slow shutter speeds.

6. Trip the shutter with a remote release if you have one; if you don't set the camera's self timer to take the picture. Using the self timer gives the camera time to stop shaking after you press the shutter release.

7. Add light. Supplemental light can greatly improve your flower photography in many ways. First, using a flash helps you get the small apertures you need for maximum depth of field, while helping to freeze any plant movement. Supplemental lighting also helps fill in shadow areas and balance light, and, if used properly, can help bring out more of the flower's detail. To achieve this last benefit, you need to position your light(s) to rake across the flower from the side.

8. Use reflectors or diffusers to modify an existing light source. You don't always have to rely on supplemental lighting to modify your light. You can position a reflector to bounce light into shadow areas, or you can use a diffuser placed between your light source and the flower to soften the light falling on it. Either way, you save the trouble of buying an accessory flash and getting it to work with your camera. Best of all, you can make your own reflectors and diffusers cheaply from stuff you probably already have.

 See Chapter 7 for more detailed information about sidelighting and light modifiers.

Summary

How you manipulate your camera's controls can go a long way toward creating more interesting pictures. Try to take your exposures to the extreme and don't be afraid to get closer to your subjects.

To make better photos, begin experimenting with your shutter speed and aperture selections. Take the same photo several times—once the way your camera suggests, once with a fast shutter speed and larger aperture opening, and once with a slow shutter speed and small aperture. Compare the results. Experiment. Film's cheap, digital's even cheaper.

Expanding Your Horizons: Panoramic and Bad Weather Photography

There's a comfort zone we all find ourselves in sooner or later. We've developed habits that work for us. We've figured out how to get the job done.

We've gotten in a rut.

Call it whatever you want. You've hit a plateau, you're going through the motions, and you're doing the same things over and over.

There are ways to expand your photographic horizon, but you have to start by trying something different. This chapter offers some ideas on how to get out of your photographic rut by approaching your photographs from a couple of different perspectives, such as the panoramic view and the view you see when Mother Nature throws some weather your way. Somewhere in here should be something you haven't tried before. Maybe it gets you out of that rut and on your way again.

Creating Panoramic Images

Using your digital camera to create panoramic images certainly is a way of expanding your photographic horizons in at least one sense of the word. There are two parts to creating striking panoramic images: the technical challenges and the creative ones. The following sections consider both to these.

Handling the technical challenges

A panoramic image is one whose longer side is usually at least twice its shorter side. Common panoramic print sizes are 3 x 6, 6 x 12, and 12 x 24. More extreme versions are also used. When you get right down to it, the only real limitation on the size of panorama shots is the imagination of the photographer.

Panoramic images can be a striking tool in the photographer's bag of tricks. Because this format is so seldom seen, images created this way automatically leap out at the viewer. In addition, the panorama's extreme dimensions can be perfectly suited for subjects that don't quite fit the normal photographic frame.

The biggest technical challenge to working in panoramic format is that your camera isn't shooting a panoramic image, although some cameras may offer a panoramic mode. This means that you're wasting space at the top and bottom (or sides) of the image that you're only going to crop out. Fortunately, this problem isn't insurmountable. Ways of dealing with the issue are discussed later in this section.

Handling the creative challenges

You can pick just about any subject for a panorama, but finding subject matter that truly works with the extreme dimensions is a bit more difficult. These are good challenges though. Remember, you're trying to stretch yourself creatively here, so finding a task that fires your imagination isn't a bad idea.

Here are some potential subjects for panoramic shots:

✦ **Lighthouses:** These tall, slender structures cry for panoramic treatment. Just remember you're creating a vertical panorama.

✦ **City skylines:** Instead of including lots of sky and foreground, turn the cityscape into a panorama.

✦ **Shorelines:** Many images made at the shore show an empty sky forced upon the image by the tyranny of the standard photographic image dimensions. Changing to a panoramic format means the photographer can show what's important and leave the rest out. Beach photos are a good example of this kind of thinking.

✦ **Natural wonders:** Sometimes the best way to show a grand sweeping vista is by shooting a panoramic image. This format helps isolate the landscape against a small sliver of sky, making the scenery stand out.

✦ **People events:** Events such as the Indy 500 or the Punkin Chunkin contest offer large numbers of people and contraptions. If you can position your camera on an elevated vantage point, you're in position to create an effective panoramic composition that better shows the event than the normal photographic image.

You can create a panoramic photo with a digital camera in two different ways, and the following sections explain these techniques. These methods also work with film cameras, but they're easier with a digital camera. The exception, of course, is if you invest in a high-end film camera made specifically to take panoramas or buy a cheap, disposable panoramic camera.

Creating panoramic images the standard way

The usual approach to creating a panoramic image with a nonpanoramic format camera is to create a series of photographs of a scene while rotating the camera a fixed amount after each image, and then stitching the photos together into one large, long panorama.

This technique isn't new. Film photographers have been doing it for decades, but in fairly limited numbers. The resulting images were more like collages than photographic prints, with the seams from one print to the next being readily apparent.

The advent of digital photography, first through scanning photographic prints and later with digital cameras, made it possible to create virtually seamless panoramas. This capability has resulted in a huge increase in the number of photographers trying to create panoramic prints.

The digital process is a natural for this kind of thing. You can bring the images together in Photoshop, line them up and blend them together seamlessly. Once satisfied, you can then order a print, which looks nothing like a series of pictures stitched together. There are also plenty of programs on the market that will do all the work for you, including Arcsoft's Panorama Maker, Photo Vista Panorama Maker, and Spin Panorama to name a few.

Visit this book's companion web site for links to software that does the stitching for you.

Making the process even easier, a couple of equipment makers have created tripod heads designed specifically to handle panoramic shots. Ipix and Kaidan both offer equipment designed to use your camera properly for panoramic photography (see Figure 6-1). One of the most important considerations for this kind of shooting is to position the camera lens so that it revolves around one single point.

The best way to visualize this is to consider how your camera would normally sit on your tripod and maneuver. Normally, the rear end of the camera is mounted to the tripod head. This means that as you rotate the camera, its sensor spins over the same axis. At the same time the front of the lens swings through a much larger circle.

To get the best results for a panoramic image, the camera needs to be positioned so the front end of the lens stays over the exact center of the tripod head instead

Figure 6-1: A digital point-and-shoot camera with add-on lens mounted on an Ipix 360-degree tripod head.
© 2004 Dan Simon

of the back of the camera. It's possible to create panoramas without doing this, but the results aren't quite as good or quite as easy.

The Ipix and Kaidan systems are built to help you position the camera this way. Their tripod heads will also have built in "detents" to help you more exactly position the camera for each image. The Ipix system is usually used with a 180-degree fisheye lens so you only need to make two images to create a 360 panorama. Special software stitches the image together in an Ipix format file that lets the viewer maneuver through the panorama in all directions. Or, you can just stitch the two images together in an image-editing program such as Photoshop to create an extreme panorama (see Figure 6-2).

Figure 6-2: A panoramic photo created by using a digital point-and-shoot camera and fisheye lens mounted on an Ipix tripod head.
© 2004 Dan Simon

In the shot shown in Figure 6-2, I created two images, captured them to my home computer, pasted them together, and cropped to this rectangular image. This image provides a 360-degree view.

Creating panoramic images the easy way

One advantage of using the method discussed in the preceding paragraphs is that it helps you to create huge, high-resolution files. Suppose you don't consider that an advantage? Suppose you're just interested in making panoramas for the web or your computer screen, or perhaps getting smaller prints made.

There is an easier way to create a panoramic image. One that you can even stretch a bit to allow for reasonably large prints. It's called *cropping*, and I introduced you to this concept in Chapter 1. You can crop any image into panoramic dimensions, as I explain in the following example.

During a Canada/New England cruise, I shot the Boston business district from a harbor tour boat (see Figure 6-3). When I shot the image, it was saved under JPEG compression making a 1.7MB file. But when you open the photo in your image editing software, it decompresses to its actual size. Consequently, this image—shot on a Canon EOS 1D camera—opened in Photoshop as an 11.6MB file.

Figure 6-3: Boston skyline shot from a harbor boat.
© 2004 Dan Simon

I wasn't thrilled with either the gray sky or the gray water in the foreground, so I decided to crop this image down to a panorama. To do this, I selected Photoshop's cropping tool and then dragged the sides in until I had cut out much of the gray sky and water (see Figure 6-4). The image ratio of this particular photo is about 5 to 2. Cropping reduced the file size, too, so the resulting image file ended up being slightly less than 7MB.

A 7MB file is more than large enough to make a good quality 15-inch by 6-inch print (at 180 dpi). If you want to go larger than that, there are some options.

 For more information on file sizes and resolution, turn to Chapter 2.

Figure 6-4: The Boston skyline photo cropped to a panoramic format.
© 2004 Dan Simon

One technique that's popular in the digital imaging community is called *Stairstep Interpolation* in Photoshop. The idea is that the program can do a better job of increasing resolution (*upressing*) in a series of small increments than it can in one big adjustment. The method works as follows:

1. Open your photo. From the Photoshop File menu, choose Image ⇨ Image size. Make sure that the bottom drop-down menu is set to Bi-cubic and the Constrain Proportions and Resample Image boxes are checked.

2. Go to the Resolution setting and add 10 percent to the number that's already there. (Frequently this number will be 72 ppi because that's a fairly standard default for digital camera images.)

3. Click the OK button. Photoshop now resizes your image to be 10 percent bigger.

4. Repeat Steps 1 through 3. Generally, you can do this about five times without noticeably degrading your image.

At least one article I've read on this subject maintains that you get the best results by upressing in one percent increments. It probably will work better than in 10 percent chunks; but I'm middle-aged and have to get my pictures finished before I'm retired. If you're young, by all means, give this method a try.

Visit this book's companion web site at www.wiley.com/compbooks/simon for a Photoshop action (a repeatable sequence of steps) that performs this tedious chore for you.

Upressing Software Options

If you anticipate needing to increase image resolution on a regular basis (for any reason, not just making panoramic images), consider one of the programs created specifically for that purpose.

A couple of good ones are Pixel Smartscale by Extensis and Genuine Fractals by the Altimira Group, both of which work as a Photoshop plug-in. I particularly like Pixel Smartscale because it doesn't require a separate file format, but either program is a good choice.

Chapter 15 (and this book's companion web site) offers more information about programs that enable you to increase image resolution.

 Project: **Assembling a high-resolution panoramic image**

As you might expect from the word *assembling*, this project explains the process I discussed earlier for stitching together multiple photographs to form one large panorama.

Practitioners of this method range from the ultra-serious, who invest in special tripod mounts and software packages to make the process as exact as possible; to the casual dilettante, who just wants to make the occasional panoramic image as cheaply and easily as possible.

The advantage of this method is that it enables you to create a very high-resolution file. High-resolution files are necessary if you want to make large prints without it looking like you enlarged your file too much.

Here's how you shoot the multiple shots for the panorama that you will then stitch together:

1. *Plan your shot carefully*. Doing this step right will really make your life a lot easier later on. Try to visualize your composition (a technique pros rely on) and then position your camera and tripod as precisely as you can. Shooting a panorama this way really requires a tripod. You need to position and move your camera as precisely and levelly as you can during the picture taking process.

2. *Make sure your camera is as level as possible*. There are several ways to make sure your camera is as level as possible. One of the best is to use a level made to mount in your camera's hot shoe (a place to mount a flash unit). If your camera doesn't have a hot shoe, or you can't find such a device, you can use a standard level to level the tripod's camera mount before mating the camera to it. Be sure to level it in multiple directions. (The camera needs to be level on all axis.) By the way, most of us normally orient the camera vertically and take extra shots. This requires you to make more images, but increases the overall resolution of your panorama.

3. *Set up the camera appropriately*. Getting the exposure right for a panorama can be a little bit tricky. It's best to set your camera for manual exposure and set one consistent exposure to use for every image in the sequence. Base your setting on the brightest part of the scene, underexposing a little if you need to so you can maintain highlight detail.

4. *Start making photos*. Each time you take a shot, rotate the camera to its next position, taking care to overlap your previous shot by about 25 percent. (This gives you some leeway when assembling the image later.) Some tripod heads are marked incrementally so that

Continued

Project *(continued)*

you can be precise. If yours doesn't have incremental markers, use landmarks such as telephone poles or tree limbs to help you judge where the overlap is.

> **Tip**
> Many of us prefer to start from the right and work our way left when shooting multiple shot panoramas. This way, when you bring the images into Photoshop or a stitching program, the images are lined up properly at the beginning of the sequence.

5. *Mark the end of your sequence somehow, even if you take a shot with your hand sticking in front of the lens.* This way you'll know when you've gotten to the last shot of a particular sequence. This is particularly important if you follow Step 6.

6. *Always try to shoot at least two panoramic sequences to improve your chances of getting a workable sequence.* This is a good time to re-level the camera and tripod if you've had any doubts about how well you did that job the first time too.

7. *Capture your images to your computer and either import them into your panoramic stitching software or open them in Photoshop.* If you're using a panoramic stitching program such as PhotoStitch or Panorama Maker, follow your program's directions. You can also create panoramic images by stitching photographs together in an image-editing program with a layers capability such as Photoshop.

Here's a simple description of how you can stitch images together to form one larger panorama.

1. Open the images in your image editing software.

2. Create a master document for your new panorama. This is a new document you will use to build your panorama. Choose File ➪ New. A dialog box opens asking for the dimensions of the new file. Make it slightly taller than the height dimensions of your images and make it as wide as you want.

3. Place the first image in the master file preferably to the left edge of the frame (it's easier to work from left to right, so choose the left most image in the sequence).

4. Place the next image into the master document. Reduce its opacity so that you can make out details of the first image underneath the second. Using the program's move tool, superimpose the second image over the first until the two images line up properly. (Note: you may need to slightly rotate the second image to get it to match up properly.)

5. Once the images are properly aligned, use your editing program's eraser tool (set to a soft edge brush) to erase the line created by the edge of the second image. Try to work to areas where there's a hard line occurring in the image (say the edge of a building).

6. Repeat this process for the remaining images.

7. Once you've aligned all your images properly, save a copy of the master document in an editable form (layers intact) so you can go back to it later if you decide you want to make changes. Then flatten your working version of the file.

8. Crop as necessary. At this point you can tweak the overall contrast (tonal range from brightest white to darkest black), saturation (richness of the image's colors), and sharpness of the image just as you would a newly captured photograph.

9. Using the cloning tool or healing brush, go over small imperfections in alignment to clean up any obvious stitching areas.

 Chapter 15 offers more detailed information about cropping and image correction tools.

At this point, you have a finished panoramic image. Figure 6-5 shows a panorama image that I stitched together.

Figure 6-5: A panorama shot created by stitching images together using PhotoStitch.

© 2004 Dan Simon

Oh, the Weather Outside Is Frightful

Another way to expand your photographic horizons is to make photographs in weather you wouldn't normally shoot in. Granted, this means going out in bad weather, but from a photographic standpoint, bad weather is frequently good weather.

Bad weather makes for dramatic images. I love going out near the end of a snowstorm. Our normally colorful world has turned monochromatic. This is time to look for spots of color in an otherwise gray landscape. Storms are Mother Nature's version of working in Photoshop to change the way the environment looks. A creative photographer tries to take advantage of that (see Figure 6-6).

 Visit this book's companion web site at www.wiley.com/compbooks/simon to view the color version of this photo.

Figure 6-6: A lake near my home shortly after a snow storm. Most of the world has gone monochromatic, but the flag and the house still show their color, making the eye leap to these two elements.

© 2004 Dan Simon

Dealing with the elements isn't as hard as you might think, even with today's cameras packed with electronics. Still, to make the experience more comfortable for both you and your gear, here are some tried and true tricks I've followed during a career that has taken me literally from the extremes of Guam to Antarctica.

 Remember, ensuring a stable camera is critical in bad weather. See Chapter 2 for more information about tripods, monopods, and other stabilizers.

Dealing with the elements 101 (for humans)

Head, hands, feet—it's amazing how often these vital areas are under protected. You can bundle up in a huge parka, but if your head is and hands are exposed and your feet are barely clothed, you will be cold.

It's more effective—and easier—if you adopt a head-to-toe approach to winter dressing. Dress in layers (preferably ones that will wick moisture away from your body) and include thermal underwear for both your upper and lower body.

Synthetic materials such as Polypropylene and Pile will move moisture away from your skin and help keep your body warmer as compared to cotton, which absorbs water and makes you feel even colder. Wet cotton is about the worst thing you can wear under cold conditions.

✦ **Head:** I still use the expedition weight Balaclava (refers to a style of pullover wool hat) I used when I served with Operation DEEP FREEZE in Antarctica. This marvelously warm chapeau can be used as a watch cap (rolled up to just cover my head), rolled all the way down to cover everything except my nose and eyes, or pulled under my chin to cover all but the bottom half of my face. I combine this with a polypro facemask to provide extra protection and prevent the itchy feeling wool gives me. There are even more advanced (and complicated) hats currently on the market.

✦ **Hands:** One nice trick for photographers is to combine a lightweight set of polypro glove liners with a heavier pair of either fingerless gloves or one of the glove/mitten combinations. These wonderful mittens convert to fingerless gloves just by lifting the hinged outer mitten to reveal the fingerless section underneath. The lightweight glove liners allow enough fine control to operate the camera, but still give you some protection against the elements.

✦ **Feet:** Wear an inner polypro sock liner under heavier wool socks, ideally inside Gore-Tex hiking boots. It's especially important to protect your feet because they're in constant contact with the ground. Don't underestimate how much heat the cold ground can suck from your body, particularly if you're standing in the same place for an extended period of time.

 Visit this book's companion web site for more information on dressing appropriately for the elements and links to vendors who sell cold weather gear. The site also provides detailed information about cold weather clothing materials.

Concerns are a bit different when you're dealing with warmer temperatures and lots of rain. Your primary concern then is staying comfortably dry. The easiest (but most expensive) way to do this is with a Gore-Tex rain suit. The advantage to this material is that it keeps rain out but still allows body sweat to wick through the material and away from your body, keeping you more comfortable. Gore-Tex clothing is very nice if you can afford it.

If you can't quite justify the expense, a basic nylon rain suit is cheap and effective. Nylon is just not as comfortable; you tend to feel like you're in a sauna. Polypro thermal underwear will wick the moisture away from your body, making you a little more comfortable, but you're still going to be warm. (Maybe too warm.)

Carry either a package of paper towels (in Ziploc bags) or one of those super absorbent towels that backpackers use. This kind of item is vital for drying off your hands before using your equipment.

Dealing with the elements 101 (for cameras)

The secret to staying comfortable when you are out in bad weather is finding ways to stay warm and dry; your camera wants the same treatment. Too cold and it will malfunction; too much moisture and it won't work. Your goal as a bad weather photographer is to make your camera comfortable enough to keep working. The following list provides some recommendations:

✦ **Fresh batteries:** Cold weather reduces the effectiveness of most types of camera batteries. Start out with a fresh set and carry several more for backup. It's best to keep them someplace warm (like inside your parka near your body). In extreme conditions, it may be necessary to keep switching between battery sets as one warms up and another gets too cold. Lithium-Ion Nickel Metal Hydride (NiMH) and Ni-cads do better in cold weather than regular alkaline batteries, with NiMH probably being the best choice.

✦ **Camera raincoats:** Some manufacturers make raincoats designed for specific camera and lens combinations. These can run anywhere from $45 to $200 each and do a good job of protecting your gear. Still, even a working pro can't afford to buy—or carry—one for every camera and lens in his bag. I have a couple for special circumstances. The rest of the time I just take a plastic shopping bag and some artist's tape or duct tape and tape the bag over the camera. I make a hole for the lens to poke through and tape around the lens hood to hold that end in place. It's ugly as sin, but it keeps my gear dry. It's even easier for a digital point-and-shoot camera. Just take a plastic Ziploc bag and put your camera inside it. Then make a hole for the lens, tape the bag around the lens, and zip the bag's seal between the ends of the neck strap.

✦ **Desiccant packets:** These annoying little packets seem to show up in every package of electronics gear you buy. Save these critters and keep a couple in your camera bag. This will help prevent any moisture that does find its way in there from doing too much harm. You can buy larger versions at many camera stores. If you have several equipment cases, it's a good idea to keep some desiccant packets in them, particularly if you store your gear in your car trunk.

Some Final Thoughts

The key to expanding your photographic horizons is to try to break out of your established habits and try something new. Trying new techniques and shooting under extreme weather conditions are a couple of ways to do this. Here are some more ideas to stretch your creativity.

✦ **Pick a word:** Choose a word and spend an afternoon or a week trying to portray that word photographically. Simple words such as *color, fun, small,* work very well. Keep this up, and you'll find you're developing a growing portfolio of images that are completely different from what you've shot in the past.

✦ **Pick a scene:** Find an interesting location near your home and then shoot it regularly over the course of a year. Document its moods and its changes of wardrobe. Visit the site at different times of day and night.

Finally, just take pictures. One of the best photographers I ever worked with had what he called his "minimum daily requirement." He shot at least a roll of film a day, every day. This doesn't mean going out and firing off 36 quick snapshots. I mean 36 carefully composed and thought out images. He worked every day at becoming a better photographer, and it showed in his portfolio.

With a film camera, this much shooting would be pretty expensive for someone whose job didn't supply the film. But with today's digital cameras, you don't have that problem. You can shoot a quantity of images and capture them to your computer at minimal cost.

Shooting every day will make you a better photographer. I promise.

Summary

If you feel you've gotten into a photograph rut, don't be afraid to try something new. Digital cameras make it easy to experiment without incurring a lot of extra costs because you don't have to make prints unless you want to.

Don't be afraid of bad weather; instead, see it for what it is, an opportunity to make better pictures.

Let There Be Light

Photographers tend to obsess over light, and for good reason. Without proper light, you can't take good pictures.

I was on an assignment one Saturday afternoon shooting a high school soccer game, when one of the fans struck up a conversation.

"Perfect day for photography isn't it!" he said.

I gritted my teeth.

It was noon; there was a bright sun right overhead. It's one of the most difficult types of light there is to work with when you're shooting digitally. It's no picnic with film either, yet most people think it's a "picture-perfect" day.

Years ago, film technology was limited to slow speed, fine-grain films that required a lot of light for effective photography. As a result, a whole generation of photographers learned that they need a lot of light to take pictures, which doesn't really apply to today's photography.

With higher ISO settings, better quality films, and sensors, it's possible to take good photos in relatively low amounts of light. Yet many people still think they need lots of light to take good pictures. In reality, it's not usually the amount of light that's important, but the quality and the direction of that light.

In this chapter, I cover how to identify quality light, and how to use and manipulate light to your advantage. I also show you how to use light to your advantage and create more dramatic photographs as a result.

Finding Quality Light

Sunrise and sunset produce the best light of the day. During these times, the sun is low in the sky, and the light produced is rich in color and generates dramatic shadows. *Golden light*, as it's known, doesn't guarantee better pictures, but it can have a spectacular effect on your photography. Figures 7-1 and 7-2 show golden light's dramatic effects.

 Morning light is at its best from just before sunrise to about an hour afterward, while evening light is best from one hour before to just after sunset. Rather than changing your approach to photography, simply change the time of day you take photos!

Figure 7-1: Sunset at Brigantine, NJ. Although you can't tell in this grayscale image, the sunset produced a rich palette of colors in the evening sky, further reflected in the water.

© 2004 Dan Simon

 Visit this book's companion web site at www.wiley.com/compbooks/simon to see more images, and in full color, that use the power of light to evoke a mood.

As the sun travels higher in the sky, contrast increases, shadows get smaller and the light loses color until it becomes white. This is generally the poorest light of the day (unless, of course, you count the darkest part of the night.)

Handling high-contrast lighting

Contrast refers to difference between the brightest white and the darkest black within the scene you want to photograph. This difference is usually measured in f-stops.

Figure 7-2: Sunrise. This image uses sunrise and back lighting to produce a beautiful sunrise photo of a bird watcher at Hawk Mountain, the nation's oldest raptor sanctuary.

© 2004 Dan Simon

Different recording media have different contrast limits. Depending upon the particular type, color negative film can generally handle a contrast level of seven f-stops or more. Digital camera sensors on the other hand, can only manage five f-stops difference from darkest black to brightest white while holding detail at both extremes. Any more contrast, and the photographer is forced to give up either highlight or shadow detail.

Recognizing high-contrast lighting can be difficult because the human eye adjusts to light so quickly, whereas cameras oftentimes don't.

You can deal with high-contrast lighting either by judging light more carefully before taking a photo, or by checking your LCD screen afterward. Some digital cameras even flash highlight areas that are overexposed. If your camera doesn't offer such a feature, you need to examine the LCD image very closely to try and determine if the highlights have any detail to them.

However, if your camera doesn't identify overexposure, managing difficult lighting conditions can be a real challenge for digital photographers. Fortunately, there are several things you can do to deal with high-contrast lighting.

✦ **Recompose your image:** Try to find a different composition that eliminates really bright or really dark areas from your scene.

✦ **Balance light:** One of the most common solutions professional photographers use to deal with high-contrast lighting is to increase the light hitting shadow areas to balance them with the scene's brighter areas. In simple terms, turn on your flash unit, or rig some accessory lights to bring out detail in areas that are too dark to show up on a properly exposed image. To see what I mean, check out Figure 7-3.

Figure 7-3: Lisa backlit by a bright sunset. I used flash to keep her from being silhouetted.
© *2004 Dan Simon*

 Visit this book's companion web site, www.wiley.com/compbooks/simon, to see a full color version of this image.

✦ **Filter light:** Graduated neutral density filters are popular with digital photographers because of their ability to hold back bright sky areas while not affecting shadow areas. Graduated neutral density filters are half dark and half clear. Position the filter so the dark section is superimposed over the bright area and let your built in light meter (see sidebar below) set the exposure. See figures 7-4 and 7-5 to see the results of using a graduated neutral density filter.

Figure 7-4: I shot this image with no filtration.

© 2004 Dan Simon

Figure 7-5: I used a graduated neutral density filter to reduce the light striking the water. I also reduced the exposure by one f-stop to reduce the scene's overall brightness, knowing I could bring back the highlights in the top half of the image in the touch-up process.

© 2004 Dan Simon

 To see more clearly the difference between these two shots, visit this book's web site, www.wiley.com/compbooks/simon.

✦ **Block light:** Sometimes you can block an overpowering light source to reduce overall contrast in a scene. Blocking light works for portraiture where placing a diffuser between the sun and your subject will both lower the overall contrast ratio and soften the light hitting your model.

Using Your Camera's Built-In Light Meter

All digital cameras come with built-in light meters, or sensors that measure light in any one of several different ways, depending on how advanced your camera is. Here's a listing of the most common metering systems.

✦ **Center-weighted averaging** assumes that the most important subject matter is in the center of the viewfinder, and it measures the image's overall brightness and weights its reading to slightly favor the viewfinder's central portion. Center-weighted averaging is a good general-purpose choice.

✦ **Center metering** bases its light reading on the center part of the image only. If you follow the rule of thirds religiously, center metering can emphasize to the wrong part of the composition as a result.

✦ **Evaluative, multisegment, or matrix metering** are more sophisticated metering systems that break the image down into zones and measure and evaluate each segment before calculating a best exposure based on typical photographic compositions. These are very good general-purpose metering methods. If your camera offers one of these three modes and you don't want to be bothered with figuring out how to meter manually, this is your best choice.

✦ **Spot metering** reduces the metered area to a very small spot (the center circle) of your viewfinder. It's useful for difficult metering conditions because you can point the spot sensor directly at the most important element in your scene and take a light meter reading off just that spot. Sophisticated cameras such as the Canon EOS 1D enable you to take a series of spot meter readings and then average them together for an overall value.

It's important when taking light meter readings to make sure you're properly measuring the light falling on your subject. If your subject is strongly backlit, then odds are that the strong light behind your subject will fool the light meter and return a reading that's too high for your subject. It's better to either zoom in close to meter directly off your subject or to dial in a couple of f-stops worth of exposure compensation (to +1 or +2) to correct for the backlighting.

Considering light's direction

Another important consideration when taking pictures is the direction of your light, which affects the resulting images. Here are the most common directions light comes from:

✦ **Front lighting:** Front lighting is the direction most photographers work with. Your light source is behind your back and shines directly on your subject. Front lighting is nice and safe. It provides decent illumination and solves most exposure problems.

✦ **Side lighting:** Position your camera and your subject at a right angle to your light source, and you have side lighting. Side light is great for bringing out texture and detail. It can also create a moody sort of image where your subject appears to be emerging from the shadows. See Figure 7-6 for an example of side lighting.

Figure 7-6: Side lighting creates two different worlds in this shot: the world of light and the world of shadow.
© 2004 Dan Simon

✦ **Back lighting:** Beginners are all taught to avoid this one. Put your light source behind your subject and you have a difficult (but sometimes rewarding) kind of lighting known as *backlighting* (see Figure 7-7). If you're working with a backlit subject, it's particularly important either to meter off your subject (rather than letting the strong light behind it determine the exposure) or set your exposure compensation control to add an f-stop or two of extra exposure. Although too strong a light source behind your subject can overwhelm the image, carefully controlled backlighting creates a lovely effect known as *rim lighting*, which produces a beautiful glow around your subject.

Don't forget that you can see all the images in this book in full color at www.wiley.com/compbooks/simon.

Improving the Lighting in Your Photographs

Another way to improve the quality of your photographs is to use supplemental lighting.

Most of the time this means using either your camera's built-in flash unit or an accessory flash unit, but sometimes it's as easy as repositioning a couple of lamps to throw more light on your subject. The idea is simple: Throw more light on a poorly lit subject to create a better photo.

Most of the time extra light is beneficial, but you do want to avoid lighting your subject from below, a style known as *ghoul lighting*. This casts strange shadows and produces an otherworldly appearance that can adversely affect your photographs. In fact, cinematographers have been using ghoul lighting for years; it's the lighting used in those old black and white horror movies your parents and grandparents might have watched.

Figure 7-7: Back lighting gives an ethereal presence to any subject.
© 2004 Dan Simon

When applied judiciously, supplemental lighting is one of those things that can make a huge difference in your photography.

A flash, for example, is just as useful under bright light as it is in low light. In fact, its careful use in high contrast conditions can go a long way toward solving some of the most common photographic problems.

Getting good results from flashes doesn't have to be difficult. You need to understand that the camera is competing with one of the finest optical instruments ever devised—the human eye.

Your eyes quickly compensate for fairly severe changes in illumination, so you tend to view a scene without realizing your film or digital sensor doesn't see it the same way.

Part of what makes using supplemental lighting challenging is recognizing when to use it in the first place.

Built-in flash

Built-in flash is self-explanatory. It's literally the flash built in to your camera, and it's very useful for cleaning up shadows caused by baseball caps and other hats. If you're shooting a group of people and somebody's wearing a hat, turn on your camera's built-in flash. This is one of the most effective ways to use your camera's built-in flash.

Flash is also helpful if there isn't enough light to create a photo without blur from camera shake, but the quality of such photos is mediocre at best. Still, flash can be the difference between being able to take a photo and not being able to take one at all.

Unfortunately, your camera's built-in flash can cause just as many problems as it solves. For one thing, the flash is located just above the lens. The flash's location is what causes red eye (when your subject's eyes appear to glow red in a photo) as the flash's light reflects off your subject's eyes back into the camera lens.

Another problem with built-in flash units is that they're woefully underpowered. These flash units are generally good for a distance of about eight feet, usually just far enough to handle a group of people you're shooting for a souvenir photo. This limitation, however, doesn't stop people from trying to use these flash units to light major sports arenas or the Grand Canyon.

Using supplemental flash

Supplemental, or accessory, flash is simply an external flash you use separately or in conjunction with your camera's built-in flash unit. There are several ways to use supplemental flash:

✦ **Hot shoe mount accessory flash:** If your camera has a hot shoe (a mount that triggers your flash when you press the shutter button), then a hot shoe mount accessory flash is a great addition to your photographic arsenal. These units are frequently designed to work specifically with your camera model, and usually described as *dedicated* flash units. The best of these models swivel and tilt in a variety of ways to permit bounce flash and can receive information from the camera lens to tell it the exact distance your subject is from the camera.

✦ **Slaved flash units:** A slaved flash relies on a built-in photoelectric cell that triggers the flash unit when another flash goes off. Although slaved flash units or slave triggers (devices that attach to non-slave flashes to make them slaves) have been around for a long time, digital cameras require a special type of slave technology because digital camera built-in flash units operate differently than built-in flash units on regular film cameras. These flashes fire a special pre-flash to calibrate some camera settings and trigger traditional slaves before the lens opens. Check out the Digi-Slave flash line for slaved flashes made specifically to use with digital cameras. (Visit this book's companion web site, www.wiley.com/compbooks/simon, for a link to Digi-Slave's web site.) Keep in mind, if you have a DSLR, regular slave units will work just fine.

✦ **Reflectors:** Sometimes the answer isn't necessarily an extra light source but simply a matter of redirecting an existing one. Reflectors serve this purpose. You can either use one of the many photographic reflector systems (many of which are collapsible and have different coverings to change the color of the reflected light), or you can make your own reflector with a sheet of white foam core board, or even aluminum foil glued or stapled to a lightweight sheet of plywood. Then you position the reflector so it bounces your light source into the shadow areas (see Figure 7-8).

Figure 7-8: A reflector held below these tulips reduces the shadow caused by diffuse overhead light.

© 2004 Dan Simon

✦ **Diffusers:** Photographers place diffusers between their subject and the light source to soften the light and reduce its intensity. Commercial versions are available, or you can fix a sheet across a sunlit window or stretch a pillowcase over a window screen or homemade wooden frame to create your own diffuser.

Summary

Next time you're out taking pictures, take a moment to consider light. Ask yourself: What direction is it coming from? What color is it? How intense is it? And, most importantly, how can I use it to my advantage?

Budget some time one morning or evening to visit someplace near your home and take photographs at sunrise and sunset. Spend about an hour or more, planning your time so you're there both before and after the sun's appearance. Watch how the light changes during that time.

Reflectors and diffusers can make all the difference in your photography as they help balance the light between highlight and shadow areas. If you place a diffuser between your light source and your subject, you'll create a much more pleasing outdoor photo.

Tackling Different Photographic Subjects

We live in a photogenic world filled with an amazing array of subject matter.

To acquire the skills and knowledge necessary to document this wide array of subjects, a professional photographer must be willing to dedicate countless hours to practice.

Hobbyists seldom have the time necessary for such mastery. This part of the book shows you ways to approach various types of photography so that you get good results with just a little effort and practice.

Photographing People

Poor people pictures plague poorly prepared photographers. (Okay, I'll stop now.)

Seriously, most people buy cameras in order to photograph other people and to document those special moments in their lives: births, marriages, graduations, trips, and family gatherings. Each special moment revolves around including another human being in the photo.

Yet so many of these pictures are, if not flat out bad, certainly underwhelming.

But people photos don't need to be dull. People are wonderfully interesting photographic subjects when approached properly. They do many interesting things, present many interesting looks, and connect with you on an emotional level because we're all members of the same species.

Many of the problems you run into when photographing people may be due to bad photography habits you've developed over the years. If you never receive feedback about these habits, you just keep on making the same mistakes and taking the same bad photo over and over. The result is that unfocused, undirected picture of someone that's too far away. There's no real emotional content to the picture and there's probably no real clue as to why the picture was even made.

Just doing something as simple as tightening your composition can make a big improvement in the quality of your people pictures. During the next few pages, I show you some other ways that you can improve the pictures you take of people.

Choosing the Type of Photo You Want to Take

In photographing people, the first thing you have to decide is the type of photo you want to take. Although a good, basic digital camera can deliver nice results in any type of photography, some types of cameras are better suited to one style of photography or another. In addition, a number of accessories can give your images a more polished look.

The important thing is to choose equipment that gives you high-quality results while providing you with enough flexibility to explore other kinds of photography. Fortunately, finding this happy medium isn't hard to do.

You can create a high-quality formal portrait with just about any digital camera offering even the most modest of zoom capabilities. Fancier cameras can make your life easier, particularly if you're trying to crank out a large volume of portraits. If you're a hobbyist who's more interested in experimenting with various lighting and portrait looks, almost any camera will do.

The ways you can photograph people fall into several different categories: portraiture, candid, and glamour. These categories describe the feeling that each type of image hopes to convey. Each type of photography has its own requirements and considerations, and I touch on these differences throughout the rest of this chapter. It's not unusual for a photographer to find a special aptitude or preference for one type of photography over another. If you discover such an aptitude or preference, by all means pursue it.

Formal Portraiture

In simple terms, a *portrait* is any image in which the subject is an active part of the photographic process. Simply put, subjects are posing for a photo of themselves.

The first category of portrait photography is the formal portrait. This is the classic go get dressed up, visit a photographer's studio, sit up straight, smile, and get your picture taken shot, as shown in Figure 8-1.

 Don't forget, you can see each figure in full color on this book's web site, www.wiley.com/compbooks/simon.

This type of photo wants to show you at your best. If the photographer can pose you so you look thinner and neater and better dressed than you ever look in everyday life, she will certainly do so. Likely too, the better she makes you look, the more pictures you will buy.

A good formal portrait is something of a study in contrasts. People dress up in clothing they seldom wear. They pose in a manner in which they seldom, if ever, stand in real life. And finally, they hold positions they never maintain in real life. Back when I did a lot of these, I used to joke that formal portrait sittings were

Figure 8-1: A formal portrait.
© 2004 Dan Simon

incredibly tense and uncomfortable, even though when done right they depicted a family that looked relaxed and comfortable. "You only have to look comfortable," I used to tell clients, "not actually be comfortable." Needless to say, I don't do a lot of formal portraiture anymore.

Camera requirements

Before you get started photographing people, consider the following list of necessary camera requirements for serious portrait work:

- ✦ **Capability to trigger studio lighting.** Usually this means a PC sync cord outlet that connects the camera to the lighting kit. One alternative is if your camera has a hot shoe; then it's possible to mount a wireless or infrared transmitter to the camera to fire the studio strobes. A second, less desirable approach is to simply use your camera's built-in flash to trigger slaved lights. (This is undesirable because it drains your camera batteries faster and also because the built-in flash takes longer to re-cycle than the studio lights, delaying your next shot.)

- ✦ **Capability to be mounted on a tripod.** This may not be mandatory, but I'd hate to have to shoot portraits without being able to mount my camera on a tripod. It's nice to be able to set up your shot, get the composition just right, and then have the freedom to walk up to your subject to adjust the head position, straighten clothing, or do any of the other things you frequently need to do. It's easier to shoot portraits from a tripod mounted camera.

✦ **Remote control.** Like many portrait photographers, I prefer to hold a remote behind my back so that my subject can't see when I'm about to make the picture. All too often, even with this approach, you end up with people who can anticipate the flash going off and blink fast enough to ruin the picture. It gets much worse if they can see your hand on the shutter button. A remote cable release lets you move around a bit if you want to have your subject looking off in the future. It also enables you to lean in, adjust the subject's pose, and quickly lean back out while taking the photo. If you're not using the remote shutter release, you end up taking your eye off your subject, finding the shutter button, and then looking back at your subject. This generally doesn't work as well.

Necessary accessories

Formal portraiture also requires certain accessories to help you create the best possible image. Here are the most important ones:

✦ **Lighting:** Improved lighting is one of the things that sets the formal portrait apart from the informal version. There's a direct correlation between the quality of your light and the quality of your portrait. It's possible to create a nice portrait using one master light in a big soft box fired straight at your subject, but a multiple lighting setup gives you a much nicer product. Most portrait pros work with a three to four light arrangement, which provides a main light, fill light, back light, and hair light (see Figure 8-2).

Figure 8-2: Studio lighting, complete with umbrellas and soft boxes, makes a big difference in the quality of your portraiture.
© 2004 Dan Simon

✦ **Light modifiers:** Because direct, unmodified flash is harsh and unforgiving, it's best to plan on some form of light modification. This is usually done through accessories known as *diffusers* (a flat panel positioned between the light and your subject) and/or *soft boxes* (a panel mounted on your studio light that provides soft, even lighting), that soften the light.

✦ **Reflectors:** These tools are used to bounce some light towards your subject. Bouncing light softens it, helping to produce a nicer looking portrait. Umbrellas are a type of reflectors. They're mounted directly in front of the strobes (flash units), which are then pointed away from the subject and toward the umbrella. The strobes fire into the umbrella, which reflects the light on to your model.

✦ **Backdrops:** Most often, the backdrop is something designed to distract as little as possible from your model. Occasionally, the backdrop complements the event, such as a Christmas tree and presents for a holiday image or the Titanic's grand staircase for a cruise ship portrait.

✦ **Posing aids:** There are a variety of objects available to help your model pose comfortably. These range from pneumatic chairs, which can be raised and lowered as necessary, to posing blocks (for positioning feet), to stylized objects such as large numbers (popular for senior photos where you have the student pose against a large number representing the graduation year).

To make shooting portraits less cumbersome, you can set up a home studio in any extra room or space you have. (I tell you how to do that later in this chapter in "Project: Setting up a home portrait studio.") Obviously, the larger the space, the more things you can try. But don't worry, many very effective home studios have been set up in tiny rooms. It may limit your portraits to head and shoulders shots, or tight compositions of just two or three people, but you can still create interesting images.

Making interesting portraits

Creating a nice formal portrait isn't that hard. The secret lies in helping people look their best for the photograph, something that isn't necessarily synonymous with simply looking their best.

Things such as good posture and a neat appearance are important. All too often, your subjects may not have paid the level of attention to these requirements that's necessary for a professional quality portrait. This is where you come in.

Setting up the formal portrait

Most formal portraits are done with the subject in a seated position (multiple people in one image usually requires a mix of standing and seated). Professional portrait photographers tend to prefer pneumatic chairs that can be raised and lowered as needed, but this isn't a requirement. What is important is for you to be able to seat your model in a way that is comfortable and flattering. Normally this means that the subject's feet are resting flat on a flat surface. That's where a chair that raises and lowers comes in handy. If you work with a regular chair, having a set of posing blocks will make your life easier. These are simply nesting wooden blocks of different sizes that you can place under your subject's feet. An added benefit of these blocks is that you can have people stand on them if you need to make them taller. You can make your posing blocks by hammering together a variety of sizes of wood blocks. Just make sure the blocks are strong enough for a heavy person to stand on.

 Project: **Posing your subject for a formal portrait**

Remember, the formal portrait process is about making someone look the best they possibly can. Follow these steps as you set up a formal portrait shoot and you're likely to be satisfied with the results:

1. Look over the subject's clothing to ensure that the clothes will display well (keep a lint brush handy) and the hair and make-up (if the person is wearing any) are properly fixed. It's always a good idea to have a mirror handy so that your subjects can check their appearance.

2. Give your subject some idea of how the process works without overloading her with technical detail. I like to give subjects an idea of how long the sitting will take and how many different poses I'm planning to shoot. Telling people ahead of time that I'm making half a dozen shots of a pose helps them stay relaxed and patient. Most amateur photographers take one shot and they're done, so people begin to get impatient after the third shot is taken if you don't warn them ahead of time. You can always take fewer shots once you get started if you feel
you nailed a shot. Just tell your subjects they did a super job for you, so you don't need the extra images after all. I also ask if they have a particular shot or pose they're interested in (many do).

3. When you have the subject seated properly, it's important to make sure she is sitting up straight. Most people don't normally sit up properly, so you may have to encourage this. The easiest way is to press two fingers into the small of the back while gently pushing on the front of the shoulder. Have your subject lean slightly into the camera, as shown in Figure 8-3.

4. Position your subject so that her shoulders are lined up properly. Proper alignment normally means at a slight angle to the camera because the turned shoulders give a sense of movement to an otherwise static pose. Turn her head so that it faces the camera, and angle her face down slightly.

5. After you create the basic pose, return to the camera or to your shooting position if you're not using a tripod. From here, you can still offer some slight direction such as asking the subject to adjust her head position as needed and telling her where to focus her eyes.

6. Decide how to compose the shot. Vertical works best for most portraits. Then zoom in. Unless your subject is wearing a wedding

gown or a prom dress, odds are it's best to compose a tight shot. Most portraits begin a little above the head. This extra space is referred to as *head room* and should always be found in a classic portrait. The shot extends either to the shoulders—the typical *head and shoulders shot*—or down to slightly above the waist. An even tighter composition (called the *head shot*) is used for model portfolios and identification images.

If you have a particular reason for wanting to show the entire body, back up as much as possible rather than zooming out to a wide-angle focal length. Although this may be impossible in a small, home studio, every bit of extra focal length helps to flatter the subject. Exercise care with the full body shot that your lights provide enough coverage. Also be careful that the edges of your background aren't apparent.

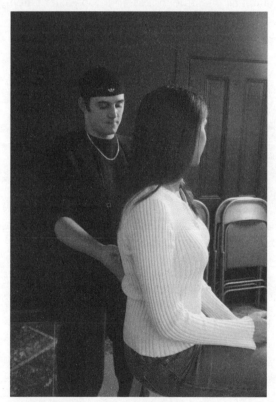

Figure 8-3: The "magic button."
© *2004 Dan Simon*

7. Decide how to handle the subject's eyeglasses and the potential for reflected glare off the glasses. In the days before the digital darkroom, glasses were the portrait photographer's worst enemy. All too often, an excellent image was ruined by the reflected glare. Conventional retouching could only go so far and was prohibitively

Continued

Project *(continued)*

expensive. It's easier to fix such a problem in an image-editing program these days, but it's still better to do everything you can to minimize the glare in the first place.

When it comes to dealing with glasses, you have several options for making your life easier. Sometimes, a subject is comfortable having her photo taken without glasses. More often, however, glasses are a part of her identity (as in "No one's going to recognize me without my glasses"), so it's better to try to adjust them by sliding them a bit forward on the bridge of the nose (see Figure 8-4). This changes the angle of the glass and frequently minimizes the reflection. Another option is to try repositioning your lights slightly, also to change the angle of the reflection. Even if you can't get rid of it completely; reducing glare as much as possible makes your job easier when you try to fix the rest of it in the digital darkroom.

Figure 8-4: Lisa's glasses were a problem (photo on left) until I asked her to tilt her head down slightly (photo on right). (Note: Repeated firings of the studio strobes actually caused her light-sensitive glasses to darken as the shoot went on.)

© 2004 Dan Simon

8. Check the appearance one last time. If your subject's clothing is bunched anywhere, a quick tug should fix it. Hair out of place? Have a brush or comb handy for fast touch-ups. How does the tie look? Check the line made from the dress shirt's outer layer down through the zipper of the trousers. The two should match up. Poor alignment of these items in a formal portrait is distracting, so ask your subject to align these items before taking his place.

9. When you're ready to snap the shot, ask the subject to smile or give you the expression she wants to convey. Although most people choose a portrait of themselves smiling, you do run into the occasional subject who's better photographed looking focused and

serious. Just remember that setting the expression should be the last step you take before making the photo because it's hard for the average person to hold an expression for very long. It's incredibly frustrating when a photographer gets you to smile and then putters about doing other things, while you feel that smile slipping away. Get the subject to smile and make the photo! If you have any doubts, take another shot.

10. Take the picture. If possible, keep the camera remote behind your back so that your subject can't tell the exact moment you make the photo. Quickly scan the face. As soon as the expression is ready, take the photo.

Maintaining a Professional Demeanor

Your attitude is important in bringing out the best in your subject, and how you relate to your subjects can make or break a sitting. Always be positive, upbeat, and enthusiastic. Remember that people sitting for a portrait are usually self-conscious. They need to feel confident in your skills as a portrait photographer. Never let the situation get to the point where it becomes a competition between you and the subject to make them look good. If it reaches this point, you've already lost.

Posing a group

You can choose from any number of poses and arrangements when creating formal portraits. When working with a family, it's customary to make a shot of the full family; a couples shot of the parents, and then photograph the child or children. Most families are quite satisfied with these poses, but there's no reason you can't pose mom with her daughters or dad with his sons if that's what the subjects prefer. You can offer a wide range of poses for your subjects to choose from. Just bear in mind that the average person has only a certain amount of patience, energy, and enthusiasm for having a portrait made.

The basic group pose begins with your seated anchor. When posing families, that anchor is usually mom. Seat her and get her posed. Then bring dad in behind her, seated halfway to one side. Now you have the beginning of the couple's pose. Arrange their heights so her eyes are roughly level with his mouth (this is why pros favor pneumatic posing stools). Have dad lean forward slightly so his head is as close to being on the same plane as mom's face. Try to do this with every person in the composition. The closer faces are, to being on the same plane, the more in focus everyone will be.

Now bring in the shorter child and set him up next to mom. Use posing blocks to make him taller if need be, but get his height up to where his mouth is level with her eyes (and thus equal to dad's). If he's too tall for this, you'll have to raise mom up to get her mouth and his eyes right. This puts dad's position out of line, so you'll have to adjust the posing stool to get his height right too. Avoid the temptation to have someone "scrunch" down or rise up a little. This is very uncomfortable and impossible to hold for more than a few seconds. Take the time to get the heights right.

After you get these three together (and you can use this as a pose for a group of three people) bring in the fourth person. Place her behind mom and raise her so that her mouth is even with dad and person number three's eyes (or slightly higher). This gives you the *diamond* pose, the basic building block for group portraiture. From here, you can add additional people by using dad or person number three as the anchor for a new diamond and building outward the same way you constructed the first diamond. Add one person behind and halfway to dad's right so that this person's mouth is even with dad's eyes, and then place another person behind dad and high enough that his mouth is even with the eyes of the person you just posed to the right of Dad. Do the same on the other side with person number 3, working to the left; then build upward to complete the diamond. As a general rule, you can give a little extra space for the top person in each diamond, so try spacing this person so that his chin is level with the eyes of the two people right below (see Figure 8-5).

Figure 8-5: The diamond pose.

Lighting the formal portrait

It's lighting, more than anything else, that makes the formal portrait look professional. Let's face it, there's a huge difference between the impromptu family portrait done with a camera mounted flash and one done with a multi-light studio setup. Lighting is what separates the amateurs from the pros.

The essence of the studio lighting look is the multiple-light arrangement. It's possible to create this look outside the studio using multiple slaved flash units, and many photographers do use just such an approach. The reason portrait pros use studio rigs is these units put out more light, recycle faster, and keep going longer. For the amateur just making a few portraits, the flash method works just fine. For the pro cranking out the volume or whose reputation depends on the best possible results, the studio lights meet that need.

Basic portrait lighting setups

When it comes to lighting portraits, you can arrange multiple lights in a number of ways. These variations create different looks and moods and each serves a different purpose. The type of lighting you use also depends on the direction in which the model's face is turned.

Here are two versatile lighting setups that work for producing flattering, useable light. These basic arrangements are quick to set up and work for one person or groups of up to 20 people depending on how powerful your lights are. If you're running a home studio, you can leave either of these arrangements set up all the time so that you're always ready to create a professional looking portrait:

✦ **Main lighting plus fill:** This is a simple two or three light setting. Position your main light about six feet from your subject and at least three feet to the right of the camera (see Figure 8-6). Point the light directly at the posing stool (preferably through a soft box) or reflect the light into an umbrella, which reflects the light onto the subject.

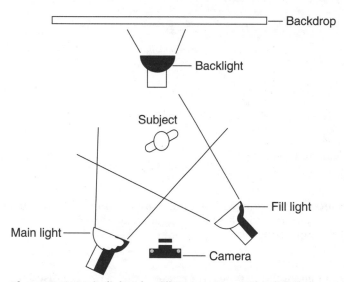

Figure 8-6: Main light plus fill arrangement. This lighting setup includes a small backlight to separate the subject from the background.

Position your fill light (a light used to fill in shadows created by the main light) opposite your main light so the two lights and posing stool form a triangle. If you have a third light, set it behind the posing stool, directed at your background with the light angled upwards to provide some separation between the model and the backdrop. Each light should be raised so that it's angled slightly downward at your subject. (This requires some adjustment as the size of your group increases.)

If your lighting kit is limited, you can substitute a reflector for the fill light for small sittings (limit is about four people). The reflector bounces the light from the main light into the shadow areas, improving the lighting ratio. Place the reflector closer to the posing stool because the reflected light output won't be as strong as a strobe unit would be.

✦ **Butterfly lighting:** This setup calls for your main light to pointed straight at the posing stool, usually through a soft box (see Figure 8-7). You can then add a backlight to provide some separation from the backdrop. Your main light should be raised high enough so it can be angled slightly downward at your model.

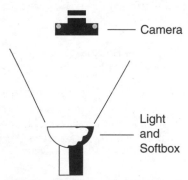

Figure 8-7: Butterfly lighting setup.

Figure 8-8 shows a photo in which a butterfly lighting setup was used. One strobe was fired through a soft box mounted directly above the camera and pointed straight at the model.

Lighting variations

In addition to these main lighting types, there are some variations used primarily for individual poses, which are designed to minimize or hide flaws:

✦ **Short lighting:** This technique positions the subject so her head is turned slightly to one side of the camera. The main light is then positioned so it illuminates the side of the face not facing the lens. This will slim broad faces.

✦ **Broad lighting:** With this technique, the main light illuminates the side of the face facing the lens. This will make narrow faces look wider.

Figure 8-8: An image made with butterfly lighting.

© *2004 Dan Simon*

✦ **Rembrandt lighting:** This technique uses Butterfly and Short lighting together. The main light is placed above the subject to the side of her face angled away from the camera. In Figure 8-9, the main light was placed to the left of the model at about a 45-degree angle, and her face was turned slightly toward the light.

Lighting options

As noted earlier, lighting is the key to professional looking portraiture. The good news is that you can set up a decent studio without breaking the bank. The following list gives you several ways to do this:

✦ **Photographic lighting:** You can invest in a decent to high-quality main light, fill light, light modifier, and stand for a reasonable amount of money ($200 to $500). Add a good quality reflector ($30 to $100) on either another light stand via a clamp ($50 to $100) or use an extra tripod (free, because you already own it) with a Bogen super clamp ($20 to $30 if you don't already have one). This takes care of your main and fill lights. You can either make do with this minimalistic setup, or invest a little more money to add a modest backlight ($100 to $200.)

This setup will give you a reasonable amount of flexibility, but it won't help you do a good job with large groups. Still, for a home studio where you just want to experiment, it will give you options. The added advantage is you can build upon this arrangement over time, adding more or better lighting as you can afford it.

Figure 8-9: An image shot with Rembrandt lighting.
© 2004 Dan Simon

✦ **Photo floods:** Unlike the photographic strobes discussed earlier, these are simple floodlights that stay on all the time. They tend to be cheaper, than photographic spots (one catalog offers a unit with stand for $55.49 sans bulb that can be used as a back light or fill light; main light versions were listed for about $90). These systems frequently produce more heat than strobes because they're on all the time, but do produce workable light.

✦ **Garage work lights:** The digital darkroom has made using halogen work lights more practical for many hobbyist photographers simply because it's easy to white balance for these lights in the computer. As a result, a cheaper, double duty option is available for amateur photographers trying to set up a home studio as cheaply as possible. Three of these can give enough light to create many studio lighting arrangements. Just make sure you white balance your camera properly when using them. You can improve the quality of this lighting by bouncing (reflecting) the light off a white ceiling or reflector or putting a diffuser between the lights and your subjects (not too close to the lights).

 You can find more information about color correction and white balance in Chapter 15.

Backgrounds

Background choices run the gamut from basic seamless paper up to fancy hand-painted muslin cloth backdrops, which depict scenes appropriate for various times of the year.

The professional portrait photographer may rely on such finery because the different backdrops can help increase sales as he creates a summer sports portrait followed by a fall foliage one, followed by a Christmas one, and so on. The pro goes this route in hopes of increasing sales. The hobbyist can pursue such options as she sees fit.

The easiest (and maybe the cheapest) approach for a home studio is through the use of seamless backdrop paper. This is available in a variety of colors and comes in long rolls. You just hang the paper from a set of wall-mounted rollers and unfurl however much you need for your portrait. When the bottom section gets too soiled or crumpled to use (usually from the model standing on it for full-length photos) you just cut off the soiled end and unfurl some more. Because the paper is relatively inexpensive (a 50-foot roll of nine-foot wide white paper runs less than $100) photographers can build a variety of colors fairly easily. Usually white and black are the first elements of the collection, but if you expect to do a lot of digital magic, blue and green screen versions are available that make it easier to remove your model from the background so that you can drop her into a new image.

 Blue screening and *green screening* are techniques where the model is photographed against a particular shade of blue or green background that is easy to eliminate digitally. The television and movie industries have used this method for years to create various special effects. Thanks to the home computer revolution and programs like Photoshop, hobbyists can do this kind of thing too.

 Project: **Setting up a home portrait studio**

A basic home portrait studio doesn't have to be difficult to set up. The following steps can walk you through the process:

1. *Determine the basic light sources you must have.* Aim for two sources and three if you can afford it. You could conceivably use an off-camera flash and a reflector, but you probably won't have the light output necessary for anything more than simple one-person head and shoulders shots.) The more lights (within reason) and greater light output you have, the more varied your lighting can be.

   Your lighting kit can be floods (always on) or strobes. Floods do raise the temperature of the room and use more electricity, but also let you see how shadows will fall while you're posing your model. Strobes need time to recycle, and unless they have a built-in modeling light (a lamp that stays on so you can see shadows during the posing process), you have to check your images to discover any

Continued

Project *(continued)*

shadow problems. Because strobes can discharge and recharge, they generally can produce a greater output than photofloods. This means you can usually shoot with smaller apertures than when using floods.

2. *Mount your lights.* The easiest way to accomplish this is through telescoping light stands. Each stand needs an adapter to mount the strobe or flood on the stand. These can be raised and lowered as needed and collapse small enough to fit in a small bag. Figure one stand for each light. You need stands that telescope up to about seven feet for your main and fill lights, but you can get by with a smaller stand for your backlight. Homemade substitutions are possible, particularly if you're the type that's good at making things yourself. Much depends on how portable you want your studio setup to be. If it's never going to leave the house, wall mounting a light might be an option.

3. *Provide seating for your subjects.* Although pneumatic posing stools are popular with the pros, you can get by with stuff you already have. A good three-legged stool isn't bad because it enables your subject to rest his feet on one of the rungs. A basic wooden chair can also be put into service. Try to buy or make a set of posing blocks that are sturdy enough for people to stand on.

4. *Add a backdrop.* Start with either seamless paper or dye an old sheet. If you or a friend is artistically inclined, look at hand painting your own canvas backdrop.

5. *Add a tripod to your equipment list.* My preference is always to work with a tripod, and if you plan to work with one, be sure to have one that works with you. This means that it needs to be sturdy enough to hold your camera steady, but light enough to move easily. It should also be fairly simple to raise and lower the camera as needed. If your budget allows for one, consider mounting the tripod on a dolly. A dolly makes repositioning the camera a much simpler task.

6. *Buy or make some props.* These fall under the "nice-but-not-necessary" category. Yes, they can add something to a portrait, but they won't be missed if they're not there either. If you like this sort of thing, use your imagination. Oriental fans, athletic gear, fancy lace gloves, and flowers all offer interesting possibilities.

7. *Decide on what kinds of reflectors and light modifiers you need.* These handy tools help you bounce light from your light sources and/or soften your lighting. It's usually best to try to avoid using unmodified light because it tends to produce a less forgiving quality of light. Either shoot through a diffuser or soft box, or bounce light off an umbrella or some other reflector.

After you have gathered all the gear for your studio, set it up so that it's readily useable. Here are some things pros do to make sure their equipment works with them instead of against them.

✦ Use gaffer's tape or duct tape to mark off the position of your basic lighting arrangement. This way, if you reposition for a particular shot, you can get your lights back in place quickly.

✦ Tape down power cords and sync cords to ensure that people don't trip over them as they move about the studio. Even worse, a leg hooked through a power cord can bring your lights (or even your camera) crashing to the floor.

✦ Hang a mirror somewhere near the posing area so that subjects can quickly check their appearance. It's nice to also have a shelf nearby with combs, hairbrushes and tissues for other quick touch ups.

Informal Portraiture

Informal portraits are the most popular and common type of portraiture. They are much more spontaneous than the formal kind. Informal portraits are the pictures you make when you are out with a group of friends and just want a nice picture to remember the occasion or the person. Frequently,you want to combine the person and the location to produce a memory shot of some vacation or road trip.

Unfortunately, informal portraiture is done poorly by most people. Indecision over what to show and what to leave out usually results in a futile attempt to show everything, resulting in an image that shows nothing.

Informal portraits tend to be ho-hum photos. Your subject is standing there staring at the camera, forced smile pasted on her face. Often, the subject is standing in front of some sort of tourist attraction or at some event and you're taking the picture to immortalize a special moment in time. Some day, 40 years later, you may look back at that image and say, "Who's that, and why did I take her picture?"

Or, all those years later, you may gaze fondly at the image and a flood of memories and emotions will come rushing back as you remember who the person is and why you took the photograph. Such is the wonder of photography that it can serve that purpose. When it does, it's just for you. When you try to share that photo with someone who wasn't there, the picture doesn't convey the same power. Your audience doesn't have the same memories and emotions as you, so the power of that image is lost.

Yet it is possible to create images that both preserve your memories of that friend or loved one and also provide the necessary information to interest someone who was never at the event. In Figure 8-10, for example, instead of shooting Lisa and our friend, Heather, holding Heather's new baby and staring into the camera, I caught this natural moment that offers much more emotional content.

There are times too, when the spontaneity of the informal portrait gives enough life to your subject that its content supercedes it banality. My wife Lisa, and her

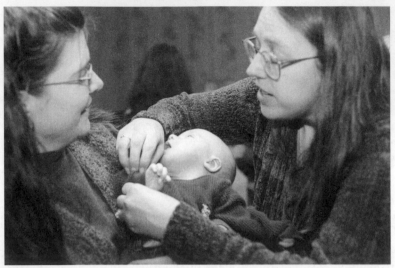

Figure 8-10: A more natural way to capture two friends with a new baby.
© 2004 Dan Simon

sister for instance, make a habit of sticking their tongues out at me every time I point a camera in their direction. You'd think this would ruin the photo. But actually, it reminds me of the characteristics I enjoy about them: spontaneity, impulsiveness, sense of humor, and enough self-confidence not to worry about how the shot will turn out.

When you're taking an informal portrait, remember what's important: your subject's face with the background scenery. Create a tight composition of your friend (concentrate on the head and shoulders) positioned to the right or left edge of the frame. You can then budget the rest of the frame to the landmark you want to include in the photo. Here are a couple of other things to keep in mind when shooting informal shots of people:

✦ **Balance the light:** There may be a distance of several miles or more between your subject and the scenery, so there's a good chance the light levels will be different. Determine which element of the composition is brighter and do your best to help the other element get more light. If your subject is in shadow and the background is brightly lit, the answer is easy—turn your flash on and fill in the shadows. If your subject is brightly lit and the background is in shadow, it's a bit tougher. Try to reposition the subject so that he's in the same shadow your scenery is or try to block the light (try a sheet of cardboard or a car windshield's collapsible sun shade) to reduce the light.

✦ **Lens choice:** Make your friend and the scenery look like they're closer together by choosing a short telephoto focal length over a wide angle one. This decreases the apparent distance between the two. Don't go for too long a telephoto though; the resulting loss of depth of field may render the background too out of focus to be recognizable.

✦ **Depth of field:** Try to select an f-stop that gives maximum depth of field while still allowing a fast enough shutter speed to prevent blur from camera shake or subject movement. If you manage a small lens opening (say f8 or smaller), you can focus on a point somewhere between your friend and the scenery and keep both in focus. (It really helps if your camera has a depth of field preview function.)

Try to create a relaxed looking pose. The vacation portrait shown in Figure 8-11 was made during a sailing trip in the Bahamas. I zoomed out a little to show the sailboat canopy, but still framed the shot tightly enough to make Lisa the most prominent part of the image. The late daylight was relatively even (not high-contrast), so I didn't need to use a flash. When possible, consider including some kind of prop that helps identify where you area, such as a guidebook or map.

Figure 8-11: Good example of a relaxed pose. You can tell the shot takes place on a boat, but the subject is still the prominent part of the image.

© 2004 Dan Simon

For non-travel related photographs, try to include something that shows why you were making the picture in the first place. Was it a holiday? How about a barbecue or some other type of family get-together? All too often,you get caught up in the excitement of the moment and forget that you may be looking at these photos 20 or 30 years from now and won't immediately remember what was going on when you took the photo.

Look for props or elements that make it obvious where your subject is and what's going on. This will add meaning and insight into the images decades from now when you're looking at them and reminiscing.

Personally, I think people are most interesting when they don't know they're being photographed. You can find out more about this type of photography in the "Candid photography" section a little later in this chapter.

Environmental Portraiture

The environmental portrait is a cross between a formal portrait and an informal location. The idea behind this type of image is that by showing the individual in his work environment, you provide some insight into his world.

This is terrific when your subject is a blacksmith or a rodeo cowboy; it's not quite so exciting when he's an office worker. Still, the idea is to produce a casual looking image of a person who seems to be busy working and just stopped for a moment to pose for a picture.

Environmental portraits can make a nice souvenir photograph for someone who is proud of his profession and finds his identity through his work. Because this picture is as much about what the person does as about who the person is, it certainly provides us with more information than does the traditional formal portrait.

Yet, there's a whole world of people photography beyond the posed stuff. This next category, candid photography, is my favorite style of people photography, and the kind I do the most.

Candid Photography

The candid photo is one where your subject either isn't aware that the photo is being taken, or isn't actively posing for the image because she is too busy doing whatever she was doing that made you want to photograph her in the first place.

In candid photography, you are actually capturing a moment in time (see Figure 8-12). The idea is to show what people and their lives are really like. These are the photos that show whoyou are and whatyou do. If done right, they can help tell someone who's never met us what we're like.

Candid photography is all about catching people being themselves. It requires no special props, posing, backdrops, or any of the many things necessary for successful formal portraiture. Sounds easy huh? Well, not quite.

Candid photography comes complete with its own set of challenges. First and foremost is finding ways to photograph people without them being aware that you're taking their photo. Then add this to the challenge: you're also trying to make them look good—or at least natural.

Figure 8-12: Candid photos give us a glimpse into the lives of others.

© 2004 Dan Simon

Candid photography becomes most interesting when you catch people caught up in the things they do. The unexpected shot produces natural moments that show an individual's true nature. For the shot shown in Figure 8-13, I got down to eye level for a more pleasing photo.

It can be hard to make good candid photos. This isn't because the process itself is difficult—it isn't. Instead, the challenge comes from the change in persona necessary to do the job well.

Most people go to an event or get-together to have fun and maybe take a few photos. This approach is fine for producing snapshots, but of limited value for producing quality images. Being a good candid photographer means spending more time observing than participating.

The good news is that people-watching can be a lot of fun. This is your opportunity to get to know what your friends and family are like from a slightly different vantage point.

As noted earlier in this book, good candid photography calls for a variety of tactics from the photographer. Although people do get so caught up in what they're doing, that they forget their picture is being taken, it's also frequently necessary to resort to stealth tactics for really interesting images. The following section tells you how to become a stealth photographer.

Figure 8-13: A child opening a Christmas present is usually too occupied with what he's doing to notice you're taking his picture. A telephoto zoom (80 to 200mm made it possible for me to create a tight composition without distracting the subject.)
© 2004 Dan Simon

Stealth photography

An amateur candid photographer can often blend more easily into a crowd than a pro can, simply because an unobtrusive point-and-shoot camera is less noticeable than the loads of equipment a pro often carries. Yet pros who specialize in candids have their own ways of blending in. Whether you're an amateur or a pro, however, here are some points to keep in mind when you're trying to snap candid shots:

✦ **Be sensitive to your subject:** Candid shots show people behaving naturally, so the results can sometimes be embarrassing. Be sure to keep this in mind when shooting candids. Although it's important to capture naturalness as much as possible, the goal isn't to catch someone in an unflattering pose. It's often desirable to delete shots that while eye-catching, are also humiliating.

✦ **People tend to forget you're there after a while.** They may notice you at first, especially if you take a lot of photos and use flash, but if you go work another part of the room, eventually people get so wrapped up in having a good time, they forget about the photographer. This is the perfect time to come back to their area.

✦ **Develop a sense of stealth.** I frequently use a modest telephoto (about 200mm equivalent) to isolate people in a crowd. Most people aren't familiar enough with lenses to know what angle of view they have, so unless the lens is pointed right at them, they don't realize you're taking their picture. Focus on a person or object the same distance away and then swing the camera on to your subject and quickly take the photo.

✦ **Use your zoom lens to its fullest.** This one plays upon the same idea as using a telephoto lens, namely people don't really recognize that a camera lens is trained on them unless it's pointed right at them. Use your lens at its widest setting (adding a wide angle adapter if you can) and position people away from the center of the image. (Remember the rule of thirds, too.) Because the lens isn't pointed right at them, most people don't realize you're taking their photo.

✦ **My personal favorite.** Go with the widest focal length you can (the wider the better) and don't even look through the viewfinder. Just lift your camera up to your chest (you can even look down at it to make sure it's level. If you wear a puzzled look, people will just think you're distracted.), and point it in the direction of the person you want to photograph. All you have to do at this point is trip the shutter! The wide angle lens will give you a large enough field of view that someone standing a couple of feet away from you will still be in the frame. Be ready to pop off a second shot as the person realizes you just took their picture! I use this technique in the photo shown in Figure 8-14.

Figure 8-14: This image shows a family's natural behavior on Christmas morning.
© 2004 Dan Simon

The key thing to remember in candid photography is that you want your subjects to look as natural as possible. Unless you're working with a professional model (whose job is to look unposed and natural), you've got to photograph people when they've forgotten you're around. The next section gives you some tips on how to accomplish that.

Striving for naturalness

What's important to remember is that good photography is more than just tripping the shutter a lot. If you want to make better people photos, it helps if you truly understand your subjects.

Whether you're trying for that great sports photo or looking to make interesting people images, developing a sense of anticipation is vital. In sports photography, you study the game and learn how things work. The same principle applies to candid photography.

If you see a pair of teen-aged girls in animated conversation, it's pretty likely that sooner or later, one of them is going to raise her hands to her face in an "Oh mi-god" moment. If you're anticipating this, your camera is pre-focused to her distance and the exposure settings are already locked in. You can just lift your camera and make the photo.

On Thanksgiving Day, while dinner's being prepared, I know my brothers-in-law will be gathered around the TV watching football. Because they're excitable types, I can anticipate that sooner or later, they'll shout and gesture at the TV and can be waiting for the shot. (Well, I could if I wasn't slaving away at a hot stove making dinner.)

At any family gathering at my one brother's house, I know that after dinner, David will settle down in his favorite chair for a nap. I also know that my nieces and nephews will be down in the rec room either playing games or plotting mischief. These are all good possibilities for interesting candid photos and all rely on your ability to anticipate behavior.

The type of photography I discuss in the next section, "Glamour photography" is the complete opposite of candid work.

Glamour Photography

Glamour photography is usually the first one that comes to mind when you think of models and professional photographers. This type of photography is all about making people look glamorous (see Figure 8-15).

Once, glamour was strictly the specialty of the pros, both photographers and models. But as anyone who's walked through the local shopping mall may know, this style has an appeal for everyone. These portraits make popular gifts.

Glamour goes a step beyond formal portraiture in the sense that it tries to show the sex appeal of your subject. Clothing, makeup, and hairstyles tend to be more pronounced and some additional lighting tools are used.

Categories of glamour photography

The glamour approach can be adapted to many styles of photography. Some of the most popular include the following:

 ✦ **Portraiture:** Glamour lighting, sexy clothing, teased hair, and more makeup are all elements of this style of glamour portrait. Sometimes the model adopts a more sensuous expression, but smiling versions are also popular.

Figure 8-15: A glamour shot.

© 2004 Dan Simon

✦ **Swimsuit:** Ever since the classic bathing beauty shots of the 1920s, pictures of people in their swimsuits have been fair game for photographic study. The glamour version of this image emphasizes the beauty of the human form. Typically, swimsuit portraits are shot with longer lenses (sometimes 300mm on up) because the extreme focal length flatters the model's face (see Figure 8-16).

✦ **Boudoir:** Bedroom photography, usually complete with lingerie. This style glories in the sexuality of its model and portrays her as an object of desire.

✦ **Nudes:** The dividing line between "Glamour" and "Fine Art" nude photography appears to be getting blurrier every day. I know I see a lot of "fine art nudes" that should more certainly be described as "glamour" style. Fine art nudes almost treat the human body as an abstract form. Although you may be able to recognize certain features, the idea isn't so much to reveal, as it is to question. Glamour style nudes celebrate the beauty of the human figure. Their goal is to present something beautiful for your enjoyment.

Whole books have been written about each of these styles of glamour photography. This book touches upon the first two (because the editors and my wife wanted to keep a PG rating).

Figure 8-16: Swimsuit glamour shot.
© *2004 Dan Simon*

Portraiture

As I mentioned in the preceding section, glamour portraits portray sex appeal. Shirts can be tight fitting or more revealing with buttons undone. Frequently the photographer uses soft-focus effects to create a kind of dreamy look. These can be created either during the photo shoot through the use of soft focus or diffusing filters, or afterwards in the digital darkroom using filters such as those by Power Retouche or The Imaging Factory.

 The Imaging Factory is discussed in more detail in Chapter 15 in the context of image editing.

Glamour lighting

Lighting for glamour portraits tends to be based on the butterfly lighting style (described earlier in this chapter), particularly for women because it tends to be quite flattering. A popular variation of this lighting style is known as Clamshell lighting.

Clamshell lighting is popular for glamour portraits because it adds a sensual glow to the model's face. This style begins with butterfly lighting but adds a reflector below the model's face to bounce some light back up into the shadow areas (see Figure 8-17).

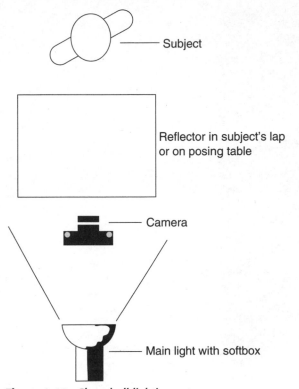

Figure 8-17: Clamshell lighting setup.

Figure 8-18 shows an example of an image shot using a clamshell lighting setup. In this photo, the model was lit normally with a strobe fired through a soft box positioned directly above the camera. At the same time, a reflector was held in front of and below her face (out of sight of the camera, of course) to bounce some light back onto her face.

Fancier lighting setups may include a second light below the main light with a colored gel to provide an interesting color cast to the image.

Swimsuit photography

Swimsuit photography shot indoors can use the same basic lighting setups as discussed earlier in this chapter. It's natural to want to shoot these images outdoors as well, and done properly, location photography can produce attractive results.

Now for the bad news. Most of those great swimsuit photos you see of models at the beach or at the pool are created in the early morning hours right after sunrise. (Here's a quick way of telling if your kid really wants to be a model, see how enthusiastic she is about getting up at 4:30 a.m. to prep for a sunrise photo session.)

Figure 8-18: A glamour shot using Clamshell lighting.
© *2004 Dan Simon*

Still, there are some ways to make swimsuit images during a more sane time of day. One way is to shoot on overcast days. The flat lighting works pretty well.

You can also work with large reflectors and diffusers. These will help soften the light (diffusers) and also bounce some light into shadow areas (reflectors) to balance the light a bit better.

Favor the longest focal length you can reasonably work with for these shoots. I like to work with a 300mm telephoto whenever possible because it creates a very pleasing image. There's an added benefit in that the extra distance between you and the model can help an inexperienced or nervous subject feel a bit more comfortable (see Figure 8-19).

Shooting at Family Gatherings

After you get comfortable with the various techniques for photographing people, family gatherings become the perfect training ground for you to practice your skills. Reunions, holidays, weddings, and birthdays, give you all the opportunities you need to work on your "people skills."

Figure 8-19: Swimsuit portrait made with a 300mm telephoto.
© *2004 Dan Simon*

Shoot your portraits early while everybody is fresh and neat (especially the kids!). After you've done the portraits and group shots, start working on the candids. Family get-togethers are fertile ground for memorable candid photos because you're capturing people in the roles you've known them in for years.

Document the preparation that goes into meals. Photograph the kids as they get re-acquainted and play together (remember to get down to their level). Catch the card players or conversations, and frame your images tightly to create a greater sense of intimacy.

   Project: **The window-lit portrait**

Using light coming through a window makes for an easy and beautiful one-person portrait technique. Developing an awareness of this kind of directional lighting can also help you create nicer candid images as you learn to look for this type of light in everyday situations.

Continued

Project *(continued)*

The following steps walk you through the technique for shooting a window-lit portrait:

1. First off, you need a window, but not just any window will do. You need one facing the sun for it to serve as your main light source. Especially bright sunlight, however, may be too much for this type of portrait.

2. Position your subject so that she is bathed in the light coming through the window. You can pose your subject so she's looking into the light (putting them in profile to your shooting position) or looking directly toward the camera.

Figure 8-20: Sunlight pouring through the kitchen window illuminates my sister-in-law's face, producing a lovely image.
© *2004 Dan Simon*

3. If possible, turn down the other lights in the room. You're looking for a pronounced lighting ratio where one side of the subject's face is

illuminated, whereas the other side is in shadow. You can use supplemental lights to try to keep the ratio under control. (If the window light is too bright and other illumination is too dim, the shadow side of the face goes completely black.)

4. Meter off the side of the face illuminated by the sun. This is the main part of your subject and you want your exposure to show detail in this part of the face. If you screw up here, you end up with a big white splotch where your subject's face is supposed to be.

 See Chapter 7 to find out more about using a light meter.

5. Do a test shot. Pros used to do this with Polaroid film in the days before digital, but now you can just try a shot and check your LCD screen to see how it worked. If there's too much contrast (pure white face on the sun side and dark black on the shade side) find a way to balance the lighting better. Some suggestions are to add more supplemental lights or to use a reflector to bounce some of the sunlight back onto the shadow side of your subject's face. You can find opportunities to utilize window lighting almost anywhere. With this technique, you can produce beautiful, thoughtful images without investing in expensive lighting equipment. Figure 8-20 shows an example of the soft illumination sunlight often provides.

Summary

Your fellow human beings are about as interesting a subject for photographic study as you can find. One photographer I know even treats the pregnant female body as a topography for landscape portraiture!

Whether you pursue portraiture or candid photography, there are opportunities for amazing results and a fulfilling hobby or profession. Get good at photographing people and you'll have a wonderful collection of photographic memories depicting your family and loved ones.

Photographing Sports

Sports photography is one of the most exciting types of photography you can do. There's a real challenge to capturing peak action during fast-moving competitions.

Of course, there are a lot of different sports out there. Experienced pros spend years learning the best vantage points to shoot from and the peak action to look for. This information is earned the hard way, by dodging running backs and ducking foul balls, by shivering in the cold during football season, and by overheating in steamy gyms during wrestling season.

In this chapter, I share some of my hard-learned secrets with you and tell you how to take better sports photos. I tell you how to anticipate the action, how to prefocus so you're ready for that perfect shot, and what lens to take with you on the shoot. I also give you specific tips for the various sports that you may be shooting. When you are done, you'll know everything about sports photography except the secret sports photographer's handshake. (If you want that, send $19.95 to the address at the end of this chapter and I'll be glad to e-mail you the instructions.)

The Essence of Sports Photography

"Three rolls of butt shots."

I was standing on top of the vert ramp (the big, U-shaped ramp skateboarders do their tricks on) at the X-Games in Philadelphia a few years ago and chatting with a fellow photographer I'd been shooting with the day before. We'd been in the same position that day, blazing away as athletes such as Tony Hawk, Bucky Lasek, and Andy MacDonald did their stuff.

He was shooting film; I was shooting digital. He'd burned three rolls of film thinking he'd made good photos, but never really knowing until he processed his film and could review the results.

Me, I'd figured out my timing was a little bit off after viewing my first few butt shots. I made the adjustment and had plenty of great photos to show for it.

By now, you already know I prefer digital to conventional photography, so I don't have to bang that point home. Instead, the point I want to make here is that timing has got to be right on for capturing peak action in sports photography. Get it a little bit wrong, and you end up with three rolls of butt shots.

Sports photography is all about documenting action. Often, freezing the peak moment of excitement does this. Pros rely on fast shutter speeds and quick auto-focus systems to produce memorable results. As point-and-shoot digital cameras improve, such photography becomes more and more possible for amateur digital photographers. More affordable DSLRs put even greater power in the hands of budding sports photographers. The following sections offer some techniques that can help photographers at all levels really get in the game when it comes to shooting sports.

Capturing the Action

Sports photographers use a variety of techniques to document the various events they cover. Sometimes, the most interesting images have little to do with sports action and instead focus on small details (see Figure 9-1).

Intense moments of action, frozen in time, however, still represent the images you most often see in newspapers and magazines. These tend to be the shots you remember. This section gives you some tips on how to capture the shots that portray the drama and thrill of athletics.

Anticipating the shot

A key to good sports photography is anticipation. Good photographers actually begin taking the photo before the peak moment occurs. This is necessary because of the speed of modern athletes and the objects they throw, kick, or strike.

The more you know about a particular sport, the more effective a sports photographer you can be. Your knowledge can enable you to anticipate action and also have a better understanding of how to position yourself. This chapter details much of this information for a wide variety of sports, but that doesn't mean you can't follow your own instincts. Use your experience to plan the kind of photos you want to make.

Your ability to anticipate key moments improves with practice. Good sports photographs happen the same way good athletic performances do—the participants practice their sport or craft to get better at it. This doesn't mean you have to be out every day photographing a sporting event just to improve

Figure 9-1: I was photographing a bike race when I
noticed the piles of energy-boosting snacks.
© *2004 Dan Simon*

(although that is one reason why pros become so good at this kind of
photography). Instead, make use of down time during a game. Follow the action
and make some shots even when the athlete you're following isn't in the game or
isn't near enough to photograph. The more images you make, the better you'll
get.

Concentrate on following either the ball or a specific athlete, and work on
tripping the shutter just before the athlete strikes the ball. As you do more and
more of this, you'll improve at capturing the peak moment. Thanks to your
digital camera, you can afford to waste some photos as you improve.

In the days before digital, amateur photographers—always aware of the cost of
film and processing—photographed sporting events while carefully rationing
their shots. As any working pro can tell you, that's not the way to cover a
sporting event.

It's the opposite that's true. Sports photography calls for the unrestrained use of
motor drives or sequential shooting capabilities. This is no time to be stingy.
Thankfully, digital cameras relieve the cost issue.

Prefocusing the shot

Even the fastest auto-focus systems aren't perfect. Athletes move so quickly and in many sports are part of such a confusing jumble, that sensors get fooled, directions change, and both photographer and camera miss plays completely.

There are some things you can do help improve your chances of having the camera, lens, and your eye aimed at the right place at the right time.

In the preceding section, I talked about anticipation as a way of tripping the shutter in time for a great photo. Anticipation is also important in giving your camera a head start on the action. Here's an example of what I mean. Take a corner kick in soccer. You know where the play is going to begin—the soccer player off the field charges to the ball resting at the very corner of the playing area. If that player is your son or daughter, here's a chance to catch him or her in action. Prefocus your lens on a spot just before the ball, and you'll already have the key point in focus before the action happens. As the athlete begins his kick, trip the shutter and you've got your shot!

A more difficult example of prefocusing is at the other end of the corner kick. You know the ball is going to head toward a cluster of players near the net, so prefocus your lens to the group of players waiting for the ball. When it comes time to put the ball into play, follow it with your camera (without activating the focusing mechanism) until it reaches the net area; then start shooting (see Figure 9-2). Because you already prefocused your lens on that area, it won't have to waste time refocusing from a completely different point.

Prefocusing for cameras with shutter lag

Prefocusing to where you think the action is headed is most effective with cameras that respond quickly to the shutter button being pressed. You can focus on the group in front of the net and then wait for the action to start. If your camera suffers from pronounced shutter lag, taking a long time to make a photo after you press the shutter button, then a different technique is in order. Instead of following the ball from the corner to the group in front of the net, your best bet is to keep your camera focused on the group and to keep your autofocus on by holding the shutter down halfway. By focusing on them the entire time, the camera is ready to fire as soon as you press the shutter button.

When I use this technique, I try to keep my left eye open so I can see the beginning of the kick. Then I start shooting once I know the ball is in the air. With a fast motor drive, I can usually get off two to three shots during the entire sequence of events.

Following motion

Another key to making good sports photographs is realizing that a stationary camera and a moving athlete don't combine for the best images. Instead, you should follow the athlete in the viewfinder as she travels so the camera moves in concert with the motion—a technique known as *panning*. Then, when the time comes to trip the shutter, you'll be in sync with the action.

Figure 9-2: Anticipation and prefocusing made this image possible.
© *2004 Dan Simon*

Panning in low light

You can also use panning, when light levels are too low to permit fast shutter speeds. By following the motion of the athlete, you increase the likelihood of keeping her in focus even though your shutter speed may not be fast enough otherwise.

Panning can also help you produce an interesting photo. When you pan at a slow shutter speed, you throw the background out of focus because of motion blur (see Figure 9-3). This creates a sense of speed and motion that the frozen image lacks. It's a nice alternative technique when you want to create a different sort of image.

Figure 9-3: I photographed this skateboarder by panning the camera while using a slow shutter speed.

© 2004 Dan Simon

Keep in mind, you'll have a higher percentage of wasted shots with this technique. If you want to try panning (and I hope you do), plan on lots of experimentation and repetition. If I need to get a panning shot as a planned photograph, I plan to take at least eight or ten sequences of shots using this technique to improve my chances of getting one good image. If enough opportunities exist, I shoot even more.

Stopping motion

Fast motion calls for fast shutter speeds. Although the speed varies from sport to sport, shutter speeds of 1/250th of a second or faster are the bare minimum needed for stopping action. Keep in mind that this is the recommended minimum speed for human motion sports. If you're shooting auto or motorcycle racing, much faster shutter speeds are mandatory. Figure 1/750th to 1/1000th of a second as a minimum. Furthermore, faster shutter speeds are also necessary for motor drives to function at their fastest.

You can also freeze motion by using flash. The burst of light from an electronic flash unit lasts only about 1/10,000th of a second, so its brief duration stops the fastest motion. Be warned though, that if you combine electronic flash with a slow shutter speed, the combination produces an effect known as *ghosting*. This is where the shutter remains open long enough for the ambient illumination to register an image on the sensor. The result is a ghost trail with the main one your flash recorded.

The other problem with using flash to freeze motion is that its range limits its effectiveness. Most sports action takes place farther away than your flash can reach. Don't bother using your built-in flash for this kind of thing either, it really won't have the range. Instead look for a powerful accessory flash. Many of these can pump light out to a distance of 100 feet or more provided you're shooting with fast aperture lenses (f2.8 or better). Even an f4 lens combined with one of these flash units will give you some distance (perhaps 70 to 90 feet).

Choosing the right lens

It's hard to discuss sports photography without at least mentioning equipment. You've probably seen the sideline shooters at major sporting events with their huge lenses and multiple cameras. It's easy to look at such gear and think that you don't have a chance with your point-and-shoot camera or entry-level DSLR and modest optics.

The truth is you don't. At least you don't if you want to take my job from me. If all you want to do is get good photos of your kids playing sports, that's a different story. Your gear is good enough if you know how to use it.

Telephoto lens: King of the sports world

Unless your kid's a top chess or backgammon player, odds are their sport puts them at a distance from your shooting position. Let's face it, most sports take place on pretty large athletic fields.

Even with big telephoto lenses, there are still lots of times when I'm just standing on the sidelines because the action is taking place too far away. Still, a good telephoto (and many digital point-and-shoot cameras these days have powerful telephoto capabilities) can improve your chances of making a shot. So can a second camera.

Carrying a Second Camera and Shooting from the Hip

Many pros carry more than one camera when they shoot an athletic event. For instance, if I'm on the sideline of a soccer or football game, I usually have one camera with a long lens on it (300mm or longer) and another with a modest zoom (28–70). This way I can follow more distant action with the telephoto yet still be able to grab the camera with the short zoom and bring it up to shoot a play coming toward my sideline. (Of course this is the moment when sane people start running away from the action.)

Continued

Continued

If you have a second digital camera, try carrying it with you. Set its zoom for its widest setting and have it where you can grab it in a hurry. Plan on shooting from the hip. In other words, just pick it up and point it in the direction of the action without bothering to bring it to your eye and compose the photo.

I suggest you try this multi-camera technique with something like soccer or field hockey—a sport in which the participants don't try to tackle each other at the sidelines. When it comes to football, leave this approach to the pros. The risks of a player/photographer collision are much greater in this sport.

Shooting from the hip takes a little practice, but can really increase your chances of making good photographs. Here's how it's done. As the athletes get bigger and bigger in your viewfinder, keep shooting until they're too big to photograph. At this point, pull the camera away from your eye and look at the athletes while grabbing the camera with the short zoom. As you backpedal away from the potential collision, point the camera at the players and hold down the shutter button. Frequently, you end up with a lot of garbage this way, but often mixed in among the bad shots is a keeper or two.

Medium zoom lens: Shooting indoor sports

A medium zoom is usually considered to be a range of focal lengths running anywhere from 24mm at the wide end to about 135mm at its longest telephoto.

This is a handy optic for many indoor sports, such as cheerleading, basketball, volleyball, and wrestling. The biggest problem with such lenses is that most of the affordable ones (at least for DSLRs) are too expensive for the typical amateur user. More and more point-and-shoot digital cameras are offering this range of focal lengths at reasonably fast maximum apertures, but be sure to check what the maximum aperture is at the extreme end of the lens. Telephoto lengths usually have smaller maximum apertures than wide angle ones.

Still, the action in these sports frequently takes place at a distance where an accessory flash can be effective, so that can compensate for smaller lens openings. Be careful though, some sports (such as volleyball) don't permit the use of flash because it distracts the players.

Medium range zooms are also handy second camera optics. Rack them out wide and shoot from the hip when action comes your way. They're also good for shots of athletes on the sidelines and from behind the bench for pictures of coaches coaching.

Wide-angle zoom focal lengths

These lenses have limited use in sports photography, but when they are effective, they provide a much-needed different perspective on things. They're useful for shooting from the hip and to frame certain sports, such as skateboarding.

Wide-angle focal lengths are also useful for sports portraiture because their distortion and great depth of field can grab your attention with a very different sort of portrait. Add elements of the sport into the photo and you can create an interesting sort of image. One example is to photograph a baseball player by having him hold the bat as if in mid-swing. Position your camera so the end of the bat is right in front of the lens and make the photograph with the athlete looking up the barrel of the lens towards your camera.

Photographing Individual Sports

The list of potential sports a professional photographer can end up covering is a long one. That list begins with adventure racing and makes its way through the alphabet up into the *W*s with white water rafting and wrestling (sorry, I couldn't think of any sports beginning with Y or Z).

For the remainder of this chapter, I give you a rundown on techniques for photographing all the major sports and most of the minor ones. First, however, here is some general advice that will help no matter what sport you're photographing:

✦ **Get as close to the action as you safely and reasonably can.** Obviously, there are limitations, but often you can get fairly close to the action, particularly for junior high school (and younger) sports. This is good because it's the junior high and under age groups that are the most in demand markets for sports photography picture sales these days. (And if you're the parent of a middle school student you probably already understand firsthand why these pictures are so important to you.)

✦ **Shoot at the highest resolution possible.** This way you can use the extra pixels to let you crop in tighter when your lens isn't long enough to fill the frame.

✦ **Try to place yourself near likely action spots where the person you want to photograph is likely to be.** I'll give more specific information for each sport, but there are predictable patterns for just about every sport.

✦ **Never be satisfied with just a couple of good images.** Keep plugging away. Pros with all their expensive gear rip through hundreds of photos in the course of a single event.

If you're really interested in making the best sports photos you can, study both the sport you're following and the coverage of that sport. The more you look at published photos made by top sports photographers, the more you get a sense of what good sports photos look like. This can help you anticipate particular moments or situations that lead to these kinds of photos.

Keep in mind that it's not unusual for a working pro to be sent to photograph a sport he's never even seen before. You still have to make useable photographs even though you have no experience to fall back on. This happened to me at the Philadelphia X Games, a couple of years ago, when I had to shoot the wakeboarding event (see Figure 9-4). The key to effective photography under such circumstances is to figure out where to position yourself to catch the action and then get a feel for the timing of the event.

Figure 9-4: I'd never photographed a wakeboarding event before shooting this one, but the basic advice I cover in this chapter helped me make this image.

© 2004 Dan Simon

The following sections provide an alphabetized list of sports and my advice on how to shoot each one. This information comes from my personal experience; conversations with other sports photographers, and advice I've seen given on sports photography and photojournalism related web forums. If, after reading the following sections and checking out this book's companion web site, you still have a specific question on sports photography, feel free to e-mail me at `dgsimagery@hotmail.com`. My hope, however, is that I'll answer your question somewhere in the next few pages.

Visit this book's companion web site (`www.wiley.com/compbooks/simon`) for links to web forums on sports photography.

Archery

One of the more interesting archery photos is also one of the more dangerous. Use a telephoto lens to photograph the archer head on. This is a *posed* shot, which should be very carefully coordinated. Even then, I like to be standing behind a tree when I try this one.

Another good photo is from the side with the drawn bow framing the archer's face. An even better shot is to zoom in tight and photograph the head from above the eyes down to slightly below the hand gripping the arrow. Try to be even or slightly forward of the archer (no more than a foot or so) for this photo. You can try a similar shot from nearly head on remembering the bit about being really, really careful.

Badminton

One of the fastest sports in the world (based on the speed of the shuttlecock), badminton, is challenging to photograph because player movement is so unpredictable. Adding to the problem is the poor lighting found in most gyms.

If your circumstances permit, set up a shot before competition. Get up on a ladder and shoot down on a player poised for an overhead slam. (Try to be fairly close so you can shoot almost straight down).

Once competition starts, try to be as close to the floor as the game will allow. Use a medium focal length for wide shots of the court and a longer lens to isolate the players. If you have a fast telephoto, this is a good time to use it. Prefocus on the net and then back out another couple of feet. You can do this with an interchangeable DSLR lens, but maybe not with a point-and-shoot digital camera. If you're using a point-and-shoot, prefocus on the net; that will at least get you close.

If you're interested in making a picture story, get some close-ups of the racket and shuttlecock. Also photograph spectator interest. Mix up horizontals and verticals.

Dealing with Poorly Lit Gyms

When shooting in a gymnasium, you may not be able to use flash. So plan on ratcheting your camera's ISO setting up to around 800 ISO or higher, if possible. Keep in mind that setting your camera to manual exposure mode and choosing an f-stop/shutter speed combo that's a full stop below what the camera's light meter recommends is effectively doubling your ISO setting. This means you can "force" your camera beyond its normal ISO capacity.

Another way to force it beyond an ISO limit is to adjust your exposure compensation setting. Note, however, that you don't gain any improvement in your image quality this way. In fact, you're deliberately underexposing your images with this technique. What this does do is let you shoot at a fast enough shutter speed to make sharper underexposed photos. It's possible to salvage a sharp, but underexposed photo in the digital darkroom, but it's impossible to sharpen a blurred photo, so this approach at least gives you a chance to get a useable photo. It doesn't work miracles and will reduce the final quality of your image, but it may also save an otherwise impossible situation.

Adventure racing

Look for loops, switchbacks, or goosenecks in the course. This will enable you to photograph a specific athlete then cut across the gooseneck and be in position for the racer to pass you by again.

Zooms rule for this kind of photography. A long zoom range will let you start shooting the racer coming toward you and keep shooting as the racer continues to move toward you. Vary your shots between tight compositions and slightly longer views to include some of the scenery in order to create a sense of place. The majority of your compositions should be vertical because the human form is a vertical one.

If circumstances allow, plan on making some shots from above and some from a low angle. If you can photograph the start from above you can make a shot of a mass of heads and feet all moving in the same direction. Shooting from a low angle can make for a dramatic shot too, but be wary of the sun's position or you might end up with a badly backlit photo.

Auto racing (NASCAR style)

This is one of the fastest growing sports in America and deservedly so. With its mix of fast action, colorful automobiles, and even more colorful personalities, auto racing offers a visual feast for the photographer.

Sadly, the average amateur is often too far away to be able to photograph top-level races well. If you can get yourself in position to cover the track, plan on using very fast shutter speeds. NASCAR autos move so quickly that shutter speeds of 1/1000th or 1/2000th of a second or even faster may be necessary.

Other things to consider are access during the days leading up to the race. Pit tours provide a nice opportunity to photograph some of the other elements of racing such as the mechanics areas and the tools necessary to keep these high performance machines working at peak operation.

Don't forget to make some wide shots of the whole track environment and capture the immensity of a race and its thousands of fans.

Auto racing (small track)

Lower-level competitions can be a lot of fun to photograph because fans can get closer to the action, the equipment, and the drivers. Here you can hope to create images that rival those made by the pros.

Capture the race start by positioning yourself behind the starter. Compose the shot so the starter fills less than half the frame leaving room for the cars. Choose a modest shutter speed around 1/100th of a second. This will blur the flag and the cars while keeping the start and surroundings acceptably sharp.

Photograph the racing cars near a turn where they're slowing down a bit can give you more time to make photos. Use a telephoto lens to compress the field of cars and make the cars appear close together.

Wander the pit areas photographing mechanics at work and disassembled autos. Look for drivers in their race clothing, many of whom are agreeable to posing for a photo. Make these tight compositions (headroom to waist).

If your wife isn't looking, photograph the racetrack beauties who are usually wandering around the track.

Every now and then, turn your back to the track and use a wide-angle lens to catch the fans' excitement. Try to get a shot of screaming, cheering people.

Auto racing (hot rod, funny car)

Create an interesting portrait of the racer by using a telephoto lens to isolate him inside the cockpit of his dragster. Make this a vertical composition and crop it tightly from headroom to the top of the cockpit. Because these machines are so unusual, make close-ups of some of their parts. Look for interesting reflections in the metal and use them to artistic effect.

Use a bugs-eye view with a wide-angle lens while photographing a dragster. Place the car's front wheels in the foreground and let the body of the car recede into the background for a composition that sucks the eye in.

Baseball

There are real challenges to photographing baseball, particularly because of the distance photographers are placed from the action and the unpredictability of the action. If your main subject is playing the outfield, your task is beyond difficult. Your best bet is during the warm-up at the start of each half inning. Otherwise, you face a long wait hoping to see a ball hit close enough to an outfielder for you to get a good photo of the player.

There are some more predictable shots available if you're just working to make good photos. The easiest position to photograph is the pitcher, and there are several good ways to make such an image. One is in profile from headroom to waist if your lens will bring you close enough. Photograph the entire sequence from the beginning to the end of his delivery if your motor drive and buffer can handle it. Shoot from the side that gives the best view of his face. This should be the opposite of his delivery side. (Left for a right-hander and right for a left hander.)

Another good view is from directly behind the backstop. Here you can compose an image looking directly at the pitcher with the umpire serving as a frame on one side and the batter on the other. Time it just right and you'll be able to see the ball too! This shot's a bit tricky because everybody's moving around and shifting positions. Umpires make it particularly hard because they stand up till almost the last moment, blocking your view.

Batters provide another predicable and relatively easier subject to photograph. Position yourself across from the hitter (line-ups with frequent switching from lefty to righty drive you nuts because you can't quickly get from one side to the other). Now you're ready to photograph the swing, ideally catching the ball actually striking the bat.

At the pro level, a neat photo is created by mounting a remote controlled camera at the top of the backstop positioned to shoot down on home plate. Fire away to try and catch the ball streaking over the plate.

Photographing the bases is manageable with a long lens. To photograph these positions in such a way as to show players' faces, you need to be on the other side of the field shooting across the playing area. Prefocus on whichever base you're covering and wait for something to happen in the area. Be alert. A runner on first base means you can cover second base hoping for a play there with a sliding base runner; a runner on second means a possible play at third; a runner on third means a potential play at home plate. This last one is the best of all because you can position yourself down the third base line and prefocus a couple of feet up from home plate. If you're lucky, you may be able to catch the catcher diving forward, ball in hand, to try to tag the sliding runner out.

If you're concentrating on the first or third baseman, remember to be ready for balls thrown in their direction. This is far more common with the first baseman, and if you plan it properly, you can make a photo of the player stretched out, mitt and arm extended, to catch the ball as the base runner flies by behind him.

Atmosphere shots of players sitting on the bench watching the action make for good secondary images, as do close-ups of bats, balls, and mitts lying around.

Basketball

This is a relatively easy sport to photograph because much of the action takes place at predictable locations and within the range of shorter focal lengths. Although you can justify a 300mm telephoto to photograph backboard action at the other end of the court, you can normally manage just fine without the big lenses. Usually a 28–70 and 80–200 (in interchangeable lens terms; many point-and-shoots cover this range, too) are more than enough to shoot this sport.

Start at the baseline and use the 80–200 to make shots of the guards bringing the ball up court. Switch to the 28–70 to capture lay-ups and the fight for rebounds (see Figure 9-5). Stay to one side of the backboard rather than directly under it, and be ready to shift positions as referees can sometimes move in front of you.

For a change of pace, head to the mid-court area. This gives you a different look at ball handlers and puts you in position to make shots of the bench and the coach coaching. Here is where you can focus in on the coach screaming at her players. Time-outs give you a particularly good opportunity to document coaches talking to players.

Flash is helpful in photographing this sport although there is growing antagonism toward its use. Some parents have blamed the blast of a flash for missed shots. The average high school gym generally provides enough light to allow for shooting at 800 ISO, with settings around 1/150th to 1/200th of a second at f2.8. Sometimes you get lucky and the light is better, but more often it's worse. Under such conditions, maximum apertures of f2.0 (which quite a few point-and-shoot cameras offer at their wide-angle end) are becoming necessary. If lighting is a big problem, remember that it's better to be a half stop or a stop underexposed and stop action than it is to have properly exposed pictures that are blurry.

Figure 9-5: Basketball action photographs well and doesn't require a big investment in expensive lenses. This photo was made with an 85mm lens.
© 2004 Dan Simon

Pros sometimes mount a camera at the top of the backboard triggered via remote control to get bird's eye view–images of players going up for rebounds. If you're ever in a position to try such a rig, the important parts include mounting the camera via a super clamp and having a backup tether securing the camera to the backboard with wire in case the clamp fails. A wireless remote is mandatory for this sort of rig.

Biathlon

Cross-country skiing and riflery combine in the biathlon for a demanding sport. The athletes do the hardest work, of course, but it's no day in the park for the photographer.

Start at the start. (See the benefits of hiring a professional writer for a book like this? A non-professional might have written something stupid here.) Photograph the mass of racers starting up the course. Use a telephoto lens to compress the mass of athletes.

A good position for dramatic photos is at the high point of a hill. Here the racers are moving at their slowest and look their most exhausted. The rifle firing stations are also good places to photograph. Although a direct head-on-shot is very powerful, it's the kind of shot you have to set up outside the actual race because photographers aren't allowed in the shooting area. Instead, try to find a position where you can photograph the shooters in profile. A long lens lets you make a tight composition concentrating on the face and weapon.

Biathletes, like any of the cross-country sky distance athletes, reach the finish line near exhaustion, completely spent from their efforts. This is a great opportunity to create powerful images. Find an area near the finish line where you can set up for such shots and be ready with a telephoto zoom so you can back your lens out as they get closer to the line. Look for shots of recovering athletes after the race, too.

One other concern: all that snow can throw off your light meter. Set your exposure compensation to increase exposure from one to two f-stops to properly expose your subject.

Billiards (and pool)

Photographing billiards and pool is easy when you're shooting in your basement or at a recreational facility. It's a whole other story when you're shooting a professional competition.

For times when you can use flash and move about freely, get close to the table and set up a shot where the target ball and pool cue form a line leading up to the shooter's face. Shoot low, from table level rather at a normal standing eye level. Because depth of field will probably be shallow, decide whether you want the ball or the shooter to be in focus. Another nice shot is from above—shooting straight down on the pool table and shooter.

If you're shooting at a professional event, expect to have to work without flash and probably from a distance where the players can't hear noise from your camera. This means you need a longer telephoto (probably greater than 300mm). Long focal lengths coupled with indoor lighting means that blur from camera shake will probably be a problem. Plan on using a monopod, tripod, or some other support to prevent that problem. Remember, long focal lengths magnify the effects of vibration, so even though you may be using a lightweight point-and-shoot, blur from camera shake is much more likely than you probably expect.

If the noise from your shutter firing becomes a problem, wrap your camera in a towel to muffle the sounds it makes.

Bobsledding

Use a telephoto lens to shoot the bobsled and rider head on. Make low-angle shots with a wide-angle lens before the start of the run. Use flash to expose subject and sled under bright sunlight and plan on giving one to two f-stops exposure compensation to make up for your light meter's tendency to underexpose people because of all the ice. If you can get overhead, shooting straight down on the sled creates an interesting image.

Spectator access is frequently a problem at major events. If a photo is important enough to you, be on site ridiculously early (by several hours). If you're a serious amateur shooting something less than the Olympics, it may be possible to get a press pass to the event. See if your local paper has any interest in photos from the event; this way, you can justify press credentials.

If you can't get press access, then your best bet is to be at the frontmost part of any of the spectator access areas that gives a clear view of a long stretch of track. This gives you enough time to spot the sled coming toward you and make the photo. If your camera allows it, prefocus on a spot on the track and trip the shutter early to catch the bobsled as it travels past your focussing point.

You can try your camera's autofocus for such shots too, but most point-and-shoot cameras don't offer fast enough autofocus to catch top-level sleds and riders. Remember to prefocus and have your autofocus activated before the sled comes into view.

Bowling

Shooting in a bowling alley involves typical low-light problems. In fact, if you can't shoot with flash, you're generally in serious trouble. Most bowling alleys are so poorly lit that even 800 ISO isn't enough to guarantee action stopping shutter speeds.

It's usually better to shoot the bowlers warming up. Then you can use flash and get out on a neighboring lane or access walkway and photograph the bowlers releasing their balls towards you.

Secondary photos include a wide shot from the scorer's table showing a bowler throwing the ball with some of the other lanes included. Add another photo of a bowler polishing a ball and a close-up of the balls on the return and you have a basic package of images.

Boxing

This is usually another low-light indoor shoot, although occasionally matches are held outdoors. If you're above the ring, flash helps. If you're below the ring, flash will blow out the ring's ropes (overexposing them), and they'll broadcast shadows onto the fighters. Try to boost your ISO and shoot without flash instead. Because you're below the fighters and the lights are above them, use your exposure compensation control to boost exposure from 1/2 to one full f-stop.

Try to frame the shot tightly (from headroom to waist) and to trigger the camera as the fighter starts his punch.

Be ready for a knockdown. If you get one, look for a shot of the ref directing the standing fighter to a neutral corner while the downed fighter lies on the mat.

Bullfighting

Because you will likely be positioned at a distance, come prepared with a long lens. If you don't expect to be a long distance away, come prepared with more life insurance. (Unless you have really great seats.) Under those (close-up) circumstances, an 80–200mm lens or equivalent can cover shots on your side of the arena, while a longer focal range takes you into the action.

Canoeing/kayaking (flat water)

Flat water canoeing can be quite picturesque. The trick here is to overcome the distance between the canoe and the shore (or the boat you're shooting from). One very effective shot is to compose vertically and zoom in tight enough to frame from headroom (just above the paddlers' heads) down to either the top of the boat (showing enough to make it obvious they're in a canoe) or down to the water far enough to include a reflection of the boat and paddlers.

Get another striking image by finding a bridge over the waterway and shoot straight down on the canoe as it passes underneath.

Canoeing/kayaking/rafting (white water)

In addition to the flat-water shots (which you can shoot while the boat is in "flat water" mode), capture peak action while the craft is in a rapid. It's difficult to give general advice because each rapid is different. Generally, it's best to shoot from a slightly elevated platform so you can get the faces of the paddlers in the image, but some rapids may dictate standing downstream and waiting for the boat to dip into and then pop out of the rapid.

Keep in mind that white water paddlers wear a variety of colorful and interesting safety garb including life vests and helmets. These can make for an interesting portrait. Make sure you compose tightly. Figure headroom to the top of the boat.

White water canoes (both open and closed deck) and kayaks can practice a self-rescue move known as an *Eskimo Roll*. This is an exciting and demonstrable move, one I had to do several times each river trip for my guests back in my days as a river guide. The trick to photographing it is either being able to photograph it head on to the front of the boat, or being on the same side of the boat on which the paddler is surfacing.

Cheerleading

A telephoto lens lets you make a tight composition. A wide-angle lens gives you the big picture. One very nice image is when the entire team jumps into the air. Use a wide-angle lens and position yourself in the center of the formation (see Figure 9-6).

Try at least a few tightly composed images when the cheerleader is yelling. These images should key on the cheerleader's face, preferably looking straight into the lens.

Figure 9-6: Cheerleading offers the potential for exciting team photos.
© 2004 Dan Simon

Particularly exciting are the aerials. To make shots such as these you need to key on one of the athletes and focus on her while she's at the top of a stack. This way you're ready for the toss or drop and can photograph the cheerleader in the air.

Cricket

First, brew a cup of tea. Then unlimber your long telephoto to cover the long areas of the field. This will also help you focus in on the batsman. You can also take position behind the batsman to photograph the bowler as they pitch. Make sure you take some wide shots to show the expanse of the playing field. Close-ups of the equipment will add to your photo package.

Curling

Make some wide shots to show the playing surface, but otherwise concentrate on using your telephoto to key in on the participants. Shoot from a low angle to bring together rocks (also called stones) and the athlete when they're low to the ground sizing up the shot. If the competition allows, use flash. If not, go with a high ISO setting (800 is high enough). You'll get some benefit from the light reflecting off the ice and bouncing back up to illuminate the athletes.

Cycling

This is a fast-moving sport, so be prepared to use fast shutter speeds. If your auto focus is fast enough, use a long focal length to shoot the cyclists head on as they ride toward you, as shown in Figure 9-7. If your auto focus isn't fast, switch to manual focus and prefocus on a point where you expect the riders to reach. Trip the shutter while the rider is still a few feet from that spot.

If you can position yourself so that riders pass by your location, switch to a wide-angle lens and photograph the line of riders as they go by. Try some shots with slower shutter speeds in order to blur the riders and show how fast they're moving. Also try panning with the riders to keep the cyclists in focus while blurring the background.

Play some angles too. Shoot from low down (see Figure 9-8) and straight down from above. Either of these shots is easy to make with even a basic point-and-shoot camera.

Figure 9-7: A telephoto lens and fast shutter speed captured this rider as he rode toward me.

© 2004 Dan Simon

Equestrian (You shoot horses, don't you?)

Sorry, I just couldn't help myself. If you're photographing an equestrian competition, plan on using long focal lengths. From an impact standpoint, a shot of the horse and rider heading, straight toward the camera provides an interesting photo. Frame this one from the rider's headroom to the ground to show the entire horse, or crop a bit tighter to show just the rider and the horse's head.

Profile shots of the horse are important for establishing the horse's appearance and stud potential. Photograph the horse in mid-stride with the foreleg closest to the camera extended forward. Ideally, all four legs should be in an extended position.

Figure 9-8: A wide-angle lens held low to the ground while the cyclists move toward you can provide an interesting image.
© 2004 Dan Simon

Equine portraits can be made with a telephoto lens shot straight on and composed vertically. A more unusual portrait can be made using an extreme wide-angle focal length (20mm or wider in the case of 35mm equivalent lenses). Here you can position the horse's mouth and nose at the bottom of the frame and lead the viewer's eye up to those of the horse's.

Fencing

Light's a problem because most meets are indoors and flash use may be discouraged as a distraction to the competitors. There's the added problem that you can't see anybody's faces while they're fencing.

Use your telephoto for action shots. If circumstances permit, shoot from behind one fencer so you can create a head-on shot of the other. Use the fencer whose back is toward you to frame the one you can see.

During downtime, create portraits of any specific participants you're interested in. Have them hold their mask in one hand and rest their foil across their chest diagonally. (Odds are they're already very familiar with this pose and will create it for you on their own.)

This is another sport that photographs dramatically when shot from above. You can also make an interesting overall image by shooting from the side away from the crowd. Use a wide-angle focal length, get low, and show the fencers with the crowd in the background.

Fishing

Much of your approach to fishy photography depends on the type of fishing you're documenting. Fly-fishing, boat fishing, sport fishing, and surfcasting are all so different that they could easily be covered as separate entities.

Here are some general ideas. Apply them as they fit your situation.

Shoot the fisherwoman head-on while she's in mid-cast (if possible). Create a profile close-up of the hobbyist checking her bait or fly. Make close-ups of the lures, flies, and other equipment.

Shoot from above when possible. This is frequently possible for fly-fishing because it's done on a river and you may have a bridge handy. It's sometimes possible to shoot from above for bass boat fishing when the event takes place on a river, and may even be possible for deep sea fishing when you can climb to a higher point on the boat.

Look for interesting lighting opportunities. Backlighting a fly fisherwoman and her line can result in beautiful rim lighting on the line but is very difficult exposure-wise. Side lighting will show detail well and help you capture the overall scene.

Don't forget a portrait of the fisherwoman proudly holding her catch. Frame the picture tightly from headroom (hatroom since they're always wearing hats?) to chest. (The subject should be holding the fish about level with the face.) If your fisherwoman is wearing an interesting hat, a tight head shot that shows the face and hat can also be a nice image.

Football (American style)

This is one of those sports that pro photographers make look harder than it is. You see them all the time, the guys (and gals) with the big lenses, multiple cameras, and bags of equipment. Well, if you're a working pro trying to cover as big a chunk of the field as you can, these are necessary. On the other hand, if you're a parent who's just interested in getting shots of your kid, you can get by with much less gear.

One thing you do need is to be on the sidelines (see Figure 9-9). Trying to make useable images from the stands only works if you're willing to settle for wide shots. It's frequently not that hard to shoot from the sidelines though. It all depends on the level of competition that's going on.

Figure 9-9: Football is best photographed from the sidelines.
© 2004 Dan Simon

Forget it for the pros and upper division college level play. Here you need special access and it's not that easy to get. High school games and below, on the other hand, are a different story. It's usually possible to get on the sidelines of a high school game so long as you don't get in the way.

You have two approaches. One is to get permission ahead of time by checking with the school's athletic director or football coach. It helps if you offer to share your pictures with the team or the school for use in the yearbook. (Odds are, that if you're a parent of one of the players, it won't be a problem.)

The second approach is a little sneakier. When I feel like practicing (and practice is as important for a sports photographer as it is for an athlete), I just go down to one of my area high school games, march through the gate, and take up a position on the sideline.

I'll admit, it probably helps that I look like I'm supposed to be there because I'm carrying a lot of pro gear. It also helps that I walk through like I belong there. If asked, I say I'm a freelance photographer just shooting the game for practice, and that usually satisfies the questioner. Two things to consider: First, I usually don't get asked, and second, there's no certification process to become a "freelance" photographer. In simplest terms, it means you're an unemployed photographer because you don't have an employer guaranteeing your paycheck. In other words, anybody can say he's a freelancer.

Now that you're on the field, here's what to look for.

Start by positioning yourself about level with the line of scrimmage. This gives you the chance to photograph the quarterback as he's barking out signals. It also puts you in place for shots of the handoff and the running back coming toward your side of the field. (Of course, if they run to the other side of the field you're out of luck.) Usually an 80–200 lens or a bit longer will give you the coverage you need. I usually have one camera with a 300mm telephoto lens, another with a 80–200, and a third with a 20–35 for hip shots. As I mentioned earlier in the chapter, hip shots are photos made when players are headed for the sideline and you just grab the camera and point it in their general direction and start shooting.

Drop about 5 to 10 yards behind the line of scrimmage if you want to focus on the pass rush. An 80–200 or equivalent focal length range works here.

Move about 10 to 15 yards up field of the line of scrimmage for pass plays and also to get a different position on running plays. From here, you can shoot the handoff and the running back going into the center of the line (and hopefully breaking through). It also puts you in position to turn and follow any pass receivers on your side of the field.

Once teams get near the goal line, you can position yourself behind the goal posts and shoot straight ahead. This is a hit or miss type thing, but sometimes you're perfectly positioned for a running play straight into the line.

For punts, you can try for a shot of the punter kicking or position yourself for the returner catching the ball and then making the return. I usually don't bother shooting the kickoff, but instead focus on the return. Of course, if the kicker is your son (or daughter?) go right ahead.

Look for shots on the sidelines of coaches yelling instructions and players watching the game intensely. If it's cold enough, get shots of the steam coming off the players' heads and the fog of their breath.

Look for interesting shots in the crowd. People with signs and banners provide possible title information or useful reference photos. You can also take a shot of the scoreboard.

If you're keying on a certain area, such as the quarterback/running back exchange, remember to prefocus on the specific athlete.

Knowing the tendencies of the team you're photographing is also a big help. If they're primarily a running team, you can spend more time keying on the running back. If they're pass oriented, focus on the quarterback, the receivers, and the opponent's pass rush.

Golf

Golf is well within the range of the typical point-and-shoot digital camera. Start out by making some photos at the putting green where you're apt to be forgiven if camera noise throws off a put.

Compose vertically, and tight enough to show the golfer from headroom down to the golf ball. Time the photograph so you shoot when the golfer brings the club head back and starts to move it forward.

After the golfers hit the tee, line up about 50 feet down the course from them. I usually stay in the cart path because this is a relatively safe and permissible area to work from. Timing a shot to catch the ball coming off the club head is incredibly difficult. In fact, many of the shots you see in advertisements and brochures are shot by having someone toss a ball in front of a photographer during the golfer's practice swing. (This technique is definitely not used in news and sports photos. Those shots are real.)

Gymnastics

Gymnastics is a very difficult sport to photograph because of poorly lit gyms, rules prohibiting flash, and the distance photographers are usually kept from the performances.

As usual, lower level competitions provide more leeway than higher level ones. Sometimes practice is the best time to make good photos because things are less intense.

The best action shots usually involve catching the athletes while they're in the air, preferably inverted. You can create more dramatic images though by following the athlete during slower moving events such as the balance beam where you can focus in tightly on the concentration on the gymnast's face.

Prefocus where possible and remember that some events—the vault, for example—require an explosion of movement from the athlete. If you're photographing such an event, you're going to need to trip the shutter a little earlier to compensate for the speed of the athlete's movements.

Shoot the balance beam from equal height (climb on something) and also from below with a wide-angle lens (being careful to compensate exposure because overhead lights will throw off your light meter).

Shoot the floor apparatus from the same height as the floor if possible. Look for tumbling routines for great action shots. Some tumbling runs may include several different speed tumbles. If you can find out ahead about a slow tumble or flip, it can give you a better opportunity to make a good shot. Don't forget to try some panning shots with slow shutter speeds (1/100th of a second or less) to create a sense of motion.

When shooting the rings, try to get high enough to be even with the athlete's face when they're doing an iron cross (this is where they extend their arms out to the side, parallel to the floor, and hold the position). You can create a dramatic image this way as you document the strain and concentration on the athlete's face. If circumstances permit (meaning that you're shooting during practice and have the coach's okay) lie flat below the gymnast and shoot straight up.

Make portraits of the athletes while they chalk up and take close-ups of chalk-covered hands and gymnastic slipper-clad feet. Look for dramatic shots of athletes watching their teammates perform and also look for emotion as scores are posted or routines are completed. Keep an eye out for coach/athlete interaction, particularly if you have a big coach bending over to get to eye level with a diminutive athlete.

Hockey (ice)

You can cover this sport effectively with an 80–200 lens or equivalent (unless you're focusing on the goalie, in which case you'll need a longer lens). The biggest challenge is dealing with fast moving players who are constantly changing directions and getting in each other's (and your) way. Expect a lot of wasted shots as your auto focus will frequently be a tad too slow or another player will dart in front of your camera just as you're making a shot. Try to have plenty of camera memory with you or some way of dumping images to an external hard drive or laptop, because *chimping* (taking quick breaks to examine your shots) wastes valuable shooting time.

It's better if you can shoot from a location where you're free from the protective Plexiglas at most rinks. This usually means close to the players' area where you may or may not be able to get access. If you have to shoot from the stands, you'll need a longer lens. It's harder to show athletes faces from a higher up position, so if at all possible, shoot from rink level (see Figure 9-10).

Figure 9-10: Ice hockey is a fast-moving sport best shot from ice level if possible.
© 2004 Dan Simon

Trying to follow the puck around the rink is challenging, particularly because there will be lots of times when the action will be taking place too far away for your lens to be effective. When you get these times, consider turning to the bench and making some head shots of the players. At the rink I usually shoot at, the player's area receives about two f-stops less light than the ice, so plan accordingly. One other thing about ice hockey is that the overhead lights reflect off the ice and bounce back up on the players, creating nice, even lighting.

Hockey (field)

Another fast moving sport, field hockey can be photographed with a variety of lenses depending on what part of the field you want to cover. When I shoot this sport, I usually work with two or three cameras using a long telephoto (300mm f2.8 or longer), a telephoto zoom (80–200), and a wide-angle zoom (20–35) for hip shots. During the course of the game, I move from sideline to sideline and also take shots from the end lines where I can get the players charging directly towards the goal.

This is another sport where athletes move quickly, change directions constantly, and are always getting in your way. Bring lots of memory if you have it.

If your camera's auto focus isn't particularly quick, rely on prefocusing and waiting for the action to come to a particular area. Another option if your auto focus is truly bad is to switch to a wider optic and small enough aperture (probably around f5.6 or f8) so that your depth of field will keep things sharp. Then wait for a play to take place near where you're standing.

This isn't a bad approach if watching the game is as important to you as shooting. All you have to do is keep one hand on your camera and then when the action gets close, fire away, hip shooting if necessary.

Keep one other thing in mind when shooting field hockey. Because players can't carry the ball, they're almost always looking down. Consequently, you can get better shots from a kneeling position than you can from a standing one (see Figure 9-11).

Lacrosse

The techniques I mentioned for field hockey also apply to lacrosse, because both sports involve roughly the same playing field and involve athletes running around with sticks trying to score goals.

One nice difference is that players can run while carrying the ball. This means you can shoot standing up and even better, can look for shots of athletes running straight toward the goal. This is a nice shot for a telephoto lens 200mm or greater because it flattens out the players, making them look closer together. Keep in mind that you need to be on the end lines for this shot.

Motorcycle racing

This sport is distinguished by fast bikes and lots of dust—at least if the event takes place on a dirt track—. Photograph the start with a telephoto lens to compress the riders into one big mass of people and machines. Then isolate individual riders as they come toward you.

Figure 9-11: Action takes place low to the ground in field hockey.
© 2004 Dan Simon

Make close-up shots of the riders before the race in their racing garb (which tends to be colorful and visually interesting). Although recognizable portraits require them to take their helmets off, you can make some neat looking pictures by shooting straight into the helmet while they're wearing it. Ask riders to raise their visors so you can look directly into their eyes.

Photograph the mechanics working on the bikes, and take close ups of the machines and parts. Also use the reflections in motorcycle chrome to make unusual images.

Try some panning shots to show the speed of the riders. Also see if you can get elevated and mount your camera on some form of support. Then make a slow speed photo to show a sharp track and blur of motorcycles, once again to show how fast they move.

Motorcycle stunt events (Moto X, Big Air, X-games)

These events tend to feature bikes flying through the air, so there's the opportunity for some very exciting images. Because the jumps take place at predictable points in the course, it's possible to turn your auto focus off and instead prefocus on a specific point. You then just wait for the rider to come to you. This works really well on something like Step-up, which is a kind of high jump for motorcycles. Here you can focus on a point about five feet on the other side of the step-up bar and wait for the biker to make his attempt.

If the event is indoors (and many are), you can take advantage of the area to get up high enough to be level with the bikes as they fly through the air. You can even try to get up higher and shoot down on the bike to show just how high they are in the air. Get down low and shoot straight up at them too, although this may create problems for you when it comes to dealing with the arena lights overhead (see Figure 9-12).

Figure 9-12: An X-games athlete during the Moto-X competition pulls off a trick stunt.
© 2004 Dan Simon

Paintball

Fast moving and colorful, paintball is a fun sport to photograph. If you're shooting from the course boundaries, make sure you have some protective coverings for your camera and yourself because errant shots can reach your location.

A telephoto zoom is the lens of choice for this sport because it lets you re-compose quickly for different spots on the field.

Look for profile shots of players shooting next to course obstacles. If you can get a shot right down the barrel of a paintball gun into the player's eyes (or mask) you've gotten a good image. This is a tough shot to get during play. It might be a one you have to pose.

Do some portraits after the match, particularly of some of the players who've been hit and have readily visible splotches of paint on their clothing. Also make close-ups of the guns and the tubes of paintballs.

If you're covering a tournament, try to show the speed and agility of the players. This means slow shutter speed photos that blur their movements. For an interesting technique, try zooming the lens while the shutter is open. This trick takes lots of trial and error, and you'll waste plenty of pictures before you get good, but give it a try.

Racquetball

Let's see, name a sport that's fast moving and confined to a small space—seemingly perfect for exciting photography! Now, just to add a twist for the photographer, fix it so most the action takes place with the players turned away from the camera. Yep, that's racquetball for you.

You have a couple of choices. Stay on the floor outside the court and wait for times when the players play a shot off the back wall, which only works if the court has see-through Plexiglas back walls. Or, shoot from above looking down into the court, which only works if the court has a second level observation deck.

Suppose the court you're stuck with doesn't have either. Your only choice then is get permission to photograph the players during a warm-up or practice session. Hunker down low and photograph the players while they drive shots all around you. (Wear protective clothing and remember not to make disparaging remarks about the sport or its participants.) Experiment with shutter speeds to find one that keeps faces and bodies sharp while blurring the ball and racquets.

Running

Shoot the start from straight ahead with a telephoto. Then concentrate on individual runners. Try to catch the runner fully extended with his forward leg just striking the ground.

If you're shooting cross-country runners, look for a spot on the course where there's a hill and position yourself near the top. This way you'll catch runners at their slowest and be able to get more shots if you need them. A telephoto zoom will let you reframe as they come closer to your position.

Also look for places on the course where runners change direction or double back. Not all courses have them, but if the one you're shooting does, you may be able to photograph runners multiple times as they pass one point and then another.

Look for shots at the finish line. Here the runners are frequently spent and exhausted, and it shows. You may see them collapse or need support to clear the finish area because they've given all they had in the race. Photograph the same athlete a few minutes later looking tired but satisfied.

Also make shots before the race. This is the time to get pictures of the athletes preparing mentally (usually listening to music) and stretching.

If you're shooting track, position yourself about 20 feet beyond a turn. This way you can shoot the runner in profile and then continue photographing them as they round the turn and come straight towards you.

Sculling/Crew

Shooting crew can be a challenge, even for pros armed with long lenses. For parents trying to grab a shot of family members competing in the sport, it can be nearly impossible.

Spectators at rowing meets frequently vie for a spot at the finish line in order to enjoy the excitement of the race's end, making this vantage point crowded and difficult to shoot from. Even worse, the boats approach sideways to the photographer and a great distance away, so making a good action photo is virtually impossible.

Photographers, however, can benefit more from being at the race's start, particularly if it affords them a head-on view of the athletes. Some venues even launch from near the shore, which is the case for events taking place at Camden, NJ's Cooper River. Under such conditions, photographers working with limited gear can frequently obtain exciting and dramatic action photos.

Race starts require an explosion of power and energy by rowers who are comparatively close to shore. With little competition for viewing space (remember, everyone else is at the finish line), the few photographers who've chosen to shoot the start can make tightly composed images that show the power, tension, and beauty of this sport.

Start with the tightest composition you can manage with the understanding that the racers will be moving away from you once the event begins. You have only a brief period to shoot a particular boat before it pulls out of range of your lens, so have your camera set on fast shutter speeds and its quickest continuous shooting and focusing settings. Make sure you've prefocused before the race begins.

Family members hoping to get good pictures of loved ones in competition can find no better way to make use of limited photographic equipment than at such a moment when modest zoom lenses can get as close as possible to a favored athlete. Another good vantage point occurs when boats pass under a bridge. Here the photographer can get fairly close and shoot from an elevation, which offers a good view of the rowers' faces.

One of the very best places to shoot from is the chase boats that teams use to follow their boats. Although access to these is limited, sometimes a skilled amateur photographer with ties to the team can make arrangements ahead of time to ride along. Contact the team's coach or school's athletic director well in advance of the meet to see if this is possible. Often, a promise to make pictures available for the team's web site or school yearbook makes getting access easier.

Sculling meets are rarely cancelled because of bad weather, so come prepared for difficult shooting conditions. Have a camera raincoat or plastic trash bags and masking tape available to protect your gear, along with paper towels or a chamois cloth to dry off your gear and your hands. Consider buying a set of polyropolene gloves, which wick moisture away from your skin and help to keep your hands dry. Toss a cheap, disposable rain poncho in your camera bag or car trunk so you have some protection for yourself.

Bad weather isn't just a hindrance to race photography, it's an opportunity for interesting photos. Make tightly composed pictures of rain soaked hair and faces. Show the athletes wiping or toweling off water. Look for scenes around their base area such as members of the team crowded into a van to stay dry amidst a jumble of gear, clothing, and personal stereos. Find the really dedicated one who's out getting his or her running in even though the weather is miserable. Take close-ups of the equipment and boats and look for jumbles of color in the personal items such as hats and stereos. Show the mud and the jumble of footprints around the team bus or staging area. Shoot the spectators, too.

Before races begin, the athletes usually have a fair amount of set-up work to do. This can include changing the position of foot cups in the boat and staging gear, such as oars, near the water. All of these tasks provide interesting photo opportunities to supplement the main action shots. Another classic sculling photo is the tightly composed picture of a team lifting and carrying their boat above their heads (see Figure 9-13).

Skateboarding

A wide-angle lens is the popular choice for skateboard photography. Shooting from a low angle is also a good technique. These unusual views probably help mirror the counter-culture feel of the sport. Personally, I like the change of pace the sport provides to more typical sports photography.

Because skateboarding is all about spectacular jumps and tricks, it's a sport that photographs well, as shown in Figure 9-14. Whether you're shooting in a park or street setting, or photographing vert (vertical) ramp action, the opportunity is there to create some fun images.

Don't forget to look for graphic compositions of boarders against a clear sky. Here you can separate the athlete from his surroundings and focus in on the unusual moves he makes.

Figure 9-13: If you can't get close enough to photograph the action out on the water, look for images on land that show the athletes working as a team.

© 2004 Dan Simon

Skiing (cross-country)

Both downhill and cross-country skiing require you to consider the effect of all that bright white snow on your light meter. Set your exposure compensation for as much as two extra f-stops compensation to make sure the skiers are properly exposed; otherwise, the camera will show gray snow and dark skiers.

Photograph cross-country skiers head on with a telephoto lens. Make close-ups of the colorful clothing the athletes wear and of the colorful waxes they use. Include shots of them working on their skis if possible.

Isolate the loneliness of the sport by showing one skier against a large barren backdrop.

Figure 9-14: A skateboarder executes a board flip during an X-Games competition.

© 2004 Dan Simon

Skiing (downhill)

Because downhill skiers move much faster than their cross-country brethren, it can be a real challenge to photograph them well. Be prepared to react quickly and plan on prefocusing on a specific part of the course or trail instead of hoping your auto focus is fast enough to catch them.

Soccer

If you have a super telephoto (500mm or greater), shoot from the area behind the goal so you can get players from all over the field coming straight toward you. Have a second camera with a modest zoom for when players get too close for the super telephoto.

If you're a parent or friend with more modest equipment, walk the sidelines concentrating on your specific player. Most players have a certain area and side of the field they cover, so put yourself as close to this action area as possible. Shoot vertically. If your player consistently comes close to the sidelines, try zone focusing (pre-focus on a point where you think the player will be, set your aperture to about f8, and turn off your autofocus if you can). Take the shot when the player comes close, and you should have enough depth of field to get a sharp image. Just make sure you'r shutter speed is set to at least 1/250th of a second.

Softball

Refer to the section on photographing baseball. The techniques are the same for these two sports.

Swimming and diving

Flash isn't allowed during a dive competition, but it is usually allowed during practice. Flash is almost always allowed during the swimming portion of the meet.

Arrive early (at least a half an hour) to give your equipment a chance to get used to the humidity. If you show up at a big indoor swimming pool and just snatch your gear out of your camera bag, your lenses and viewfinder are going to fog over and you'll not be happy. No amount of wiping will solve this problem. (Some pros carry small travel hair dryers with them for just such an emergency.) The easiest solution is to get there early and leave your gear inside the camera bag until it's had a chance to acclimatize. (It takes about a half an hour.)

To photograph swimmers, shoot from the end of each lane for strokes where the swimmer's head comes out of the water centered and looking toward the lane end (butterfly and breast stroke). Shoot from the side of the pool for strokes where the swimmer isn't looking ahead (backstroke and crawl).

Shoot diving in profile and also head on with a long lens. Another exciting moment is at the start of the race when swimmers dive into the pool (see Figure 9-15). You can shoot this from the side and use flash for good results.

Tennis

When photographing tennis, shoot through the fence with a long telephoto or get up at the net with a medium zoom. Time your shot for the moment before the racket hits the ball, and don't be afraid to compose tightly. Look for moments of peak excitement, such as when the server tosses the ball up in the air and freezes just a moment.

This sport usually calls for a telephoto in the 300mm to 400mm range if you're shooting from behind the fence. The narrow angle of view makes shooting through chain link easy. Use an 80–200 zoom if you're sitting up at the net following players at the baseline. Use a shorter zoom if you're covering a serve and volleyer (alas, a dying breed) from the net (see Figure 9-16).

Figure 9-15: The start of the race is an exciting time to make photos.
© 2004 Dan Simon

Figure 9-16: Long focal lengths are necessary to capture dramatic tennis action from behind the court.
© 2004 Dan Simon

Most tennis action is covered horizontally, making it a problem to find strong vertical compositions. Look for verticals when the player serves and makes overhead slams. Timing calls for you to trip the shutter shortly after the player begins her back swing. Be prepared for very fast action when the player is at the net. Frame the shot loosely because you can't tell which way the players will move until the last instant.

Many indoor courts and even some outdoor venues offer elevated viewpoints of the courts. Although this is not the best choice for your main coverage, these spots can give you an alternative viewpoint. If it's possible to shoot almost straight down on the player while she is serving, you can create an unusual shot looking down into her eyes. More often than not, you need to set up this photo during practice by standing on a ladder and staging the action.

Track and field

A track and field meet offers a smorgasbord of sports for you to follow. And, just to make things a little more challenging, multiple events are going on at the same time.

The good news is that track and field can be covered quite well with just an 80–200 lens, although longer focal lengths can come in handy. The hard part is picking and choosing your spots so you can make images at as many different events as you need to.

A track and field meet typically includes various running events, hurdles, high jump, long jump, javelin toss, discus throw, shot put, pole vault, and occasionally events such as the triple jump and steeplechase. It's not unusual, though, for a smaller meet to run less than a full slate of events.

Hardest to cover are the short relays because you can't be at every relay point. If you position yourself near the exchange point for the first exchange, you can photograph the first runner coming around the curve towards you and then shoot the exchange. If you're really quick, you may be able to sprint across the field and catch the fourth runner coming down the homestretch.

When you get to the longer races, your opportunities to photograph every runner increase, although sometimes two runners are in such close proximity that the front runner screens the rear one the entire time they're in range of your camera.

I usually try to be near the exchange point. That way, I can photograph one runner coming toward my position, document the exchange (which is one of the more interesting shots in running), and rack out my zoom to get the next runner. I usually do this with a 28–70 zoom, but this is one time where something like a 35–105 or some similar zoom is really nice. If you're shooting with a point-and-shoot whose zoom is too slow to recompose for each of the preceding suggestions, concentrate on the exchange. It's a much more exciting shot than one of the runner just running.

Hurdles photograph well, but this event can be difficult if you're trying to photograph each participant. The "money" shot in this sport is the athlete flying over the hurdle, shot from straight on (see Figure 9-17). I have a 170–500 zoom and like to use it for this event because it lets me cover three hurdles worth of action.

Figure 9-17: The hurdles call for quick reflexes and good timing—and that's just for the photographer.
© 2004 Dan Simon

The long jump is my favorite event and probably the easiest to photograph well. You know where the athlete is starting from and where she's going. And because she's moving in a straight line, she's easy for your auto focus to track. You can even prefocus on the expected landing point if you have to. To make things even better, you can photograph the jumper while in mid-air for a very dramatic image. Shoot this one from straight on while kneeling if possible (see Figure 9-18).

Pole vault offers at least two interesting shots. The first is to photograph the athlete head-on as he races down the approach, shooting straight down the pole into the vaulter's face. Compose this shot fairly tightly; you don't need to show the entire pole or the athlete's legs.

The second shot is the athlete going over the bar. You can get this from behind the pit, but look for nearby stands that will enable you to get level with the bar. This vantage point will give you the best opportunities.

Shot put, discus, and javelin all photograph similarly. Because of safety concerns, you can't photograph the athlete's head on unless you're using a very long lens. Usually, you can position yourself down one of the diagonal lines leading away from them. This means you'll only be able to get the participants who are throwing from the opposite hand of the side you're on. Because each athlete throws at least three times, you have the opportunity to get a shot of everyone if you want. An alternative view for the shot put is behind the pit. Here, you can compose a photo of the athlete with the shot pressed against his cheek the moment before he begins the throw. Use a long lens to compress the image and also to put some space between you and the athlete. (It's important to remember that you don't want to interfere with the throw.)

Figure 9-18: The long jump is an attractive sport to photograph because you can predict the athlete's movements.

© 2004 Dan Simon

Steeplechase is an unusual event that features a number of jumps over what I can only describe as odd barriers. This event isn't held all that often at the high school level. I generally like to station myself near the water jump because it's the most dramatic location on the track. An 80-200 zoom works just fine and gives you some play for different compositions.

I've only seen this event held once at a girl's high school track meet, but it was pretty fun. Because this isn't a regular event for them, a lot of the athletes want to enter just for the novelty. Very few could clear the water jump so there was lots of splashing (which photographs well). It even reached a point on the last lap where one coached yelled to his runner to do a cannonball into the deep end of the hazard.

Volleyball

Outdoors, this is a relatively manageable sport to photograph, and you can make good pictures from behind with a very long lens or from the sides and up in the stands with an 80-200 zoom. As the level of play improves, you can more reliably predict who will be the second and third players to touch the ball and be ready to photograph them.

Indoor volleyball is more challenging because of mediocre light and a ban on using flash, because it distracts the players. This means that even with high ISO settings (800 ISO, maybe even 1000 ISO), you're shooting at barely adequate shutter speeds to stop action (see Figure 9-19).

Figure 9-19: Volleyball can provide some exciting action shots. Higher-level play can make it easier to predict where action will occur.

Your best bet is to see if you can use flash during warm-ups or practice and then do the best you can during the match. This is another sport where you should plan for large numbers of wasted exposures and have plenty of memory on hand.

Wakeboarding

The ideal position is to be on the boat towing the wakeboarder or on a pier jutting into the water so you can photograph the wake boarder straight on. If you can't be in this position, find a spot on shore near, but slightly beyond, one of the jumps. Use a long lens (300mm or greater) and keep a slightly loose composition. This is another sport with lots of wasted pictures. Running short of memory shouldn't be a problem though. Odds are you'll only have a chance to fire off a few shots for each run.

Weightlifting

Light is a problem, and the odds of your being able to use flash are pretty small. If you were lifting a few hundred pounds over your head would you want a bunch of flashes firing into your eyes? The good news is that the athletes don't move that quickly and you know where they're going to be and how they're going to be moving. Plan a tight composition from just above the extended weights to down to slightly below the athlete's chin. An even more dramatic image is to make a shot when the bar is resting on the athlete's chest and he's concentrating on his next move. Make this a very tight composition of just his face and the bar and wait for the moment he starts to push the bar up.

Close-ups of chalk covered hands and stacks of weights make good secondary shots. If you can get directly above and shoot straight down, this makes for a good view, but the opportunities for this kind of shot are rare.

Wrestling

This is another sport that's played in poorly lit gyms. The good news is that you're almost always allowed to use flash. This makes wrestling fairly easy to photograph well.

Get low for this sport. Sit on the floor and be ready to lie flat when the wrestlers are doing the same. Look for a photo of one wrestler staring at his opponent arms out ready to attack. Also look for shots of the two athletes down on the mat. Compose photos tightly and remember what's important: the faces and particularly the eyes of the participants.

Summary

Sports photography is one of the most exciting and fun types of photography I know. Not only is it challenging, it's also a terrific feeling to know that in the midst of all the action, you've made a great photo. There's an added bonus, too. As someone who shoots lots of high school sporting events, I get to meet and interact with the current generation of young people. There are a lot of nice kids out there, and you'll find plenty of them at your local athletic field.

Try to learn the basics of the sport before you go on the shoot. If you know how a game or event will unfold, it's much easier to be prepared to snap a great shot of the action. The best advice I can offer to anyone who wants to shoot a sporting event is to shoot a lot and shoot often. The more time you spend photographing a sport, the better you can learn to anticipate action and the better your timing will become.

Photographing Nature

N ow that you're familiar with composition and your camera's technical aspects, you're ready to put your knowledge to practical use.

For some people, practical use means venturing into nature photography. The effort to photograph living things is an exciting and challenging pursuit, one that entails using your skills to capture the great outdoors in all its glory, which includes birds in flight, animals at play, or the beauty of wild plants and flowers.

You don't have to run with lions in Africa or hunker down in Arctic snow to take great nature photos; you can find some of the most intriguing subjects in your own backyard. In this chapter, I tell you about ways you can take interesting photos without having to travel the globe. It's even possible to take exciting photos without having to become an expert outdoorsman! Of course, the more you know about your subjects and the outdoors, the more effective you can be.

The good news here is that you can get started without having to spend a fortune on equipment. In fact, many digital point-and-shoot cameras are already capable of making good pictures of wildlife and outdoor scenes.

Be forewarned: Nature photography can become addictive! If you decide to pursue nature photography as your passion, it can lead to early wake-up calls and an investment in more expensive equipment if you decide you want to take your hobby further. But first, the basics.

Nature Photography Basics

Timing and preparation are vital to taking good nature photographs. Animals move quickly, particularly wild ones. Most are also afraid of human contact and can be skittish, ready to flee at the slightest sound or movement.

If you can minimize the number of things you have to do in order to bring your camera to bear on your subject and snap off a picture, the better off you are. No matter where photography falls on your priorities list, there are some things you can do to improve your chances of getting an image.

Equipment readiness

Timing and preparation alone aren't enough to capture good nature photos; your equipment must also be ready. Here are some other considerations:

✦ **Keep your camera out of its case:** There's no way to quickly take a photo if you have to root through your bag to find the camera. If you always have your camera at the ready, you're less likely to miss a shot and regret it later!

✦ **Keep your camera turned on:** Most digital cameras offer an energy-saving mode: after a period of inactivity, the camera goes to sleep, so to speak. A quick tap on the shutter button is usually enough to wake it up, which is much faster than having to turn the camera on. Test this process with your camera to get a sense of how much of a time difference there is between waking the camera from sleep mode and turning it back on. Some cameras handle the wake-up more quickly than others.

✦ **Load a fresh set of batteries:** You should load fresh batteries for two reasons. First, you don't want to waste time changing batteries when you find something worth photographing. Second, your camera performs better with fresh batteries than it does with partially drained ones. Keeping fresh batteries in your camera shouldn't be a problem if you're using rechargeable ones. But it can get expensive if you aren't. If your camera uses a proprietary rechargeable battery, try to make sure it has been recently charged before your excursion. Some batteries lose their charge over time; others don't. My Canon EOS 1D batteries drain over time, but my wife's Canon EOS D30 batteries don't. Battery life varies from camera to camera.

✦ **Pre-set controls:** Consider the type of photography you expect to do and pre-set as many controls as you can before starting out. If you're photographing birds in the wild, fast shutter speeds and long optics are the way to go. If you're at the zoo or a captive animal display, you can worry more about depth of field concerns and maybe even close-up work. In a captive animal situation, you can sacrifice shutter speeds for smaller aperture settings and maybe even be close enough to use flash effectively.

 Pre-setting controls usually includes your ISO settings, exposure automation mode, and situation-specific settings. For example, if I'm photographing animals in the wild, I usually choose aperture priority and a wide open lens aperture. This way, I know I have the fastest possible shutter speed for the conditions. Once I'm at a stopping point, I frequently change to manual exposure and meter for specific conditions. Be sure to also double-check that you've selected the proper resolution setting.

✦ **Pre-focus:** Although it's not possible to know exactly where a surprise subject might be, it's generally safe to pre-focus farther away rather than closer. If your camera allows it, pre-focus the lens to a point about one third back from infinity (∞ on your lens). This should give the focus mechanism less distance to travel to achieve proper focus.

✦ **Fresh memory:** Make sure your camera's media card or internal memory is ready for photography. This means ensuring that there's a memory card in your camera, your media card is reformatted, and you've captured to your computer any images still on your media card.

 Some cameras will still operate without a media card. Make sure that your media card is in your camera so you don't lose any of the shots you worked so hard to get!

✦ **Camera position:** Even when wearing my camera by neck strap, I usually hold it with at least one hand (usually my right hand so I can have a finger on the shutter release). This way I can bring the camera up to shooting position and grab a shot quickly.

✦ **Know your camera:** Every camera is different, so it's hard to offer specific advice. Your camera probably has some little tricks that help speed up its operation. In many cameras, faster shutter speeds let sequential shooting modes work their fastest, and pressing the shutter button halfway prevents the camera from going into sleep mode and also keeps auto focus operating.

Read the following sidebar on being prepared for an example of how preparation can pay off.

Quickshooting

After an early morning of photography, I was heading back to my car when I caught a break that only happens to photographers who put themselves in a position to get the unexpected image.

Often when I combine hiking and photography, I wear a combination of a Lowepro Street & Field system chest pouch, belt, and harness system (separate items that can be combined to work as one), coupled with a camera backpack for my tripod and extra gear. I wear my basic lenses in pouches that hang from the belt and keep my camera with lens attached in the chest pouch. This way, I can do most of my photography without having to remove the backpack, but still have my heavy gear if I find a spot where I want to spend some time.

This particular morning, I'd decided that the early light was just about played out and it was time to wrap up. Since I had a quarter mile to hike and would pass several ponds on the way to the car, I chose to keep my 80–200mm lens mounted on the camera (many point-and-shoot cameras can approximate this is a focal length range these days). Instead of inserting it into the chest pouch, I rested the camera

Continued

Continued

and lens on it horizontally while gripping the camera with my right hand. My thumb was near the autofocus activation button (my camera was tweaked so autofocus was activated by the exposure lock button instead of the shutter button), and my trigger finger was holding the shutter button half-depressed to keep the camera awake and ready to go (a tried-and-true technique for minimizing shutter lag time, explained in Chapter 9).

This setup let me walk comfortably with the weight of the camera and lens borne by the chest pouch instead of my wrist, yet I was able to bring the camera to bear fairly quickly.

My habit paid off as I rounded a bend and heard a loud honking to my right. As I glanced over, I saw a Mute Swan angrily confronting another bird that had invaded his pond. Turning, I lifted the camera while simultaneously activating autofocus with my thumb. I was able to get the camera up to my eye and start shooting before the bird was completely out of the water. The D30's modest motor drive managed a three-shot burst before the bird passed me. Of the three, the second shot was the best and is displayed in the following figure. I never would have gotten this photo if the camera had been turned off, in a camera bag, or even if it was just hanging by the neck strap because of the D30's normal shutter lag time. This shot was only possible because I was holding the camera in a way that minimized its response time.

© 2004 Dan Simon

Equipment concerns

If you're working with heavier equipment or just want to add some extra stability, the following list provides some useful pieces of equipment you might want to consider:

✦ **Monopods:** Monopods are single leg (usually collapsible) devices that are more portable than tripods. Monopods are great for bearing the weight of a heavy lens and can increase stability enough to give you a one f-stop bump in steadiness. Monopods can also double as hiking staffs while you're on the trail (n fact, many hiking staffs offer a camera mount). If you decide to give the monopod a try, remember to choose one that works best with your camera. Although some of the lighter models are fine for point-and-shoot cameras, they don't handle the heavier weight of a DSLR and accompanying lens very well.

✦ **Mini-pods (also called table top tripods):** These are exactly what they sound like: miniature tripods. If you expect to do a lot of ground-level photography (or anticipate lots of surfaces off the ground such as rocks, walls or ledges), mini-pods are lightweight alternatives to full tripods. Try to avoid extending the legs or column posts, which increases the effects of vibration.

✦ **Beanbags:** Beanbags are higher tech these days, with all sorts of fillers, but the basic idea is the same. A beanbag gives you a softer surface to rest your lens or camera on while cradling your equipment enough to keep it steady. Beanbags don't work miracles, but they can be helpful if you're using the roof of a car or a boulder or a tree branch as a steadying platform for your camera. Best of all, you can carry them empty and fill them with sand or dirt when you get to your shooting location.

Types of Subject Matter

Potential subject matter abounds when you venture into the great outdoors. Nature photography encompasses the spectrum of living things, including plants, flowers, insects, birds, animals, and more. Some subjects are easier to photograph than others. This section provides some tips on photographing various subjects found in nature.

Spiders and insects

Insects can be one of the easier subjects to photograph. Butterflies in particular make beautiful subjects and most point-and-shoot digital cameras offer a close focusing mode that captures these colorful creatures in all their splendor. Most point-and-shoots require you to compose the photo using the LCD screen instead of the viewfinder. Even if your camera doesn't require this, go ahead and do so anyway. Butterflies are less likely to be disturbed and fly away if your camera gets close to them than they are if you get close to them. If you can get close enough without scaring them off, here are some things to consider when shooting butterflies:

✦ **Light direction:** Pay careful attention to light direction, and remember to consider using flash to fill in shadows. You can also carry a folded up piece of heavy-duty aluminum foil to reflect some light onto them.

✦ **Butterflies are lightweight:** Since these delicate creatures are so light, wind conditions tend to determine how much success you can have photographing them. Days with calm to light breezes usually give butterflies the greatest freedom of movement. During especially windy conditions, they try to hunker down when possible, but they don't always succeed!

✦ **Early morning activity:** Butterflies tend to be active in the early morning, just after the sun comes up (which, coincidentally, provides some of the day's best light). One enthusiast I know describes them as "little solar panels." They need the early morning sun to warm up enough to start their day.

✦ **Migration:** Some butterfly species, such as the monarch, are known for their migrations. If you live along a monarch migration route, you can count on finding butterflies to photograph. Sometimes, you may even be able to find large numbers clustered together in the trees, as shown in Figure 10-1.

Figure 10-1: Using a flash helps to display the detail on the wings of this cluster of monarch butterflies.

© *2004 Dan Simon*

 Be sure to check out this book's companion web site at `www.wiley.com/ compbooks/simon` to see full-color versions of the images in this chapter.

Photographing other insects can be more of a challenge. Spiders and their webs can make for very interesting images. If you find arachnids worthy subject matter, plan a few early morning shoots while webs are still covered with dew. Side and back lighting create beautiful effects, so experiment with different camera positions.

If you have the choice, it's best to keep some distance between you and the spider, mainly because they tend to scurry off and hide if you get too close. If you're shooting with a DSLR, a telephoto lens and extension tube combination is a good choice. If you're working with a point-and-shoot camera, understand that you may only get one shot before the spider hurries off. Fill flash is a good idea because it helps bring out the detail in both the spider and its web.

Flying insects such as bees and dragonflies are difficult to catch in flight. In fact, it's almost impossible if you're trying to do it with autofocus; it's more doable if you're using flash and depth of field to ensure sharp focus. Your best bet is to photograph flying insects while they rest on a flower or plant, which only enhances your overall composition.

Insect photography can create images ranging from the terrifying to the hilarious. You never know what you're going to find when you peek into their world, evidenced by Figure 10-2.

Figure 10-2: I think there's a little more than organic gardening going on here!
© 2004 Dan Simon

Plants and flowers

Plants and flowers make wonderful photographic subjects, particularly when you capture them in their natural surroundings. Making attractive images of this subject matter is quite easy because they don't run and hide at the sight of you.

Early morning is an especially good time to photograph wildflowers. Strong directional sunlight helps bring out detail in the plants, plus the morning light's color bathes them in a warm glow. Best of all, you frequently find morning dew glistening on petals and leaves.

Here are some things you can do to help take better pictures of plants and flowers:

✦ **Carry a reflector/diffuser combo:** These are collapsible panels that can be used to either soften the light hitting your subject, or (when its reflective covering is fitted on) reflect light onto it. If you're not interested in buying a reflector/diffuser combo (they cost between $30 and $90, depending on size), heavy-duty aluminum foil can be pressed into service as a reflector. Additionally, a pillowcase stretched over a rectangular frame serves as a makeshift diffuser. If you're concentrating on smaller plants, a small mirror may also work.

✦ **Create a backdrop:** You can use a piece of colored cloth as a background to separate the plant from distracting surroundings. This won't give you the feel of a good wilderness image, but it is useful in making plant portraits.

✦ **Manipulate plants to improve composition:** You can use twist ties or short strips of cloth to gently tie back plant stems to improve your composition. Just remember to remove them when you're done shooting. You can also use a plant mister to create dew if none is present.

✦ **Experiment with extreme focal lengths:** Giving your shots a different look is always fun. Extreme focal lengths bring out detail and create interesting compositions, as shown in Figure 10-3.

Figure 10-3: I shot this close up with an 8mm fisheye lens and re-mapped it to a rectangular image with Power Retouche, a Photoshop filter. The extreme angle lets the flower remain prominent while still allowing me to keep Lisa in the image.
© 2004 Dan Simon

✦ **Take some low-angle shots:** Use a wide-angle lens or focal length (28mm or wider) and put a flower in the foreground close to the lens. This creates an interesting composition, one that pulls the eye deeper into the image. With taller plants, you can create interesting images even when the light isn't good. By shooting from below the flower (using a bug's eye view), you create an unusual composition. As an added bonus, the flower petals may take on an astonishing translucence.

Birds

Photographing birds can be a challenging and exciting hobby. Indeed, some of the leading practitioners of this art have raised the bar to an incredibly high level. Spectacular images of birds in flight are now the norm.

Pros manage shots such as these thanks to expensive optics and high-speed motor drives. They also understand the best times of day to take such pictures, and they learn enough about their subject's behavior to understand what they do in various situations.

Hobbyists hoping to make memorable bird photos don't have to feel left out, however. More and more point-and-shoot digital cameras offer focal lengths long enough for effective bird photography. Add-on lenses, which increase the magnification of your built-in zoom, can boost reach even further.

 A subcategory of hobbyist bird photographers, known as *birders,* are legendary for their zeal and enthusiasm, and deservedly so. Many of them work incredibly hard at their obsession. People in this category are more interested in spotting a particular bird than necessarily photographing it. Although they hope to create good pictures, most would rather spend a fortune on spotting scopes and binoculars than they would cameras and lenses.

As cameras improve, so do their autofocusing speeds, making it possible to expect better results. One area where point-and-shoots still trail pro lenses is in light-gathering capability at longer focal lengths. This deficiency can make photographing birds in early morning or late daylight difficult because you might not be able to use fast enough shutter speeds to avoid camera shake with long focal lengths.

Birds vary greatly in size. Larger birds, such as the great blue heron, are big enough that you can get frame-filling photos of them from a reasonable distance. Smaller birds, like robins and cardinals, present a much greater challenge. Generally, it's best to try to photograph them as part of an overall composition instead of trying for a full-frame portrait.

In the wild, birds tend to be skittish. Like most other animals, they have a certain zone of safety they want to maintain. If a wild bird sees a human beyond this safety zone, it tends to keep at whatever they're doing. If you move inside this safe area, however, the bird usually flies away or at least moves enough to re-establish the required distance.

Unfortunately, the safety zone for most birds tends to be longer than the effective range of many telephoto lenses. This means you have to combine optics with technique to get close enough for good photography. One way to overcome this obstacle is to understand their movement and adapt to their patterns.

For example, after shooting geese at a wildlife sanctuary for a while, I could discern a pattern of travel. All the birds would follow a set direction of travel, and swinging around the lake would position me so that the next group of birds to fly off would pass close by overhead. Made with a 300mm telephoto lens and 1.4x teleconverter, Figure 10-4 shows that my diligence paid off!

Figure 10-4: Proper positioning, in addition to a 300mm telephoto lens and a 1.4x teleconverter, captures geese in flight.
© *2004 Dan Simon*

Waterways are also good places to find birds. Often, if you're patient, you can be in position to photograph them when they come in for a landing (see Figure 10-5).

Figure 10-5: A shot of large birds landing, as they use their bodies to help slow their air speed, can produce quite a dramatic photo.
© *2004 Dan Simon*

Late winter and early spring are good times for bird photography. Many trees aren't yet filled with view-blocking leaves this time of year. It makes it easier to spot nests and even the birds themselves.

Early morning is the best time for bird activity, but you can also see movement late in the day before sunset. You can expect more landing opportunities as flocks settle down for the night. If you have a nice sunset, look for birds silhouetted by the sun.

If you're shooting in late daylight, keep in mind that light levels fall rapidly, so keeping a fast enough shutter speed becomes a problem. Boosting your ISO settings and mounting your camera on a tripod will help you squeeze the most out of the diminishing light.

Land animals

One of the toughest challenges a nature photographer can tackle is photographing wild animals. Many of these creatures are nocturnal, so photographing them by conventional means is just about out of the question. Instead, a dedicated nature photographer can set up a camera near an animal path or suspected den and rig the camera with a motion sensor that fires the camera and its flash unit when an animal passes the sensor.

Some DSLRs, such as the Canon 1D, have a built-in function that fires the camera automatically when something is in focus. Problem is, the camera only fires once in this mode. If the animal that triggers it isn't the one you were hoping to photograph, oh well, try again tomorrow night.

Few point-and-shoot digital cameras can be rigged this way, so this is area of nature photography beyond the bounds of most amateurs. At best, however, such images are more recording than great art, anyway.

Perhaps the best way to tackle the challenge of catching wildlife in its natural setting, is to be out at the day's margins. The time just before sunrise and right after sunset is a transition period where the nocturnal and the diurnal occasionally cross paths. Look for game trails near water sources and make an effort to be inconspicuous. Remember, animals see better in the dark than you do, especially the animal shown in Figure 10-6.

Animals that are active during daylight hours make things easier for the photographer. Here, you at least have the light on your side. Daylight is a prime time for cold-blooded animals in particular, because they need the sun's warmth to bring their body temperature up to functioning levels.

Look for dark rocks in direct sun. These solar receptors attract all sorts of reptiles, like the lizard shown in Figure 10-7, who soak up the warmth stored in these rocks.

Good nature photographers learn to look for animal *sign*, which is a fancy way of saying droppings. The presence of sign indicates that you're in an area frequented by a particular creature. As you get better at reading sign, you should be able to tell what type of animal left it. You can also tell roughly how long ago

Figure 10-6: Shooting at dusk, and with a little luck, you can capture the denizens of the night.

© 2004 Dan Simon

Figure 10-7: Despite feeling threatened by nearby humans, this lizard is reluctant to leave a comfortable spot!

© 2004 Dan Simon

an animal passed your area based on how warm the sign is. Use the information you glean from sign to plan your next shoot and pick out a potential hiding place to set up and wait for the animal's approach.

Some places offer better opportunities for success than others. Over the next few pages, I cover various locales available to people who want to take good nature photos.

Nature Preserves and Wildlife Sanctuaries

There are many wildlife sanctuaries and preserves across the United States. These sites offer a safe haven for wildlife and a resource for animal lovers and nature photographers, not to mention offering the opportunity to photograph animals you wouldn't otherwise see. See Figure 10-8 for just such an animal.

Figure 10-8: Short of going on safari, you're not going to encounter a gorilla except in a game preserve or safari park.

© 2004 Dan Simon

Taking photographs at preserves or sanctuaries is much more challenging than shooting at zoos and captive animal demonstrations (discussed later in this chapter) because the animals are wild and go where they please, even scurrying off it suits their mood.

Although preserves and sanctuaries significantly improve your chances of getting photographs of wild creatures, this is a "training-wheels off" exercise. If you take a great photo of a wild creature at a wildlife preserve, you've simply taken a great photo, and no explanation is necessary.

Photography at a wildlife preserve makes things easier for you than trying to photograph an animal in the wild. Because these preserves offer the animals protection, they're frequently a little bit less skittish than they are in their natural surroundings. They also tend to see more humans and consequently are a little less afraid. Don't expect miracles though; these are still wild animals.

Animals in the wild

When you're pursuing wildlife in its own territory, you're working at a big disadvantage. You're in the animal's home. They know the territory intimately and their senses are more in tune with their surroundings than yours are. Animals are also smart enough to be scared of people and will generally run or hide long before you've had a chance to see them.

Seems ironic doesn't it? You can be driving down a rural highway and lose count of how many deer you see feeding by the roadside, but just try to find one while you're hiking.

Knowing your area of exploration and its wildlife is helpful. If there's a particular type of animal you hope to see, it's good to know its habits, particularly whether it's nocturnal or diurnal. But sometimes that's not enough. As stated previously, animals tend to be migratory, which means photographers also have to be migratory.

Wildlife photography on the move

It can be a challenge to cover ground (or water) and find wildlife to photograph at the same time. Animals are sensitive to sounds and sights and tend to flee at the first indication that something is amiss.

One thing that can make your efforts more successful is finding regions where hunting is prohibited. Animals that haven't been hunted are much less afraid of people than those who have been hunted.

Some places are more conducive to wildlife sightings than others. Mule deer in the Grand Canyon show very little fear of humans (too little, actually). It's not hard to get within effective lens range of them.

Bears become a little less afraid of human beings every year, which isn't a good thing. Even relatively timid bears, such as the brown bear, are dangerous. Yet all too often, careless people let themselves get dangerously close to these wild animals. By all means, plan on photographing them if you get the opportunity, but keep your distance. Never try to entice a bear closer by offering food or calling to it. And don't assume that you are safe inside your car if one of them comes after you.

Some animals are a bit more approachable. On a sea kayaking trip off the coast of New Zealand, I paddled out to a seal colony at one of the small islands and got within 15 feet of the seals. One of them even came in the water to check out my kayak. Later in that same trip, a possum rummaging through my gear woke me up. The animal showed no fear of me, whatsoever, even though I was just a couple of feet away!

Here in the United States, I've had bear and deer walk into my camping areas. I've also caught sight of foxes, wolves, and the occasional member of the cat family while driving on the highway (hard to tell a cougar from a mountain lion at 65 mph at night). It's best to have someone else driving, a ready camera, and a fast shutter speed ready if you hope to shoot from a moving car; even then, this method has a low likelihood of success. Certainly any chance you have depends on your ability to shoot quickly.

As I mentioned earlier, when you're out looking for them, wild creatures can be mighty hard to find. One thing you can do to improve your chances, is letting them find you, as discussed in the next section.

Wait for them to come to you

Sometimes wildlife photography is about finding a location that animals frequent and then waiting for them to come to you. Some things to keep in mind include understanding that most animals are active when the sun is low in the sky. This gives them a break from the heat and also makes them a little less visible. Animals (just like you and me) tend to wake up hungry and thirsty, so they usually head for water after they wake up.

Look for game paths heading toward a water source and position yourself a safe (from the animal's perspective) distance away. Make sure the wind is blowing toward you and stay alert. It's best if you wear clothing that helps you blend into the background.

 Wearing camouflaged clothing might be ideal when you're on a hike, but it's not the best idea during hunting season, especially if you're in an area where hunting is permitted.

Blinds: A way to stay out of sight

Some photographers also resort to using a device known as a *blind*. A blind is simply a shelter used to hide you from an animal's sight. Many preserves and sanctuaries have permanent observation points located in areas where animals are common. You can just plan on using these permanent shelters if one is available. If it isn't, you may want to invest in a portable blind.

Blinds come in many different versions, some designed for hunters and others for photographers. They can be tent-like, offering room to move around, or even relatively formfitting, designed to fit around a seated photographer, his chair, and his tripod-mounted camera and lens.

Animals tend to fear anything that looks like a human, so anything that reduces your resemblance to one helps. Although this may sound like a far-fetched idea, it isn't. Even the family auto can be pressed into service as a blind if you're looking for wildlife near a roadway. Birds in particular are known for their willingness to come much closer to a car than to a person. Just remember to turn off the engine and your stereo sound system!

Some preserves receive enough use that wildlife almost becomes approachable. This is an even more common occurrence with birds.

The Meadows

I occasionally shoot at a preserve known as the Meadows, not far from the Cape May lighthouse in southern New Jersey. This Nature Conservancy site is popular with both birders and photographers and has a number of benches and observation platforms.

Birds here have become used to people watching and photographing them and are slightly less afraid of humans than they might be at other locations. As a result, if you're patient, you can get photographs of the birds without having to resort to the huge lenses serious bird photographers rely on. Certainly, if you can manage the equivalent of a 300mm lens or just a bit longer, you have a chance to fill the frame with a great egret or other mid- to large-sized bird, as I did in the following photo.

© 2004 Dan Simon

I made this photograph of a fishing great egret with a Canon D30 and 170–500 zoom set at 232mm. The image has been cropped some (about 50 percent) because I was maintaining a fairly loose composition, which was necessary because the bird was moving quickly through the water looking for food.

I'd been shooting this particular animal for about 12 minutes. After making some recognition photos (nice pictures that show I'd actually seen a great egret), I started trying to capture some action shots.

This bird was busily earning his breakfast, and so I set upon earning mine. It took several tries, but I was finally able to time my shot to catch his strike. I should note that I was out early this day, timing my arrival at the preserve for before sunrise. In fact, I was done shooting before 9 A.M.

An animal can go from hunter to hunted without notice, so they are always on their guard. And their senses are usually far more acute than ours. Here are some things to keep in mind when you're trying to photograph animals in wild settings:

✦ **Smell:** Cigarette smoke, colognes, and other strong scents shout out loud and clear that a human is in the area. Even your cup of coffee and breakfast sandwich let wild creatures know something is out of the ordinary.

✦ **Sight:** Many animals see things differently than you and I do. Species that spend their lives as prey usually have wide-set eyes. Although they can't pinpoint things as sharply as you (as a predator species) can, they have the amazing peripheral vision necessary to see hunters approaching. You may think you're out of their sight, but in reality, you're not. Species that spend their lives hunting, on the hand, have close-set eyes. (Notice which category humans fit into?) Hunters are attuned to the slightest movement and can focus on that movement quickly. The more you move around, the more likely you are to give away your position.

✦ **Sound:** Yeah, animals also hear better than humans do. If you're moving around, not only can they see your movement from a distance, but they can hear it too. Try to wear softer clothing that doesn't make as much noise if it brushes against something. Avoid loud conversations and activities, such as lighting cigarettes, opening cans of soda, or typing on your laptop computer.

✦ **Touch:** Okay, if they can touch you, you're no longer the hunter. Drop this book and climb the nearest tree. (Don't forget your camera!)

 It's a good idea to be prepared for bad weather when you're shooting in the wild. An unexpected rainstorm can leave you far from your car or the nearest shelter while wearing a neck full of expensive gear. Protecting your camera against the elements isn't that hard. You can make an effective raincoat for a point-and-shoot camera out of a Ziploc bag and some masking tape. In a pinch, a plastic shopping bag and some duct tape also fashions protection for an interchangeable lens camera. Flip to Chapter 6 for more detailed information about shooting in bad weather and protecting your gear.

Another form of nature preserve: Your backyard

Sometimes you don't even have to leave your own property to find nature photography opportunities. Suburban backyards support a reasonable amount of wildlife on their own.

You can turn your backyard into a mini nature preserve of sorts. At the very least you can make it an animal friendly environment that provides shelter for wild creatures. Put out food and water, and you can expect additional company.

Simply putting out a birdfeeder can attract more birds to your property. You can choose specific types of feed to attract particular types of birds. After you set up your feeder, you can learn birds' feeding patterns and develop a plan for photographing them.

I have several bird feeders hanging from different spots in my yard. One feeder hangs from an overhang right outside my kitchen. I keep a woodpecker mix in this feeder, and it has paid off more than once with close-up views of different birds. One morning I photographed a red-headed woodpecker by using an 80–200mm lens. I chose this focal length because I'd be able to get fairly close to the bird photographically while keeping my distance physically. Despite shooting through window glass, I still ended up with a nice photo, shown in Figure 10-9.

Figure 10-9 Red-headed woodpeckers are just some of the birds that frequent backyard bird feeders.

© 2004 Dan Simon

Squirrels and chipmunks are also easy to attract (sometimes too easy) and many suburban lawns also provide homes for rabbits. Try to shoot from behind a doorway or from your car. Since these guys are skittish even though they're used to people, use a doorway on the other side of the house to get outside and quietly walk around to your shooting position. Opening a doorway in sight of these creatures causes them to scatter.

Rabbits tend to freeze when spotted. Hoping you won't notice them is their first line of defense. Take advantage of the rabbit's momentary stillness; once they decide their ruse hasn't worked, they're off.

Setting Up a Remote Camera

Sometimes the answer to your nature photography dilemma is to get your camera close to your subject while you still keep your distance. This solution is effective, but calls for an investment in assorted accessories to make it possible.

The camera needs to be set up on a tripod (usually with some form of protection, such as a camera raincoat, to safeguard it) and triggered remotely either via an extension cord or wireless trigger. Fancier setups include supplementary lighting for best results.

Setting up a remote camera is another one of those things that probably calls for a DSLR, but if your point-and-shoot offers a remote triggering accessory, then it's probably worth a try.

Once you're ready to start photographing, plan on making lots of images. Capturing photos of birds in flight is very difficult. If you're working with fixed conditions where you know where the bird is coming from and where it's going, you can prefocus on a particular point in its flight path and try to maintain enough depth of field to give you a little margin for error.

Although the idea of knowing where the bird is coming from and where it's going may sound unrealistic, it frequently isn't. In my backyard, a family of sparrows has taken up residence in an ivy-covered fence. We've set up a bird feeder about four feet away from the fence. By using a remote-controlled camera, I get many opportunities to photograph birds flying from the fence to the bird feeder (see Figure 10-10).

Figure 10-10 Capturing birds in flight with a remote camera can be quite simple and can produce some nice results.
© 2004 Dan Simon

Captive animal demonstrations

Animal sanctuaries and game preserves offer a chance to photograph animals in a controlled setting. These environments let you create images you wouldn't normally be able to get in the wild.

Hawk Mountain, in Kempton, PA, for example, sometimes offers afternoon displays of educational raptors from the Lehigh-Trexler Game Preserve. Educational birds have been injured and can no longer return to the wild. Sometimes raised as pets, these bird no longer have the proper fear of humans necessary for their survival.

 Visit this book's companion web site, www.wiley.com/compbooks/simon, for links to web sites for the organizations mentioned in this chapter.

These educational birds are sometimes displayed for extended periods of time so that visitors can see them up close and learn about their habits and artists and photographers can study and use them as models. The cost for this, by the way, is usually free!

Captive demonstrations sometimes last for hours and may display as many as eight to ten different avian subjects—including hawks, falcons, and owls—handled by knowledgeable handlers who can answer your questions. Because of the safeguards, you can get close to the birds. And when I say close, I mean *close.* I nearly backed into a pair of screech owls while photographing a falcon! Under these conditions, you can use any digital camera on the market to take a close-up portrait of one of these birds, such as the one shown in Figure 10-11.

Figure 10-11 Lisa using an Olympus C2000 to photograph a rough-legged hawk up close.
© *2004 Dan Simon*

Captive demonstrations are a great time to work on creating portraits of these creatures. You're close enough for your flash to do some good, and you can make frame-filling images.

Zoos and Aquariums

Zoos and aquariums can be fertile grounds for photography since you know where the animals are and might not have to travel very far. Keep the following advice in mind to improve your chances of getting good photos.

Zoo photography

Animals are most active during the cooler times of the day (makes sense doesn't it?). So plan to arrive early when they're up and about. Even better, call ahead and try to find out the feeding schedule for the animals you're most interested in photographing. Animals are the most anxious and active when they're anticipating a meal.

If you're planning a zoo visit, expect a mix of opportunities. You might be able to get fairly close to some animals, but you probably can't get very close to the dangerous ones, so plan accordingly. While I've made some nice shots with an 80–200mm lens, if you have a longer lens, you'd be wise to take it along.

Some zoos, such as the Philadelphia Zoo, make a photographer's life easy. Many of this zoo's animal exhibits offer clean lines of sight that are perfect for animal photography. Clean sight lines make your photos look like they were actually shot in the wild, as in Figure 10-12.

Figure 10-12 You'd never know it, but I took this giraffe portrait during a visit to my local zoo.
© 2004 Dan Simon

Take your time when shooting at zoos and make sure you take lots of images. Spend some time watching the animals and always have your camera ready.

The Making of a Family Portrait

Some of my favorite animal photos are the result of little more than pure dumb luck.

I'd just about finished making some head shots of a lion, when I saw a lioness approaching him. I'm a cat lover myself and noticed something familiar in her expression, so I stood by waiting to see how the pair greeted each other. As she nuzzled him I brought my camera up to my eye in order to frame the pair (thankfully still focused to roughly the same distance as they were).

I was already triggering the shutter button when she turned parallel to the male and they both held the classic "gazing off into the future" pose that portrait photographers sometimes use. I quickly fired off two photos of this tender moment, and one of them appears below.

© 2004 Dan Simon

Even though luck was involved, this anecdote illustrates an important point. I don't know how many times I've seen people (myself included) miss great images simply because they weren't ready at the right moment to take a picture.

You can plan your schedule down to the last detail, spend the day walking the zoo, and do everything possible to optimize your chances for a great shot. Then you're walking to the exit, all done for the day, when a peacock crosses your path, turns for a moment, and spreads his tail—for only an instant! By the time you reach for your camera, the moment is gone and you've lost the shot—unless your camera is up and ready to go. At the zoo, I always wear my camera, always have it turned on, always set a fast shutter speed and prefocus the lens, and more often than not, hold it in my right hand with my finger near the shutter release.

Aquarium photography

Underwater shots aren't limited to the kind you might take on a snorkeling expedition. Aquariums also allow you to shoot aquatic animals underwater—but from dry land. Photographing at aquariums, however, poses one significant obstacle: shooting through glass.

Shooting through glass

Shooting in an aquarium presents its own challenges, mostly because you're shooting through Plexiglas walls, which reduce image quality and bounce reflections back at you. This bounce back effect only gets worse if you try to use flash to brighten up the animals on the other side of the Plexiglas.

Here are some techniques you can use to shoot better photos through Plexiglas:

✦ Choose a higher ISO setting so you can shoot without using flash. See Figure 10-13 for a photo shot under these conditions.

✦ Use a polarizing filter to minimize reflections.

✦ If you're going to use flash, attach a rubber lens hood and position your camera so the lens hood rests on the glass. This will help block much of the light reflected by the flash. Make sure it's not against aquarium rules to do this.

Figure 10-13 I set my camera for a higher ISO before shooting through this Plexiglas window so that I could shoot without flash.
© 2004 Dan Simon

Underwater photography

If you expect to shoot a lot in bad weather, or if you plan to do a little snorkeling and would like to take pictures while you're at it, consider purchasing one of the entry-level waterproof cameras on the market. Many of these cameras sell for less than $400 and can manage anything from just a few feet underwater to as deep as 200 feet. Figure 10-14 shows an example of a photograph taken using an underwater camera.

Figure 10-14 Even a modest underwater digital camera can help you bring back shots like this.
© 2004 Dan Simon

An alternative to buying an underwater camera is to buy an underwater housing for a digital camera that you already own. Depending on whether you want a molded Plexiglas housing (very expensive) or are willing to go with a soft plastic housing (modestly expensive), your options range from just a couple of hundred dollars to well over $1000. Still, if the soft plastic housing meets your needs, you can find one to handle most DSLRs for less than $300.

Light Falloff

One of the biggest hassles of underwater photography (besides keeping your camera safely dry) is the problem of *light falloff*. Once you get more than a couple of feet below the water's surface, the amount of light reaching your subject decreases dramatically. This means that if you want to take good underwater photos, you need to use some sort of supplemental lighting. It might be the camera's built-in flash (short distance) or an accessory light (medium distance).

Water is much denser than air is. As sunlight travels down through the water, its strength is reduced significantly. Indeed, you can lose as much as three f-stops worth of light just by dropping below the surface. Water conditions such as a choppy surface can rob you of even more light. The amount of light falloff varies depending on time of year, time of day, and geographic location.

If you're snorkeling and don't get too far below the surface, you may be okay if you set your camera to a higher ISO setting to make up for the lower light levels. Better still, use the camera's built-in flash to help light your subject matter.

One problem that can result from using flash underwater is known as *backscatter*. Light reflecting off particles in the water creates a snow-like effect. More advanced underwater systems place a diffuser over the flash head and post the light high off the camera to change its direction. This can help reduce backscatter. As a rule, you make things easier by being close to your subject and shooting with a wide-angle lens. This makes your flash more effective and reduces backscatter. (Of course it may not be safe with certain types of undersea creatures!). Even at a mere three feet below the water's surface, backscatter caused the specks and particles floating above the stingray shown in the following figure.

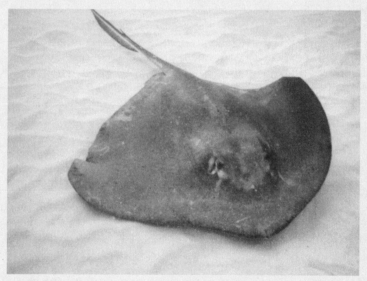

© 2004 Dan Simon

Ethical Considerations

Certain ethics are involved when you take nature images for a magazine or book. First and foremost, they can't be faked in any way. This doesn't just outlaw Photoshop trickery, it also means not using captive animals, not shooting under controlled conditions, and not manipulating the environment in any other way. There is even heated debate about the ethics of setting out food to attract animals. You're not strictly forbidden from doing any of these things, but you must identify that you've done them. Editors don't hold that against you, but you're competing with photographers who might actually create their images out in the wild. Guess whose stuff gets picked?

When you're shooting pictures for yourself, these concerns aren't as important. Taking a great picture of an animal at a zoo or captive animal display simply gives you a great picture for display in your own home. But just because you're not held to the same ethical standards as professional photographers doesn't mean you should dismiss ethics entirely.

There's another set of ethical concerns that deal with how you interact with nature. As lovers of the outdoors,you have a responsibility to make sure your actions don't damage the wilderness or threaten the wildlife. Please follow the appropriate guidelines for the wild areas you visit. Remember the request "Take only photographs, leave only footprints." Make sure they're good photographs, too.

Summary

In this chapter, you discovered how to take interesting nature photographs without having to invest in expensive equipment or travel great distances. Opportunities to photograph nature and wildlife exist everywhere. From zoos to nature preserves—and even in your own backyard—photographic subjects abound if you take the time to search them out (or let them come to you).

Photographing Landscapes

Landscape photography is where you show the power and beauty of the physical world. This type of shooting is classic photography. It's where you capture a side of your world that isn't always readily apparent to the casual passersby.

This type of photography appeals to almost everyone. How often do you see someone holding up a camera to photograph that magnificent vista, which seems to go on for unimaginable distances?

Sadly, many of those pictures turn out to be pretty underwhelming once you get back home and have prints made. It shouldn't be too surprising when this happens. Let's face it, you're trying to compress a huge three-dimensional scene into a tiny, two-dimensional 4 x 6 photograph.

Yet truly gifted landscape photographers do manage to find ways to document the beauty and scale of the landscape. What's their secret? This chapter helps you see how to shoot great landscape photos. You just need to follow the basic rules of composition, make the light work to your advantage, use seasonal weather conditions to break out of the typical "postcard" image, and include a foreground element to make an image feel more three-dimensional. And that's only the beginning. Read on to find out more secrets of the landscape photography pros.

Getting Started in Landscape Photography

Okay. Now that I've spilled the beans on some of the secrets of how great landscape photos are made, you're ready to go out and make your own masterpieces, right?

In This Chapter

Rural/natural landscapes

Urban landscapes

Industrial landscapes

Unfortunately, it isn't quite that simple. So, first, here's a basic primer on landscape photography.

Landscapes come in a variety of types. They can be real. They can be imagined. Here are the basic categories of landscapes:

✦ **Rural:** This is one of the stereotypical types of landscape images. It can be the covered bridge, the farm scene, or great rolling hills of pastureland. Rural landscapes take advantage of graceful curves and soft lines. They can show vast expanses of land or particularly familiar icons. Rural landscapes look like they can be used to illustrate America the Beautiful.

✦ **Urban:** There is beauty to be found in the urban landscape too. City skylines at sunset provide one such example. Interesting architecture and vast manmade canyons also provide interesting subject matter.

✦ **Industrial:** Although it may seem difficult to find beauty in industry, many industrial settings do create interesting landscapes. Large imposing edifices and big complexes make good subject matter for industrial landscapes. As impersonal and alien as mechanical structures can be, sometimes the human connection makes the scene that much more powerful.

Landscape photography is about finding beauty in the world around us. All the elements of composition discussed earlier in this book are particularly important tools in showing that beauty.

Just like the landscape painters and artists who came before, photographers, both pro and amateur, pursue landscape images to fulfill a need inside to create works of beauty. Whether you're working with a high-end DSLR or just a basic point-and-shoot, it's possible to make memorable landscape photos with a digital camera.

Features of nature such as mountains, lakes, and rivers are some of the ingredients in creating landscape images. Compositional elements such as leading lines and the rule of thirds are some of the tools you use to arrange them. Light is the glue that holds everything together.

Technical Considerations

Razor sharp depth of field from foreground to background is a prime concern for landscape photographers. Sharp focus helps show the beauty of the land and lets the eye drink in all the details of a scene.

Landscape photographers often focus on a particular lens's *hyper-focal* distance. Hyper-focal distance is an optimum focusing point determined by the focal length of the lens you're using, the f-stop the lens is set to, and the size of the digital sensor your camera uses.

In simple terms, knowing the correct hyper-focal distance lets you use depth of field to set a zone of sharp focus that begins as close as possible to your camera and ends at infinity. Achieving such depth of field is quite easy, particularly with a wide-angle lens.

Say you're shooting at f4 with a 50mm lens. If you focus on a point 90 feet away, everything from 44.5 feet to infinity will be in sharp focus.

 I came up with the numbers in these calculation examples thanks to a hyper-focal length calculator I found at `www.outsight.com/hyperfocal .html#hyper`. Just plug-in your data and this online calculator figures the calculation out for you.

If you take the same photo at f8 with a 20mm wide-angle lens, you can focus on a point 7 feet away, and everything from three-and-a-half feet to infinity will be in sharp focus.

Using hyper-focal distance is a lot more practical with prime lenses than it is with zoom lenses or point-and-shoot cameras because to be really precise, you need a depth of field scale on your lens that lets you adjust your focal point accordingly. If you're a math whiz, you can also figure it out on your own, but it's not easy. In fact, some people pick up extra money by creating hyper-focal distance charts for individual lenses.

 Be sure to check out this book's companion web site at `www.wiley.com/ compbooks/simon` for links to web sites that offer online hyper-focal distance calculators.

Fortunately, you have some easier options.

If you're using a point-and-shoot camera, your options are limited. Pick your camera's landscape mode because this setting is designed to maximize depth of field. Identify the foreground point you'd like to have in sharp focus and the background scene you also want rendered sharply. Focus the lens at a point about one third of the way past the foreground point. If your lens opening is small enough (a high f-stop number), you should have enough depth of field to bring both foreground and background into focus.

You can improve your chances of accomplishing sharp focus and large depth of field by using your widest focal length. If you mount your camera on a tripod or other stable surface, you can also slow your shutter speed for the maximum possible depth of field.

The same approach works for DSLRs, but depending on your particular camera, you may have some other tricks you can try. If you're shooting with a Nikon DSLR, for example, and are working with older prime lenses, you may actually have a depth of field scale engraved on the lens. If you do, you can simply use it to find the hyper-focal point. Just choose your f-stop and then find the two markers for that f-stop on the engraved scale. Turn the lens until your far point meets the f-stop marker on the right and then see what distance comes up next to the f-stop marker on the left. If it's still too far away, choose a smaller f-stop for your exposure.

Photographers working with one of Canon's high-end DSLRs (the EOS 1D, EOS 1DmkII, and EOS 1Ds), have a very useful tool known as the DEP mode. (DEP mode is also found on Canon's high-end film cameras.) You can access DEP mode via the mode button on the left side of the camera's top deck in the same way you change any of the camera's exposure modes. In DEP mode, you point the focusing point at the far target and half press the shutter (to acquire its distance via the autofocus sensor). Then you find the near point you want in focus and half press the shutter again (same reason). The camera then calculates the appropriate hyperfocal distance for the lens and picks the correct f-stop. You can also switch to manual mode at this point and close the lens down one more f-stop with appropriate change in shutter speed to ensure enough depth of field for a sharp enlargement.

Canon's other DSLRs offer something known as A-DEP mode. This isn't quite as good, because it requires placing one of the side autofocus sensors on your far point and the other side's autofocus sensor on the near point and then half pressing the shutter. This is fine if the two points line up that way, but they seldom do.

Rural Landscapes

Landscapes. Scenic vistas. Sunsets. These are the pictures you may take while you're on vacation or going for a weekend drive (see Figure 11-1).

Figure 11-1: Mountain sunrise shot before 7:00 a.m. after a one-mile hike.
© 2004 Dan Simon

The image shown in Figure 11-1 combines several classic elements of good landscape photography. The curved line of the mountain provides a sense of grace while the orange and blue of the sunrise are complementary colors. Photos like this rely on early morning light for their magic. At 6:45 a.m. this scene was magical. A couple of hours later, this vista was still beautiful but much less photogenic. The light had lost most of its color and the atmosphere had become hazy, obscuring detail.

Although landscape photography documents the environment, it's also more than just creating a record of a scene. Instead, you use light, weather, and composition to show your vision of the landscape.

Landscapes don't have to rely on *good* weather—those bright sunny days so perfect for picnics and romance. Instead, what you generally consider *bad* weather can produce some very interesting images (see Figure 11-2).

Figure 11-2: Winter landscape after a snowstorm.
© *2004 Dan Simon*

An always-interesting time to do landscape photography is during the calm right after a snowstorm. The landscape is still and calm. There's little or no movement from wildlife, which is hunkered down because of the storm. It's your chance to capture a monochromatic snowscape and the alien environment your world has become. I shot the landscape in Figure 11-2 in color, even though the result is an almost completely grayscale image. No color manipulation was done to this photograph.

Photography under such conditions isn't very difficult. You just need to make sure you're dressed warmly enough for the weather and that you keep your camera protected from the snow. It's an opportunity to find color elements and make them stand out because they form small islands of color inside an otherwise bleak environment.

 To find out more about protecting yourself and your gear in difficult weather conditions, see Chapter 6.

One thing about weather conditions, they tend to change pretty quickly. The same morning I made Figure 11-2, I also shot Figure 11-3. This shot was made about two hours later. Although it's not easy to tell in this grayscale reproduction, the light was beginning to take on some color. What's also interesting about this composition is the clump of reeds in the foreground at the right edge of the frame. This gives something for the eye to lock onto in the foreground before traveling through the image to the far side of the pond. Layering compositional elements this way helps create a more three-dimensional effect.

Figure 11-3: Winter lake landscape a few hours later.
© 2004 Dan Simon

Be sure to check out this book's companion web site at www.wiley .com/compbooks/simon to see a side-by-side comparison of these two images. And remember, color versions of all the photos in this book can be found at this URL.

Urban Landscapes

The same principles you use to make compelling landscape photos can be used to make winning urban landscapes. Look for strong lines, graceful curves, and interesting reflections. You can also shoot into the sun to create strong silhouettes, taking advantage of the lines and shapes created by city skyscrapers and urban canyons.

Look for strong graphic elements and interesting shapes. Architecturally interesting buildings can provide a focal point for your compositions. As shown in Figure 11-4, city skylines can provide a variety of graphic shapes.

A good urban landscape can show the beauty in a manmade scene. It may be an abstract image representing Anyplace, USA, or it may be possible to tell exactly where the image was made right down to the photographer's exact location.

When you're shooting an urban landscape look for conditions and features that work toward your advantage. Backlighting gives you silhouetted buildings, side lighting brings out the detail in the building's construction.

Figure 11-4: Boston from the harbor. Strong lines and sharp angles make city skyscapes attractive subject matter for landscape photography. Harbor tour boats can make an effective shooting platform and give you a clean view of the city.
© 2004 Dan Simon

If you can find a body of water within the scene, try to include a reflection of your skyline or scene in the water. This is a technique that landscape photographers use for mountains and forests, and it works for buildings too.

Industrial Landscapes

With massive furnaces and imposing machinery, industrial sites can be big enough and interesting enough to create their own landscapes, which are well worth photographing (see Figure 11-5).

Just like natural and urban landscapes, lighting is a key element in creating interesting images. Often, the large windows and skylights that big industrial structures rely on for light make your job more interesting. Windows and skylights provide strong directional lighting and dramatic shadows that you can use to make interesting images.

Use sidelighting to bring out detail in machines and texture in walls and ground. Backlighting makes for interesting silhouettes.

If you're shooting inside an industrial structure, consider using a tripod in order to close down your lens for greater depth of field, which keeps everything in the shot sharp and brings out the detail in heavy machinery and big equipment.

Also look for patterns and strange shapes you can use to make the scene look even more otherworldly.

Figure 11-5: The small cutoff I-beams form a curving line that leads the eye into the sunrise at Bethlehem Steel.
© *2004 Dan Simon*

Industrial landscapes also provide you with a variety of unusual shapes and forms, which can lead to dramatic silhouettes and abstract forms. In Figure 11-5, the massive furnaces at the Bethlehem Steel facility in Bethlehem, Penn., provide an unusual graphic element when silhouetted by the rising sun.

Summary

It's not hard to create landscape photos that break out of that boring picture postcard look. The secret is to do things differently than everyone else. Although this sounds like a no-brainer, all too often, it isn't that simple.

Quality landscape photos are heavily dependent on quality light. Unfortunately, this means that for the best results, you either have to get up earlier or stay out at inconvenient times during the day.

The other way to find interesting landscape images is to go out and shoot when the weather's interesting ("bad"). Sadly, this is the time when many people put away their cameras and hunker down at home.

Try going out right after a winter storm to see what your neighborhood looks like. Take a camera and a tripod and make some photos. You might be surprised at the results.

Photographing Travel Destinations

There are two kinds of people in this world: Those who go on vacation and want to bring back some nice pictures, and those who go on vacation specifically to take pictures. Vacations are probably a bit easier for the first group. You just concentrate on having fun—your attitude is mostly "oh yeah, let's get some pictures while we're here." For all of us in the second category, travel is a bit more work.

This chapter shows you what you need to know to create better travel photos.

Planning and Preparation for the Trip

Planning is the key to maximizing your photographic opportunities while traveling. You don't want to turn your vacation trip into a highly structured and regimented effort, but you don't want to show up at your destination and spend time figuring out where you want to go and what you want to do when you could be out shooting photos. Fortunately, there are some compromises that will help make your visit better all around. If you have access to the Internet, doing some research and preparation before you leave can actually help you start enjoying your trip months in advance.

As a vacation photographer, you operate under a couple of fairly serious handicaps, particularly if you're visiting a location for the first time. Local photographers have spent years learning the best locations and best times of day and year to photograph a particular spot. So here you are, with maybe half an hour to a couple of hours at a famous scenic overlook to come up with an interesting image. Maybe you're not hoping for professional results, but you do want to make an image that looks good and brings back fond memories when you pull it out later. By doing some research ahead of time, you can have a plan for where you want to be at specific times of the day so that you can get those memorable shots and still enjoy a relaxing trip.

Resources

When you're doing your research and planning, be sure to take advantage of the following resources:

✦ **Guidebooks:** Both general purpose and photographic specialty guidebooks are available for many regions, parks, and countries. Such books can provide detailed information on shooting locations, ways to beat the crowds, and even where to find a good meal or a replacement piece of equipment. Even a non-photographic oriented guidebook should have good information about photogenic locations, plus high-quality images of the area.

✦ **Chamber of Commerce publications and visitor guides:** These tend to be designed to promote local businesses and attractions, but they're also illustrated with pictures that show the area to best effect. One very useful aspect of these publications is that they can put you in touch with tour guides and companies that show you the area. This can be a good idea if you're visiting for less than a day and have to make the most of your few hours at a location.

✦ **Brochures:** Local tourism boards often hire professional photographers to create brochures that show a popular tourist spot at its best. You can benefit from their hard work by studying their images for composition and potential vantage points.

 Does this sound like cheating? It isn't. I suppose you can argue that part of photography's challenge is creating something new, not copying what someone else has done. If you're a working pro hired to photograph a site for an ad campaign, you probably shouldn't copy existing work, but if you're a hobbyist who just wants to take some nice vacation pictures, there's nothing wrong with this approach.

✦ **Working the web:** When you're visiting a new place, it's a good idea to learn from those who've already spent a lot of time in the area finding the best vantage points for photography. A wide variety of travel web sites, chat rooms, and message forums exist that provide information and advice on how to photograph your destination. Often, you can actually make contact with another photographer who lives and photographs in the place you're planning to visit and ask for advice.

 Visit this book's companion web site, www.wiley.com/compbooks/simon, for more information on this topic and links to some useful sites.

What to take

Planning what photographic equipment to take with you on vacation can be a real challenge. You want to have enough equipment to take the photos you want, without being burdened with too much unnecessary gear. In this section, I offer some perspective on what gear is worth taking on your next vacation.

Cameras

Obviously you want to bring a camera with you, but have you ever considered bringing a backup? Because vacations cost so much and you get to take them so rarely, it's not a good idea to risk your memories to one piece of gear. Even if it means taking your old film camera or a couple of disposable cameras, make sure you're covered if your main camera breaks down.

If you've had your digital camera for a couple of years, consider sending it in to the manufacturer for a basic cleaning and lubrication service. If you've only had it a short time, give it a good, but gentle cleaning yourself. Use compressed air and a blower bulb to blow away dust from the camera's controls and lens.

It's tempting to buy a new camera just before a special trip. If you can, make your purchase a couple of weeks before your vacation so you have time to familiarize yourself with your new toy.

Fun with an Underwater Camera

Just before writing this chapter, Lisa and I enjoyed a Caribbean cruise aboard the MS Norwegian Sun. Fleeing a Nor'easter, we left for Miami a day earlier than planned and spent some time shopping at the city's Bayside Marketplace. Giving in to an impulse, we bought a Sony DSC-U60 waterproof digital camera. We liked the idea of a camera that could withstand the elements, and it gave me the opportunity to snap this photo of Lisa snorkeling at Grand Cayman Island. Notice how tightly I composed this image? It wasn't necessary to show her full length to make it obvious she was snorkeling.

I also liked the idea of using the camera while working on the travel section of this book. The DSC-U60's capabilities are much closer to those of typical amateur cameras than they are to the gear I normally shoot with.

The DSC-U60 actually offers less than most point-and-shoot digital cameras. It has no zoom capability—not even a digital zoom—and only offers a modest 2-megapixel resolution. It does have a small built-in flash unit and a few user-controlled shooting modes, but really not all that much. These are the trade-offs a manufacturer has to make when building a digital camera that functions up to five feet underwater. If this camera was intended only for dry land, these would be serious shortcomings.

Continued

Continued

© 2004 Dan Simon

Laptops

One problem unique to digital photography is the need for extra media during a multi-day vacation. Most photographers buy enough media to get through a normal day of shooting. Normally this works fine. You go home at the end of the day and capture your images to your computer and re-format your media. It doesn't work as well when you're on a multi-day vacation, unless you bring your computer with you.

Bringing your computer isn't a bad idea because it gives you a way to enjoy a large-screen view of your images.

Laptop alternatives

It's nice to be able to bring the digital darkroom along with you when you travel, and that's what traveling with a laptop computer does for you. Taking along a laptop can also help you manage the problem of storing and reviewing all the photos you create while on a trip without having to resort to buying extra memory cards. I take a laptop with me on every trip I make. I even lugged it along on a 10-mile hike through the Arizona desert to reach and photograph Havasu Falls at the Western Rim of the Grand Canyon!

Portable hard drives, however, are smaller alternatives to laptop computers when you're traveling. If you like gadgets or are looking for multi-purpose gizmos, a portable hard drive might be right for you.

At the bottom of the scale are the portable hard drive units that do nothing more than give you some place to dump images. In fact, some of these devices even come without a hard drive so that you can install your own. I have one of these, a Sima Image Tank. The advantage is that this is the least expensive way to go. The downside is that there's no confirmation that my files have transferred successfully. So I usually don't use the Image Tank for anything more than a way to back up files in the field. I just don't have the necessary level of trust in this device to consider reformatting a card full of images after I think I've captured files to the Image Tank. You transfer images by inserting your memory card into the appropriate slot in the Image Tank and pressing the copy button. Once it's done copying, the device shuts off.

At the other extreme is the FlashTrax, a portable hard drive made by SmartDisk (see Figure 12-1). I borrowed one of these for our recent Caribbean cruise and found it to be a big improvement over the Image Tank and other similar devices. To use the FlashTrax, simply pull the card out of your camera and insert it into the device's card slot. Press and hold the copy button and the unit's LCD screen

Figure 12-1: Lisa takes a break at the Mayan ruins at Tulum, Mexico, to start up a FlashTrax portable hard drive and review some of her images.

© *2004 Dan Simon*

lights up. After a short delay, a scroll bar indicates the progress the device is making in copying your files to its hard drive. Once you're done, you can view your files via its LCD screen.

 Don't' forget that you can find full-color images on this book's web site at www.wiley.com/compbooks/simon.

The FlashTrax has a built in LCD screen where you can preview images. This is the best confirmation I can think of to ensure that your photos have indeed safely made to the hard drive. The FlashTrax has output connections so that you can hook it up to a TV for playback, and it also serves as an MP3 player. You can even zoom in to check details in your images. The device uses USB 2.0 for fast data transfers and works easily with both my Mac and my PC. The Image Tank, on the other hand, works just fine with my PC, but not nearly as well with a Mac. Its USB is the slower 1.0 version.

Of course you pay a premium for such quality. The FlashTrax currently goes for about $459 in stores (with a 40GB hard drive capacity) while you can get a bare bones Image Tank for about $69, plus the cost of whatever size laptop hard drive you install yourself, or a model with a 40GB hard drive installed for $200. There are also other versions of the Image Tank available that come with hard drives already installed. Still, if you need to travel light, and you don't want to take a laptop computer with you, the FlashTrax is a great alternative.

One thing to keep in mind for any of these devices is that their battery life can be limited, making a set of spare batteries important. Some portable hard drives use off-the-shelf consumer batteries (AAs usually), whereas others rely on a more expensive proprietary style battery. Battery life may be another consideration in picking a particular unit.

Other companies that offer portable hard drive devices include Kanguru, Vosonic, and Minds at Work. Some things to consider when buying a portable drive are media compatibility (does the drive accept the type of memory card or device your camera uses), data transfer method and speed (USB 1.1 versus USB 2.0 or FireWire), cost, and ease of use. The biggest requirement for me is simply being sure that my images actually did transfer successfully.

Portable CD drives

Another burgeoning option is the portable CD-RW drive that can write directly from media cards. As these devices become more common, they can represent a nice solution to the traveling digital photographer's dilemma.

The savvy traveler can also take advantage of another choice: the photo kiosk. These do-it-yourself printing stations are popping up more and more often in drugstores, supermarkets, and other retail establishments. Many (but not all) offer a CD-backup option that lets you burn a CD from your memory cards. Although it costs more than burning CDs on your home machine, it might make the least expensive solution to the problem of not having enough camera memory for an extended vacation.

The biggest weakness to using the CD kiosk is that you can't always count on finding one everywhere you go. They're becoming common in the United States, but it's hard to say how likely you'll be to find one in remote locations. Something else to consider is that finding a photo kiosk and burning a CD takes time out of your vacation that you'd probably rather spend enjoying yourself.

Miscellaneous items

Keep in mind that equipment and supplies will usually be cheaper back home than in many places you travel once you leave the country. Although you may be able to find AA or AAA batteries overseas, finding memory cards (particularly at affordable prices) to fit your camera may be nearly impossible.

Getting to Your Destination Intact

People used to say that getting somewhere was half the fun. Now a days with heightened security, crowded flights, and smaller seats (or bigger fannies), getting to your destination seems a lot more like work.

For an amateur who's just carrying a point-and-shoot and some accessories, transporting your photographic gear isn't a big deal. If you're a working pro or serious amateur though, it can be more of a challenge.

Getting through security

Never pack expensive camera equipment in checked luggage. There's a greater risk of equipment being stolen or damaged this way, plus, there are concerns that the X-ray machines used for checked baggage are so powerful that they can damage digital media and maybe even camera sensors. (The machines for hand carried luggage aren't a problem.) This means if you're carrying a camera bag's worth of equipment or more, some careful planning may be in order, particularly if you're also bringing along a laptop computer.

You can be extra careful by keeping your camera gear in something that doesn't look like a camera bag. Sometimes you can buy a camera bag insert that has padded pockets you can fit your gear into while stashing the insert inside a bag that doesn't scream "expensive gadgets."

Carrying all your stuff

In this new digital age, camera bag makers have recognized that digital photographers don't just carry regular camera gear these days. So combination camera/computer bags are now available that can haul a lot of gear, plus enable you to slip a laptop into a special compartment. The best of these bags are also designed to fit within the confines of an airplane's overhead luggage compartment.

Ironically, such a bag may work against you, at least if you're a man. Most airline carryon rules limit you to one carryon bag plus a laptop computer case or woman's handbag. (It still amazes me to see what my wife can carry on board with the understanding it's her handbag.) If you resort to the combination camera/computer bag, you'll lose the extra laptop bag you could normally bring. I usually bring both, keep the laptop in the laptop case and use the laptop compartment of the backpack for other storage. Once we're at the hotel, I rearrange things so the laptop is with the camera equipment, and off I go.

Creating a Sense of Place

One of the goals of any travel photographer is to give a sense of the uniqueness of the place you're photographing; otherwise, why bother traveling?

Photographers create a sense of place by looking for things that stand out as different. Sometimes it's a local road sign, sometimes it's the vegetation. One good example is the pastel-colored houses found in the Caribbean and Mexico (see Figure 12-2). Homes just aren't painted in quite the same way here in the United States, so it's immediately apparent that you took your photos somewhere else. Home design and architecture are noticeably different too.

Figure 12-2: One look at this photo from the window of a cab while on the way to Mahahual, a Mexican fishing village a few miles from Costa Maya, and you know you're not in Kansas anymore!
© 2004 Dan Simon

It's important to remember that your vacation photos represent a collection of work, so not every image you shoot needs to give a sense of place. But keep in mind, if you create a standalone image that doesn't have that sense of locale, viewers might not have any idea where the photo was taken.

You can use any number of visual cues to make it obvious that you didn't take your pictures at home. It's a bit more difficult to show where you actually took the photos, but it's certainly worth the effort. Here are some handy tools you can work with:

✦ **Landmarks:** Including a recognizable landmark in your travel photos is a surefire way to show locale. Mayan ruins are likely in Mexico or South America. The Eiffel Tower is in Paris. If you've got one of these in your picture, well, you're not in Kansas are you?

✦ **Signs:** Governments all over the world display signs that tell you where you are, or at least where you aren't. People also tend to wave signs at big events, and businesses are fond of them too. Sometimes, a sign warrants its own photo—such is the case with the lobster sign shown in Figure 12-3—and words often aren't necessary to communicate that you're looking at a seafood restaurant in Maine. Wordless images usually work best as part of a scrapbook or presentation where they can serve as a title page or transition image.

Figure 12-3: If it's a giant lobster sign, you must be in Maine, right?
© 2004 Dan Simon

✦ **Foods:** Certain foods are peculiar to a specific locale. Indeed, if you're looking at a palm tree and coconuts, you know you're somewhere tropical. Fruit Bat and red rice is a treat saved for special occasions on the island of Guam in the South Pacific. You might feel squeamish about actually tasting such a dish, but it sure makes for an interesting photograph!

✦ **Local customs and dress:** Although photos showing local dress aren't as striking as they once were (especially because you can see this kind of thing on TV all the time), there are still times when someone's garb tells you where they're from. Certainly cultural festivals provide good opportunities to photograph people wearing indigenous clothing.

Not every culture, community, or individual has a beneficent view of photography. Before shooting a landmark or someone in ceremonial costume, be sure you're not offending anyone's sensibilities by doing so. The U.S. State Department's web site at `http://state.gov/` is a great resource for information on foreign policy and customs.

Shooting from an Airplane

Aerial photography offers a drastically different perspective than you get on the ground. Although it's easy to create images that look different from all the other shots you've taken in the past, there are some challenges to creating good images while you're in the air:

✦ **Vibration:** Airplanes and helicopters vibrate a lot. Forget about the reciprocal of the focal length rule for shutter speed here (discussed in Chapter 3). Plan to use a shutter speed of at least 1/500 of a second or fasterwhen shooting from a moving airplane. (You can get away with a slightly slower shutter speed, but why take the chance?).

✦ **Plexiglass:** Airplane windows are made of Plexiglass, so they're a pain to shoot through. Plexiglass doesn't possess the same optical qualities as normal glass, so expect quality to diminish if you're shooting through an airplane window. The best solution is to open the window whenever possible. Obviously you can't do this on commercial jet flights, but it may be possible if you're on a sightseeing flight. Be sure to ask permission of the pilot before throwing the window open. Figure 12-4 is typical of a shot you might get through an aircraft's window.

✦ **Preparation:** Most helicopter flights are short, particularly if you're flying on a helicopter for transportation and not for touring. So as not to miss any great photos, get your gear set up while you're on the ground waiting to board rather than once you're in the air (see Figure 12-5).

Scenic flights can be a great way to see a location from a completely different perspective and make some memorable photos. Just remember to choose fast shutter speeds and take lots of pictures!

Figure 12-4: Shooting through aircraft windows presents some obstacles (like shooting around your neighbor's arm), but it can also result in some interesting images.
© 2004 Dan Simon

Figure 12-5: Be sure to have your camera gear ready to go before you get in the air!
© 2004 Dan Simon

Some Tips on Shooting from the Air

If the pilot offers to take a slow pass around a particular landmark, politely decline. Although slowing the aircraft's speed gives you more time to take pictures, it often creates excessive vibration that even fast shutter speeds can't overcome. This same vibration makes it hard for you to keep your camera oriented for proper composition.

This is also a good time to use a polarizing filter if you have one, because the higher up you are the more ground haze becomes apparent. A polarizing filter can help penetrate this haze.

One last thing: This is one occasion where bracing your camera against a wall or cabin isn't a good idea. Aircraft (particularly helicopters and small fixed wing planes) vibrate tremendously. Bracing you camera against the wall of the cabin will increase camera vibration instead of reducing it.

Shooting from a Train

Most of us don't travel all that much by train anymore. Sadly, modern train cars don't offer the same character and elegance as they once did. So why even worry about this type of travel photography?

Well, trains can still be fun to travel on, particularly if you're riding one of those antique trains that are so popular in many places.

Trains, particularly the older ones, can make interesting shooting platforms. Although modern trains may offer picture windows, you still have the problem of shooting through glass or Plexiglas. With older trains, you can get lucky and find yourself shooting off an observation deck or through open picture windows. This can make your images that much more appealing. Certainly, if you ever have the choice between shooting through glass versus being out in the open, choose the latter.

When shooting from a train, it's important to remember that you're still in a moving vehicle. So you need to use fast shutter speeds to compensate for the train's movement and vibration. Try not to shoot at anything slower than 1/500th of a second if possible. Slower shutter speeds may be okay if the train is heading up an incline and has slowed its pace, but there will still be plenty of vibration.

One nice shot to look for is the front of the train as the engine rounds a bend in the track. This gives you a chance to photograph the engine while you're inside one of the trailing cars.

Photographing the train itself

Although train travel photography may not be that exciting when you're using the train as a means to get from point A to point B, there are still many interesting trains plying the tracks across the country that have nothing to do with basic transportation.

Railroad enthusiasts have done much to keep a variety of antique trains up and running, and you can ride them pretty cheaply. These trains provide a wonderful opportunity for travel photography that teases us with a glimpse of a different era (see Figure 12-6).

Figure 12-6: Steam locomotives can provide some interesting photographic opportunities.
© 2004 Dan Simon

Here are some ideas to consider when photographing these marvelous old trains.

✦ **Details:** Don't forget close-ups of interesting details in train design and construction. There are many abstract images you can pull from such machines and the play of light and reflections from their metal surfaces can provide even more interest.

✦ **Lens magic:** Telephoto shots of the train heading straight at you present an eye-catching image that's just perfect as a standalone or lead photo. Turn to your widest focal lengths to get up close and create a sense of the power of the locomotive.

 Refer to Chapter 4 to find out about other creative uses for focal lengths.

✦ **Speed:** Make some slow shutter speed exposures to show the train in motion.

✦ **People:** Often the people who run these trains dress in period garb. Make sure you get some pictures of them as they operate and service the machines.

✦ **Shoot the curves:** Some trains have passenger cars where it is possible to lean outside the windows and shoot up toward the front of the train. (*Warning!* This can be dangerous, however, so approach this technique very carefully and at your own risk.) If you can manage this safely, it's possible to get a nice shot of the front of the train as it rounds a curve. You'll probably need a short to medium length telephoto to get this photo.

Trains evoke memories of a different time and attitude. And old train stations can be wonderful photographic subjects on their own, particularly if you photograph them during early morning or late in the day.

Shooting from Your Car

Not only are automobiles practically a second home for many of people, they're also great platforms from which to conduct photography.

Wildlife photographers frequently use their vehicles as shooting blinds. For some reason, a wild bird or animal is less afraid of a Pontiac than a person. Cars can also serve as protection from the elements while allowing us to shoot through open windows or hatchbacks.

If you're traveling by car, your photographic road trip has all sorts of opportunities for great photography. Here are just a few ideas:

✦ **Reflections:** Cars are loaded with reflective surfaces, many of which can be put to good advantage by creative photographers. Use your auto's mirrors or chrome surfaces to capture the reflection of a member of your group or some famous landmark you've visited on your trip. Another cool option is to do at least one self portrait (try a wide angle focal length) in a nice curvy spot of chrome.

✦ **Night lights:** If you can make a long exposure with your camera, then find a vantage point overlooking a crowded roadway. Set a nice long exposure (multiple seconds if possible) and turn the headlights and tail lights of the moving vehicles into neon ribbons tying the roadways together. This can be one way of photographing a destination that shows how busy and popular it is. An example of this kind of shot could include a picture of the Arc d' Triumphe in Paris at night with ribbons of light winding through and around the structure. It would certainly be a much more interesting photo than an image created at noon with static cars depicting a typical French traffic jam. Bridges are another good subject for this kind of photography, but make sure it's okay to photograph a specific bridge before you show up with your camera and tripod.

✦ **Neonville:** Nighttime is the right time for neon signs. Find an interesting one on the roadside and frame it against the night sky.

✦ **Road to infinity:** Find a deserted stretch of road and position your camera on the ground with its flash turned on. Pop off a shot and see how the road surface disappears as the light from your flash dissipates.

There are some handy gizmos on the market to make shooting from your vehicle easier. Particularly useful are window mount/ball head combinations. These devices let you mount your camera on your car's window and then maneuver it with the attached ball head. Using a window mount/ball head combo works well with point-and-shoot digitals as well as small DSLRs. I definitely don't recommend using such a device with heavier pro-level camera bodies, particularly when heavy lenses are attached. Too much weight on too small a window mount can break your window.

Using cars as mobile photography platforms

Automobiles make splendid vacation transportation. You have the luxury of setting your own schedule and picking the destinations you want to visit. This can maximize your shooting opportunities.

Cars also make it possible for you to get to out of the way places that other forms of transportation might not visit. Sure, you can book a guide service or hire a driver, but that gets expensive. Best of all, if you discover a particularly magical place for photography, you can change your schedule and spend extra time there.

Sometimes the nicest alternative is to fly to a location and rent a vehicle to go exploring with. This also lets you pick a car, van, or truck based on what you expect your needs to be. Here are some things to consider when deciding the best vehicle to rent:

✦ **Cars:** Your basic family auto handles civilized roads quite well. It can carry people and gear comfortably, is reasonably cost efficient compared to heavier vehicles, and can be rented from any auto rental company. These tend to be the least expensive option depending on how luxurious a car you want to rent.

✦ **Pick-up trucks:** Underrated and unsung in this day of the SUV, pick-up trucks can be terrific mobile photography platforms. You can carry a lot of gear in the bed of the pick-up, make room for a sleeping area there, and then set up a tripod and blind at a moment's notice. Best of all, these rugged vehicles can handle more difficult roads than cars. In fact, a skilled driver can take a good pickup on some fairly difficult backcountry dirt roads.

✦ **Sport Utility Vehicles (SUVs):** SUVs are immensely popular these days for their ability to carry extra people and gear and also for the psychological boost their owners get from driving one of these "King of the Road" vehicles. They certainly have some advantages: lots of cargo space, can handle more rugged terrain than the typical family sedan, and provide a good photographic platform. Lift the back tailgate and set your camera up inside the SUV, you don't even need a photographic blind. Be careful though. Just because you're driving a four-wheel drive "go anywhere" vehicle doesn't mean you can do anything you want with it. Operating one of these vehicles in some of the backcountry areas of the American Southwest requires a lot of skill. If you never do more than drive to and from work and the local supermarket with your personal SUV, don't think you can handle a backcountry trip without getting some training in off-road vehicle handling.

Anytime you head into wilderness areas on your own, there are some important safety precautions to consider. First and foremost, make sure you have a supply of emergency food and drinking water. For information on other emergency supplies you should consider taking with you, refer to the "10 Essentials" for backpackers discussed in Chapter 10. Cell phones don't work reliably in the wilderness (if at all), so consider renting a satellite phone. These devices have become much more affordable in the past few years. You may be able to rent one for a few days for less than $100.

Shooting from a Cruise Ship

As a former sailor in the U.S. Navy, I love being at sea, particularly as a passenger on a modern luxury cruise ship. Gourmet meals, comfortable surroundings and a new city, country, or port almost every day! What's not to like?

Traveling on a cruise ship certainly offers some unique photographic opportunities and advantages:

✦ **Equipment:** You can bring more luggage (I mean "equipment") on a cruise ship than you can bring on a commercial flight. The more equipment you have at your disposal, the more diverse your travel shots can be.

✦ **Perspective:** You can photograph the shoreline from the sea and reverse the more common seascape photo. These images can really stand out in a photo collection because it's such an uncommon point of view. To make them even more interesting, consider setting them up as a panoramic image, by taking the shot at your camera's highest possible resolution and then cropping the image down to panoramic dimensions. (A ratio of about 2 to 1 or greater.)

✦ **Sub-plot:** Your sea voyage creates its own separate story line, namely the unique shipboard environment and community. You can document architectural details of the ship's construction or the elaborate and lavish food presentations in the dining room and buffet.

✦ **Windows:** It may sound sacrilegious to call them *windows* rather than *portholes*, but truth be told, the big glass things on modern cruise ships are more accurately described this way. Such large purveyors of natural directional lighting can be a wonderful source of mood lighting for romantic photographs.

✦ **Ship shots:** You can shoot your cruise ship as it's docked in port, you can shoot it from land, or you can shoot it at water level. All these angles offer a unique perspective of the vessel. Take a look at Figure 12-7 to see what I mean.

Figure 12-7: Shot from water level, this picture offers an interesting view of the vessel that carries you on your travels.
© *2004 Dan Simon*

✦ **Excursions:** The ship's excursions program has an assortment of planned trips available. Often, taking one of these trips saves you all the time and trouble of arranging your own transportation and logistics. This can be a huge advantage, particularly in countries where you don't speak the native language.

✦ **Variety:** Many itineraries place you in a new location almost every day, and each location presents you with a new set of photographic opportunities and challenges. You're treated to new sights and landmarks and may have to shift your focus from scenic photography to creating cityscapes or architectural images. You'll probably also be treated to a variety of weather during your trip, so you'll have to adapt to changing lighting and weather conditions. This may seem difficult, but it actually gives you the chance to be creative as you adapt to each set of conditions.

✦ **New friends:** Cruises are a great way to meet fellow travelers—many of whom are also interested in photography—and to share advice and experiences. Crewmembers who visit each port often can also be good sources of information about a particular port you're visiting. They may know of off-the-beaten path adventures or sights, or they may be able to recommend a particular driver or restaurant.

Be forewarned, photographing cruise vacations isn't all milk and honey. Because all the scheduling is done for you, you have a finite amount of time to get that perfect shot, lest you be left behind. Likewise, you have to deal with whatever lighting or weather conditions you encounter in a particular port.

Traveling by cruise ship can be a great way to quickly put together a nice package of travel photos in a short time because cruise ships get you to so many ports so efficiently. The downside is the travel photographer really doesn't get to spend enough time in any one spot to really get to know the location or photograph under enough different lighting conditions to be thorough.

It's still very possible to create beautiful travel photos when using a cruise ship as your base of operations, as I hope the pictures I include in this book will show. It just calls for some planning, creativity, and a little bit of discipline. (Not too much for heaven's sake. You are on vacation!)

Making Better Travel Photos

Taking better travel photos can be challenging. For every wonderful photo opportunity, you have to contend with throngs of tourists, distance from your intended subject, or even your own perfectionist tendencies! Here are some pointers to help you make the most of every photographic opportunity:

✦ **Define your subject:** One common pitfall among amateur photographers is to try to show too much. In doing so, they lose sight of the subject and end up with a memory card full of nondescript images.

✦ **Get close to your subject:** One of the simplest ways to take great travel photos is to get close to your subject whenever possible. Getting close captures nuances of your subject that you'd lose when shooting from far away.

✦ **Take plenty of shots:** If you find an interesting subject, don't be content to shoot just one or two images. Use different camera angles and take photos from a variety of locations. Sometimes the best shot you take is the last one!

✦ **Be patient:** At heavily trafficked tourist locations, you usually have to deal with people walking in and out of your shots. If you're patient enough to wait for a lull, great shots present themselves. It also doesn't hurt to ask politely for people to move out of your shot; they tend to be respectful when they know you're trying to take a picture.

✦ **Edit distractions out later:** If your subject is big or if you're not in a position to ask people to move out of your shot, you can edit out distractions in your digital darkroom (see Figure 12-8).

To find out more about touching up your photos in the digital darkroom, see Chapter 15.

Figure 12-8: Before and after. Thanks to Photoshop, I was able to turn the photo on the left into the photo on the right by digitally removing the tourists who had wandered onto the scene.

Summary

There are many ways to make the most of travel photography options. When visiting a new place, certainly one of the keys is knowing as much as possible beforehand about what to expect so that you can be positioned to make the kind of photographs you want.

Also keep in mind that you'll make far more photographs while traveling than you normally do at home. So having either extra memory or a storage system such as a laptop computer or portable hard drive is important.

I always try to have a camera with me when traveling, but that doesn't always mean I'm trying to be a professional photographer. Sometimes, you simply need to have a fun day in a new place. That's when an easy-to-use, lightweight second camera makes a nice option. If you don't have such a camera, or you just need a day off from photography, that's okay, too. After all, you're on vacation. Have fun!

Telling a Story with Pictures

Ever see one of those big, multi-picture frames that holds a whole assortment of different 4 x 6 pictures? People like such frames because it gives them a chance to use a lot of photos and show a lot of different ideas.

It's possible to take the idea a giant step further. Instead of randomly sticking pictures inside a frame to fit the shapes, orientations, and sizes that somebody else has determined, why not take charge of such a production yourself? Not only can you be the boss of such a production, you can use it to tell a particular story of an important event in your life.

In this chapter, I guide you through the process of creating a story through your photographs.

Planning Your Picture Story

After you decide that you have a particular event, project, or time period that you want to document with a picture story, it's important to do some planning. You're working on a series of images, so taking a haphazard approach can come back to haunt you if you miss a key shot simply because you didn't think of it at the time.

Fortunately, planning such a shoot isn't very hard. It just takes a few moments thought about the story you want to tell with your photographs.

Considering the key elements

Telling a story photographically isn't all that hard. As with any story, you need a beginning, a middle, an end, plus some photos to amplify the detail.

In theory, you can create an effective picture story with as little as three pictures. Most of us, myself included, are much more talkative image-wise. Extra pictures can show detail that enriches and complements your key artwork.

It's important to create images that put forth a logical flow of information. So it's important to start out with an opening or establishing shot. This opening shot can be a photograph showing your subject entering the site of the event or meeting with someone who plays a key role in the action. Or, it could be an image of your subject at the start of a project, say a gardener standing in front of a plot of untilled soil or a woodworker before a pile of lumber.

The following sections discuss two things that can help you plan out a picture story: the shot list and the storyboard.

Create a shot list

I do a shot list for virtually every assignment I do. It's simply a logical and ordered way of approaching a photographic shoot that helps you get the most out of the shoot.

Creating a shot list is simple. Sit down and write out a list of ideas for pictures based on your expectations of the day. Remember to plan a variety of shots for each photo idea. In other words, remember to plan on high and low angle shots plus images from both the left and right side, plus some pictures shot straight on. Plan on doing this for each important idea you want to cover. (Now you may be starting to understand why professional photographers shoot so many pictures.) Check out the picture story project at the end of this chapter for a sample shot list.

Create a storyboard

Storyboards are a valuable device used throughout the creative industry whether it be for television, movies, ad campaigns, or photographic shoots. In basic terms a *storyboard* is simply a series of sketches that show the message's progression.

The storyboarding process is frequently documented on TV or in the movies as a series of cartoon-like strips. If you sketch well, you can do this too if it helps you in planning the story.

If, on the other hand, you can't sketch worth a darn (much like me), simple stick figures will do. The storyboard is a valuable way of visualizing a potential image and, if need be, sharing that image with an assistant, friend, or model. It's not a make or break document that determines the success of your shoot.

The idea behind all this planning is to put you in the best possible position to make the most of your photographic opportunity. It's not designed to provide a rigid framework that you have to stick with. Often, while on the shoot, you'll see photographic possibilities that never occurred to you while you were shot listing or storyboarding. That's okay. Shoot away! You aren't limited only to those shots you planned beforehand. The storyboarding method is simply designed to minimize your risk of missing shots you could foresee, not lock you into a shooting script.

Take the photos

After you have created a shot list and a storyboard, it's time to go make the pictures that tell your story. The following list describes the type of shots you're looking for, although not always in this order:

✦ **Establishing shot:** Just like any other story, a picture story needs a beginning. Ideally, this is a visual that can also serve as a title photo. Frequently, the title shot shows a sign or structure that clues the viewer in to what the picture story is about. Your main subject may be in the establishing image, but it doesn't always have to be. Signs, documents, books, magazines, and other written literature can be excellent establishing shots provided you remember that copyright laws still apply. It's not a big deal if the photo story is something you're making to hang on your wall. But if you publish it in a newsletter or on a web site, you may get contacted by the document's originator.

During a recent Caribbean cruise, I followed a sign-wielding tour guide who was leading us through town. Grabbing my point-and-shoot digital, I quickly snapped off the shot shown in Figure 13-1. This will make a great title or introduction photo for a picture story on this particular tour. I was shooting my Sony DSC-U60 in program mode, 1/500 sec at f5.6.

Figure 13-1: Finding a title shot to introduce your picture story.

© 2004 Dan Simon

✦ **Beginning photo:** Although the beginning photo and the establishing shot sound like the same thing, they don't have to be. Think of the establishing shot as a sort of title slide with panache and the beginning shot as the first photo of the sequence that actually shows what the story is about. The establishing shot can be a title, such as a road sign naming the place where the story takes place,whereas the beginning photo shows your subject starting whatever project or event you're documenting. In Figure 13-2, my friend Sylvia fills out an entry form for a bike race she's entering. This kind of paperwork shot provides a logical beginning point for a picture story.

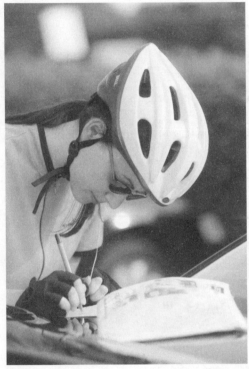

Figure 13-2: This photo of an athlete filling out an entry form makes a good beginning photo for your picture story.

© 2004 Dan Simon

✦ **Continuation image(s):** After you've introduced viewers to your topic, you need at least one, and as many as three or four images, to show the development of the idea. These pictures show the effort in progress and help viewers understand how something is happening. The goal is to accomplish this in as few images as possible if you're aiming for professional results, or in a reasonable amount of pictures if you're just trying for a personal effort that shows something important to you. (Using fewer pictures lets you run each photo bigger, maximizing impact.) Look for photos that convey a sense of the event. They can be action shots of the competition or vignettes that show a side of the event most people don't think about. Figure 13-3 shows some examples of continuation images.

Figure 13-3: These images of cyclists "in action" convey both the continuing action of the bike race and the realities of it, too.
© 2004 Dan Simon

✦ **Detail photos:** It's important to show viewers some close-ups of particular elements of the story. If you're doing a picture story on a gardening project, some close-ups of the tools, seeds, or young plants provide a visual break to a series of images. Close-ups also cause viewers to refocus, which helps to rekindle interest. For my bike competition picture story, I chose a detail shot of the bike's brake and the pile of bananas, as shown in Figures 13-4a and 13-4b.

✦ **Finishing shot:** Every story needs an ending, and picture stories are no different. You need a photo that tells the viewer you're done. If your story focuses on the act of creation, your finishing shot is the completed work (whether successful or unsuccessful). In Figure 13-5, an image of the tired but happy rider provides a nice finishing shot to the day's race.

Mixing up your images

The other key thing to consider when you're shooting a picture story is a basic piece of advice I tend to give over and over. Mix up your images to include lots of vertical shots. There are several reasons for this:

✦ Verticals are a natural part of life. If you're trying to document reality, your images should reflect this.

✦ Variety is important for keeping interest. Once again, if all your images have the same orientation, your picture story will not be as visually interesting.

✦ Whether your plan is to lay out your photo story images in a frame or compile them to send off to a commercial printer or an online printing service, including verticals can help you make better use of space and design and possibly save you some money in the bargain.

Figure 13-4: Detail photos inject an important bit of variety into the picture story. (Top) Detail shot of bike's brake. (Bottom) Bananas.

© *2004 Dan Simon*

Give your photos a sense of direction

Photographs have a direction, a sense of movement. They can lead the eye in a specific direction. It's very important to keep this in mind when you're shooting for the printed page, and it's also important for a multi-image collection for a web page. It's not quite as vital for a presentation where you're showing one

Figure 13-5: A triumphant rider at the end of his ride provides the perfect ending to your picture story.

© 2004 Dan Simon

image at a time; but keep in mind that if you're constantly shifting direction, your presentation will look herky-jerky. In the photograph of an X-Games BMX competitor shown in Figure 13-6, the eye moves in the same direction in which the bike and athlete are traveling. If, in my picture story, I followed this photo with a similar shot that moves the opposite way (as shown in Figure 13-7), viewers would need a moment to reset and re-orient.

Page layout revolves around the *Reverse S* approach. This is a classic design approach to newspaper layout designed to wind the reader's eye through the page, while never directing it off the paper. If done properly, the reader's eye begins at the upper-left corner of the page (the normal starting point for cultures that read from left to right) and slides down the page to the right side, until a photo directs her back left and up returning her to the starting point. At no time during her viewing, should any layout element move her eye off the page.

In order to make this kind of approach work, it's necessary to shoot from a variety of angles so that you can be sure to have pictures that move the eye in any direction (don't forget up and down, too). This is another reason for storyboarding and shot listing. It helps provide you with a checklist to make sure you get all the images you need, in a variety of angles.

Figure 13-6: First, I send you one way with a bike moving from right to left.

© 2004 Dan Simon

Figure 13-7: Then, I send you the other way with a bike moving from left to right. This kind of movement can be distracting for the viewer, particularly in digital slide presentations.

© 2004 Dan Simon

End the story

Closure.

It's something that you hear about all the time. Well, it works for photography too, especially the picture story. You need a good ending.

In fact, the ending photo is one of the most important pictures in the picture story. If done well, this photo should even stand on its own, as does the lead photo.

A good closing photo doesn't have to be anything complicated. It's just a summation shot. Think of the gardener proudly standing in front of his newly planted garden or the woodworker holding her new creation. The picture tells us the effort is finished and the story told by your images is complete.

A particularly effective closing shot has a tight composition of the subject looking directly into the camera. This kind of eye contact is particularly riveting.

If possible, show something that makes it obvious the mission has been accomplished. It might be your daughter holding up a plate of freshly dyed Easter eggs or a proud fisherman showing off the cooked fish in a frying pan, but it should be something that says the task has been completed.

 Project: **Storytelling with a Camera**

My wife, Lisa, and I love glass art and often visit a Southern New Jersey glassworks museum for its glassblowing demonstrations and displays. This place offers a fairly unique interactive program where participants make their own paperweight under the tutelage of an expert glassmaker. I signed Lisa up for a paperweight making session, and I decided to create a picture story as a photographic souvenir. The following steps explain the process for shooting this picture story:

1. Shoot the establishing shot. To start of this story, I can choose from a number of possible images, such as Lisa and her instructor meeting for the first time or Lisa entering the furnace. Instead, I picked the image shown in 13-8 of Lisa with her nearly completed paperweight. The image doesn't present any titling information as was included in the photo shown in Figure 13-1 earlier in this chapter, but it works as an establishing shot because it gives us a

Figure 13-8: Even though it doesn't provide any actual titling information, this works as an establishing shot because it illustrates what the picture story is about.

© *2004 Dan Simon*

Continued

Project *(continued)*

sense of what the story will be about. The glow of hot glass and Lisa's smile help draw viewers into the story.

2. Shoot a beginning photo. My beginning shot, shown in Figure 13-9, shows Lisa and the glassblower looking at different types of paperweights. At this point, Lisa decides what designs and colors she wants to incorporate into her paperweight. This image seems to provide enough information to get the story started and grab the viewer's attention.

Figure 13-9: This beginning photo shows how the project starts.

© 2004 Dan Simon

3. Shoot two or more continuing action photos to illustrate how the event or project is unfolding. My first shot is a vertical shot of Lisa shaping the paperweight (see Figure 13-10, left) because it visually describes an aspect of the actual paperweight making process. The second shot (see Figure 13-10, right) was also a vertical and showed the pair reheating the paperweight. The vertical shots bring some variety and visual interest to the story, and shooting two verticals together enabled me to create a side-by-side composite vertical shot to save space. And by stepping back to shoot the photo on the right, I was able to show more of the surroundings.

If I wanted to add another image to this sequence, I'd have gone with a wide shot of the furnace area. That would add more variety to my selection of images and give viewers a better sense of what the working environment was like.

4. Include detail or close-up photos. Close-up shots serve two purposes:

   • They help avoid a series of similarly composed photos.

   • They provide a detailed look at the project.

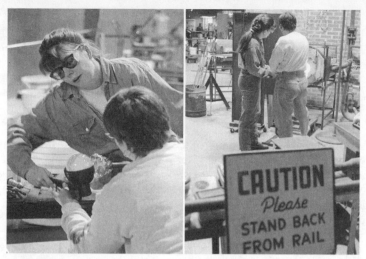

Figure 13-10: These continuing action photos document the process as it unfolds.

© 2004 Dan Simon

My story includes two detail photos, but either one of them would be enough alone. I like the close-up of Lisa's fingers practicing how to spin the glassblower's tube (see Figure 13-11, left). This is an important part of the glass-making process, so it's a nice piece of information to add to the story. The other image (see Figure 13-11, right) shows the hot glass being removed from a form. I like this image because of the color of the glass. I should note that my original picture was a horizontal composition. After reviewing the photo back home, I cropped it into the vertical you see here.

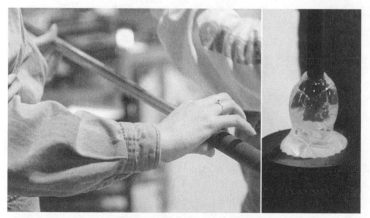

Figure 13-11: Twirling fingers and glowing glass. Detail photos help isolate specific elements of the story.

© 2004 Dan Simon

Continued

Project *(continued)*

5. Shoot the finishing shot. The perfect ending shot to this story might have been a shot of Lisa holding her brand new paperweight in her hands and beaming with accomplishment. Unfortunately, getting that shot would have also required an immediate trip to the hospital because the paperweight still had a temperature of about 1300 degrees.

As an alternative finishing shot, I opted for the next best thing: the image of Lisa standing next to her paperweight beaming with a sense of accomplishment (see Figure 13-12). Because I was shooting with available light (or *available darkness* as I call it), there wasn't enough depth of field to keep both Lisa and the paperweight sharply focussed. Other images in the picture story show Lisa in sharp focus, so I felt it was okay to put the emphasis on the creation and not the creator. I could have also saved my establishing shot to use here as a closing photo if I'd wanted.

Figure 13-12: Closure: the artist and her creation.

© *2004 Dan Simon*

6. Decide how you want to assemble and present your picture story. One option is to assemble a collection of images into a multimedia digital presentation using PowerPoint or Digital Sho. You can work in music and sound effects if you like. Limit your presentation to about 15 or 20 images (5 to 10 minutes in length).

For my picture story of Lisa's paperweight experience, I decided to create a giant composite image in Photoshop and then have a large print made to show the entire story. I'm not talking about a *collage* here. For a composite, you maintain the integrity of each image, but you place each one in relation to the others so that together they tell the story (see Figure 13-13). After creating a 10 x 15 print in my photo editing program, I can upload it to an online printing service to make a photo quality print. Online printers such as Shutterfly and EZ Prints.com can make such prints for less than $10.00.

Figure 13-13: A composite series of photos can tell the story of a special event in an eye-catching manner.
ⓒ *2004 Dan Simon*

Online Printing Alternatives

An attractive and easy alternative has become available through online printers such as Shutterfly and Sony's Image Station. This option enables you to have your images produced as a complete package in a bound form.

Continued

Continued

Shutterfly produces *snap books*, which are spiral bound booklets that offer attractive backgrounds and the option of providing caption or title information. These are a bit more expensive than doing it yourself in a home photo album, but they give a much more polished look to your work.

Image Station goes Shutterfly one better. Image Station allows you to create photo books with high-quality printing materials. Unlike snap books, which only allow one image per page, these books let you arrange multiple images in a variety of layouts. They're not cheap to produce (they start around $30 per book and go up in price based on the number of pages you want) but they can make a spectacular memory of a special trip or event. Believe me, if you've ever bored a roomful of people to death with a stack of 4 x 6 prints of your vacation (you must be one of my relatives), this is the cure. Set either one of these products up properly and maintain some discipline with the number of images you add, and you'll impress your friends and relatives with your newfound skill.

You can find out more about these two printing methods on this book's companion web site at www.wiley.com/compbooks/simon.

Summary

Next time you want to show people a collection of images from your vacation or special family event, consider packaging them as a photo story instead of just a pile of random prints.

Whether you assemble them in a conventional photo album of your own, or try a snap book or photo book, the thought you put into the process can turn a cure for insomnia into a cherished family memory.

The important thing is to have some kind of plan for your presentation. Instead of showing every picture you shoot, choose those that advance the topic. If you do this job right (and it's not hard), you'll have people asking to see more of your photos.

Doing Your Own Image Processing

◆ ◆ ◆ ◆

◆ ◆ ◆ ◆

Once upon a time, photographers not only took photographs, they also processed the film in the darkroom. Although this was a messy, time-consuming chore, it also enabled the shooter to control the entire image-making process from start to finish.

Practitioners such as Ansel Adams took this process to its zenith by making the actual shot and the processing work together to create images of great beauty. For those of us not endowed with Adams' genius and desire, commercial processing took hold.

The *digital darkroom* now offers us that same level of control, but without the mess, expense, and time spent in the dark. Programs such as Adobe Photoshop give us amazing control over our photographs. This part of the book shows you how to put the digital darkroom to work for you.

Introduction to the Digital Darkroom

Before the advent of digital technologies, photographers would have to develop their photos in a traditional darkroom, which is a daunting and time-consuming task. Dangerous chemicals coupled with long developing times don't make deadlines easy to meet (trust me on this one).

But with today's software and high-speed Internet connections, even the most rudimentary digital cameras and laptop computers can bring the darkroom right into your home. In the digital darkroom, enthusiastic beginners can now learn to process their images quickly and effectively without the hassle and hard work of a conventional darkroom.

This chapter covers various ways to transfer your digital images from your camera to your computer, and what file formats and file sizes are open to you once you have your digital photos on your computer.

Making the Computer Work for You

There are several ways to transfer images from your digital camera to your computer, a process known as *capturing*. I explore each way a little more fully in the following paragraphs, and each has its own advantages. Choosing one over another is simply a function of personal preference.

Transfer methods

There are three commonly used methods of image capture popular today:

✦ Camera to computer

✦ Media to card reader device

✦ PC card adapter to laptop PC card slot

Before choosing which method you want to use, consider each one's advantages and disadvantages:

Camera to computer

Transferring images from camera to computer is the starting point for many digital photographers. Your camera usually comes with some method of transferring images directly from your camera to your computer, usually through a USB cable, though some pro models offer faster options such as FireWire (IEEE 1394) or USB 2.0. Some older camera models, and models that don't have removable memory, use the older, slower serial or parallel connections that previous generations of computers offered.

In order to make this connection work, you probably need some form of driver or accessory program The driver is supplied with the software that comes with your camera. Some operating systems may already be able to connect to your camera and treat it like a separate hard drive, but not all do. The driver program enables your camera and computer to communicate and move data back and forth.

More advanced features of this software may also let you change certain internal camera controls. Generally these internal controls alter in-camera processing functions that manage saturation, contrast, and sharpening controls on certain camera models. The software may also allow you to tweak your images while they're still in the camera. This can be helpful if you're only transferring a few images from a shoot and can pick individual shots to manipulate and transfer. Your camera's operating manual can tell you if your camera's software offers this capability.

In many cases, the camera manufacturer provides both a stand-alone computer program (in case you don't have Photoshop) and a separate Photoshop plug-in that lets you connect to your camera through the popular image-editing program (if you do). There have also been some third-party programs that work with a variety of cameras for this purpose.

The main advantage of transferring images from your camera directly to you computer is that you don't have to buy any accessories for capturing images. On the downside, it tends to be slower than other options, drains your camera's batteries, and increases wear and tear on your camera. Still, if you don't use your camera a lot, only work with one or two pieces of media, and don't create that many images, this method works pretty well. Refer to your camera's manual for how to best set up your computer and camera for this kind of thing.

Generally you just insert the CD-ROM that comes with your camera and follow the instructions it gives you. The process is usually very easy. For example, I recently bought a Sony DSC-U60 digital camera. The CD that came with the camera did a great job of installing the necessary software in my Windows PC. It was even easier hooking up the camera to my Macintosh, which recognized the camera as an external hard drive without even installing any software for the camera.

If you want to use this image capturing method, make sure your camera has fresh batteries, or use a power cord so you have a reliable power supply for the data transfer. This way your camera won't run out of power in the middle of a transfer.

Media to card reader device

Probably the most popular method in use today is the *card reader*, a peripheral device that hooks up to your computer via one of the common connection methods. Some home computers even come with card readers already built in.

These devices are popular because they don't tie up your camera, frequently accept multiple media types, and offer portability from computer to computer, often without the need for special drivers. My favorite is a FireWire card reader that provides fast data transfer. Because I sometimes come home with four or five full 512MB compact flash cards, you can understand why I want a fast method of data transfer. See Figure 14-1 for examples of what card readers look like.

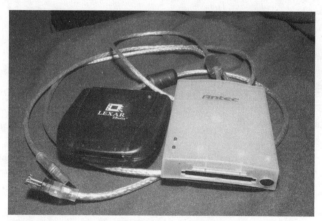

Figure 14-1: (Left) FireWire compact flash card reader. (Right) USB device that reads compact flash, IBM microdrives, Sony memory sticks, and smart media, provided that you have the correct adapter.
© 2004 Dan Simon

The positive aspects of card readers far outweigh the negative aspects. They're inexpensive (some are even downright cheap), and many are cross-platform capable and can frequently handle a wide variety of media. Keep in mind that your card reader might require a specific driver in order to work with your computer, but such a driver is often supplied when you buy a card reader. Check the documentation that comes with the card reader to see if you need a specific driver.

PC card adapters

These work in the PC card slot of your laptop computer and are a nice choice for many users. These adapters are a little longer than a business card (plus much thicker) and have a receptacle at one end that receives the compact flash card, IBM microdrive, Sony memory stick, or smart media card it's designed for. Slide the card into the PC card slot and the media shows up on your computer screen just like another hard drive.

These adapters are simple to use. They don't require any drivers, they work in both Macs and PCs, and they're generally pretty cheap. In terms of speed, they're faster than USB but not quite as fast as FireWire or USB 2.0. The biggest potential drawback is that you need one for each medium you use, which can be a hassle if you use more than one medium. The only other drawback to these handy little critters is that they only function on a laptop computer. See Figure 14-2 for some examples of PC card adapters.

Figure 14-2: Three different PC card adapters and their memory. From left to right, compact flash, IBM microdrive, and smart media.

© 2004 Dan Simon

 A new PC card adapter on the market in Japan is actually faster than both USB 2.0 and FireWire, but it's not currently available in the U.S.

File Format

Now that your images are in the digital darkroom, you have to decide what file format you want to work in and what level of quality you hope to achieve. You may be able to choose among TIF (or TIFF), JPEG (or JPG), or Raw file formats. If you decide upon Raw, then you also have a choice between either 8-bit or 16-bit file formats depending upon your camera.

TIF

Still, some cameras do offer an uncompressed TIF (or TIFF) file option. The advantage of going this route is that no compression takes place and all three primary colors are recorded, not interpolated. If the highest possible quality is paramount, then an uncompressed TIFF is your best choice.

Now, here's the bad news. Your camera has to write a ton of data to the memory card. This is a slow process and can prevent you from shooting until the image is fully written to the card.

JPEG

Virtually every digital camera on the market these days offers the *JPEG* file format. JPEG (or JPG) is an industry standard file compression format. Digital cameras usually don't record image files without compressing them, because writing data to the memory card would take too long.

Normally, when you shoot in JPEG mode, the camera performs the interpolation and creates a file that can be read by virtually any image viewer. These files are smaller in size than Raw files because they've also undergone some image compression, but at the highest quality settings, are also very good quality images.

Digital camera images are normally recorded at 8-bit color depth when they're created as JPEG files. Whatever white balance or color settings that were in effect when the picture was made are what you end up with.

Raw Format

JPEG is the industry standard file-compression format. Some cameras offer an uncompressed TIF file option, but more often, a camera offers something known as *Raw* format.

Raw format is sometimes mistakenly called a compression format, because no actual compression takes place. Instead, Raw format takes advantage of the way digital camera sensors operate.

Although digital images are made up of the colors red, green, and blue, digital camera sensors don't actually record all three colors. Instead, the sensor records a value for each pixel in the sensor and then interpolates that information through software and the camera's microprocessor to arrive at the colors you actually see in a photograph.

When you shoot in JPEG mode, your camera interpolates an image, but in Raw mode, no interpolation occurs. Instead, interpolation occurs once the images are captured into the computer and processed via a Raw converter supplied either by the camera manufacturer, or in some cases by a third party software maker.

Raw format's advantages and disadvantages

Raw format lets you squeeze every last bit of quality out of your images, but, like everything, shooting in Raw format has its pros and cons. The following points represent what's best about Raw format images.

✦ **Original data:** Your computer's microprocessor does a better job of processing an image than the microprocessor in your digital camera, and better maintains the original image's integrity. Working with original data means that your image is unlikely to contain compression artifacts (mistakes introduced by your camera's processing software), and because you're working with original data, you can change white balance settings without damaging your original file. You can tweak color balance in an image-editing program, but if you do that, you're working with pixels. This isn't necessarily bad, but you should minimize such changes because their cumulative effect can cause image degradation.

✦ **16-bit file conversion:** Color bit depth refers to the number of colors the image is capable of representing. For 8-bit depth, this means 256 colors. Digital camera sensors are capable of recording 12-bit color depth, which translates into thousands of colors. Because the computer can only distinguish between 8- and 16-bit images, these files are converted as 16-bit images even though they only contain 12 bits of information. In simple terms, a larger bit depth means an image can display a greater tonal range. You can choose an image's color bit depth, as shown in Figure 14-3.

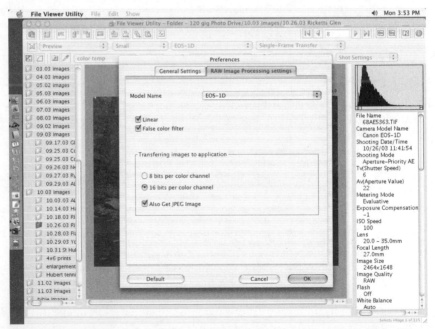

Figure 14-3: You can make Raw conversions as either 8- or 16-bit TIFFs. You can also make these conversions as linear conversions where no in-camera processing is applied.
© 2004 Dan Simon

✦ **White balance:** Because Raw files contain all the camera sensor's information, you can change the image's white balance (see Figure 14-4).

This is a big advantage of choosing Raw format, but it's not something that can't be fixed in other ways

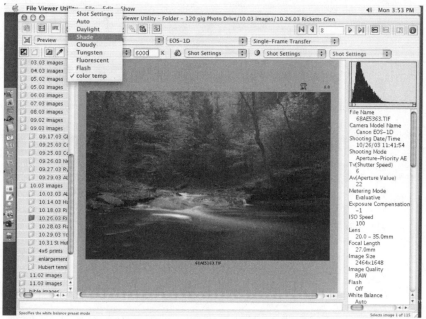

Figure 14-4: Camera makers supply Raw conversion software that you can use to change an image's white balance long after it's been created. This is Canon's file viewer utility for its line of digital cameras.

© 2004 Dan Simon

✦ **Exposure compensation:** Some cameras and their Raw conversion software allow you to change your exposure settings by as much as two f-stops either way long after you've taken the photo. See Figure 14-5 to see how.

Raw format also has its share of disadvantages too. Some of them include:

✦ **Larger files:** Raw files are larger in size than even highest resolution JPEG files, which means your memory card fills up faster and you need more media (compact flash cards, memory sticks, smart media cards) to shoot the way you're used to. You also need lots of storage space, because converted Raw files are very large.

✦ **Conversion required:** In order to work on Raw files, you have to convert them into another format. Depending upon your computer, conversion can be a very slow process. It can get even slower if you have hundreds or thousands of images to convert. Fortunately, more and more image browsers offer a *preview image* from a Raw file feature (usually because the camera maker includes a JPEG file they can read) so you can preview images and only convert the individual images you want to work on.

Figure 14-5: Adding or removing exposure dramatically affects your photos.
© 2004 Dan Simon

✦ **Software required:** Although many different cameras offer Raw mode, each has its own way of converting files, which means you have to use conversion software that works with your camera's version of Raw., Digital camera manufacturers provide Raw conversion software when you purchase a camera. See Figure 14-6 for an example.

Choosing between 8-bit and 16-bit images

If you decide to work in Raw format, you have to choose between converting your pictures to 8- or 16-bit files.

If you want to get the most out of your images, opt for the 16-bit files. As noted earlier, this file contains more image information than the 8-bit version.

Not every photographer wants to work with 16-bit files, particularly because there are only a limited number of things you can do to an image in most image editing programs. Photoshop has managed to provide more options for 16-bit files in each new version. Still, if you're working with an older version of the program, or using a different image editor that doesn't recognize 16-bit files, you may find there's not much you can do with them.

If you're using Photoshop 7 or later, check out the Raw workflow section in Chapter 16 for more information on using this format.

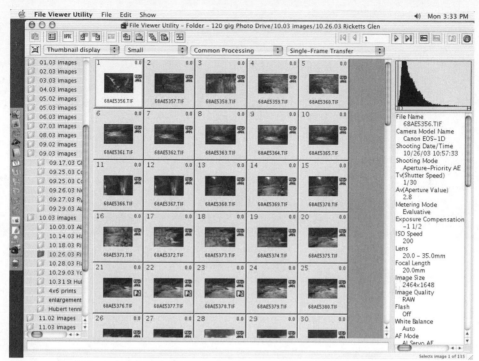

Figure 14-6: Raw files must be converted to a file format that image-editing programs can work with. Use either the manufacturer's conversion software or Photoshop CS's Raw conversion plug-in.

© 2004 Dan Simon

Summary

Although it may seem like an added complication, working in the digital darkroom offers tremendous advantages over the days of shooting a roll of film and just handing it over to the clerk at your local one-hour photo place.

You can exercise amazing control over your files with a program such as Photoshop. Combined with the power of Raw format files, the digital darkroom can help you get the most out of your files. If you're a perfectionist control freak with obsessive-compulsive tendencies and lots of hard drive space, you'll be in heaven.

Image Processing

After your images have been safely transferred to your computer, as I show you how to do in Chapter 14, it's time to start manipulating them. Depending on what type of digital camera you use, there may be a little or a lot of work ahead.

There's a difference in design philosophy between cameras intended for the casual photographer and cameras planned for the serious shooter. Camera makers know that the people who buy basic point-and-shoot cameras generally don't want to spend a lot of time working on their images, and they may not know much about working in the digital darkroom. So point-and-shoot cameras are designed to process the image while it's still inside the camera.

The result is a photo that looks pretty good as soon as you open it up on your computer screen. The quality may even be such that it can go straight from your memory card to print without stopping by the digital darkroom.

Pros and serious amateurs, on the other hand, usually do know what they're doing in the digital darkroom and are happy to be bothered with all the steps necessary to make high-quality images. Folks in this category feel that the tiny microprocessor in their cameras (even in very high-end "pro" cameras) can't do nearly as good a job as their powerful desktop computer systems. If you're a control freak, this is the category you probably identify with.

At the very minimum, you'll want to check most of your images for proper exposure, contrast, and color. Digital images in general (whether from a digital camera or scanner) need some sharpening, although many point-and-shoot cameras do this step for you. And, of course, you'll also want to repair images with any technical flaws. As in so many things in the digital world, there's frequently more than one way to perform these tasks, with no hands-down best way. This chapter looks at some of the tools and techniques that savvy digital darkroom workers employ.

File Preparation

After you capture an image to your computer and are ready to begin processing it, you need to consider the actual physical dimensions of the photograph. The idea here is that if you're going to have to crop the photo at some point anyway, it's better to do it as early in the process as possible so that you have a smaller file to work with. And by cropping early, any changes you make later on are based on the image you're creating and not the original file.

Cropping is especially important if you're working on an older or underpowered computer: anything you can do to reduce file size will make your machine's job a bit easier.

Besides cropping, file preparation includes rotating a composition and correcting any keystoning problems that might exist. After those tasks are handled, you can safely crop the image down to its final working dimensions. The following sections discuss these three preliminary tasks.

Rotating an image

Sometimes when you're taking a photo, you may find that you didn't quite hold the camera as straight as you would have liked. The resulting image is a little tilted. This is easy to fix in Photoshop.

To rotate your image, follow these steps:

1. Select the Measure tool from the Photoshop Tools palette. This one can be tricky to find because it's usually hiding behind the Eyedropper tool. Both tools are located on the right half of the tools palette, in the tenth position, just above the Magnifying Glass tool. If the Eyedropper tool is in the top position, click and hold on the tool. A moment later a small menu opens up showing all the tools in this particular slot. Select the Measure tool (the one that looks like a ruler).

2. Try to locate some kind of straight line in the photo, one that stretches across as much of the image as possible. This line can be a window sill, building ledge, or street curb, but it should be something you know is physically straight in the real world. If the photograph doesn't contain such an element, try to find two points that would represent a straight line if connected. The idea is to provide Photoshop with a left and right reference point that show how the photograph should be leveled.

3. After locating the reference points, position the Measure tool on one and click and drag the cursor to the other one. Release the mouse, and you'll see a line stretching across the image (don't worry, it's not permanent).

4. Choose Image ➪ Rotate ➪ Arbitrary. This brings up a dialog box that shows the angle (which was found by the Measure tool and entered in here for you by Photoshop) and radio buttons for CW and CCW (Clockwise and Counter Clockwise). One of these should already be checked (CW).

5. Click OK, and Photoshop rotates the image for you.

At this point, notice that the image has been rotated and you no longer have a rectangular photograph. Instead, you have an image that seems to be titled out of its frame. You fix this problem by cropping, which is covered in the following section.

Keystoning

Now is also a good time to deal with the problem of *keystoning* if this is applicable to your image. Keystoning is an effect created when you tilt your camera up to photograph a tall structure. From this upward angle, the structure seems to be falling away from the camera.

Keystoning used to require advanced skills and equipment to solve the problem at the time the picture was made. Fortunately, Photoshop makes it possible to deal with this problem later, in the digital darkroom much more easily.

To deal with the keystoning effect, follow these steps:

1. When you take a photo from an angle that is likely to cause keystoning, be sure to allow for some extra space at the edges of the frame on each side of the building. You need this extra space later on when you're working in Photoshop.

2. Capture the file to your computer and open it in Photoshop.

3. Select the image (Ctrl+A on a PC and Command+A on a Mac).

4. Choose Edit ➪ Transform ➪ Perspective.

5. Click one of the edit handles at the top corner of the image. (The edit handle is a small rectangle.) Click and drag to the side, away from the image, until the building is straight. It may take some experimentation to get this just right.

6. When the building is as straight as possible, press Enter and the change takes effect. This leaves you with a funny-looking photo with the bottom squeezed in. Don't worry, you fix that in Step 7 when you crop.

7. Crop the image to fill the frame (see the next section for help with cropping). This was why you needed to leave that extra space on the sides when you took the photo.

This fixes your keystoning problem and gets you ready to begin trying to improve the quality of the image.

Cropping

The first thing to consider is whether or not your photo needs to be cropped. This is the act of removing unnecessary space around the edges of the photograph. Let's say your lens wasn't long enough to fill the image with your subject, resulting in a lot of wasted space at the edges. Cropping cuts off that extra space, making your subject fill the frame and reducing the size of your photo.

To crop your image, follow these steps:

1. Find the Cropping tool on Photoshop's Tools palette. It's on the left side, two spaces down from the top. The icon for this tool is a set of cropping *L*s that replicate the tools used in the pre-digital darkroom days to crop photos.

2. Place your cursor at a point where you want to start your crop. (Remember, you're defining what you want to leave in the image, not what you want to cut out.) Click and drag down to the point where you want to end the crop and then release the mouse button.

3. At this point, you'll have a cropping rectangle on-screen. You can click and drag on any of the little rectangles on this cropping rectangle and adjust your crop. When you're satisfied, either press the Enter key on your keyboard or click the Checkmark button on the Tool's Options palette at the top of your screen.

The Cropping tool actually offers you an option for creating crops. You can perform a freeform crop (as just described), or you can specify the dimensions of your crop. This second choice is useful if you have a specific use in mind for your image, such as sizing it for a standard sized print.

To specify the dimensions for your crop, go up to the Options palette and enter the print size you want in the boxes marked Width and Height. Then click and drag the Cropping tool. Notice that the tool lets you drag only to the ratio you created by entering the Width and Height values. This is a handy way of ensuring that your print is sized properly before printing.

Exposure Correction

To help you understand the image correction process, I use one particular example photo throughout this chapter. I took this shot last October at a small lake near my home in Southern New Jersey. This image file (568752 fg1501, shown in Figure 15-1) is available for download from this book's companion web site (www.wiley.com/compbooks/simon). That way, you can follow the steps documented here on the same image that's represented in this book.

Download the example image file from the web site. Then open the image in Photoshop or another image-editing program. The first thing you need to do is set the image's black and white points. You do this by examining the image's

Spring Flowers

We were shooting at a botanical garden when we came across this display of spring flowers. The explosion of color was beautiful and presented some interesting possibilities. I began by making an overall shot of the display, focusing on a cluster of pink tulips about half-way down. After making that image, I decided to try a tighter shot of just the tulips, and I switched to a telephoto lens.

Pink Tulips

Pink Tulips. This photo of pink tulips was made with a 400mm telephoto lens, an extension tube, and the help of an assistant holding a reflector just out of sight of the camera. The long focal length served to make the flowers look closer together while throwing the foreground and background out of focus. The result is that your eye is drawn directly to the flowers. Because the flowers were bathed in overhead light through greenhouse glass, it was only necessary to bounce some additional light onto the undersides of the petals to lighten shadows. We did this by angling a reflector underneath and slightly to the side of the tulips.

Daffodils
The addition of a second extension tube allowed an even greater close-up for this composition of yellow daffodils. The combination of a long telephoto lens and extreme close-up minimized the depth of field so that only the two flowers are in focus.

Fireworks Zoom
A long exposure (several seconds) combined with slowly zooming the lens produced this unusual effect during a fireworks display. This kind of manipulation can be very effective if done properly. It helps to have the camera placed on something solid such as a tripod, the roof of a car, or a tabletop.

American Dream
Colored lights, darkness, and a body of water to provide a reflection make for a nice combination, particularly when you add a pensive figure at the water's edge. The camera was mounted on a tripod for a 1/3 of a second exposure, long enough to record the light on the water, but brief enough for the model to keep reasonably still.

Fall Creek
Moving water blurs beautifully when shot at slow shutter speeds. Here an exposure of four seconds gives the water the texture of spun glass while a solid tripod meant the camera stayed steady enough to keep the rocks and leaves sharp.

Waterflow (before)

Sometimes when you're working with challenging lighting conditions, it can be difficult to get exposures right. In this scene, the camera's built-in light meter recommended a setting of 4 seconds and an f-stop of 22.6. This combination was fine for exposing the background, but caused the white water to lose all detail.

Waterflow (after)

One approach would have been to deliberately underexpose this scene in order to retain information in the highlights. The shadow areas could then have been adjusted in Photoshop to bring back detail. Because it's better to fix problems in the field when possible, I chose to add a graduated neutral density filter to block some of the light striking the bottom half of the frame. I also added a color-intensifying filter to bring out the fall colors. You can use your digital camera's LCD screen to evaluate such situations and make corrections in the field, saving you extra work in the digital darkroom.

Havasu Falls

Havasu Falls is located deep within the Western Rim of the Grand Canyon. This spectacular waterfall is part of an area known as "America's Garden of Eden," and is a beautiful place for photography. There are many places from which to document the falls; by shooting straight on near the water level, I was able to place this small travertine falls as a foreground element. Neutral density filters were used to permit a longer shutter speed (about eight seconds) and also to reduce some of the light at the top of the composition. It's usually a good idea to place a strong foreground element in a landscape; this helps the eye travel through the image, creating a sense of depth. This image was made with a DSRL (Canon EOS 1D) so some processing was necessary in the digital darkroom to make it look its best. See the original on the next page for a comparison.

Brigantine Sunset
Combine water and late daylight, and you have the makings for a beautiful image. In this photo, the last light of the day has caught two boys enjoying the cool evening air as a boat returns from a day out on the water. The rich blues and purples are accurate representations of what the scene looked like and were not created by filters or software manipulation.

Havasu Falls (RAW)
Here's the photo of Havasu Falls as it looked when I first transferred it from my camera to my computer for processing. As you can see, the original image is darker and has some dust spots that need cleaning. I set black and white points for this photo, adjusted its levels, cleaned up the dust spots, did some minor dodging and burning, and then sharpened the image twice — once to burn off digital haze and once to sharpen it for printing in this book.

Washington's Crossing Morning Glow

Rivers at sunrise often give off mists because of the difference in temperature between the water and the air. Add the colored light of sunrise and the early morning fog, and you have the ingredients for an unusual photograph.

Hawk Mountain Sunrise

Sometimes it's tough to tell whether fog is your friend or foe when shooting at sunrise. Often a heavy fog will ruin your opportunity for a beautiful sunrise image because it mutes, or even obscures, the brilliant yellows and oranges you expect from this time of day. Sometimes though, the fog can work in your favor, as it did for this photo. Here the blues created by the fog contrast nicely with the orange of the sun trying to burn through the mist. Blue and orange are complementary colors; they work well together when you marry them in an image.

Sunrise at Bethlehem Steel

You can also combine an orange sunrise with a dark blue sky to get that vibrant match of complementary colors. This may produce problems for your overall exposure because you're underexposing an f-stop or so to make a dramatic sky. In this shot, it wasn't a problem as the imposing furnaces of Bethlehem Steel were perfect for a dynamic silhouette in the morning light. The lines of the buildings converge on the sunset, pulling the eye deep into the image.

Workday Morning

Industrial landscapes can be difficult to photograph without the help of dramatic lighting. Here, sunrise and back lighting help make this scene more interesting. The line created by the I-beams in the street helps draw your eye deeper into the photo. This is another useful compositional element known as a "leading line" because it moves your eye through the photo. Once again, a strong foreground element helps lend depth to a two-dimensional image.

American Lake

Patriotic themes make for good photos. Someone painted an American flag on a sheet of plywood and placed it on this lake near my home. Every now and then I stop by to photograph the scene, trying different ideas and documenting its changing look during the seasons. This photo, made during the fall, is probably my favorite. The sweep of the trees and the shoreline in the distance add grace and depth to the image; the juxtaposition of the flag and the house beyond it give the image a symbolism I like.

Long May She Wave

Learn to look for compositional elements wherever you are. This picture was made while we were riding the Cape May-Lewes Ferry. It was late in the day and easy to concentrate on making pictures of the sun setting on the water. Photographers should always remember that ferries and tour boats fly the national flag off their stern, providing you the chance to make a patriotic image. It was cold, and there was a pretty good breeze blowing. This meant it was necessary to take quite a few shots before recording this one with the flag positioned perfectly over the sunset. The image has the complements of blue and orange working for it, plus the flag is backlit, making it appear translucent. There's an added advantage to shooting when the sun is low in the sky; its rays are less intense, meaning that even though the flag is backlit, it's not in silhouette. If this were a photo of just the sunset, it would still be a pretty picture, but the addition of the flag adds emotion to the shot.

Christmas Train
Travel offers lots of exciting opportunities for photography. Sometimes, even the mode of transportation can be photogenic, as is the case with this antique train.

Fishing Boats
At other times, a quick peek out a taxi window can provide a perfect photo opportunity. Our cab was crossing a bridge in Jamaica when we spotted this scene on the river below. We had our driver stop for a moment so we could make some photos of the colorful fishing boats.

"The King"
You never know who you'll meet while traveling. This gentleman was our cab driver in Grand Cayman. He was quite willing to pose for photos and happy to sign a model release so that I could use his picture in this book. Later on, back on the ship, we looked at his signature. Sure enough, he'd signed it *Elvis*.

Underwater Lisa

You do things on vacation that you probably don't get the chance to try at home, so try to be ready to make photos under any circumstances. You can find digital underwater cameras for less than $300 (sometimes a lot less), and soft plastic housings that will protect your camera a few feet underwater are also quite reasonable (less than $100 depending on your camera model). I don't have any experience with underwater photography, but I was still able to use a basic underwater digital point-and-shoot camera to make this picture of Lisa snorkeling during a recent vacation.

Mayan Ruins at Tulum

Try to anticipate photo opportunities by studying travel brochures for the areas you're visiting. In the course of planning our visit to the Mayan ruins at Tulum, Mexico, I came across several images that showed an undulating coastline with one structure jutting out over the sea. Once we reached the site, I knew to look for a vantage point that would enable me to create a similar photo, resulting in this image. Don't be afraid to take ideas from post cards and travel brochures if you're only visiting a location for a couple of hours. These ideas can help you make the most of your limited time for photography.

Port Nassau (after)

Don't be afraid to include signs or labels inside your images when you can. Here, the ship's life ring tells you exactly what vessel I was on when I shot this picture of the port of Nassau in the Bahamas. Early morning light bathes the port beautifully, bringing out the pastel colors of the homes and buildings. By adding a foreground element (the life ring) the two-dimensional image takes on a three-dimensional feel because the eye moves from foreground to background to take in the whole image. In order to keep both the life ring and the port sharply focused, I chose a small lens opening and slow shutter speed to maximize depth of field. I then focused on a point in the water about a third of the way into the scene to keep everything in the zone of sharp focus.

Port Nassau (before)

This is what this image looked like before processing. In addition to the basic processing the image required, it was also necessary to lighten up the life ring, railing, and deck that were in the shadow of the deck above. This was done by creating a levels adjustment layer in Photoshop and then activating a mask over the adjustment layer. I then used a brush tool to remove the effects of the adjustment layer from the top half of the image. This way, the adjustment layer only lightened the portion of the image that was in shadow.

Portland Head Light

Portland Head Light is a wonderful subject for photography that can be photographed well from several different vantage points. Interestingly, few people seemed willing to walk down to this spot during our visit. When you photograph something like a lighthouse, try to help provide context for its existence. In this case, I included the sea and rocks that make the Maine coastline particularly treacherous. Try photographing the subject from different angles and take some shots from a distance so that you can show the surroundings.

Portland Head Light (no warming filter)

Here's a shot from the same sequence. This image hasn't been processed yet, but more importantly, was made without using the warming filter I used in the image above. I used the warming filter to reduce some of the blue from the sky and water. The effects of this filter can be reproduced in Photoshop if you don't have a warming filter for your camera.

Other Views of Portland Head Light

Two more views of the Portland Head Light. The process of creating a memorable photograph involves going exploring with your camera. Even if you think you've got a great picture, walk around, take a few more shots from other angles and directions. We even made pictures of this lighthouse from the ship as we sailed by it while leaving the harbor.

Port Nassau Panorama

Don't be afraid to try unusual angles, crops, and printing dimensions. Some scenes lend themselves to panoramic display, such as the photo of the Port of Nassau in the Bahamas. This shot was originally a full-frame composition from a 3mp camera that was cropped down into panoramic format. Although the resolution isn't high enough for the image to be made into a big print, it's still perfectly fine for a 3x7 or even a 4x9.5 print.

Peggy's Cove Panorama

I used the same cropping technique for this photo of Peggy's Cove in Nova Scotia, Canada, as I used for the Port of Nassau shot. I used a 4mp camera for this shot, and the crop isn't quite as severe. The result is a file that can be printed to 6x12 without needing any increase in resolution.

New Hope Train Station Panorama

I made this image by stitching multiple vertical photographs together to create a high-resolution 180-degree panorama. The final version of this image produced a 32.6MB file capable of being printed to a size of 6x26 at 268 ppi.

Lilies

Using high and low camera angles also makes for eye-catching photos. This picture of a cluster of lilies was made with an extreme wide-angle lens held underneath the flowers and pointed almost straight up. The result is an interesting image made during a time of day when the light was not particularly good for photography.

Lovely Moth

Close-ups also produce a different kind of look. Many digital cameras offer a close-up mode, and add-on lenses can increase this capability. DSLRs, with their interchangeable lenses, offer even more versatility. This image was made with a Canon EOS 1D with an extension tube and 400mm telephoto lens.

Monarch Butterfly
DSLRs don't have all the fun. This close-up of a monarch butterfly was made with an Olympus C2000 in close-up mode. A digital camera's LCD screen makes such photography easier because you can compose the photo using the LCD instead of the viewfinder. This keeps you farther away from the insect (which thinks you're kind of icky, anyway) and gets you to lower the camera a bit, making for a better composition. If you think you'd enjoy doing this kind of photography, plant butterfly attracting plants, such as the liatris shown in this photo, and increase the likelihood of a visit from these creatures.

Misty Foliage (after)
Take full advantage of color as it occurs in nature. This picture of fall foliage was made early in the day, before the morning fog had completely burned off. The softer lighting gave the fall colors a beautiful glow.

Misty Foliage (before)

This is what this image looked like before processing. The fog has muted the colors of the fall foliage and dulled the image. By setting a white and a black point, adjusting levels, burning off the haze, and sharpening the photo, I was able to create the final image shown above.

Red Tulips
Springtime provides its own share of color, including a perennial favorite, tulips. Even if your own garden doesn't look like this, plan a visit to the nearest botanical garden and take advantage of their hard work to produce colorful images such as this one.

The Early Bird

Shooting into the sun can make for dramatic and colorful images. Adding a human element can evoke a mood of contemplation. When shooting into the sun, be careful to make as many pre-exposure settings to your camera as possible. This will minimize the time you spend looking through the viewfinder with the camera pointed toward the sun.

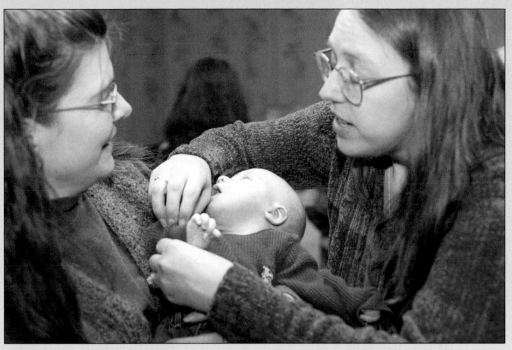

New Baby
Remember when you're photographing people to get in close and capture what's important, facial expressions and emotions.

Goofy Nephew
Of course, sometimes you can get a little too close.

Lisa Portrait

Pleasing portraits call for a medium close photo. Start by giving your subject *headroom,* leaving some air above their head and zoom out until just above the mid-section. Have your camera even with your subject's eyes (or just a hair above so you can tilt down ever so slightly). Position your light (or preferably lights) at a 45-degree angle and higher than your subject. If done properly, you produce a nice "catch light" in your subject's eyes.

Glamour Portrait

When posing your subject, it's best to have her body weight placed slightly forward. Here the model was using a posing stool to lean forward on her hands. The glow of light behind her was created by a third light positioned directly behind her upper back.

Misty Glamour

Here's another photo of Gina from this same shoot. Often when you're making glamour-style images, it's nice to use a soft focus filter or shoot through a black neckerchief stretched tight over the lens. This softens the overall look of the image and creates a sort of dreamy, romantic look. For this image, I created a similar affect in Photoshop by using a soft focus filter from a set of filter plug-ins made by The Imaging Factory.

Yellow Flower
Use longer focal lengths to flatter facial features. In this portrait, a 300mm telephoto lens was used.

Admit One

People can be most interesting when you photograph them doing things that they enjoy. Shooting people in action is certainly much more challenging, but the rewards are greater.

Heads Up
Capturing peak action is difficult, but it can produce memorable images. It takes fast shutter speeds and long focal lengths to isolate action such as this, but you can improve the odds by anticipating events. This soccer photo was the result of a corner kick. I pre-focused on the mass of athletes at the net and waited to trip the shutter until the ball was kicked to them.

Flying
Good action photography requires proper technique. Besides fast shutter speeds and the ability to anticipate action, the sports photographer also learns to track the athlete in motion, following his movements with the lens.

"I Made This!"
Don't forget that people at work can provide interesting subject matter. Intersperse shots of the individual with close-ups of what they're working on for added interest.

Hot Glass
Close-up of the paper-weight.

TV Crew
Use a foreground element such as these bottles of dish soap to draw the eye deeper into an image.

Hidden Tiger
Consider the way light plays upon your subject.

Figure 15-1: Example image you can download and use to follow along as I go through the image correction process.
© 2004 Dan Simon

histogram to determine the location of the darkest black and the brightest white. A *histogram* is a graph that charts the distribution of pixels throughout the image's exposure range.

Reading the histogram

This graph is a useful tool for understanding exposure and applying corrections both in the field and back home in the digital darkroom. Higher end digital cameras frequently offer a histogram view via the camera's LCD screen. If you have such a camera, learning how to use this tool can help you avoid some common exposure problems, such as underexposure (see Figure 15-2).

The histogram for this image shows that the majority of the pixels are distributed to the left of center with a peak near the far left side of the graph. The photo it represents was underexposed by almost a full f-stop to try to keep detail in the sky. If you were reading this histogram just after making that photo, you'd know you should adjust your exposure to create a brighter image. If the pixel distribution was reversed, with the majority of pixels to the right of center, you would have an overexposed image and would need to adjust accordingly.

A "good" histogram shows a distribution of pixels throughout the tonal range of the graph with information in the highlight range (right side of the graph) being particularly important because this is where a lot of highlight detail can be found.

Fortunately, an underexposed image like this can be saved in the digital darkroom, and you can use the histogram to help you fix it. The next few paragraphs show you how to make the necessary adjustments.

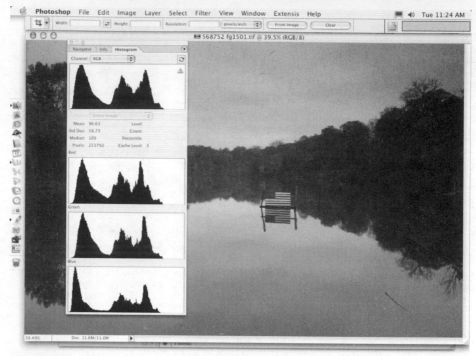

Figure 15-2: Histogram of an underexposed image.
© 2004 Dan Simon

Setting levels

One simple way to correct exposure problems in Photoshop is via the program's Levels function. Although not the most powerful way to tackle the problem, tweaking levels can be done quickly and easily, and the method generally produces good results.

Follow these steps to manipulate the highlight, shadow, and midtone levels in the image:

1. Choose File ➪ Image ➪ Adjustments ➪ Levels. The Levels dialog box opens. (You can also open the Levels dialog box by pressing the keyboard shortcuts Command+L on the Mac or Ctrl+L on the PC). Notice the histogram and the little triangular sliders just below it.

2. In the Channel drop-down box at the top of the dialog box, you can choose the option that designates the color channels that make up the image you're working with. RGB should appear here by default because that's the type of file digital cameras typically create. If you are working on a grayscale image, Gray appears here; if you are working on a CMYK file, CMYK appears in this box. If you click the down arrow, you can see the individual choices for the color channel that appears. For RGB, the color choices are Red, Green, and Blue (see Figure 15-3).

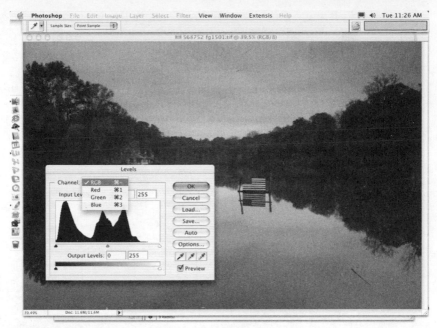

Figure 15-3: The Levels dialog box in Photoshop.
© 2004 Dan Simon

3. Select Red from the Channel drop-down box. This brings up a histogram that shows only the distribution of red pixels throughout the image. This histogram may be significantly different from the combined RGB one. Because this image is underexposed, as I mentioned in the preceding section, there are no pixels in the highlight area at the right edge of the histogram. Notice the line under the histogram with the three triangles distributed along it? The triangle to the far right, controls the image's highlights and is known as the *highlight slider* or *white point.* Move this triangle left until it meets the first significant amount of highlight pixels (the first place where the graph begins to rise). This should put it somewhere around 179 in the highlight section of the Input Levels boxes above the histogram. At this point, the image takes on a reddish cast. This is only temporary. Next, check the *shadow slider* (the triangle at the far left, also known as the *black point*), which controls the image's shadows. In this case, it's already lined up with the leftmost collection of pixels so no adjustment is necessary.

4. Select Green from the Channel drop-down box. Move the highlight slider accordingly (somewhere near 175 should be appropriate). Once again, the black point is fine. Notice the tint changes again.

5. Select Blue from the Channel drop-down box. Adjust the highlight slider as needed (to about 175). Once again, the black point doesn't need to be changed. Notice the image's color is now closer to what the original image looked like.

6. Select RGB in the Channel drop-down box. Notice in Figure 15-4 how the histogram shows small gaps in the graph? A normal RGB image contains 256 levels, which describes the image's tonal range. By adjusting the white point and black point sliders (when necessary), you effectively compress the image's tonal range. These gaps reflect the missing information as a result. If too extreme a correction is made, your image can become posterized, resulting in loss of detail. This is why it's better to capture an image with a full tonal range—in other words, make an accurate exposure—than rely on fixing things in the digital darkroom afterwards. Fortunately for this image, the underexposure was not extreme enough to ruin the photograph.

Figure 15-4: A damaged histogram—note the gaps in the graph.
© 2004 Dan Simon

7. Adjust the middle slider (known as the *gray point*) to bring out the middle tones of the image. A setting around 1.30 seems to work best for this photo.

8. At this point, I like to save the file under a different name. That way, I still have the original image, plus my working version of the file. I do this for a couple of reasons. As computers and software keep evolving, there's a good chance I may be able to do even more with the original image file later on. Secondly, I learn more about digital photography, the digital darkroom and Photoshop and other programs regularly, so a year from now, I can probably improve upon the work I did today. Under such circumstances, I never want to abandon the original image.

Find out much more about naming and saving images as part of a planned workflow in Chapter 16.

Working with curves

One of Photoshop's most powerful tools is the Curves option. If I described the Levels controls as a steak knife, this precise control is the digital darkroom's version of a razor-sharp scalpel!

Before opening the Curves dialog box, choose File ➪ Window ➪ Info to open the Info Palette. Position this palette so it is near one of the corners of the screen.

Choose File ➪ Image ➪ Adjustments ➪ Curves. This opens the Curves control dialog box. Alternatively, you can press the keyboard shortcut Command+M (Mac) or Ctrl+M (PC).

After you open the Curves dialog box (see Figure 15-5), you may notice that Photoshop's tool palette jumps from whatever tool you were using to the Eyedropper tool. This is because you're going to use the eyedropper to find the black, white, and gray points of the image. (Note the little eyedroppers on the lower-right section of the dialog box, with the corresponding black, gray and white point choices.) This is where having a two-monitor set-up on your

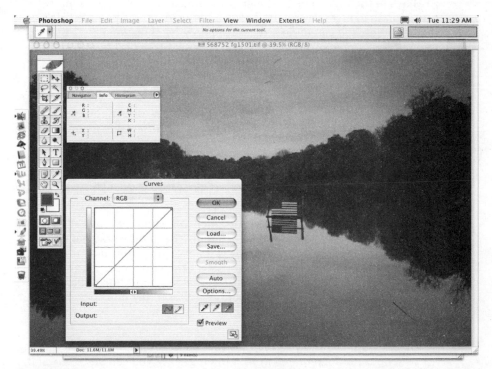

Figure 15-5: Using the Curves control and Info palette.
© 2004 Dan Simon

computer is worth its weight in gold, by the way. With two monitors, you can have the Info palette and Curves dialog box open on one monitor while you enjoy an unobstructed view of your image on the main monitor. Fortunately, you can move the Curves dialog box around the screen, you just can't move the Info palette around while the Curves dialog box is open.

Setting black, white, and gray points using curves

At this point, the image needs some color baselines set. First on the list is telling Photoshop what the darkest black and brightest white points are in an image. Then, if possible (it frequently isn't), you want to show the program where a neutral gray appears in the image. With this information, Photoshop can adjust tonal information and color balance more accurately.

Follow these steps to set the white, black, and gray points:

1. Search for the image's correct white point. This is the area of pixels as close to 256, 256, and 256 on the Info palette as possible. Be careful though. Avoid metallic reflections or glare because these don't provide an accurate representation. In an underexposed photo, such as the example I've been using in this chapter, the white point will be fairly far away from the 256, 256, 256 coordinates. Select the white eyedropper and then maneuver the cursor over the brightest spots of the photo, noting the readings in the Info palette. This method helps you search with more precision than just viewing the image and deciding one point is brighter than another. You can undo a reading simply by choosing File ➪ Edit ➪ Redo Color Sample (Command+Z on the Mac; Ctrl+Z on the PC). After you find the brightest spot, click the mouse to have the program set the white point. For this image I found the brightest spot to be at 201, 201, 199 in the sky above the trees, slightly left of center.

2. Find the image's black point. Select the black eyedropper and move the cursor over the dark areas of the photo looking for a value near 0, 0, 0. Because this image is underexposed and reasonably contrasty, odds are good that you can get pretty close. I found a shadow area to the lower right of the image within one cluster of trees with a value of 5, 7, 2. Click on whichever point you find that comes closest to 0, 0, 0. This will adjust your image once again.

3. Look for the mid-tone gray point. Although you should always set a white point and a black point for an image, finding the middle gray isn't as vital—in part because not all images will have an appropriate gray value. It's still good to look for one, though. Select the gray eyedropper and examine the image looking for a value in the neighborhood of 90, 90, 90. I found a value of 88, 76, 71 and embedded (clicked my mouse on) that point for middle gray for a subtle color correction.

By the way, if you use a gray card (available at any photo store catering to serious photographers) in your photography, you can place one at the edge of the image and make the photograph. Make your middle-gray reading off the card and then crop it out of your image.

Adjusting the curve

After you set the white, black, and gray points, you need to adjust the actual curve for best exposure. The Curves dialog box lets you set individual points on the line from black to white. You can then make corrections to specific tonal ranges of the image.

To adjust the curve, follow these steps:

1. When you open the Curves dialog box (it's under Edit ➪ Adjustments ➪ Curves), you see a grid with a diagonal line going through it. You can use your mouse to embed multiple points on this line and move small portions of the line to affect the contrast in different areas of your photograph. Unlike the Levels control, which offers three control points (Highlights, Midtones, and Shadows), Curves offers as many as 15 user-managed control points. (You seldom use more than 3 or 5 on an image, though.)

2. Start by clicking the mid-point of the diagonal line. You can then click and drag this point. Move it upwards and it lightens the image, move it downwards and it darkens it. (Whoa! Just a small amount, dragging the point halfway up or down the box will really mess up your image.)

3. Embed additional points above and below the center point. You can then move these points around individually to further tweak your image (small adjustments work best). While working in RGB format, your adjustments affect contrast and tonal values. You can also use the Curves box to make color adjustments.

4. At the top of the Curves dialog box is a pull-down menu marked "RGB." If you click on this menu and pull it down, you'll see individual choices for Red, Green, and Blue, in addition to the RGB offering. These choices refer to individual color channels (*channel* is the way Photoshop distinguishes color layers from regular layers). You can work in each of these individual colors separately from the rest, enabling you to get rid of color casts or make other changes in the color quality of your image. Color adjustments are made the same way tonal ones are, by embedding control points on the diagonal line and moving them around to change the color value of the particular channel.

Fine-tuning the color in the Variations dialog box

After you set the white, black, and gray points, your image should be pretty close to useable. Sometimes, however, the color may seem a little bit off. If this is the case, Photoshop has a very useful tool known as *variations*. You choose File ➪ Image ➪ Adjustments ➪ Variations to open the Variations dialog box. This tool provides a sort of digital test strip showing lots of different versions of your image (see Figure 15-6). You can just work through the examples, fine-tuning as you go.

The process I just documented works well but is *destructive* in nature. In other words, the image's original pixels are changed, resulting in a loss of original data.

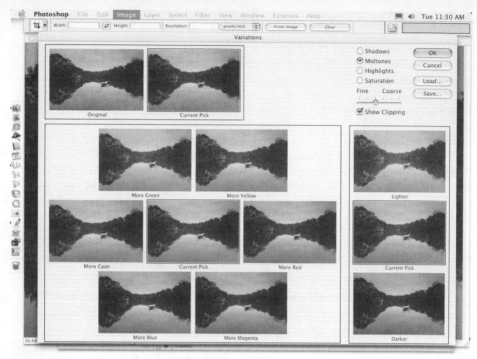

Figure 15-6: Various versions of the image, shown in the Variations dialog box.
© 2004 Dan Simon

See the sidebar about "Nondestructive Editing" in this chapter to find out ways to keep your original images intact.

Nondestructive Editing

Finding ways to improve digital image files while causing as little alteration to the underlying original files is currently a major drive among many Photoshop enthusiasts. As I noted earlier, many feel it's important to preserve the original file as much as possible, so the more things you can do that don't alter original image data, the better.

Programs such as Photoshop that offer the capability to work in layers lend themselves to nondestructive editing. Many photographers start their image editing process by creating a duplicate layer of the original image. This lets them manipulate to their heart's content, secure in the knowledge that they can always have immediate access to the original file if need be.

Working on a copy layer of the file instead of the original is a good practice, but only if your computer has the RAM and processor speed to work effectively with the larger files this technique creates. If your system isn't up to that challenge, save this method for your next machine. Just make sure you archive an original version of the image somewhere safe.

Using adjustment layers:
A nondestructive approach

Fortunately, Photoshop offers a nondestructive approach to image adjustment. This is through a feature known as *adjustment layers*. These are layers that can be used to apply levels or curves controls (as well as the program's other image adjustment tools) without changing the underlying pixels. You can manipulate an image to your heart's content with adjustment layers, and then turn the layer off and still have your original image. You can save the file as a Photoshop file or a TIFF file with layers intact, and you can come back to it a year later and still be able to change the original levels or curves adjustment as desired. Another benefit of using adjustment layers is that you tweak the opacity of the effect, giving you even more control.

An even bigger advantage to working with adjustment layers is that you can activate a mask (explained in the next section) and then selectively apply the adjustment to selected portions of the image rather than the entire photo (see Figure 15-7).

Masking

One of Photoshop's most powerful features is its capability to mask out portions of an image while leaving others unaffected. Think of a mask as a user-defined

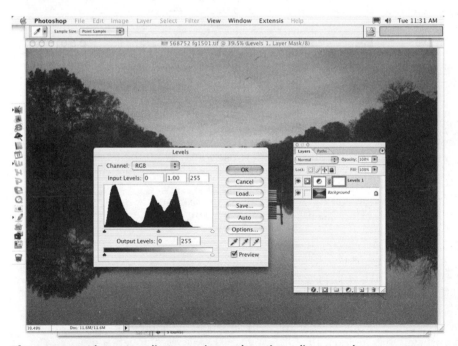

Figure 15-7: When you adjust your image by using adjustment layers, you can always go back to your original settings, something you can't do if you apply the affect directly to the original layer.

© 2004 Dan Simon

overlay. You can apply the mask to certain areas (say shadow areas) so they're protected from a particular effect, whereas leaving other areas unmasked (say highlights) so that you can change their intensity.

Masks let you fix one part of an image without having that correction mess up another area. Masks are one of the things that make Photoshop great.

Dodging and burning

Sometimes your overall image is pretty well balanced exposure-wise, but it has one or two areas that need a little work. Maybe a highlight's a little too bright or a shadow area or mid-tone that's a bit too dark. You can't tweak levels to fix this problem, although you could create an adjustment layer and then activate the layer mask to tweak those spots. The problem is, you're masking a lot of area just to fix a couple of little problems.

As it happens, Photoshop offers some tools to deal with this sort of problem. They're known as *Dodging and Burning tools*, which is what they are also called in the conventional darkroom. As a matter of fact, the principles are the same. By design, Photoshop's creators wisely tried to keep the feel of the digital darkroom comparable to the conventional one for all of us old geezers who got our start the conventional way. Photoshop also offers a third tool—the Sponge tool—that can increase or decrease image saturation. This one's based on the old photographer's trick of taking a developer soaked sponge or piece of paper and rubbing it on a portion of the image to overdevelop it.

In the conventional darkroom, a dodging tool is used to block light from the enlarger from reaching a specific area of the print, making that area lighter. The Dodging tool in Photoshop does the same thing, lightening the area it's applied to. The burning tool in the conventional darkroom does just the opposite. It adds light from the enlarger, increasing the light striking the paper and making the burned area darker in the print. The Photoshop Burning tool works in the same way, darkening the area it's applied to.

Generally, it's best when using either of these tools, to set the exposure to a small percentage and build up the effect in an area rather than using the tool at 100 percent and probably overdoing it. Using the Dodging and Burning tools results in destructive editing, by the way, as these changes affect your original pixels. The next section discusses a nondestructive method for using dodging and burning.

Nondestructive Dodging and Burning in Photoshop

Dodging and burning through Photoshop's tools is a bit on the dicey side. For one thing, you're changing original image information; for another, it's difficult to be precise with this method. The following steps walk you through another way of tackling the problem that keeps your original image intact:

1. Create a new layer by choosing File ➪ Layer ➪ Create New Layer.

2. Double-click the layer to bring up the Layer Style palette. Change the Blending mode to Overlay and the Opacity to 50 percent. Leave the advanced blending section alone, but make sure the Blend If drop-down menu is set to Gray. Click OK

3. Select a brush (not the Dodging or Burning tool) a bit smaller than the area you want to work on. Set your foreground/background colors to the default black and white by typing the letter *d*. Use black to burn in (darken) areas of the picture that are too bright and white to dodge (lighten) areas of the image that are too dark. It's usually best to set the brush opacity to about 50 percent or less so you don't overdo the effect. You can always increase it by painting over the same area a second or even third time.

4. If you overdo a spot, just paint over it with the opposite color and remove some of the effect!

5. If you have a particularly difficult area to work on, consider creating a selection to isolate the part of the image you want to correct. This will prevent you from spilling over into areas you don't want to change. Selections and masks are covered in greater detail a little later in this chapter.

Other Methods of Image Tweaking

Photoshop offers a number of different ways to tweak your images. Some of these are as simple as creating a new layer and filling it with a color and then adjusting the blending mode and opacity (useful for adding or removing color casts). The following sections discuss some of my favorite image tweaking techniques.

Gray fill (for increasing tonal range)

By filling a new layer with 50 percent gray and applying it through the color dodge blending mode, you can bring out detail in an image. This is a nice little nondestructive editing technique that can help improve the tonal range of your image.

To fill a new layer with gray to increase the tonal range, follow these steps:

1. Create a new layer by choosing Layer ➪ Create New Layer.

2. Choose Edit ➪ Fill, and in the Fill drop-down box, choose 50% gray. Click OK.

3. On the Layers palette, change the Blending mode to Color Dodge.

4. Adjust Opacity as desired. I'd suggest bringing it down to 0 to see your original image and then sliding it to the right to see the effects.

5. Use the Eraser tool from Photoshop's Tools palette (set to a soft-edged brush at a low opacity) to dial down the effect in areas that don't need too much help.

6. Save a version of the image with layers intact so you can come back later and make changes if need be.

Contrast masking (for salvaging high contrast images)

Contrast masking is an old conventional darkroom technique for pulling detail out of images shot under contrasty lighting conditions. This simple Photoshop technique gives you the same result that you would get in the darkroom, and you can convert it into an action for easy use.

 Visit this book's companion web site and download the free contrast mask action.

Follow these steps to use a contrast mask on your image:

1. Create a duplicate of your image layer by choosing Layer ➪ Duplicate. Alternatively, you can select the image layer with your mouse and drag it onto the new layer icon on the bottom of the Layers palette

2. Desaturate the new layer by choosing Image ➪ Adjustments ➪ Desaturate. This removes all color from the image because you're going to use this layer to help create a mask of the image.

3. Invert the image by choosing Image ➪ Adjustments ➪ Invert. This places highlights over shadows and vice versa.

4. On the Layers palette, change the Blending mode to Overlay. Blending mode is the pull-down menu at the top of the palette. Its default is Normal.

5. Choose File ➪ Filter ➪ Blur ➪ Gaussian Blur to apply a Gaussian Blur filter, choosing a radius of about 40 (you can tweak this number as needed).

6. Adjust Layer Opacity as desired to tweak this effect. This is a subjective call, so experiment until you've made the image look the best you think you can.

Digital color filters

Warming and cooling filters have always been useful tools for photographers trying to compensate for less than desirable lighting conditions. Photoshop makes it possible to solve the same problems back in the digital darkroom long after you've made the original image.

To create a warming or cooling filter effect, follow these steps:

1. Create a new layer by choosing File ➪ Layer ➪ New Layer.

2. Use the foreground color picker on the Tools palette and pick the color you want to add to the image (orange for warming, blue for cooling). Just

click on the foreground color on the Photoshop Tools Palette (it's the upper square on the lower part of the palette), and it takes you to the color picker. Here you pick exactly the color you want to use.

3. Fill the new layer with this color by choosing File ➪ Edit ➪ Fill and then choosing Foreground color from the drop-down list.

4. On the Layers palette, change the Blending mode to Color. (Blending mode is the pull-down menu at the top of the palette. Its default is Normal.)

5. Change the Layer Opacity as needed. Usually it only takes a tiny fraction (10 to 15 percent) to achieve the desired effect.

 See how Photoshop CS offers an easier way to apply warming and cooling filters in Chapter 16.

Spotting and Image Repair

Back in the days of the wet darkroom, dust was a nightmare. You either labored to keep the darkroom and its equipment as dust-free as possible or you resigned yourself to spending time using a camel's hairbrush and special dyes to hide dust spots on your prints. The specks of dust on the negative would block light hitting the photographic paper, producing white spots. You'd dab the brush on the paper, gradually building up enough dye to get the spot to blend in with the surrounding image.

Well, even in the digital age, dust is still a pain in the neck! It's particularly bad for DSLRs and their interchangeable lenses. If dust gets into the camera body and lands on the imaging sensor (or the filter covering it), it shows up on your image as a black spot or streak.

As you may have noticed, our working image has some ugly dust spots and streaks on it. It's now time to get rid of them.

Photoshop offers several different ways of dealing with dust spots and other dirt on the image. You can use the Cloning tool to paint over dust spots with similar areas of the image that are dust free. The program's Healing brush offers an even more attractive alternative because it tries to keep some of the same underlying texture. Each tool has its advantages, and if you're using an older version of the program, you may not even have the Healing brush available to you. Keep in mind, if you use the Cloning tool approach, adopt a nondestructive method. You can do this with the Cloning tool by creating a new blank layer above your image file, checking the Use All Layers box option in the Cloning tool and then cloning over the dust spots on the new layer. When you're done, you can save a master version of the image as a PSD file with layers intact, that you can return to when needed, yet flatten the working version of the image for other uses. This solves the dust problem but still gives you an easy way to revert back to your original file.

Project: **Dust spotting—An alternative technique**

Here's a technique I use when I have to remove dust from a particularly challenging image. This method takes advantage of Photoshop's History palette and History brush. If the History palette isn't visible when you open Photoshop, you can choose the Window tab on the menu bar and cursor down to the History option to open it. You choose the History Brush from the Photoshop Tools palette.

To spot dust an image, follow these steps:

1. Open the Dust and Scratches filter by choosing Filter ⇨ Noise ⇨ Dust & Scratches. Begin with the Radius set to 1 pixel and the Threshold set to 0. Use the cursor to find and select the worst piece of dust or mark on the image. Click that mark to bring it up in the dialog box's magnifier. I chose that ugly black streak in the lower right-hand corner of the image.

2. Slowly move the Radius slider to the right, pausing a moment at each increment. Find an amount that makes the streak disappear completely. (I took it to 13.)

3. Move the Threshold slider to the right until the streak reappears. Then one level at a time, move the slider back left until the outline of the streak disappears completely. (I moved it to 3.) This is a particularly bad dust streak, so extreme settings were necessary. Click OK.

4. Go to the History palette and click the rectangle next to the Dust & Scratches event. This loads that event into the History brush.

5. Click on the event immediately before the Dust & Scratches event. Your image will return to its dusty, but clear state. Now select the History brush. (You can type the letter *Y* as a shortcut, and the program automatically selects the History brush.)

6. Select a brush size that's just a little bigger than the dust spot you're trying to remove. If it's a scratch or hair, pick a brush that's just bigger than the scratch is thick. Paint over the blemish. This should remove most dust spots and other marks, but may not work completely on really bad ones. Finish cleaning up everything you can with the history brush, then return to the remnants of the troublesome ones and use either the healing brush or cloning tool to finish up the job.

Sharpening

It's not at all unusual for digital images to need some sharpening. Although many novice-oriented digital cameras perform their sharpening in-camera, you still may find the occasional photo that needs help. If you're using a higher-end camera, odds are it will leave more of the decision in your hands, because oversharpening an image can degrade image quality.

There are a number of ways to sharpen an image in Photoshop. The most basic method is to choose Filters ➪ Sharpen and then choose one of the program's sharpening tools: Sharpen, Sharpen Edges, Sharpen More, or Unsharp Mask. The method that those who know the program prefer, using Unsharp Mask, is explained in the next section.

Unsharp Mask filter sharpening technique (destructive)

The alternative method is to choose the Unsharp Mask filter. This is the only one of the four that lets you exercise precise control. Although this is not necessarily the best way to sharpen an image, the Unsharp Mask filter does a decent job.

The Unsharp Mask filter has three controls: Amount, Radius, and Threshold. A simple method of sharpening with these controls is to take the resolution of the image, divide it in half, and move the decimal point two digits to the left. For example, here is how this would work for an image with a resolution of 300 ppi:

```
300 ppi ÷ 2 = 150.00
Move the decimal point left: 1.5
```

In this example, you would use this figure for the radius setting. Set the Amount setting to 100 percent, and then adjust the Threshold slider to tweak the overall effect until you're satisfied. The lower the threshold number, the greater the sharpening effect. You can turn the preview box on and off by clicking the check mark. This helps you to judge the effect on the image. Also be sure to preview the effect at the actual print size of the image.

This is at best a so-so method. Most images should be sharpened as the very last step before output, because the amount of sharpening necessary depends on the output resolution and how the photo is to be used. As mentioned earlier in this chapter, destructive editing methods—those that change the original pixels—are less desirable than those that don't, and this technique falls into that destructive category.

Haze Burning

Experienced digital darkroom workers frequently use Photoshop's Unsharp Mask filter to "burn off" a sort of digital "haze" many images have. This application of the filter does nothing for sharpening, but many of us use it as an additional step in the editing process. It's helpful enough that I've created an action (Photoshop's form of a scripted mini-program) that allows me to apply this technique quickly

Continued

Continued

whenever I need it. (Not every image benefits from this technique though, so be selective in its use.)

Select the Unsharp Mask filter from the Filter menu and apply settings of Amount 16, Radius 40 and Thresholds 0. Click OK and you're done. (Go ahead and try this technique on one of your own images and see the difference it makes!)

 You can download a copy of the Haze Burning action from this book's companion web site at `www.wiley.com/compbooks/simon`.

High Pass sharpening technique (nondestructive)

This technique takes advantage of a little used Photoshop filter known as the High Pass filter. Access the filter and apply this technique by following these steps:

1. Drag your image layer down to the New Layer icon on the bottom of the Layer's palette. This creates a duplicate version of your image layer. (Or choose File ➪ Layer ➪ Duplicate Layer, which does the same thing.)

2. Set theBlending mode to H Light. (Soft Light will also work; you can experiment to see which effect you prefer.) Set the layer opacity to about 50 %. Don't worry that it seems to have a strange effect on the image. The next step will fix that.

3. Choose File ➪ Filter ➪ Other ➪ High Pass to apply the High Pass filter to the new layer. Adjust the Radius slider to vary the intensity of the filter, turning the preview box on and off to get a sense of the effect. When you find a level of sharpening you like, click OK to apply the filter.

4. At this point, you can still further tweak the effect by changing the opacity of the high pass layer or even by changing blending modes. Best of all, you can turn this layer off and repeat the entire process for a completely different sharpening effect later on if that's what you need. (Of course, you have to have saved the file with layers intact to have this option.) This is one of my favorite sharpening methods because it doesn't change the original pixels, yet it leaves me the capability to change the amount and/or quality of the sharpening effect long after I'm done working on the image. (In fact, I used this sharpening method for many of the images in this book, sending them to the publisher with layers intact so the company's graphic artists could make adjustments if needed.)

Skilled Photoshop workers have multiple ways of sharpening images, each worth considering for their individual merits. Space doesn't permit me to cover them all here, but other methods of image sharpening are discussed at this book's companion web site.

Handling Noise Problems

The easiest way to solve noise problems is to turn off the power to your teenaged kid's stereo. That particular issue is beyond the scope of this book, so this section will actually deal with the issue of digital image noise.

Noise is caused by individual pixels in the imaging sensor misfiring. This happens all the time, but less often at lower ISO settings and in better shooting conditions.

Noise typically becomes a problem when you're shooting in low light and have to crank up your ISO setting. As the camera sensor pumps up its sensitivity to light, it also causes more image noise. (Noise is characterized by off-color pixels—usually reddish to yellowish—in the shadow areas of your photo.

There are several ways to deal with noise problems. One simple technique is to find the channel where the noise is the worst (usually the blue channel) and then apply a blur filter to that channel by choosing File ⇨ Filter ⇨ Blur ⇨ Blur More. This softens the image a little, but you can correct for that during the sharpening process.

Because noise is such a problem for digital cameras (particularly, consumer grade cameras with smaller sensors and lower maximum ISOs), a number of third-party options have shown up to help photographers deal with this problem. These options show up as Photoshop plug-ins, such as Nik Multimedia's Dfine, which is a complete image-processing filter (see Figure 15-8), and The Imaging Factory's noise reduction and noise reduction pro filters. Some additional third-party options can be found as Photoshop actions such as those by Digital Deluxe. These applications try to simplify the process of dealing with this problem, and each does a good job of handling noise issues.

Visit this book's companion web site for links to these noise-reduction resources.

Masking and Making Selections

So far, you've been looking at the big picture. Most of the corrections this chapter has discussed have applied to global changes in the image. But suppose you want to affect just one or two parts of a photograph?

Photoshop just happens to offer some very powerful tools for isolating areas of an image and once you begin to understand these tools, they can significantly alter the way you process your images.

The idea behind a *mask* is to block out the portion of the image you don't want to change, leaving areas where some effect will take place. *Selections* are a different approach to doing the same thing. A selection delineates the area where an effect is applied without changing areas outside the selection. The reason for lumping these two together is because Photoshop lets you move back and forth between them quite easily.

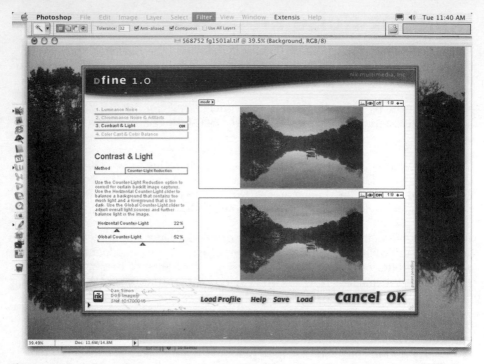

Figure 15-8: Dfine offers a noise reduction filter that can be applied to several different types of noise. (Sorry, there is still no filter included to block out your teenager's music.)
© 2004 Dan Simon

The program offers some simple selection tools such as the Magic Wand, Marquis tools, and Lasso tools, which are all found on the Photoshop Tools palette. Any one of these can be used to create a selection, identified by the program's "marching ants" effect in Figure 15-9.

Although these tools are a good starting point for making selections, they provide only a weak glimmer of Photoshop's true masking promise. Fortunately, it takes little more than pressing the *Q* on your keyboard to get there. *Q* is a hotkey that puts you into Quick Mask mode. This option turns your selection into a mask. Press *Q* again, and you're back to a selection.

The advantage to working in Quick Mask mode is that you can select an appropriately sized brush, set your foreground and background colors to the default black and white by typing the letter *D*), and then paint with white to expand your mask or black to remove parts of it. The beauty of this approach is that you can fine-tune a selection to exactly the area you need to isolate. Too much selected? Just paint with black to remove the excess. Need to isolate two different parts of the image? Paint out one and then paint out the other. Press *Q* to return to Selection mode. Now you have altered the two distinct selections you had previously selected, as shown in Figure 15-10.

Be sure to check out the full color versions of the figures presented in this book at the companion web site (www.wiley.com/compbooks/simon).

Figure 15-9: Two selected areas in Photoshop.

© 2004 Dan Simon

Figure 15-10: You can use Photoshop's Quick Mask mode and the program's brush tools to expand or remove areas of the mask.

© 2004 Dan Simon

Photoshop lets you save selections for later use. Just choose File ➪ Select ➪ Save Selection and save your selection under an appropriate name. Later on, you can return to the Selection menu, choose Load Selection, and pick the appropriate selection from the drop-down list. You can even return to Quick Mask mode and make changes to the selection before returning to Selection mode and re-saving the selection under a new name.

When you want to correct an image shot under high-contrast lighting, having the capability to save a selection can be very handy. To fix blown out highlights, follow these steps:

1. Make a selection of the area that's overexposed and copy and paste it to its own layer.

2. Apply a levels or curves adjustment layer to the layer containing the overexposed area and tweak it for best effect.

3. Press and hold down the Option key (Macintosh) or Alt key (Windows) and click the line between the adjustment layer and the selection layer. This limits the adjustment layer's effect to the selection layer only.

4. Make a copy of the underexposed area and paste it into its own layer above the adjustment layer for the overexposed area.

5. Apply a levels or curves adjustment layer to this selection and tweak for best effect.

6. Lock this adjustment layer to its selection so the effect is only applied to the underexposed portion of the image. You lock the adjustment layer by holding down the Alt key on a PC or the Option key on a Mac and positioning the cursor on the line between the adjustment layer and the layer next to it. Then click the mouse on that line.

Theoretically, you could keep using this technique on any number of areas of the image individually tweaking each element of the composition for best effect.

Third-Party Software: Mask-Pro

As terrific as Photoshop's masking and selection capabilities are, if you have to do a lot of this kind of thing, Extensis makes a Photoshop plug-in called Mask-Pro that takes masking to the next level. This plug-in is available for both Macintosh and Windows computers and a link to the company's web site (where you can download a trial version) is located at this book's companion web site. (www.wiley.com/compbooks/simon).

Programs That Do the Work for You

So far, I've been showing you how to tackle the various elements of image correction individually and through your own efforts. If you're not comfortable with this approach, or if you have to process a lot of images and you want to simplify the task a bit, one of the two plug-ins discussed in this section may work for you.

Unlike most of the plug-ins I've mentioned up to this point, these two, Extensis Intellihance and Nik Multimedia's Dfine, do it all. They fix exposure problems, sharpen images, clean up noise, and do all the other tweaks you need for a good final image. These Photoshop plug-ins cost from $100 to $200 each, so they may not be for everyone. But for those who don't mind spending the money, they can make a world of difference—particularly if you're just making the switch from film to digital photography.

Intellihance

The Extensis Intellihance plug-in offers a lot of options. You activate the filter from where it installs on the Photoshop menu, and you are then greeted by a multipanel screen. Each panel shows a preview of a different processing option, and there are 24 options in all. If you don't like any of the options, drop-down menus in each panel let you preview other choices until you find one you like, or you can individually set eight different parameters for things such as contrast, sharpness, and dust control just by clicking the appropriate down arrow. Intellihance also provides options for the type of paper you're printing to or the type of print process (newsprint versus fine art, for example) being used (see Figure 15-11).

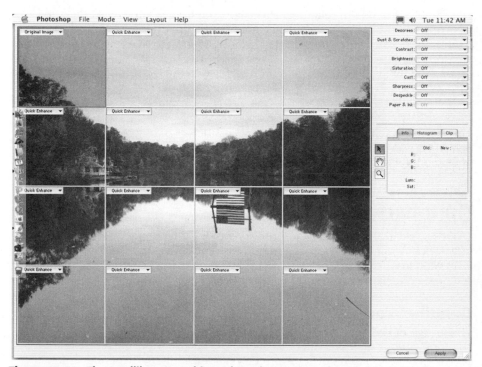

Figure 15-11: The Intellihance multipanel preview screen of processing options.
© 2004 Dan Simon

Dfine

Another plug-in, Dfine by Nik Multimedia, takes an entirely different approach to image processing but still offers lots of choices. The application works through a series of screens that lets you choose the type and level of correction for each of several categories, including sharpness, contrast, color saturation and noise reduction. Each choice provides a sample preview of the correction's effect. An additional benefit of this program is that its manufacturer, Nik Multimedia, also sells profiles for specific digital cameras, thus offering the best possible performance from the software.

Increasing Image Resolution

It's not unusual for a photographer to need to increase an image's file resolution, either to allow for a greater crop than normal or to make a bigger print than the camera's normal resolution output is capable of making.

There are a number of ways to tackle this challenge, with varying degrees of success, and this section touches on several options.

Using Photoshop's bicubic interpolation

You can use Photoshop to increase file size (sometimes known as *upressing*). Basically, the program makes an educated guess and creates new pixels to stretch the resolution of your image file. You implement this technique through the program's image size function by choosing File ⇨ Image ⇨ Image ⇨ Size, picking Bicubic Interpolation, and then increasing the resolution as much as you dare. Unfortunately, this is only good for about a 50 percent increase in resolution at best.

There's also a school of thought that says it's better to increase resolution this way in very small steps, rather than in one big jump. If this sounds good to you, download the free action from this book's companion web site.

Third-party solutions

There are several alternatives for people who need more serious upressing power than what Photoshop can offer. These programs aren't cheap, running from $150 to $200 apiece or more, but they do offer the promise of 200, 300, and 400 percent increases in resolution or more.

Genuine Fractals

This program has been around a while. It uses fractal math (don't ask me, I'm a communications major) to increase file size. This program, currently offered by LizardTech, also uses its own proprietary file format (.stn). Genuine Fractals works both within Photoshop and also as a stand-alone program.

Pixel Smartscale

Extensis recently announced a new Photoshop plug-in called Pixel Smartscale (see Figure 15-12). This tool claims to be capable of up to a 1600 percent increase in resolution. Although that seems a bit ambitious, Pixel Smartscale certainly does a great job of tripling and even quadrupling resolution.

Figure 15-12: Pixel Smartscale gives you control over various aspects of the upressing process. Whereas working in the program you can also manipulate image sharpness and contrast.

© 2004 Dan Simon

 Visit this book's companion web site (www.wiley.com/compbooks/simon) for more information on increasing image resolution and for links to the products discussed in this section.

Summary

Once upon a time, taking the photo was only half the process. Photographers finished their images in home darkrooms, frequently completing a photographic vision only partially realized when the shutter was tripped.

Great masters such as Ansel Adams created as much magic in the darkroom as they did in the field. Adams—who built his own enlarger with two dozen individually controlled lights for maximum control over his prints—would probably have loved Photoshop and the control it provides over image quality.

The difference now is that you don't have to be a darkroom master to be effective in the digital darkroom. Programs such as Photoshop have made image processing and correction possible for even the casual hobbyist. No formal training is even necessary.

This chapter provided an overall look at the many ways you can use Photoshop to improve quality or repair problems in your digital files. As you work with the program and become familiar with these techniques, you can enjoy more and more control over the quality of your photographs.

I've covered different ways of sharpening an image, masking, adjustment layers, noise reduction filters, and much more. It's a lot to go over in a single chapter, but it will get your digital darkroom efforts headed in the right direction.

Setting Up a Workflow

Now that you're blazing away with your digital camera, making images left and right, it's time to consider how you're going to manage those photos. Ideally, you're going to have a set process, called a *workflow*, to manage an image from the time you shoot it through its display, printing, and storage so you can find that same image again years later.

Back in the days of film, you would take your photos, send the film out for processing, and have your prints returned. From that point on, you may have displayed your prints in photo albums and stored your negatives in shoeboxes in the closet—neat, workable system that offers some sense of organization, and one that still applies to digital photography. Today, you can drop your memory card off at the local department store, get prints and CD-ROMs made, and store the CDs in storage cases (or shoeboxes if you prefer).

This basic system represents the simplest form of workflow possible. It treats digital photography about the same as film photography and keeps life simple. What it doesn't do, however, is take advantage of digital photography's power.

Developing a digital workflow is all about developing good image management habits. Remember, you're not just dealing with the handful of images you're processing today, you're positioning yourself to manage the images you accumulate over the years. Picture your situation a decade from now, when you may have thousands or hundreds of thousands of images to search through in order to find one specific shot. Good habits now can help you find that picture later.

In this chapter, I help you find the quickest, most thorough, and most efficient way to process your photos. I discuss JPEG/TIFF and Raw format workflows, as well as image-processing workflows for each format.

Determining Which Type of Workflow to Use

Workflow should be a fairly personal thing. Although certain guidelines about task placement are absolute, such as making sharpening your last step and sharpening for a specific use, there is enough flexibility overall for you to design a workflow system consistent with your needs and preferences.

Depending upon your needs, you can tailor the following steps to meet your own requirements. A workflow should take care of these tasks:

1. Capture images from your camera to your computer

2. Let you evaluate your files to determine which you want to keep and which you want to delete.

3. Provide an initial archive of your original files. (You can switch the order of steps 2 and 3 if you feel saving a copy of every photo you shoot is important.)

4. Keyword your images. *Keywording* is the process of attaching keywords to a file so an image-cataloging program can search through files looking for a user-specific keyword. For instance, if you keyword regularly, and someday you need to search for every picture you've ever taken of your cat Fluffy, you can just enter a keyword search for Fluffy, and the image cataloging program locates all photos containing the keyword Fluffy. This process can be automated in Photoshop so you don't have to manually enter these keywords into every photo yourself.

5. Select files for processing. (You may or may not want to process and print every photo you take.)

6. Process your photos for universal use. You can perform certain processing steps on your images that are the same no matter how you plan on using the images. Save use-specific steps (such as setting resolution and sharpening) for later because these steps will vary depending on whether you're using the files for the web, multimedia presentations, or simply getting prints made. Some people feel this is a good time to make a second archival CD-ROM, because you've taken your images about as far as you can, while still keeping them available for any use.

7. Process your files for their specific use.

8. Archive the final files if necessary. Depending on how much work you do to your files as a result of step 7, you may or may not want an additional archive of these images. Of course, you may be saving your files to yet another CD, anyway, so you can deliver them to a printer or take them to another computer for creating a multimedia presentation .

9. Add your files to a master image catalog. You should perform this step somewhere in your workflow. This way your master images catalog remains an accurate resource.

Many digital cameras offer a choice between JPEG, TIFF, or Raw capture, so this chapter covers the JPEG/TIFF workflow and the Raw workflow methods. Feel free to tweak the suggested workflows, as you like, keeping in mind that some tweaks affect your final image.

JPEG/TIFF workflow

Often, the quality returned by digital cameras shooting in JPEG mode is more than good enough for your needs. Because JPEG mode lets the camera process faster and store more images than TIFF or Raw modes do, JPEG mode is certainly an attractive option. It's also a slightly easier workflow because the camera may do some image processing for you beforehand depending on whether or not you've changed its internal parameters. (Refer to your camera's owner's manual to see if you can change internal parameters with your specific model.) This workflow is divided up into three distinct phases of the workflow process: capturing, processing, and printing images.

Phase I: Capturing and reviewing the images

For most photographers, image transfer is fairly straightforward. You can transfer your images from camera to computer, media to card reader, media to card adapter, or possibly someday in the future, through transmission from camera to computer. (Image capturing is discussed in greater detail in Chapter 14.) The following steps walk you through transferring your images to the computer and reviewing them for quality:

1. Capture your images to a hard drive (preferable), partition, or folder specifically created for photo storage. I usually create a sub-folder for each month's work, and then nest sub-folders by date and identification for each specific shoot, for example 01.04 images ⇨ 01.15.04 Longwood Gardens.

     It might be helpful to review your images without capturing your entire shoot to your computer. This way you can delete bad shots and only transfer the keepers. Many image cataloging programs will let you view the images while they're still on the media card. You can then select the ones you want to capture to your hard drive.

2. Review your images. You can review images through Photoshop's file browser or through a third party image browser/cataloging program such as ACDsee for the PC or iView for the Mac. (There are many image browser/cataloging programs available for each platform; I discuss them in greater depth later in this chapter.) I prefer to use an image browser/cataloger that lets me view full screen preview files quickly, which is why I don't use Photoshop's file browser for this task. I should note that I frequently have to view hundreds of images, so anything that speeds the process is very important. But if you typically only look at a couple of dozen images, a file browser might be all you need. A good image browser/cataloging program, like the one shown in Figure 16-1, helps you move files, reorganize them, and add notes, among other things.

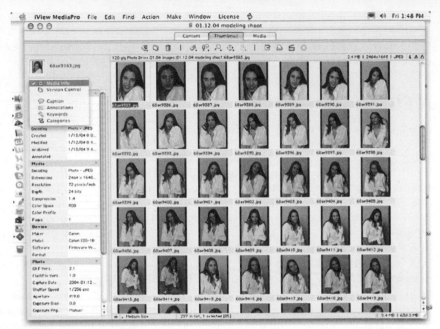

Figure 16-1: An image browser/cataloger can make your file management chores a bit easier by giving you a chance to view your photos as thumbnails or full screen previews.
© 2004 Dan Simon

3. **Cull rejects from your shoot.** Even with JPEG compression, one- and two-megabyte image files start to add up on your hard drive. If you're the type who can't bear to throw any image away; burn a CD of the complete shoot now, and cull the rejects later. By burning a CD, you have at least one complete record of everything you shoot, while still maximizing space on your hard drive. (Making a CD backup early in the process is a good idea, too.)

4. **Rename your files.** Should you rename your files or leave them in your camera's nomenclature? If your camera repeats numbers after reaching a milestone such as 1,000 or 10,000 images, then it's probably smarter to rename your files. Otherwise, you can search for one image and end up with a completely different one with the same filename. Fortunately, image-browsing/cataloging programs usually offer renaming capabilities. Photoshop users can also create a batch processing setup to rename their files. Although this step isn't vital, renaming your files can simplify finding a particular image later on.

> **Cross-Reference** To find out more about batch processing, see Chapter 17.

5. **Make a backup CD (if you haven't already).** Not only is it a good idea to make a backup CD of your original files early in the process, it's also a

good idea to make a backup CD at the end of the process. Ideally, you should make multiple backup copies of each shoot with the idea of having one set of backups at your home or studio (in case your hard drive dies) and a second set offsite (in case of fire or natural disaster). Implementing a workflow process that builds in a couple of CD burning sessions helps make sure you create multiple layers of safety in your archives. I usually create a CD for each shoot (because most of my shoots create enough images to fill one or more CDs). If your shoots don't produce enough files to justify burning a CD, create a subfolder marked Burn to CD (or something similar) and stage files there until you have enough images to fill a CD. Once you burn a CD, make sure you label it in such a way that facilitates finding it later.

 If you have a computer with a DVD burner, by all means, use it. I personally prefer to burn a CD after culling rejects, and later write files to a DVD-RAM disc for a second backup. I've also added a DVD-R/-RW drive to my computer so I can burn DVD-R discs for additional backup. If you're confused about DVD formats and want to wait a while before committing to one style, by all means, take your time. My opinion is that a combination of CDs, DVDs, and backup hard drives is the safest way to go, but the needs of a professional photographer and a hobbyist aren't quite the same. Hobbyists can make do with a pair of CD backups.

Phase II: Processing the images

Now that you've captured, reviewed, and backed up your images, they're ready to be processed in Photoshop. The following workflow tweaks your photos nicely. It's not the most complicated system in the world, and it's not designed to be. It's fast and simple, and you don't have to have a graphic arts degree to follow it.

To help you better understand the image processing workflow, I use one particular example photo throughout this section. This photo of a butterfly will do nicely. This image file (568752 fg1602, shown in Figure 16-2) is available for download from this book's companion web site (www.wiley.com/compbooks/simon). By working with this example image, you can follow the steps documented here on the same image that's represented in this book.

Follow these steps to begin processing the image:

1. Crop your files. Reducing file size as early in the workflow as possible makes image processing much easier, particularly if you're using an older or less powerful computer. If you plan to upress (increasing the image's resolution) an image you can always wait until after you've performed steps that can be done before increasing the image's resolution. Cropping first is a good idea, but it doesn't have to be a steadfast rule: You want to make other image-processing decisions based on information in the cropped image.

Figure 16-2: The example file to use for image correction.

© 2004 Dan Simon

2. **Rotate the image if necessary.** Sometimes it's necessary to correct an image whose composition is slightly off. You can easily do this with Photoshop's Measure tool, found on the tool palette grouped with the Eyedropper and Color Sampler tools. Click and hold on whichever tool is showing until a sub-menu of the three tools appears. Choose the one that looks like a ruler. Find a horizon line or baseline in the image that represents true horizontal. Place the Measure tool at one end of the horizon line, then click and drag until you reach the other end of the horizon line. Release the mouse button. Choose File ⇨ Image ⇨ Rotate Canvas ⇨ Arbitrary to enter the value discovered by the Measure tool. Click OK, and the image rotates appropriately. (You will probably have to re-crop at this point.) Select any other Photoshop tool to make the Measure tool's line disappear.

3. **Create a Levels Adjustment layer.** I'm a big fan of nondestructive editing techniques, so whenever I can, I prefer to choose such image processing methods. If you don't care, then just create a Levels Adjustment layer with the levels command (see Figure 16-3). I prefer to set white and black points as necessary through each of the red, green, and blue channels.

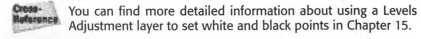 You can find more detailed information about using a Levels Adjustment layer to set white and black points in Chapter 15.

4. **Click on the small rectangle next to the Adjustment layer icon (the half black, half white circle) to activate the Adjustment layer's mask.** This mask allows you to decrease the effect of the Adjustment layer on certain parts of the image by blocking some of its effect. You do this by painting on the Adjustment layer mask as follows. Choose the Brush tool and then go to the Brush Options menu at the top of the screen. Select a soft edged brush and use black to burn in (darken) bright areas and white to lighten. Press and hold down the Option key (Mac) or the Alt key (PC) while you click on the line between the layer and the adjustment layer. This locks the adjustment layer to the original layer.

Figure 16-3: Use adjustment layers rather than applying adjustments directly to your image.
© *2004 Dan Simon*

5. Create a new layer. Set the Layer Blending mode to Color Dodge. Choose File ⇨ Edit ⇨ Fill, and select 50 percent gray from the drop-down box. Set Layer Opacity to about 10 percent. This will give the image some extra pop.

 For more information about creating new layers, turn to Chapter 15.

6. Check for dust spots or other imperfections you need to clean up. (See Chapter 15 for detailed information on handling dust spots.) This is also the time to consider manipulating your image (adding or removing elements, changing colors, re-positioning elements, and so on).

7. Add a warming or cooling filter if necessary. I'm happy with the colors of this image. If I wasn't, I could warm or cool the image by adding a digital color filter. Access the Photo Filter tool in Photoshop CS by choosing Image ⇨ Adjustments ⇨ Photo Filter (see Figure 16-4).

 See Chapter 15 to learn more about adding a digital color filter manually.

8. The graduated neutral density filter can be re-created in the digital darkroom. Choose the Gradient tool from the Tools palette and select a black to white gradient from the options menu at the top of the screen. Apply the gradient from top to bottom (click at the top of the image and

drag downward) if you want to reduce exposure to the top part of the scene, or from bottom to top (click on the bottom of the image and drag to the top) to reduce exposure to the bottom portion of the image. Set the blending mode to Overlay (on the Layers palette) and lower the layer's opacity until you get the effect you like. Remember, at reduced opacity you can paint on this layer with a black brush to further darken portions of the image, or you can paint with a white brush to lighten portions of the image. Keep in mind, a digitally generated graduated neutral density filter isn't as good as using a real one in the field. It can only help you if your image still has some detail in the highlight areas.

Figure 16-4: Photoshop offers a Photo Filter option that simulates the effects of warming or cooling filters.

© *2004 Dan Simon*

9. Choose File ➪ File Info to add your copyright information and to store other information about the image. This information stays with the image and can be read by any program that recognizes EXIF or IPTC information (most image browsers and image editing programs). Figure 16-5 shows Photoshop's File Info dialog box.

10. Haze burn sharpening. This technique is used to burn off the haze found in digital images. Choose File ➪ Filter ➪ Sharpen ➪ Unsharp Mask to select the original image layer and apply an unsharp mask. Set the amount to 16, the radius to 40, and the threshold to 0.

Go to Step 11 if you want to do high-pass sharpening. Or choose another sharpening method and then skip to Step 12.

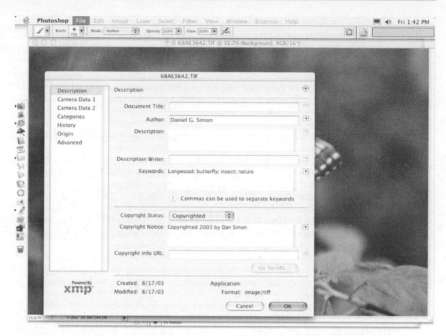

Figure 16-5: Adding information via Photoshop's File Info feature embeds information in your image file that can be read in other programs.
© 2004 Dan Simon

11. High-pass sharpening. This is a nondestructive sharpening method that provides very precise overall sharpening of your image. One of its biggest advantages is that so long as you save your image file in a format that supports layers (TIFF or PSD) you can come back later on and change the amount of sharpening you've applied to the image. It's also a good technique if you're making different versions of the image for web and print. You can adjust sharpening levels for each version very easily this way. If you're going to use high-pass sharpening, stay with this paragraph. If you decide to use another sharpening method, skip to Step 12.

It's usually best to sharpen after you size the image for final output. Because high-pass sharpening can be changed at any time, there's nothing wrong with setting your image up for this method and seeing how it works on screen. You can always change the settings later on to match your output requirements. Choose View ⇨ Actual Pixels to judge the effectiveness of your sharpening in the Actual Pixels view at the output size you plan to use. Say you plan to make an 8 x 10 print. Size the image accordingly, then set your view to Actual Pixels and apply your sharpening.

a. Create a duplicate of your original layer either by dragging the layer to the New Layer icon at the bottom of the layers palette or by choosing File ⇨ Layer ⇨ Duplicate Layer. Name the new layer high-pass.

b. Set the blending mode to hard light (you may also want to experiment with the soft light mode). Reduce the layer's opacity to about 50 percent by adjusting the Opacity setting on the layer's palette.

c. Choose File ➪ Filter ➪ Other ➪ High Pass to select the high pass filter. Look for a radius setting that seems to provide the best level of sharpening.

d. Adjust the Layer Opacity to increase or reduce the effect as desired.

e. You can reduce the amount of sharpening applied to select parts of the image by going to the Tools palette and selecting the Eraser tool. Go to the Options menu at the top of your screen and choose a Soft-edged brush and a low opacity (about 25%), and then start to erase parts of the high-pass layer to reduce the sharpening effect on those parts while leaving the areas you want as sharp as possible alone.

12. After setting up your image for high-pass sharpening, or if you prefer to use another sharpening method, create a working file. This means saving a version of the image with layers intact, so you can come back later on if you need to make changes. Although you can save this file as either a PSD (Photoshop) file or a TIFF file with layers intact, I think it's better to go with the PSD format. It's not so much that I think it's a better format, but simply as it makes life easier. If you only save flattened images as TIFF files, it will lessen any potential confusion when you try to find your working version.

 When saving multiple versions of an image, I find it helpful to employ a system of filenaming conventions. Your system can be as simple as appending a .w to indicate *working* or .f to indicate *finished* before the file appendage (.psd or .tif for instance). You can also add a .v1, .v2, or .v3 if you work with different versions of a file, but keep in mind, it can be difficult to remember what the differences among the different versions are without opening the images. (Keeping a log helps, but adds more work to the process.)

13. Archive your images again. Burn a second archive CD or make a master backup DVD.

Phase III: Printing

Now that you've done nearly all you can to a particular image, you should focus on final output, which frequently is for printing. The only work left is exact sharpening and resizing for output if necessary. Follow these steps to sharpen, resize, and print your image:

1. After you decide on print output, you need to sharpen and size the file accordingly. Keep in mind, the proportions of a 5 x 7 and an 8 x 10 are different. If you want to print one of each size, you need to crop your file twice to maintain control over the final print.

2. Choose Photoshop's Marquis tool from the Tools palette (it's the square box with the gaps in the lines). Select Fixed Aspect Ratio from the Styles drop-down menu bar and enter the appropriate values for the print size you want. Click and drag from the image's upper-left corner down to the bottom of the frame. The resulting Marquis shows the actual print area for the proportions you've chosen. Notice how it's less than the entire image area. You can reposition the marquis over the area of the image you want to print. Once the Marquis is where you want it, choose File ➪ Image ➪ Crop to crop the image. Repeat this process for each print size you want (8 x 10, 11 x 14, 3 x 5, and so on).

3. Select a high-enough image resolution. Generally, you can make good prints from a file as small as 180 pixels per inch, although higher resolution is better. (Some experts say 360ppi is ideal and 300ppi is close enough.) If you're using an online printer service or commercial printer, their specifications are the minimum you should use. Because commercial printing technology has improved considerably over the past few years (particularly in its ability to process digital files), good quality prints can be made from lower resolution files than in the past.

 Visit this book's companion web site at `www.wiley.com/compbooks/simon` for links to online printers.

If your file isn't a high-enough resolution for the size print you want, consider increasing your file size through one of the upressing methods discussed in Chapter 15.

4. If you're working with a home printer, aim for a file resolution closer to the 300ppi standard. (Don't confuse printer resolution with image resolution. Printer resolution refers to how many dots of ink per inch the printer lays down on the paper, not how many pixels per inch make up the image.) Generally your best results come from a printer setting of 720 dpi on photo-quality glossy paper. (Higher printer resolutions don't improve print quality enough to justify the extra cost in ink. Lower grade papers don't hold the ink well enough to make the savings worth it.) Keep in mind, prints need some time to dry completely (usually about 24 hours) and most are water-soluble, so don't get them wet. Standard home printer setups are not archival by the way. It's possible to see fading in as a little as a year.

 Printer makers have begun producing archival quality inks and papers, the best of which supposedly outlast prints made through conventional means. These products are tested in lab trials that simulate excruciatingly long passages of time (much like my college art history professor's lectures). If you go this route, make sure both inks and papers are of archival quality. You should also be sure you use an acid free mounting material when you display these photos.

5. If you're sizing images for use on the web or computer screen, your job's a bit easier. If you've already sharpened your image (and remember, if you're working with an image from a consumer grade digital camera, it's

done some sharpening for you), simply down sample the image using Photoshop's Bilinear Interpolation. Choose Image ⇨ Image Size. Make sure that the Resample Image box is checked and select Bilinear Interpolation instead of the Bicubic Interpolation it would normally be set to. Down sampling via Bilinear Interpolation holds the sharpening effect better than Bicubic Interpolation.

 Don't bother with Photoshop's save for web option. You get perfectly acceptable results just by saving normally. Keep in mind, smaller file sizes work better on the web, so try to keep both the image size and its file size manageable. I usually work with images that are roughly 640 × 480 in size and pick a JPEG compression around 5 for images I post on the web.

Differences between Raw and JPEG workflow

Many of the steps involved in processing a Raw file are the same as when you're processing a JPEG file. This section looks at the differences.

Phase I: Capturing and reviewing the images

Follow these steps to capture and review your Raw files:

1. Capture your images as you would in the JPEG workflow.
2. Review your images as you would in the JPEG workflow (see Figure 16-6).
3. Cull rejects as you would in the JPEG workflow.
4. Rename your files (maybe). Same as in JPEG workflow.

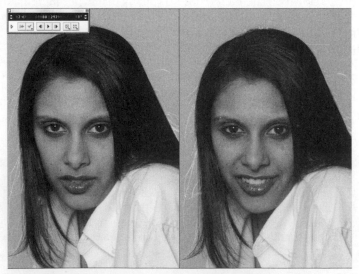

Figure 16-6: An image browser that gives you full screen previews makes it easier to examine your shots.

© 2004 Dan Simon

5. Make a backup CD as you would in the JPEG workflow.

6. Convert your images. This step is specific to the Raw workflow. Once you've picked the files you want to process, it's necessary to convert them from Raw format to a format your image editing program can work with, usually TIFF files (see Figure 16-7).

Figure 16-7: Converting a Raw file using Photoshop's Raw converter plug-in.
© 2004 Dan Simon

Usually you're presented with several choices during the conversion process depending on your camera. Some cameras, such as the EOS 1D, can create both a Raw and JPEG image for each photo, so you'll have the option of converting your Raw file to TIF format while simultaneously extracting a JPEG image. The most important choice you usually have to make, however, is whether you want your image converted as an 8-bit or 16-bit TIF file.

Since it's no more trouble to convert a Raw image to a 16-bit file than to convert it to an 8-bit file, most photographers prefer to convert the photo as a 16-bit image, at least for the first few steps of the image correction process.

 Normally, digital images are created in 8-bit color depth, which provides a total of 256 colors (as in the 256 levels made up in the histogram). Digital camera sensors are capable of recording 12-bit color data for a total of 4,096 colors. These files are brought into the computer as 16-bit files even though they only contain 12-bit depth information. If you choose to convert your image as an 8-bit file, then the extra color information is thrown away.

Phase II: Processing the images

At this point your images are ready to be processed. Raw processing does involve some extra steps over the JPEG workflow, but for the most part, it's still pretty manageable.

Slowdowns occur during the conversion process simply because it takes a fair amount of computer power to convert the file. If you're only converting one image at a time, the wait is a minor annoyance. If you have a lot of images to process, then you might plan a conversion session around a trip to the store or while having a meal.

The big advantage of working with Raw files comes when you need to salvage an image that isn't quite exposed properly. If you routinely nail your exposures, capture good tonal ranges, and manage to keep contrast levels within the capabilities of the digital imaging sensor, or if you're a studio photographer who can exert precise control over environmental conditions, then Raw format may not offer you much advantage.

On the other hand, if you frequently work under difficult lighting conditions, shoot on the fly and sometimes make mistakes in exposure, choosing Raw format can be the difference between a useable image and wasted hard drive space.

I usually set my camera up to record both a Raw file and a highest resolution JPEG file simultaneously when I'm shooting. The idea is that if everything goes properly, I just process the JPEGs and call it a day. If I have an image that needs more help, then I can convert that particular Raw file and do my best to save it.

Perhaps the biggest advantage of working in Raw format is that you can tweak exposure after you create an image and get a lot of benefit from having this capability.

For example, say you made an image during high-contrast lighting conditions. You could expose for the highlights, creating an image with underexposed shadow areas. When you get back home, you can convert the image normally once and then go back and convert it again; but this time, adjust the exposure to benefit the shadow areas. At this point, you can merge the two files together, using the highlight detail from one file and the shadow detail from the other. (A step-by-step explanation of this process can be found on this book's companion web site at www.wiley.com/compbooks/simon.)

The first phase of your editing process begins with your image in 16-bit mode. Depending on which version of Photoshop you're using, only certain edit functions will work on 16-bit files. The latest version, Photoshop CS, provides more editing tools that Photoshop 7, and Photoshop 6 offers just a couple. Fortunately the really important ones for exposure correction work in the last three versions.

Follow these steps to process your Raw files:

1. Crop your images as you would in the JPEG workflow.

2. Rotate your images (if necessary) as you would in the JPEG workflow.

3. Adjust levels as you would in the JPEG workflow.

   Photoshop CS allows you to perform many of the basic workflow steps while still in 16-bit mode, so you can keep to the methods described in the JPEG workflow. If you're using an earlier version of the Photoshop, you may have to convert to an 8-bit file a bit earlier.

   Here's a special technique if you want to work on specific parts of an image instead of applying global corrections. Choose File ⇨ Image ⇨ Duplicate to create a duplicate of your image. Convert the duplicate image into an 8-bit file by choosing File ⇨ Image ⇨ Mode ⇨ 8bits/channel.

   Now you can create a selection to work on the part of the image that needs tweaking. Save your selection (choose File ⇨ Select ⇨ Save Selection) with a specific enough name to make it obvious what file it applies to. Create any additional selections you might need and name and save them accordingly. Now return to your original (16-bit) file and choose File ⇨ Select ⇨ Load Selections to load the selections you need. You can then apply levels, curves, and other tools just to the selected areas. Even though this workaround becomes less and less necessary in each subsequent version of Photoshop, it's still helpful to realize how this trick works.

4. Some Photoshop plug-ins such as Dfine and those by The Imaging Factory work in 16-bit mode. If you're using one of these as part of your normal workflow, go ahead and apply them at this point.

5. Choose File ⇨ Image ⇨ Mode ⇨ 8bits/channel to convert your image to an 8-bit file. The process from now on is the same as if you were following the JPEG workflow.

Summary

Workflow is all about creating a logical, efficient set of procedures for processing your digital images. The best workflow for you is the one that brings out the best quality in your digital images. It's even better if that workflow can be standardized so you can repeat it over and over and over.

Whenever possible, try to make changes reversible. Improvements in editing software and printing technology make all sorts of things possible. Five years from now, that image that was only good for small prints may suddenly be good for huge enlargements. Or that photo that had too much sensor noise to be worth printing could be salvaged by new methods of reducing noise. You may need to return to the original file, or tweak edits on your working file to incorporate these advances. If all you have is an edited JPEG file, then you've lost the chance to return to your purest form of data.

Image Management and Archiving

My aunt moved from her apartment to a nursing home about a year ago. In the process of handling her possessions, we came upon a box filled with the photographs she'd kept over the years.

Talk about a treasure trove! There were wonderful images of my mother on her very first job as a waitress at the local diner, pictures from her wedding and other everyday shots that get created over the years. There were even photos of my brothers and I, including one horribly embarrassing picture of myself taken just before I left for my high school prom. There I was: baby-faced, complete with wild curly hair and crushed blue velvet rental tux. My current spouse (who didn't meet me until about 15 years later) delights in teasing me about this picture (which, thankfully, due to U.S. copyright law, can't be reproduced here).

This stash of pictures was particularly important because many of my parents' photographs were destroyed when their house burned down decades ago. As wonderful as it was to stumble on this archive, however, it would have been better if we had also discovered some information that would put the images (besides my prom photo, of course) into context. Instead, we had to rely on vague memories about images made 60 years ago. Professional photographers have always known the importance of maintaining records to accompany their images, but amateurs haven't always been so disciplined. Now, however, technological innovation is changing that.

This chapter looks at two of the issues just raised. The first is how to manage your images so that you can find them when you need to, including ways to attach information that will stay with the image file. The second issue is archiving your images so that they'll still be around in 50 or 60 years. Remember the bit about my family losing many of their pictures due to a house fire? Digital imagery is well-positioned to head off that particular risk because you can make perfect backup copies of your photos.

Managing Your Images

Digital cameras are great. Because you don't pay anything for film or processing, you can just shoot up a storm and take as many pictures as you want. No muss, no fuss, no problem.

Then one day someone asks you for a copy of a picture you took of her daughter last year while she was playing with your kids. That's when you discover that you have no idea how to find one particular photo in your collection of thousands of images.

The answer to the problem of finding a particular photo in your collection is to set up a file storage and retrieval system—ideally before you find yourself in the predicament I just described. Then, if you follow an established routine for each new batch of images you make, and if you've set things up properly, a year from now you can easily find just the photo you're looking for.

Before digital imagery became established, the conventional photographic community relied on a wide assortment of slide/negative storage and cataloging systems that ranged from shoeboxes filled with negatives to elaborate archival quality storage boxes. Dedicated photographers maintained detailed index card or file logs of their images, creating numbering systems to track and locate images within those big file cabinets of photos.

Those of us who have embraced digital photography have been spared the worst of those storage and management systems, but we're not free of the need to develop a system for safely archiving our images and finding particular images when we need them. As usual, digital photography offers some advantages and some disadvantages when compared to conventional means.

This section looks at how to develop an image management system—labeling your images so that you can find them again.

The alphabet comes to the rescue

I start this section with image management under the theory that you need to create an identity for your image before you archive it. A file management system must be built to work over long periods of time, so it's important to record important information early in the process.

It used to be a photographer had to keep a notepad to record shooting information for each roll of film she used. After her images were processed, she had to scribble data on the slide mount, the back of the photo, or on a companion index card. That way, she could pull out an image years later and know when it was made, what shot settings were used, and what ISO and type of film was used. As you see in the following section, digital photographers can skip this entire hassle.

EXIF—Leave the note taking to your camera

Your digital camera takes care of recording basic information about each shot under the heading of EXIF (Extended File Information) data. The industry standard designates what information each camera should record and how it's coded (see Figure 17-1) so that your photo editing program can retrieve the data when you review the image on your home computer.

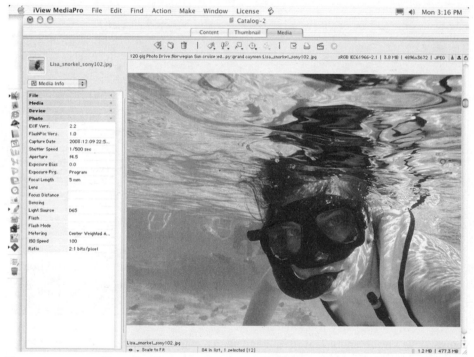

Figure 17-1: EXIF files provide a record of shooting information.
© 2004 Dan Simon

How nice to be able to tell the exact details of a particular shot! In this example, you can see that I took the photo on December 9, 2003 at 22:50 (EST) at a shutter speed of 1/500th of a second with an aperture of f4.5.

Of course, this is mostly pretty generic information. The camera has no way of knowing that you were photographing your daughter and her boyfriend leaving on their first date or your son's little league home run swing. The good news is that you can add that information thanks to the set of letters I introduce in the following section: IPTC.

IPTC—The tool the pros use

IPTC (International Press Telecommunications Council) data is the information that you can add to your image files for the sake of providing caption material. It includes stuff such as the photographer's copyright, whether a model release is available, where the picture was made, and who's in it. There's even a field for a suggested caption.

Most importantly, the IPTC data provides a place for you to enter keywords that describe the shot. Keywords, as shown down the left side in Figure 17-2, are identification tags that help categorize your images and make it easier to retrieve them later on.

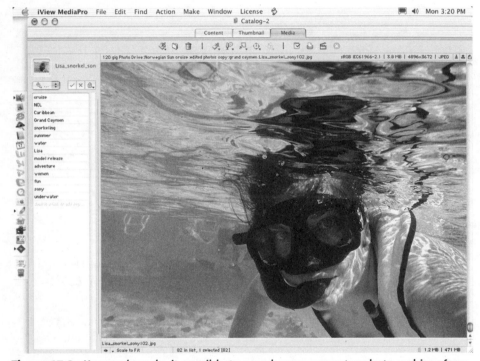

Figure 17-2: Keywords make it possible to search your computer photo archives for a particular category of images.
© 2004 Dan Simon

If you get into the habit of entering IPTC information every time you process an image, you create powerful database capabilities that make it easier to find images years after they've been made.

A few words about keywords

Your photo management task gets easier when you realize you have some powerful tools available to help you. Keywords, for example, can be extremely useful. Your photo editing software should let you enter relevant keywords through a dialog box that pops up (Figure 17-3 shows the box that opens for me

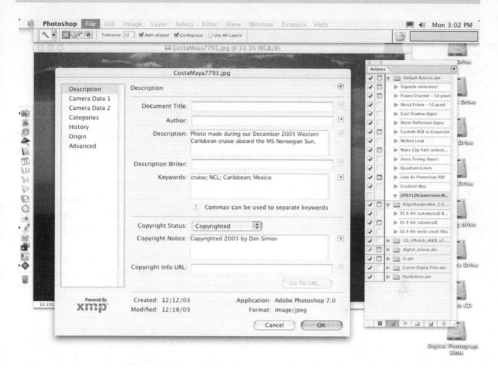

Figure 17-3: Photoshop's File Info tool provides a place to enter lots of information about an image.

© 2004 Dan Simon

in Photoshop). After you embed the appropriate words into the image file, you can create an image catalog by using a program such as iView, Extensis Portfolio, ACDsee, or any of the other excellent image cataloging programs on the market. Any one of these programs should be able to read your keywords.

The beauty of using keywords is that if you do it consistently, you can maintain a catalog of every image you have on file. For example, when I need to find pictures of Gina, a model I work with frequently, I just do a keyword search for her name. If I am trying to find a picture that I shot of her last summer in a bikini, I search for the keywords *Gina* and *bikini* and a collection of images appears. I can narrow it down even further by adding additional keywords, such as *yellow* for the color of a particular bikini and *flower* for a particular set of images in which she was posing in a yellow bikini with a flower in her hair.

As you can see, a keyword cataloging system offers a great way to locate particular images—even long after you took them and filed them away. So how could you have cataloged the photo in the example I mentioned at the start of this chapter—the photo you took of a neighbor's child playing with your child? A simple technique would be to embed the neighbor kid's name as a keyword for any image in which she appears.

Another advantage to a good keywording system is that you can use it to separate edited from unprocessed images. Just add the appropriate keyword to an image (*print*, *web*, 5 x 7, 8 x 10) and you can then refine your searches even further! I add the keyword *portfolio* to my best shots. That way, I can call up a portfolio catalog whenever I want. Even better, by combining key words, I can create a portfolio of a specific category of photos, such as sports, nature, or landscapes, to name a few.

It's a good idea to create a master list of key words in order to keep things from becoming unwieldy. Aim for one-word or hyphenated words that are reasonably short, and look for combinations of keywords to narrow down images rather than trying to come up with the perfect specific keyword or keyword sentence.

Typical key words can include: nature, sports, baseball, swimsuit, home, family, kids, yellow, summer, and school. Assigning more than one key word to an image makes it easier to run precision searches, such as the ones I can run to find specific photos of my model, Gina, that I described a few paragraphs ago.

I prefer to do my keywording in Photoshop, so that the keywords are actually embedded in the image file. Although you can attach keywords through your image browser, these won't necessarily stay with your image from catalog to catalog or if you switch browsers at some point in the future.

If you rely on your image browser to manage your photos, your best bet is to be very disciplined and thorough in maintaining a master images catalog. If you're the type that maintains one folder for print images and another for web images, this system doesn't work very well because the keywords stay with the original catalog. Say you place an image in your master catalog, and then make up a copy of it to print at a certain size. If you create a new catalog of images in your print folder, these won't have the keywords embedded in them the way they would have if you'd done it in PhotoShop instead of in the cataloging software.

Be careful not to move images to a new file or rename them after you've cataloged them (unless you rename them through the cataloging software). If you do, the image browser loses track of them and won't be able to create full screen previews of the image.

Project: Setting up a photo drive and master catalog

This project assumes that you have some form of image management software. This may be the software that came with your camera or it can be a program such as iView, Breezebrowser, ACDsee or one of the many other image cataloging programs on the market (many of which offer free trial versions you can download from the maker's web sites). Organizing your image files and setting up a proper master catalog takes a little planning. Often, if you move images after you've cataloged them, the image browser loses track of the file and can no longer create preview images.

Unfortunately, some of the steps in this project won't work if you're using Photoshop Elements because it doesn't offer the sophisticated automation tools found in its big brother, Photoshop. If you are using Elements, you have to do your keywording through your image browser.

The following steps show you how to set things up to avoid losing track of your images.

1. Set up either an empty hard drive (for heavy shooters) or a hard drive partition (for moderate shooters) just for images. If this isn't practical, or if you're a light shooter, set aside a folder for pictures.

2. Create a folder named Raw or Unedited. Here's where you'll dump all your original images, each within its own subfolder. I usually create a subfolder for each month (*01.04 images*) and nest subfolders for individual shoots inside the appropriate month's folder. I also create a subfolder for monthly catalogs for each shoot. If you open folder *01.04 images*, for example, you'll find a folder for each shoot I did in January 2004, plus the catalogs folder. Inside the catalogs folder, you'll find a catalog for each shoot for that month.

3. Use the image browser software to rename each photo according to a predetermined naming system. I use a system like this: four-digit year, two-digit month, two-digit day, short name, four-digit sequential number. The resulting name for an image named using this system is *20040112NewHope4386.tif*. From this file name, I can tell that this shot was made in New Hope, PA. I shot it on January 12, 2004, and it was the 4,386th shot I'd taken because my camera's numbering system reset (the EOS 1D resets after every 10,000 images). This system works well for me, but you may be able to create a simpler system that does the job for you.

   By setting up a catalog with various subfolders, I can preview and edit down the shoot directly within the catalog. This way I can evaluate images and cull out rejects. Generally, this leaves me with two types of photos, ones I immediately want to process and ones I don't think are worth processing, but don't want to delete either. I use the image browser to create two subfolders within the folder for a particular shoot and move images into the appropriate folder. The first is the Keepers folder for images I want to process (see Figure 17-4). The second is the Rough folder for images I'm not throwing away. I shoot a lot of images at a normal assignment, and I routinely vary the angle and direction of an image. Consequently, I may have the same photo composed half a dozen different ways. Sometime in the future, I may need to use one of those rough shots because of the direction or composition. I don't want to throw these images away, but I'm also not going to waste time processing them until I actually need one of these images. If you're dealing with a modest number of images, one folder will probably work just fine.

4. Open your photo editing software, such as Photoshop.

5. Open each image file, add basic caption information, and insert the proper keywords.

6. Save and close each image.

 You can automate much of this process by using the photo editing program's batch-processing capabilities. The next project provides a step-by-step description of how to set up batch processing in Photoshop.

Figure 17-4: An image browser such as iView, ACDsee, or Extensis Portfolio can help you keep your photos organized.
© 2004 Dan Simon

7. Process the images you've selected as keepers. If your final image is a .psd file with layers intact and processed using nondestructive editing methods, you can just resave to the Keepers folder and add the keyword *processed* to the image. If you're using destructive editing methods or saving flattened images, consider creating a Processed Images folder so as not to overwrite your original files.

 For a refresher on image processing, see Chapter 14. To find out more about destructive and nondestructive editing techniques and layers, see Chapter 15.

8. Create a master images catalog as part of your highest folder or drive. If you haven't already created one, then make a new file, name it "Master Images Catalog" and then use it to catalog your existing files. Save this file at your highest level (folder or drive partition or drive) and use it from now on as your master images catalog. Use this catalog for processed images only. Add the images you've just processed to this catalog.

All of this may seem like a lot of work (and it is.) Fortunately, Photoshop offers some powerful tools to make your workload lighter. Adobe has incorporated several functions in this program to handle repetitive tasks so you don't have to. These functions include *actions* (a scripting language you can use to automate tasks in the program) and a batch processing feature you can use to make automated image processing even easier.

Simplifying routine tasks using actions and batch processing

Photoshop's powerful automation features can save you a lot of time and effort.

Normally, when I work with the images from a shoot, I create a basic Photoshop action that attaches my copyright information and adds a basic caption and some keywords to each image file. As I mentioned in Chapter 15, you can think of a Photoshop action as a scripted mini-program—a set of specific steps that you can record and have Photoshop play back automatically at any time. Actions can save you tons of time and effort by automating particularly tedious and repetitive tasks.

After establishing the action that adds the copyright, caption, and keyword information to a file, I set up Photoshop's batch-processing function to handle the processing of an entire group of files without my intervention. This function opens each file, runs the action I created to insert the various pieces of information, saves the file, and closes the file.

The following two projects walk you first through creating a Photoshop action and then through running batch processing.

Project: Setting up a Photoshop action

Follow these steps to create an action in Photoshop:

1. In Photoshop, open an image by choosing File ➪ Open and then browsing to where your image is stored. (You must have an image open before starting the action writing process.)

2. Examine the Actions palette. Usually, there is a single folder marked Default Actions, which contains the actions that Adobe includes with the program. You can store sets of actions in particular folders, and you can create your own folders and name them accordingly. If you don't want to include this particular action in the Default Actions folder, click on the right pointing arrow in the upper right of the Photoshop's Actions palette, scroll down the menu, and choose New Action (see Figure 17-5) or New Set if you want to create a new folder. Give the action an appropriate name, such as 2003012N.Suncruise.Mexi. At this point your action is recording everything you do in Photoshop.

3. Choose File ➪ Info.

4. Type the appropriate information. It's up to you how detailed you want to be. I usually include copyright info, such as *Copyright © 2004 by Dan Simon*, and some basic caption material that works for all the images I'm keywording. I can always go back to a particular image later if I want to create a specific caption for it. I also often need to note that a model release is available for a certain image, so I include that information somewhere in the file info (usually in one of the boxes I don't use).

Figure 17-5: Photoshop actions are a great tool for automating repeatable tasks.

© 2004 Dan Simon

5. In Photoshop CS, the Keywords box is on the same screen as the copyright box. If you're using Photoshop 7, go to the drop-down menu at the top of the dialog and choose Keywords. Add as many appropriate keywords as you can. (Remember, you're applying these keywords to every image in a particular folder. If your shoot contains images from different categories, or you used more than one model, create different folders for each model or category. You can then tweak the action accordingly.) The File Info dialog box has dialogs for other entries such as the image's title, name of the author, name of the caption writer, the job name and owner's url. Other screens also offer more ways you can embed information into a file. You can make as much or as little use of this feature as you like and nothing says you have to use the data boxes for what they're labeled for.

6. After you enter all desired data, click OK.

7. Save and close the file.

8. Click the Stop Recording button on the bottom of the Actions palette. (It's the little rectangle—the first button from the left.)

After creating the action that inserts the copyright, caption, and keyword information, you could simply open each of your images and run the action one photo at a time. There are a couple of easier ways to do this job, however.

If this particular task was something you were going to return to repeatedly, you could create a droplet. *Droplets* are mini-programs that you can use whenever you have a folder of images to process. Instead of running an action for each image, droplets allow you to drop a folder of images onto the droplet icon and it launches Photoshop and runs the action for each image, processing them all until the work is done. You create a droplet in Photoshop by choosing File ➪ Automate ➪ Create Droplet.

Because the text being inserted by the action you just created won't be applicable to photos from other shoots, you won't be reusing this particular action. So in the following project, I show you how to use batch processing instead of creating a droplet.

 Project: **Creating a batch processing action**

Follow these steps to run batch processing on your images:

1. Choose File ➪ Automate ➪ Batch to launch the Batch dialog box (see Figure 17-6). At the top of the dialog are two drop-down boxes. The Set box is where you choose the set of actions your action is part of (usually this will be Default Actions, but if it isn't, click on the drop-down arrow and choose the appropriate actions folder). The Action box designates the specific action you want to run. If your action isn't already showing, click the drop-down arrow to find the action you just created.

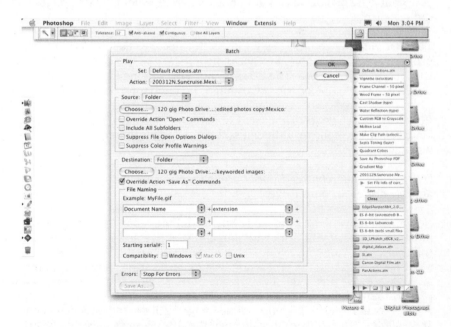

Figure 17-6: Photoshop's batch processing feature can save you a lot of work.

© 2004 Dan Simon

2. In the next section of the dialog box, click the Source drop-down arrow and select Folder from the list. Click the Choose button and navigate to the folder that contains the images you want to process.

3. In the next section, click the Destination drop-down arrow and select Folder from the list. Click the Choose button and navigate to the folder you want the images saved to. (You can use the same folder or a different one.)

4. Make sure that the Override Action "Save As" Commands box is checked.

5. Click OK and Photoshop runs the action.

6. Go have a cup of coffee and complain about how much work digital photography is while Photoshop works on your images for you.

Now that you've got your master images keyworded, organized, and cataloged, it's time to think about your archiving plan.

Making Sure Your Images Last

File longevity is a classic good news/bad news issue when it comes to digital images. The good news is that you can make perfect duplicates of any image file you want. The bad news is that nobody's sure how long those images will last on today's media.

The CDs you buy commercially will last for decades as long as you give them the proper care. For example, no CD can be left exposed to direct sunlight very long without being damaged. The CDs you burn on a home CD burner aren't quite as durable. If you're lucky, those CDs might be good for a decade or so.

That's right. Ten years. That's less time than it takes for junior to get from kindergarten to college, although still much longer than the average Hollywood marriage.

DVDs aren't much better. Neither are magnetic backup tapes, floppy disks, Zip and Jaz drives, or hard drives.

Now before anyone hits the panic button, let me remind you of the reality of most hobbyists. If you work with film and practice archival storage methods (neither cheap nor easy) your slides and negatives should last about 75 years. Most people (except for professionals and very serious amateurs) don't practice archival storage methods. If you're one of those who sticks your prints in a photo album and then tosses the negatives (still in their original envelope) into a shoebox in the closet, your original images will degrade over the course of your lifetime. (Possibly quite quickly if the place you store them is fairly humid.)

Indeed, I doubt most folks have ever gotten a print made from a negative they shot a decade or more ago. (These days, many people do scan old prints and get new prints made from the scans, however.) Instead, most people just pull out their old photo album and view the prints they had made when they originally took the photos.

If you're handling your digital images the same way you did your film ones—by getting photographic quality prints made—then your approach doesn't have to change all that much. You still have your prints (which if cared for properly can last decades or longer), and, if you plan properly, you can still have digital backups from which you can make additional prints years from now.

The trick is to understand and take advantage of digital imaging's strength—the capability to make perfect copies of files cheaply and easily. It means making multiple backups of each file, if possible on different types of media, with the realization that when new types of storage come out, you'll copy your files to that new media, too.

Let's face it, although the 10-year life span of home-burned CDs sounds brief, we haven't managed to go 10 years yet with a dominant form of removable storage. We've gone from floppies to Zip disks to CD-ROM and are now working with DVDs. Who knows what we'll be using for storage a decade from now?

I would suggest planning to copy your important files (not just photos either) to new media every time you add another form of storage technology to your system. This adds another layer of backup to your archives and because each storage format increases the amount of storage capability, it means you're using less media to store more files.

I also suggest getting photographic quality prints for those really important images. That way, you have a high-quality paper file as yet another form of backup.

A realistic look at some archiving methods

Your archiving approach is determined by such considerations as number of images you create, equipment you have available, and the money and space you're willing to commit to your archives.

The average hobbyist shoots a reasonable number of photos over the course of a year. The average pro makes considerably more. The following sections provide examples of archiving plans for light, moderate, and heavy shooters with some observations on the strengths and weaknesses of various media as appropriate.

Archiving plan for light shooters (1–200 pictures a year)

One reason for an archiving system is to provide backup for your files in case your computer becomes incapacitated (crash, hard drive failure, virus, and so on) or disaster strikes your home (fire, flood, visiting children). Setting up an archiving plan for such modest use can be a challenge, because burning a CD for just a few images at a time seems pretty wasteful. Still, when you consider how cheap CD media is these days, the peace of mind is probably worth the minimal expense.

For the light user, I suggest the following archiving plan:

1. Create a folder named Burn to CD and place an alias (Mac) or a shortcut (Windows) to your original files. When you have enough files to justify burning a CD, burn one, or copy your files elsewhere, as described in Step 2.

    If you follow the workflow process described in the previous chapter, it should be worthwhile to burn a combined CD of original and edited files. Although these files might fill only one fifth of a CD, it's still worth it for backup's sake.

2. Save a backup copy of each file to a Zip drive, CDRW (rewriteable CD), or multi-session CD. I can't stress how important it is to have at least one (and preferably more) copy of your images at an off computer location. Don't be too cost-conscious. It's worth wasting 90 percent of a blank CD you bought for $1.00 in order to protect images you want to preserve for a lifetime.

3. If you have a second hard drive (preferably an external one) save a backup copy of your files to the second drive. Or, if you have any type of rewriteable DVD recorder, add your latest crop of images to that.

4. Consider joining a web-imaging center, such as Sony's Image Station or Snapfish. These free services allow you to store photos online (ostensibly to order prints or other products). Print prices from such services can be pretty reasonable, and you can always download your stored photos later on if you need to.

   Although your storage space may be limited, if you use such a service for temporary backup until you have enough images to fill a CD, this shouldn't be too much of a hassle. (I use both Image Station and Snapfish because I like the idea of their photo books and have plenty of files stored onsite.) Just make sure you find out how long you can leave images there. Some sites only allow files to remain on site for a few months.

   Internet file storage isn't a bad idea for the casual photographer, so long as it isn't the only method of backup you use. (I've seen quite a few online storage sites disappear over the years, so never let it be your only backup.) It does offer a nice way of keeping a set of your images safely offsite. Keep in mind, however, that you usually have to work with .jpg files for these sites, so you can't keep your working files backed up this way. Use the highest quality JPEG setting you can even though this will increase your file size. Obviously, this plan works better if you have a broadband connection to the Internet. Still, if you're only working with a few images at a time, even a dial-up connection can do the job.

5. Keep a log of where your images are and how they're archived. This doesn't have to be anything fancy. You can either use a spreadsheet program, word processing document, PDA desktop software, or even keep an actual paper file.

Archiving plan for medium shooters (200–1,000 pictures a year)

For the medium user I suggest the following archiving plan:

1. Burn a pair of CDs for each shoot. You can include a set of original files and your working files, or just your working files (which contain the original data in the bottom most layer). One CD should be stored offsite if possible. (Many relatives keep backups for each other at their homes.)

2. If you have a second hard drive (preferably an external one) save a backup copy of your files to the second drive. Or, if you have any type of re-writeable DVD recorder, add your latest crop of images to that. (This can be instead of the second CD mentioned above or in addition to it, if you really want to be safe. Or, you can substitute break DVDs for CDs.)

3. Consider joining a web-imaging center such as Sony's Image Station or Snapfish. These free services allow you to store photos online (ostensibly to order prints or other products). Print prices from such services can be pretty reasonable, and you can always download your stored photos later on if you need to. It may not be practical for even the medium level photographer to try to store a copy of every image to one of these sites, but it will likely be okay to save your most important files. Remember to check on how long your files can stay on the site.

   Internet file storage isn't a bad idea for the casual photographer, so long as it isn't the only method of backup you use. (I've seen quite a few online storage sites disappear over the years, so never let it be your only backup.) It does offer a nice way of keeping a set of your images safely offsite. Keep in mind, however, that you usually have to work with .jpg files for these sites, so you can't keep your working file backed up this way. Use the highest quality JPEG setting you can, even though this will increase your file size. Obviously, this plan works better if you have a broadband connection to the Internet. Still, if you're only working with a few images at a time, even a dial-up connection can do the job.

4. Keep a log of where your images are and how they're archived. This doesn't have to be anything fancy. You can either use a spreadsheet program, word processing document, PDA desktop software, or even keep an actual paper file.

Archiving plan for heavy shooters (1,000–plus pictures a year)

If you create lots and lots of images and need a way to store them, here's the archiving plan I suggest:

1. Make an immediate backup CD(s) for each shoot.

2. Maintain a monthly backup DVD-RAM (or other form of DVD media that allows multi-session writing). Do this until the DVD is full; then start a new one.

3. Make a backup DVD. This is a second backup for offsite archiving.

4. Back up each month's folder to a separate external hard drive.

5. Consider maintaining a master images folder for your best work. These are processed images in .psd or .tif format, so they are rather large files. You should back this folder up monthly to CD and DVD-RAM.

You should also consider whether the following additional steps make sense for your needs:

6. Burn a CD (or two) of each shoot immediately after capture.

7. Make a second backup to either another hard drive, CD-ROM or DVD.

8. Consider getting a safety deposit box at your local bank and storing copies of your CDs/DVDs or backup hard drives there. It's not a bad idea to pick a bank some distance from your home either. This can help minimize the hazards from a local, or even regional, natural disaster.

9. Keep a log of where your images are and how they're archived. This doesn't have to be anything fancy. You can either use a spreadsheet program, word processing document, PDA desktop software or even keep an actual paper notebook.

Although I use Image Station and Snapfish for specific projects or to get prints made, I don't use these sites for actual image storage. The main reason for this is I simply produce too many images to make it practical. It's also harder to guarantee copyright protection of an image once it's been posted to the web. You can limit access to an online photo album via password protection, but the best safety is in not even posting a high-resolution file to the web.

A word about physical storage

Once you've burned those CDs and DVDs, you need to organize them and then put them somewhere.

You can use a home labeling system designed to make nice looking labels for CDs and DVDs or you can just simply write the date and shoot name on the disk with a permanent marker. If you go the marker route, make sure you use one designed for digital media. (Many permanent markers use chemicals that can eat through the surface of the CD or DVD and damage the data underneath, so don't use just any old marker for your archival disks.)

The other thing to be concerned about is storing your archives properly. CD and DVD media are light-sensitive, so be sure to store them somewhere out of direct sunlight.

Your archive log should have enough information to help you track an image to the proper archive disk. You can also enter the information into your master images catalog file. This way when you find an image in your catalog, you can find its archive CD or DVD. (Do I need to say it? Make a backup of your master image catalog regularly; say about once a month.)

Summary

As your image collections grow and grow and grow, keeping track of your files becomes more and more of a challenge. It's much easier to maintain an image management and archival system once you've gotten it started than it is to create one after you've accumulated thousands of images.

Once you have such a system up and running, you'll have all your favorite images at your fingertips. A few strokes of the keyboard and you'll be able to find every image you've ever made of a certain subject.

Imagine being able to find all the photos you've made of your children over the years. Now go a step further and think about being able to find all the pictures of a specific family member, maybe doing a specific thing. It only takes a little bit of work each time you capture images to have that kind of system working for you.

Photography for Professionals in Other Fields

✦ ✦ ✦ ✦

✦ ✦ ✦ ✦

Photography is a profession for some and a passion for others. But there's a third category of practitioner that falls somewhat outside these two.

This third category is the working professional—the person sometimes called upon to take photos as part of his or her job.

If you fall into this category, you know the frustrations and challenges you face. You may not have any photographic training, and you are often expected to work with little more than the most basic equipment. Yet, you are still expected to produce useable images. The chapters in this part can help you through some of the rough spots you may encounter.

Getting It Together: Help for the Occasional Photographer

For many people, photography is either a job or a passion, but for an even larger group, taking pictures is a small but necessary part of their jobs.

If you're part of this latter group—and if you're reading this chapter, it's likely you are—you're probably interested in improving your photography without having to make a big project out of it.

This chapter doesn't help you create works of art, but instead shows you how to quickly improve the specific types of photographs you need to take.

The key feature of this section are the checklists intended to help you prepare for shoots. Photographers who shoot every day develop habits and preferred camera bag arrangements that ensure they're ready for every assignment (or at least the ability and gear to quickly redesign a setup for a particular shoot). The following sections can help photographers who shoot on a more limited basis utilize some tricks of the trade.

Unique Challenges of the Occasional Photographer

Those who aren't out taking photos nearly every day shoot under different circumstances than professional or avid amateur photographers. If you fall into this category, you may go days, weeks, even months, between shoots. Even worse, many work environments share common camera gear, so you may not be the only one using the equipment. These unique circumstances can lead to all sorts of potential problems that can ruin your day if you're not prepared to tackle them as they arise.

Perhaps the biggest problem that occasional photographers face is lack of training. Depending on your subject, you may not have the specific skills to capture a good image. For example, you may lack the knowledge of macro photography you need to properly shoot a coin or a piece of jewelry. Occasional photographers also face the obstacle of unclear objectives. Often, they're just handed a camera and told that any shot will do.

To help you make the most of your photographic shoot, this chapter presents a number of checklists. The first is a basic list of equipment so that you get to the site with everything you need. As you continue to work through Part V of this book, notice that each remaining chapter contains a similar basic checklist geared toward the specific photographic needs of the professionals discussed in that chapter. Those checklists are similar to the list provided here but also include specific requirements for a particular field or business.

In addition to the basic equipment list, I also provide checklists that you can refer to before the shoot, during the shoot, after the shoot, and when you have camera problems. Keep in mind that you can combine or tailor any of these checklists to your specific needs and shooting circumstances. The important thing is to develop a reliable and workable system that minimizes the risk of forgetting something important.

To make things easier for you, these checklists are available for download at this book's companion web site (`www.wiley.com/compbooks/simon`) as PDF files (fancier looking) or Microsoft Word files (so that you can open them, edit them, and tailor them to your specific needs). Whereas the checklists in this chapter are very detailed and include supporting information on why each item is important, the versions available to download are much more concise. They offer the bulleted items without the extra material. After you download the checklists, you can edit them as necessary, print them, and store them with your camera bag. Going over the list before going on a shoot helps ensure that you don't miss the obvious, such as dead batteries and no spares, or a camera that's missing its memory card.

Basic Equipment Checklist

Before any shoot, you need to make sure that your camera's basic components are in working order and that you have all the necessary accessories. You should check the following:

Remember that this checklist and those found throughout Part V of this book are available on this book's companion web site (`www.wiley.com/compbooks/simon`) in both PDF and Microsoft Word formats. Be sure to check out the lists, download the ones that seem most helpful, and change them to fit your needs.

❑ **Check batteries:** Do your batteries need to be recharged or replaced? If your camera uses off-the-shelf batteries (such as AA or AAA), simply make sure you have a couple of sets of spares. If your camera uses a proprietary battery, you should perform this check the afternoon before, so you have time to recharge a drained battery. Some work centers keep the battery on the charger whenever the camera isn't in use. This isn't a bad idea because you're forced to take the battery off the charger before a shoot. If the camera isn't used regularly (less than once a week), its batteries should be removed because some amount of battery corrosion always occurs.

❑ **Check the camera's memory:** Make sure there's a memory card in the camera unless you have the type of camera that only uses internal memory. Going on a shoot only to find your camera has no memory is pretty frustrating. Because some cameras shoot (and display an image) without a memory card, an even worse possibility exists. You can go on a shoot, take pictures, check each shot right after you take it and never have actually recorded an image because you forgot to load the memory card!

❑ **Power cycle the camera:** Turn the camera on to make sure it's working properly. Take a test shot with the flash turned on to be sure the camera actually works.

❑ **Reformat the memory card:** This item can be adapted to your office's specific needs. Many organizations are satisfied with the memory card that comes with the camera. Because these cards tend to have a pretty small capacity, there usually isn't enough extra space on them to allow the luxury of keeping several jobs on one card. Assume that whoever used the camera last (if it's not you) captured his images to a computer.

❑ **Check accessories (if you have them):** Make sure any accessory items, such as add-on lenses or flash units, are in your camera bag. Test electronic items such as flash units or remote controls to be sure they're actually working.

❑ **Organize your gear (inside the camera bag):** If you have a camera bag for your gear, take a moment to organize it as you prefer. Also check to be sure nothing's missing. A couple of things that should be in the bag are a microfiber lens cloth (designed for camera optics) or lens tissue and cleaning fluid, extra batteries, a notepad and pencil with good eraser, and a small jeweler's screwdriver (for tightening the occasional loose screw). The camera's operating manual should also be kept in your camera bag in case you run into a problem. (If your camera's manual is too bulky to fit in the bag or take along, then copy the important pages and take only the copies.)

❑ **Organize your gear (sans camera bag):** If you're traveling light or your company doesn't own a camera bag, that's okay too. Simply follow a basic checklist to ensure that you have spare batteries, a memory card, camera instructions, and lens cloth. (I've seen people toss camera, batteries, memory cards and lens cloth in a plastic shopping bag and work from that. If it does the job for you, go for it.)

❑ **Pens versus pencils:** Should you carry a pencil or a pen in your camera bag? I always carry at least one pencil with a generous portion of eraser left on it. Pencils tend to be more valuable multipurpose tools in the camera bag. I've had the ink in my pen freeze solid while shooting in Antarctica, but I've never had pencil lead freeze. More importantly, you can use a pencil's eraser to clean your camera's battery terminal and battery contacts. Because it's not unusual for these surfaces to build up a thin film of corrosion (particularly in cameras that aren't heavily used), such a tool is indeed useful to have in your bag.

This basic list gets you out the door. Once you get to your shooting location, there are a couple more things to do to get your camera ready to shoot. Because many cameras default to factory settings when they're turned off, save this next checklist until you're ready to start shooting.

Pre-Shoot Checklist

Checking your camera's settings before you shoot is one of the most helpful pre-shoot habits you can develop. It helps ensure that the camera's settings suit your needs so the results are what you want. Here are some things to check just before you begin shooting:

❑ **Resolution setting:** I usually stress using the highest resolution setting your camera offers because you can down-sample a file without problem, but upressing (making your picture bigger) is hard. Still, if you're working with a modest memory card and have lots of work to do, balancing resolution needs with space usage becomes critical. If you need to strike a balance between resolution and space, then choose a setting that meets your company's exact needs. Don't automatically pick the lowest possible setting because that provides only enough resolution for web or monitor display. If you need to get prints from your images, the lowest setting might not be good enough. Keep in mind, even though you may originally take the photos for the company web site, somebody else may later want them for an annual report or sales brochure, so if you can shoot at a higher resolution, you may save some work later on.

❑ **ISO setting:** ISO refers to the camera sensor's sensitivity to light. ISO settings are represented by a numeric value that usually runs from 100 to 200 to 400 on the majority of point-and-shoot digital cameras. The higher the number, the more sensitive the sensor is to light (kind of like turning up the volume on a radio). The drawback is the higher the ISO number, the more noise the camera sensor generates (just as the higher volume setting on a radio produces more distortion). The rule of thumb is to pick the lowest ISO number that lets you shoot effectively. Selecting the correct ISO is very important! Too high an ISO with an inexpensive digital camera can drastically reduce image quality.

❑ **Exposure compensation setting:** Many digital cameras offer a useful control known as "exposure compensation." This feature is designed to compensate for the camera's light meter being fooled by certain lighting conditions. It also lets the user tweak exposure to meet personal preferences. Exposure compensation controls are usually set up as a horizontal scale with zero as a midpoint and one-third increments in each direction ranging from −2 and +2. Numbers on the plus side make your image brighter whereas numbers on the negative side of zero make your image darker. Checking the exposure compensation setting ensures proper exposure even if lighting conditions fool your camera's light meter. If you really don't want to be bothered, make sure this setting is either at zero or the first negative tick mark and leave it at that. If you're willing to do a little extra work in the digital darkroom to get a better image, then set your exposure compensation to −1 (or even more for very contrasty lighting). By setting exposure compensation to −1, you can still pull detail out of underexposed areas of the image, but if your bright areas have gone completely white, there is no way you can get any detail. It doesn't matter how hard you work in Photoshop. Don't be afraid to take one photo with the exposure compensation setting at normal, then another at −1. Pros do stuff like this all the time. It's a good thing to do.

Cross-Reference   Find more detailed information about exposure in Chapter 15.

❑ **Flash settings:** Many cameras offer a range of flash choices varying from red-eye reduction mode to fill flash to no flash at all. Be sure the camera's flash is at the setting you prefer. Here are some typical flash settings you might encounter:

  • **Red-eye reduction:** The camera fires off a quick series of flashes to reduce pupil size and minimize the potential for red-eye. This setting is useless for inanimate objects and can mislead human subjects into thinking their picture has been taken before the camera actually fires. It's a good idea to warn your subjects if you're using red-eye reduction mode about the pre-flashes so they don't relax their poses before the picture is actually taken.

  • **Straight or fill flash:** The flash fires as soon as you trip the shutter button. This flash setting is preferable for inanimate objects located within the flash's range, which is usually only about 10 or 15 feet at the most. This flash setting is based on your lens aperture and pumps out enough light for proper exposure for the scene.

  • **Programmed flash:** Some cameras offer another flash setting (under any number of possible different names) where the camera controls the flash output rather than simply pumping out the maximum light possible. Programmed flash is a good choice for people who don't want to fiddle around with camera settings, and it frequently does a pretty good job.

❑ **Focus settings:** It's not unusual for a camera to offer several different focusing settings beginning with an auto setting and then providing several close focusing choices. A few even offer a manual focusing choice.

Auto works for most normal uses. The majority of users probably just need to make sure the camera is set to auto. If you need to do close-up photography, this is the time to pick one of the specific close-focusing settings that meets your needs.

❑ **LCD display:** Despite being a minor concern, it's still worth considering your camera's LCD display. You can set the camera's LCD display to come on after you take a picture, or you can choose a certain length of time for the display to remain on. Longer times give you more time to review the image you just took, but also drain your camera's batteries faster. When in doubt, just leave it at the camera's default setting.

After you make it through these two checklists, it's time to take pictures, which brings you to another checklist. Relax, your life isn't about to be governed by endless checklists. I'm just being as thorough as I can in this section. You can always pick and choose the stuff you feel is important for your own checklist.

Shooting Checklist

These are some of the things you should consider while you're actually taking photographs. This checklist is fairly general, but similar lists designed for specific users appear in the subsequent chapters in Part V.

When you're ready to begin shooting, consider these things:

❑ **Where's the sun?** Be aware of the sun's position and what effect it has on your photos. If the sun is behind you, your subject is properly illuminated. Sun to your side brings out detail. Sun in front of you backlights and underexposes your subject. Set your exposure compensation to fix this, recompose the image from a different direction, or use a flash to fill in the shadow areas (but remember, flash is only effective if you're close enough to your subject for the flash to reach it). If the sun is directly overhead, you're dealing with high-contrast lighting (very bright whites and very dark shadows). Flash helps (if you're close enough) as does using a low-contrast filter. If none of this works, consider coming back another time when the light is better.

❑ **Consider the background:** Take a quick look at your background. Is it distracting? Ugly? Obscene? Political? There are so many ways a background can ruin an otherwise good photo. Consider what's there while you still have time to change your composition to minimize or eliminate the background, or change it to something less problematic.

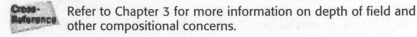 Refer to Chapter 3 for more information on depth of field and other compositional concerns.

❑ **Horizontal/vertical:** Unless you know beforehand that a certain orientation is required, plan on shooting images both horizontally and vertically.

❑ **Signs and other messages:** Make sure you check any written words that can appear in the image. In particular, look for things like graffiti or messages that can be distracting or detract from your shots.

❑ **People:** Clear out anyone who doesn't have a reason to be in your photo. Including people in your photos can be a problem because you need model releases to publish their images in any kind of commercial use situation. If your use meets the editorial use standard (that is, made for a newspaper or magazine article), then a model release isn't required, but it doesn't hurt to have one anyway.

> **On The Web** Visit this book's companion web site at www.wiley.com/compbooks/simon for a sample model release form.

Common Camera Problems Checklist

You've gone through the checklists; you've made sure you have fresh batteries and a reformatted memory card. Now you're at the job site and the camera doesn't work! What do you do?

First, take a deep breath. Often, the problem has a simple solution. Before panicking, check for one of these common culprits:

❑ **Battery failure:** There are any number of reasons why your batteries aren't working. This is why you carry spare sets. Try replacing the batteries and see if that does any good.

❑ **Battery misorientation:** You'd be amazed how often people put the batteries in upside down. When I ran a photo lab in Antarctica (imagine how that looks on a resume!), people would bring their broken cameras to me, and invariably the problem would be upside down batteries. Always, always, always double check that you've inserted the batteries properly. It's hard to tell in many of today's cameras, so this is always the first thing you should check.

❑ **Battery contact problems:** Sometimes a thin film of corrosion builds up over your camera's battery terminals. To clean off the corrosion, use a pencil eraser to rub the camera terminals and the ends of the batteries and try again.

❑ **Mis-seated memory cards:** Sometimes a mis-seated memory card prevents your camera from working. Remove the memory card, re-insert it, and try again.

❑ **Camera lockup:** Digital cameras, just like computers, sometimes lock up. If your camera locks, look for a reset button, press it (usually you need to hold the reset for a few seconds), and see if the camera reboots. Sometimes you even have to pull the batteries from the camera so it's completely without power for 10 or 15 seconds.

❑ **Dead camera:** I haven't had it happen to me yet, but it's possible your camera really is broken. If you've brought along a spare camera, now's the time to use it. If not, you either have to cancel the shoot or run to the store and buy a disposable camera (inelegant, but at least you still get the pictures). And remember, many wireless devices now offer some sort of photographic capability, so this may serve as a backup option.

I know that this chapter has been heavy on the checklists, but there's still one more to go. The next list is designed to help you manage the final details after you return to the office.

Post-Shoot Checklist

Following a standardized procedure can make your life easier and help reduce the number of problems that can occur when an office full of photographers at varying skill levels has to share one or two pieces of equipment.

The post shoot follow-up is particularly important because digital images are dangerously ephemeral at this stage. All your time and hard work can be laid to waste by someone assuming your images have already been captured and therefore it's safe to re-format the memory card. Although software exists to help recover accidentally deleted files, you introduce a whole new level of complexity to your operation by trying to use such software. It's much better to make sure your system precludes the need for such heroic measures.

Follow these steps to ensure that your photos are transferred safely from the camera to the computer:

1. **Remove the memory card.** Protecting your images should be your first priority once you're done with a shoot. Pull the memory card and store it in a safe place if you can't immediately capture its contents to a computer. It's a good idea to attach a sticky note to the memory card noting that its contents have not yet been captured.

2. **Capture your images to the computer.** Whenever possible, capture your images right after a shoot. Capturing your images immediately after a shoot is the only failsafe way to protect all your hard work, particularly if everyone in your office shares one memory card.

Good habits can help prevent bad accidents. The steps listed above are the basics for making sure your images make that final step into your computer in position for you to use them as needed.

Once in the computer, you begin the process of working on your images. I detail a complete and thorough process (known as workflow) in Chapter 16. It shows you how to get the most out of your images. Chapter 17 shows you how to manage and organize your photos so you can find them again later on.

Subsequent chapters in this section also provide workflow advice geared to the specific needs of various professions. This workflow information isn't as detailed as the process in Chapter 16, but it may be all you need to know to get the results you want. Keep in mind, cameras designed for novice photographers try to do as much of the processing as they can for you, so your camera may be relieving you of this hassle.

Summary

This chapter has been heavy on planning, preparation, and checklists. These are winning tools for working pros in any profession and particularly important for people who have to take the occasional photo as a secondary part of their job.

All too often, people are asked to create useful images without any training or guidance. There's a basic assumption that anyone can make a worthwhile picture with an unfamiliar camera and with no photographic training.

The advice provided in this chapter, and in the chapters that follow throughout the remainder of Part V, can help improve your photography without demanding too much from you in return. Follow the checklists I provide throughout, and you reduce the chance of mishaps and may even gain more confidence in your own photography.

Feel free to modify or combine these checklists to fit your particular needs. I've tried to make them as detailed as possible to anticipate every need and skill level. As a result, there are a lot of items to work through. You and your coworkers may decide some points are too obvious or too simple and don't need to be included. That's fine. Edit these lists at will to create the best tool for you and your organization.

Digital Photography for Realtors

More and more these days, homes are sold with photography. Although nothing is as important as a prospective buyer's visit to a home, good photographs can help entice that buyer to make the visit.

As a realtor, when you're preparing to make a home visit, photography is probably just one item on a long list of tasks you have before you. This chapter discusses some of the little things you can do to ensure that you're ready to get the photos you need to help sell the property. I give you tips about what to take with you and what kinds of shots you should consider taking—both inside and outside the house—to showcase the home to its best advantage.

The Basics of Real Estate Photography

Even if you consider yourself a true novice where photography is concerned, with a digital camera, a little preparation, and a few tricks from the pros, you can shoot real estate photos that showcase your properties in a positive and attractive way. The following sections can help you be fully prepared to take those great shots.

Equipment checklist for real estate photography

Before you leave the office to photograph that property you're preparing to list, be sure to take along the items provided on the following checklist:

❑ **Fresh batteries:** Digital cameras tend to drain batteries quickly, so make sure you have fresh batteries in the camera and a fully charged set of spares too.

❑ **Cleaning tools:** Keep your lens dust-free.

❑ **Memory:** Always check to make sure your camera has enough memory available to meet your shooting needs. There's nothing worse than showing up at a job site loaded down with a bag of gear only to discover that it's all worthless because your camera is missing its memory card.

❑ **Tripod (optional):** A tripod is a helpful tool. You can take good pictures without one, but having one available can make your life easier. A tripod steadies the camera at slower shutter speeds than you can safely handhold. Because slower shutter speeds allow for smaller lens openings (which provide a greater range of sharpness from front to back), using a tripod can result in sharper images that show the house better.

Remember that this checklist and those found throughout Part V of this book are available on this book's companion web site (www.wiley.com/compbooks/simon) in both PDF and Microsoft Word formats. Be sure to check out the lists, download the ones that seem the most helpful, and change them to fit your needs.

Tips for getting the best shots

Real estate photography revolves around making the house look its best. Good realtors already know how important it is to make a house show well. Doing this photographically means doing the little things. Here are some simple points to consider before you begin shooting:

✦ **Reflective surfaces:** Ask homeowners to hide polished metal and glass because these items can create hot spots within a photograph. Mirrors can create an additional problem, namely showing the reflection of the photographer (see Figure 19-1). Although you can remove your reflection in Photoshop (if you have the program and the skill to do it), it's a lot less work to avoid the problem when you make the photo.

✦ **Eliminate clutter:** What might look like an acceptable amount of knick-knacks and decorations when you're surveying the home in three dimensions can photograph as clutter in a two-dimensional shot. The less clutter in a room, the bigger and airier the room looks.

✦ **Control light:** Homeowners and realtors often want to photograph rooms with open windows in order to include views of the outside. Sadly, the resulting image is marred by a too bright outdoors that overpowers the dimly lit room indoors. Balancing the light levels between indoors and outside is a real photographic challenge. I tell you some ways to deal with this challenge a little later in the section "Ensuring the right light." One

Figure 19-1: Be careful—it's easy to catch your reflection in a mirror when you're photographing a home and not even realize it until later.

© 2004 Dan Simon

workable plan is to wait for an overcast or cloudy day, when outside light isn't quite as bright; another option is to close the curtains and shutter the blinds. It may not give you that great view of the backyard, but if the contrast levels are too high, you won't see it anyway.

Another way to deal with the difference between inside and outside light is to use the camera's built-in flash; but even this goes only so far. Often, the light outside is so much brighter than it is inside that the underpowered flash unit just can't raise the indoor light level high enough.

✦ **Keystoning:** It's important to keep your camera as level as possible when photographing a building of any kind. Otherwise, it may look like the upper corners of the structure are falling away from you. The taller the building, the more pronounced this *keystoning effect* will be, so do everything possible to shoot with your lens as level as possible. If you're shooting from ground level, you'll end up with some wasted space at the top of the frame, but you can crop that out later on your computer. Another option is to climb higher up in another building so that you can be about halfway up the height of what you're shooting. This makes a level camera more effective. If you're going to fix keystoning later in the digital darkroom, be sure to leave some extra space at the edges of each side of the image because you'll need that space to correct for the keystoning problem.

 Check out Chapter 15 for more detailed information about correcting keystoning in the digital darkroom.

Photographing the Home's Exterior

Exterior photography revolves entirely around the amount and quality of light. If the light is cooperating, photography can be pretty easy. If it isn't, you face a serious challenge.

Your biggest concern is where the sun is in relation to the shot you're making. Try to avoid shooting directly into the sun, which results in an underexposed photo. If you can't take the shot head on, try shifting a few feet right or left. Sometimes this lets you get the composition you need without having the sun affect your image quite so drastically.

Depending on the size of the house you're photographing, you may be able to get an assist from a built-in or accessory flash unit. Certainly, if you're shooting around midday when the sun is high in the sky, you're likely to have serious problems with shadows under awnings, windowsills and eaves. You can generally solve these shadow problems by using *fill flash*. This is flash you use not as your main light source but to fill in the shadow areas. It can make a huge difference in the quality of your photos.

Some cameras offer a fill flash setting (check your owner's manual for how to activate it) whereas others simply give you the choice of turning your flash on or off. In simplest terms, fill flash is setting your flash's output to match your camera's settings rather than the opposite. If you pick shutter priority or aperture priority settings instead of programmed flash, you should be okay.

Another way to avoid problems with light is to schedule the photography for times when the light is more favorable. Overcast or cloudy days provide more even illumination than sunny ones. Shooting in the early morning or late afternoon when the sun is low in the sky can be effective, provided the home is oriented in the proper direction. The problem you risk is if the sun is in front of one side of the house, it will be behind the other side, meaning one of your shots will be back-lit and the house severely underexposed.

Ensuring curb appeal

Ask the homeowner to have the property looking its best on the day of the shoot. If the owners make the effort to have the lawn freshly mowed and landscaped, be sure that yard debris has also been cleared away (see Figure 19-2) and any yard tools or trash cans hidden so that the home looks neat and tidy in the photo.

Getting the proper perspective

It's better to stand farther away from a house and use your camera's zoom (if it has one) to zoom in and create a tight composition than it is to walk in close and use a wide-angle view. A wide-angle view distorts the house unnaturally. A second problem with going for the wide-angle shot is that it's likely to create keystoning, an effect where it looks like the house is falling away from the viewer. Using a longer focal length, as in Figure 19-3, helps eliminate both of these problems.

Figure 19-2: This attractive property is marred by the plastic landscaping cloth (lower-left corner), which could easily have been covered with the landscaping stones used on the rest of the yard.

© 2004 Dan Simon

Figure 19-3: By choosing a piece of level ground some distance away to photograph this apartment complex, I was able to hold my camera level and avoid keystoning.

© 2004 Dan Simon

Don't forget, full-color versions of all figures are available on this book's companion web site at `www.wiley.com/compbooks/simon`.

 Project: **Shooting exteriors**

Successfully photographing your properties begins with solid preparation. Some tasks you need to handle when you schedule the appointment a few days or more before the shoot. Other tasks you can take care of when you arrive at the property. The following two lists can help you be prepared.

When scheduling the appointment to take the photos:

1. Call the homeowner to ensure that the lawn has been mowed, bushes and hedges have been neatly trimmed, and any yard debris has been cleaned up. Also ask if they can park cars away from the home. It's best not to have the clutter of cars in the photo if you can avoid it.

2. Check the weather forecast; look for a day with cloudy skies.

3. Check your equipment (see "Equipment checklist" at the beginning of this chapter) to be sure that you have an extra set of fresh batteries and any accessory lenses, flash units, or tripods you plan to take along. Also make sure that there is a memory card in your camera.

 It's particularly important to check the equipment in offices where one camera is shared among multiple agents. You never know when someone has forgotten to put the memory card back or drained the batteries.

4. If you haven't used the camera in a while, refresh your memory by reviewing the owner's manual. It's always better to look sure and confident than to be fumbling around with a camera as if you don't know what you're doing.

When you arrive at the house:

1. Give the exterior a quick once over to see if there's anything that might need to be spruced up or hidden.

2. If you're using a tripod, set it up and make sure it's level.

3. Check the position of the sun. If possible, try to keep the sun behind you or to one side. If circumstances require you to shoot into the sun, try angling a few feet to the side. You need to keep the sun out of the photograph. Even with the sun just barely out of the picture, you should still expect to have to compensate for the sun's bright light, causing the home to be underexposed, by adding one to two stops of extra exposure.

4. If possible, make sure that your company's sign is visible in your photo of the front of the house. If you have the right lens or zoom capability, you may be able to show the whole house and still have the sign fairly readable in the photo.

5. Take several photos of both the front and rear of the home. If it's a particularly bright day with the sun directly overhead, take at least one extra photo with the camera's exposure compensation set to –1 and another with it set to –2 (these settings will make slightly darker images in an effort to hold some detail in the image's highlight areas. Photograph any other special features, such as swimming pools and patios. Most newspaper and real estate supplements are set up for horizontal images, so you won't have to worry about shooting vertically. If this is a show house that might make the cover of a real estate brochure or flyer, take some verticals just in case.

For a really advanced technique for dealing with high-contrast lighting, refer to the section on increasing dynamic range in Appendix B on this book's companion web site at www.wiley.com/compbooks/simon.

Photographing the Home's Interior

As the following sections suggest, taking photos of the inside of a home presents its own challenges.

Ensuring the right light

Getting the lighting right for an interior can be as simple as turning on all the lights and shooting without flash, to replacing every overhead light with strobes to manage the light with precision.

Working with available light is simple and frequently effective, but does present a couple of concerns. First off, a mix of sunlight and manmade light can produce strange color shifts because each type of light has a slightly different color to it. The easiest way to manage this problem is to make sure you have something that is pure white somewhere in the image. Then when you process the image in the computer, you can use that white object as your baseline for pure white.

See Chapter 16 to find out more about using pure white as your baseline when you're trying to balance colors.

Setting the white balance

Digital sensors need to be told what pure white is. Once they know, they can calibrate for the rest of the tonal range. Although the camera's auto white balance frequently does a good enough job, sometimes more critical color accuracy is necessary.

When this is the case, manual white balance is the answer. Navigate through your camera's menu to find the white balance settings. Select *Manual white balance,* and then fill your viewfinder with something that is pure white. This is covered in more detail in Chapter 2.

Adding homey touches

You can increase the visual appeal of a home's interior by adding some of those homey touches that make a house look comfortable. Floral arrangements, brightly colored place settings on a dining table, a fire burning in the fireplace—all photograph nicely.

Photographing large interior spaces

When photographing large interior spaces, such as home offices, it's important to set your camera to produce as much depth of field as possible. If you're using a camera with manual control, go with an aperture setting of F8 or F11. This will likely result in a very slow shutter speed, so either use a tripod or set the camera on top of something solid, such as a table or file cabinet, and use a wireless shutter release or self timer if your camera comes with one. If your camera doesn't offer this level of control, try using its landscape setting (usually depicted by a mountain icon) because this setting is designed to maximize depth of field.

Flash is a mixed blessing when shooting larger areas. Although it might fill in some shadows, the built-in flash units on most digital cameras aren't powerful enough to light a large room. And many modern offices are loaded with highly reflective surfaces that can cause all sorts of hot spots in your image. It's better to turn on as many lights as possible throughout the room instead of trying to rely on flash.

Wide-angle, add-on lenses can be helpful in taking in large spaces, but be careful with extremely wide-angle or fisheye optics because they produce lots of distortion and can cause straight lines to bend at the edges of the frame. Photoshop plug-ins, such as Andromeda's Lensdoc, can make it easy to correct for such distortion, but they also add another layer of expense and effort to your workflow.

 Project: **Shooting interiors**

The important rooms are the kitchen, living room, dining room, master bedroom, master bathroom, and any special rooms, such as a Florida room or breezeway. Of course, your coverage depends on how much exposure this property is going to receive. Follow these steps, and you'll be certain to capture the important aspects of the property:

1. Favor wide-angle lenses for interior photography. Besides allowing you to show more of the room, wide-angle lenses tend to show space better than longer focal lengths that compress space, making rooms look smaller. A wide-angle lens attachment is a smart buy for real estate photography because it makes rooms look more spacious.

2. Close curtains, drapes, or blinds for all but the most overcast days. Although you may be tempted to try to show that great backyard or other outside view, the reality is that on most days, the outside is so much brighter than the inside, the camera's sensor can't handle it. If it is one of those dull, gray days, go ahead and show the view (see Figure 19-4).

Figure 19-4: This room has a nice view of the ocean, but the light outside was so bright that the camera's sensor couldn't expose both inside and outside properly.

© 2004 Dan Simon

3. Take advantage of structural features. If you're photographing a home with a second floor landing, use the landing to provide a bird's-eye view of the first floor rooms.

4. Try to maximize depth of field so the overall image is as sharp as possible. This is best done with the camera on a tripod. It's more work, but for an important property can really pay off.

5. Make sure the room is as neat as possible. It's also a good idea to remove excess furniture so things don't look cluttered. Too much furniture makes a room look cramped.

Back at the Office

After you've taken the photos, it's time to take care of the workflow process. *Workflow* is one of the hot buzzwords of digital photography these days. The term describes the process of transferring images from the camera to the computer, processing them for your particular needs, archiving the images, and managing the files.

Having a workflow for your photography is important because a good system effectively manages the entire photographic process all the way to image retrieval years later. An ineffective workflow, on the other hand, can create enough short- and long-term problems to make you consider putting away your camera and taking up a sketch pad and colored pencils.

The following steps walk you through a good basic system for managing your photos:

1. Create an appropriately named folder, such as Photos, on your computer's hard drive. Within that folder, create subfolders for Residential, Commercial, Industrial and Retail properties, as appropriate. Within the appropriate subfolder, create a new folder specifically for the property you just photographed. You can use the property's name or address or your company's file number as the folder's name.

2. Transfer the images from your camera's memory device to that folder.

3. After transferring the files to your computer, and as appropriate, rename the image files to reflect the property address, your company's file number, or the MLS number for the property. Use an image browser or image-editing program (such as ACDsee or iView) to rename your files. At this point, you can also add keywords to your files for easier retrieval later. (Keywords are a database feature that makes it easier to find a particular image later on.) Typical keywords for these types of files will identify interiors and exteriors, plus the particular room for an image. The advantage to a key-wording system shows up when you maintain a master image catalog of all the images your office has created over the years. If you've key-worded properly, you can do a search for a file number plus the appropriate keyword (*kitchen*) and immediately call up all the kitchen photos for that file number.

 Refer to Chapter 17 for more details about managing and archiving your images for easy retrieval later.

4. Copy your unprocessed files to a Burn to CD folder for burning to CD. I usually name this my "Burn to CD" folder. You should maintain such a folder so that you always have a backup copy of your original files. Keep copying files to this folder until you have enough to burn a CD. Try to back up on a set schedule if you can. Once a week is ideal, even if you don't fill a CD. This way if disaster strikes, you don't lose more than a week's worth of files.

5. After copying your files to the Burn to CD folder as a backup, take a little time to evaluate your images. Use a file browser such as ACDsee or iView or whatever program your office uses to examine each image. Eliminate out-of-focus or poorly exposed shots. Choose the ones you actually plan on using and move them to a Working Images subfolder inside your main project folder.

Visit this book's companion web site at `www.wiley.com/`
`compbooks/simon` for more information on and links to various
image browsers.

6. Process the images. Use an image-editing program to tweak your photos
if needed. Depending on the type of camera you're using, you may not
need to do any work, or you might need to do quite a bit. Higher-end
digital cameras, particularly DSLRs, are set up under the assumption that
the photographer wants to exercise as much control over his images as
possible. Consumer-grade cameras, on the other hand, are set up with
the assumption that people want the best images straight from the
camera, so they do some of the processing before the image ever leaves
the camera. Even if you're satisfied with the camera's processing, there
are still one or two things you need to do. One may be to mark the image
with your copyright depending on your firm's policy on the matter.
Another is to mark it with identification information such as address and
client info. Programs such as Photoshop have a file info function that
enables you to log such data on the image file. This is also the time to
take care of any keystoning problems you might have incurred.

 See Chapter 15 for more information on how to fix keystoned
images

7. Create two subfolders within the Burn to CD folder: Raw and Processed.
This way, you can keep a copy of both the original version of the image
and the processed version.

8. Copy the processed images to the Processed subfolder. When the time
comes, copy the contents of the Burn to CD folder (including both
subfolders) to at least two CDs. Store one in your office and the second at
a safe location off-site. At this point, you have three copies of the files,
one still on your computer in the client's file and the two CDs. This
should be the bare minimum redundancy in your system.

Summary

Photography is just one of many chores a real estate professional has to tackle in
the course of a busy day. Most companies have neither the budget nor the
interest to hire photographers to do this work, so realtors can expect to be
taking their own pictures for the foreseeable future.

Good real estate photography begins at the office with solid preparation and by
having a system that makes photography manageable for a group of people
sharing a single camera. Then, when you're ready to head out to take those
pictures, follow the pointers provided here to ensure that you take photos that
showcase your property to its best advantage.

Developing good habits and a systematic workflow can create an environment in
which everyone knows how images are handled and accessed and that makes
images available later for easy retrieval.

Digital Photography for Automobile Sales

Automobile photography is challenging. Cars are made of highly reflective materials, which can cause all sorts of problems with the photographic process. Hot spots, excessive contrast, and lack of understanding of how to photograph a car properly all conspire to make the average car ad look rather uninspiring.

In this chapter, I cover different techniques that help you capture great automobile photos. I discuss how to deal with tricky lighting situations, the advantages of photographing cars from different angles, and how to maximize depth of field so you get the best shots possible.

Automobile Photography Checklist

Begin with the basic checklists I provide in Chapter 18 to ensure that your camera is in working order and that you know how to handle simple camera troubleshooting. As always, be sure you have extra batteries and memory—getting caught in the field without power can be a hassle, especially if your camera uses a proprietary-type battery.

Although those basic checklists provide a good starting point, the biggest key to a successful auto shoot is timing your photography. Planning shoots for early morning or evening, taking advantage of overcast days, and shooting inside a showroom are ways to overcome high-contrast light and take advantage of even, usable light.

 Remember that this checklist and those found throughout Part V of this book are available on this book's companion web site (www.wiley.com/compbooks/simon) in both PDF and Microsoft Word formats. Be sure to check out the lists, download the ones that seem most helpful, and change them to fit your needs.

The following checklist provides you with the steps to take to ensure that your photos look their best:

❑ Schedule your shoot for early morning or early evening when the sun is low in the sky. Or, take advantage of overcast days when the light is even.

❑ Check the car for signs and consider whether or not you want them to appear in the photo. Also consider whether the signs will be readable in the photo.

❑ Set your camera to landscape mode to maximize depth of field.

❑ White balance your camera if you're shooting indoors or if you're going to use the photo in color.

> **Cross-Reference** To refresh your memory about how to white balance your camera, refer to Chapter 2.

❑ Select the desired shooting angle.

❑ Focus on the car's windshield.

❑ Make the photo.

Dealing with Reflections and Glare

Because reflections are such a problem in auto photography, you may want to invest in a polarizing filter. Although not as common for point-and-shoot digital cameras as they are for DSLRs, polarizing filters are becoming more available for the smaller lenses point-and-shoot cameras use.

Polarizing filters subdue certain types of reflections (like those in glass and water) but not others (like reflections off metal). Used properly, a polarizer helps reduce reflections in a car's windshield and windows, and helps to make sure that your reflection doesn't show up in the picture. Polarizers are also the only type of filter than can increase contrast in color images, so it's not a good idea to use them in high-contrast lighting situations.

 You can reproduce many filter effects in Photoshop and other image editing programs, but certain effects can only be made by the filter itself. It's not possible to re-create the effect of a polarizing filter in software.

Using a polarizing filter

Polarizing filters are two-stage filters where two different pieces of glass are rotated to find the best effect. The two pieces of glass rotate against each other and are positioned to varying effect based on their angle relative to the reflection.

In order to use a polarizer properly, you need to look through your camera's viewfinder while slowly turning the filter. As you turn the filter element, watch to see whether or not the reflection diminishes as a result. You usually have to rotate back and forth to fine tune the effect and get the best results.

You should be aware of a couple of things if you use a polarizing filter. The first is that it costs you some light. The actual amount of lost light varies depending on the orientation of the filter's two elements, but you can lose as much as one or two f-stops worth of exposure. Secondly, there are two different types of polarizing filter: linear and circular. Autofocus cameras require a circular polarizer. Only the older, manual focus cameras can use linear polarizing filters. Figure 20-1 illustrates the effects a polarizing filter can have on your shots.

Figure 20-1: A polarizing filter helped reduce some of the window glare in this photo.

© 2004 Dan Simon

Do you really need a polarizing filter? If you have to do a lot of auto photography under a wide range of lighting conditions, polarizing filters come in quite handy. If you don't have a huge workload, or if you can do all your photography when the light is on your side, then you can probably get by without this filter.

Composing an Automobile Shot

Magazine ads and new car brochures present motor vehicles beautifully. These images are brilliantly staged, precisely lit, and carefully choreographed with props and models to create a mood and stroke emotions. Although you may not need to achieve this level of sophistication, creating an attractive image of an automobile is quite simple.

Choosing an angle of view

Cars and trucks can be photographed from a number of different angles. If you're making a multi-image advertisement, you should plan on using pictures from a variety of angles. Most auto pictures, though, are run awfully small in a newspaper ad or car sales publication, so choosing the right angles becomes pretty important.

A good three-quarter view (shown in Figure 20-2) provides a nice look at the vehicle and provides the viewer a lot of information. Front views and side views are also effective, particularly if you lower the camera a little and orient it so the lens is perpendicular to the ground. Doing so helps isolate the vehicle from other background distractions.

Figure 20-2: A three-quarter view shot at eye level or lower minimizes background distractions and gives the viewer a good sense of a car's size and appearance.

© 2004 Dan Simon

In general, it's best to try to shoot about level in height with the vehicle or even a little below. This produces an angle that emphasizes the vehicle and helps minimize background distractions.

Deciding on focal length

The right focal length also improves a vehicle's appearance in a photograph. Wide-angle lenses make cars look bigger, but also more distorted. Telephoto focal lengths tend to compress or flatten your subject.

Generally it's best to choose a wider field of view, which allows you to work in tighter confines (typical of the normal car lot) and produces a more interesting view of the vehicle. Be careful, though. If you select too wide a view, you risk exaggerating and distorting a car's look. It's probably best to avoid add-on wide-angle lenses because they maximize distortion. Figures 20-3 and 20-4 illustrate the effects of different focal lengths.

Figure 20-3: Shot with a 135mm lens, this image provides a narrower field of view.

© 2004 Dan Simon

 Don't forget, full-color versions of all figures are available on this book's companion web site at www.wiley.com/compbooks/simon.

Depth of field concerns

Depth of field is an image's range of apparent image sharpness. As the photographer, you can control depth of field depending upon what camera settings you choose.

Figure 20-4: Shot with a 20mm lens, this image provides a wider field of view.
ⓒ *2004 Dan Simon*

Choosing the right settings can make your picture look very sharp or very soft, even though your focus may have been dead on. The easiest way to manage depth of field is to choose your camera's landscape or scenic setting. This setting generally produces a combination of modest shutter speed and smaller aperture that result in the greatest range of image sharpness.

Another way to control depth of field is to select a focal point about one-third of the way into the car. Focus your camera on the car's windshield instead of the front grill. Depth of field decreases the closer you get to your subject, so if you pick a spot a third of the way into the vehicle and set your camera to landscape mode, you're more likely to get the shot you want. Although depth of field varies depending upon lighting conditions, odds are that you'll have enough depth of field to cover the entire length of the vehicle by composing your shot this way.

Summary

A car salesman's life is busy enough without adding photography to the to-do list. Photographing cars and trucks for newspaper ads and flyers isn't that difficult, however. Taking advantage of the right lighting, minimizing background distractions, and getting the shot's composition right are really all it takes to create outstanding auto photos.

Digital Photography for Company Newsletters

Many companies value newsletters as an important tool to keep their employees informed. All too often though, the pictures in newsletters fall far short of professional standards.

Sadly, many in-house publications rely on that industry standard, the *grip-n-grin* photo (you know the shot; the award presenter and the award recipient stand there shaking hands and smiling for the camera), which leads to a series of photos that all look alike. To make matters worse, in an effort to avoid playing favorites, sometimes every image is run the same size and given the same treatment, resulting in a boring and unimaginative publication.

Good newsletter photography doesn't have to eschew images of award winners, but instead should show readers what the person did to earn that recognition.

The next step is to start pursuing interesting images that support the stories you're running. Images should help tell some part of the story or show the key players doing whatever made their efforts worth covering. In this chapter, I cover some techniques and considerations that can help make your newsletter the best in town!

Newsletter Photography Checklist

Begin with the basic checklists I provided in Chapter 18 to ensure that your camera is in working order and that you know how to handle simple camera troubleshooting. As always, be sure you have extra batteries and memory—getting caught out on a shoot without power can be a hassle, especially if your camera uses a proprietary-type battery.

Remember that this checklist and those found throughout Part V of this book are available on this book's companion web site (`www.wiley.com/ compbooks/simon`) in both PDF and Microsoft Word formats. Be sure to check out the lists, download the ones that seem the most helpful, and change them to fit your needs.

When you're certain you have the basics covered, here are some things you should think about related specifically to newsletter photography:

❑ **Contact the appropriate work center:** When is the best time to do photography? You're looking for a time when something is actually going on that has the potential for interesting images. Try to avoid shots of people at their desks, because those images are pretty static.

❑ **Make a preliminary visit to the work center:** Check out the surroundings and get an idea of what kind of shooting challenges await you. Consider lighting levels (will you need flash or can you get by with available light?) and potential shooting locations. Look for ways to get up high so you can shoot down on the work center for a different point of view.

❑ **Prepare a shooting script or shot list:** Spend some time thinking about what shots you should look for during your shoot. If need be, wait until after the story is written so you have a better idea what to expect. A shooting script isn't a formal document or rigid plan. Instead, it's a tool for getting your photography started. Creating a shot list gets you thinking about potential shots to accompany the story.

❑ **Go on the shoot:** It's time to start taking pictures. Shoot from a variety of camera angles and directions. Move around a lot and take pictures from many vantage points. Aim for action and try to maintain eye contact with your subjects. Take lots of photos. Mix up your images. Take close-ups, medium views, and long shots so you have a nice package of images to choose from. Don't forget to take shots from low angles too.

Here's a proof sheet from a shoot I did for one of my clients, a television production company. The images here are only a small portion of all the photographs I took during this three-hour shoot, but they help illustrate some of the points I make over the next few pages. Notice in Figure 21-1 how I take the same photo over and over, but from different directions and with a mix of horizontal and vertical compositions.

boom.ur841...　　boom.ur842...　　riverbank....　　riverbank....

riverbank....　　riverbankd...　　riverbanke...　　shoot.deve...

shoot.dl856...　　shoot.dlve...　　shoot.el85...　　shoot.er85...

tim.el8356...　　tim.straigh...　　timdr8370_...

Figure 21-1: The more shots you take, the better your chance of capturing interesting newsletter photos.

© *2004 Dan Simon*

Composing Interesting Photographs

Providing interesting imagery is key to transitioning successfully from boring to exciting newsletter photography. Here are some quick tips for better pictures:

✦ **Get in close:** Avoid head to toe images unless you have a specific reason for showing knees and footwear. Generally all you need to show is the top half of the body from waist to a little bit above the head. An even tighter composition can work just fine if the action lends itself to it.

✦ **Make eye contact:** The eyes have it. It takes some work, but it's better to catch someone looking towards the camera while they're working. The eye contact in Figure 21-2 draws viewers into the image and helps them empathize with the person in the picture.

Figure 21-2: Eye contact helps the reader make an emotional connection with the subject of your photo.

© 2004 Dan Simon

 Don't forget, you can see each figure in full color on this book's web site at www.wiley.com/compbooks/simon.

✦ **Vary camera angles:** Every picture shouldn't look like a different version of the same basic photo. Change compositions, change camera angles, zoom in, back out.

✦ **Go on location:** An active and energetic newsletter photographer can do much to improve the quality of a company publication. This often means leaving the office to tag along with a work crew or salesperson to show them at work out in the field (see Figure 21-3). It's more work, but it definitely results in more interesting images. Showing people in their actual work environment also helps other members of the company understand what their co-workers do and why they're an important part of the team. If you can document employees working in particularly difficult conditions (bad weather, remote locations) you can help inspire other workers with their example.

Figure 21-3: Shot on location, this photo communicates the hard work put in by the camera crew.

© *2004 Dan Simon*

If you're working on a freelance basis, be sure you don't interfere with anything you're trying to document.

Shooting for Layout

Because newsletters are usually laid out in columnar format, it's important to create images that support your layout.

✦ **Horizontal versus vertical:** A good mix of horizontal and vertical images provides a nice range of options when it's time to lay out your newsletter. Because most people shoot nothing but horizontals, incorporating verticals into your publication helps it look more professional.

✦ **Direction:** Pictures can have direction. They can lead the eye on or off the page. Your job as the newsletter photographer is to create photos that keep the viewer's eye on the page rather than sliding it off. The people and objects in a photograph can be moving or pointing in one direction or another. If you have someone in your photo looking to the left, then the viewer's eye tends to move in the same direction. Be aware of the direction your photo is taking and then try to shoot a similar image from the other direction. If this isn't possible, at least get a mix of images that move the eye in various directions. Look for images that move from left to right, right to left, up, down, and even combine sideways and vertical movement.

✦ **The dollar rule:** Layout artists use an old rule that says you should be able to place a dollar bill anywhere on a printed page and have it hit at least one photo. If it can't, then you don't have enough photos on the page.

Avoiding traps

Many newsletters fall victim to some classic traps that weaken their visual interest and serve to lessen their effectiveness.

✦ **Death by grip-n-grin:** It's already been discussed earlier, but it's worth repeating: Grip-n-grins do little more than take up space that could be better served by good photography.

✦ **Head shot hell:** Head shots are quite useful for identification purposes, but you don't want to bog down your newsletter with them. Problems can occur when they're run too big. Head shots should be confined to one column wide, just big enough to be recognizable. If you have more room to run a bigger photo, it's better to try to make an image of the person actually performing some aspect of their job.

✦ **Awards photos:** A sub variation of the grip-n-grin, awards photos depict a recipient displaying an award for the camera. By all means, take these photos, make prints and distribute them to the award winners, just don't use them in your newsletter unless ordered to. It's far better to show the individual doing whatever it is that got them the award in the first place.

✦ **Group photos:** Ah yes, there's nothing like a picture of a bunch of people standing in front of the camera, most of whom are smiling and actually looking towards the lens. Once again, these photos do nothing more than show what people look like. They don't provide any information as to why these people are newsworthy or what they contribute to the company. It's much better to photograph the people in the group individually while they're working.

Creating a Shot List

Putting a shot list together isn't hard. It doesn't even require you to be an experienced photographer. Once you get the hang of putting together shot lists, they become a valuable tool, particularly if you have to delegate the photography to someone else!

1. **Visualize the event:** Try to have an idea in what sequence an event might unfold. Obviously, if you can get a copy of the event schedule beforehand, you're in much better shape to visualize.

2. **Visit the event site:** Knowing a site's layout can help you figure out how hard it might be to move around, whether the location is well-lit or not, or

get an idea of potential problems that could hinder your shoot. Planning for contingencies and having a backup plan are keys for a smooth shoot.

3. **Consider event timing and your potential movements:** Can you get from one spot to another in time for a particular shot? Maybe you need to have another photographer, or at least another person with a camera covering one or two elements for you.

4. **Look for interesting vantage points:** Finding places that provide you with a different perspective only enhances your shoot. Balconies in particular are wonderful for giving you a chance to take a wide shot of the entire gathering. They also make it possible for you to get very different angles in your images.

5. **Mix up your compositions and directions:** Shoot verticals and horizontals and make sure your photos move in a variety of directions, including left, right, straight ahead, up, and down.

Summary

It takes energy and effort to create winning newsletter photos. Although it's easy to just pop in the grip-n-grins and group shots (especially because you have to take them anyway), these photos do little to enhance the quality of your publication. Make the effort to visit the trenches and show people just how hard others in your company work.

Plan your shoot ahead of time. Develop an idea of the kind of photos to look for. Scout out the work center and consider where you're going to make photographs from, making sure to move to different vantage points. Try to get some high-angle views even if you have to bring a step ladder. Variety is vital. You don't want every picture in your newsletter to look like it was made with the same cookie cutter.

Finally, don't be afraid to be aggressive with your photography. Great photos get attention. They pull the reader in, so if you have a keeper, make it work for you.

Digital Photography for Insurance Adjusters

This chapter is designed to help those who need to document accident damage. Although not the most glamorous type of photography, shooting accident damage thoroughly and accurately requires a keen eye and patience and is an extremely valuable skill.

When you're making photographs for documentation purposes, your first goal is to provide a record of something that may not be accessible, or even still exist in its damaged form, by the time decisions have to be made about it. Because you can't generally go back and re-create a shot, your emphasis needs to be on successful results each and every time you go on a shoot. The biggest challenge here is trying to represent three-dimensional detail in a two-dimensional photograph. Although you can't achieve true three-dimensional representations, you can produce images that show depth.

In this chapter, I offer some insight into how you can produce images that show detail well. I also discuss some of the challenges in working with digital cameras in this arena and how you can manage them. Because this type of photography usually has you working on tight deadlines, I introduce you to some portable field printers that can provide the instant prints you used to make with self-developing print cameras in the past.

Insurance Photography Checklist

Begin with the basic checklists I provided in Chapter 18 to ensure that your camera is in working order and you know how to handle simple camera troubleshooting. As always, be sure you have extra batteries and memory—getting caught in the field without power can be a hassle, especially if your camera uses a proprietary-type battery.

 Remember that this checklist and those found throughout Part V of this book are available on this book's companion web site (www.wiley.com/compbooks/simon) in both PDF and Microsoft Word formats. Be sure to check out the lists, download the ones that seem most helpful, and change them to fit your needs.

After you have the basics covered, here is a list of handy items to pack with your camera for trips into the field to document insurance damage:

❑ Extra batteries and memory.

❑ Portable printer, paper, and extra ink.

❑ Power inverter or extra batteries for your printer.

❑ Flash unit or low-contrast filter to help deal with high-contrast lighting.

❑ Reflector and/or diffuser to bounce light into shadows (reflector) or soften light hitting your subject area (diffuser).

 You can find more detailed information about using reflectors and diffusers in Chapter 3.

Choosing the Best Camera for the Job

Ideally, you should choose a digital camera that runs on commercially available double AA or triple AAA batteries that you can find almost anywhere. Then, if you find yourself without power, you can just zip into the nearest convenience store and buy some more. If you already have a digital camera that uses proprietary batteries, try to make sure you have an extra battery or see if your camera comes with an external power supply. If it does, you can power it from your car's cigarette lighter in an emergency (either via an adapter or by using the power inverter described a little later in this chapter).

If you're still deciding which digital camera to buy for this type of work, you need to consider what kind of property you want to photograph primarily. If your main focus is documenting auto damage, you can probably get by with almost any point-and-shoot digital camera that offers a close focusing capability and a modest zoom lens.

If you specialize in larger properties, such as homes or office buildings, you may need a bit more versatility. Certainly, it would be wise to find a camera that can at least accept add-on wide-angle lenses that can take in an entire fire or disaster scene. If you expect to routinely have to deal with large accident settings, you may want to consider investing in a DSLR and an appropriate wide-angle zoom lens.

Making Prints in the Field

Another thing to consider in building a camera outfit is whether or not you have an immediate need for prints. Many professionals in the past have relied on Polaroid cameras and their instant prints because of that need. With an instant print, you could make a visit to a damaged vehicle or property, photograph the damage, and attach a picture directly to your report.

It used to be digital photography didn't work very well for this sort of use because you still needed access to a computer to process your shots. Then, for a while, there was a digital camera on the market with a built-in printer. Unfortunately, it appears that model is no longer available. The next section tells you about a couple of portable printing options.

Choosing the right portable printer

These days, if you want to shoot insurance photos with a digital camera, you have several options. You can carry a laptop and small portable printer that runs off either the laptop's battery or through an automobile power inverter. This gives you the option of creating your report in the field and printing images as part of the actual report instead of attaching a separate print to it. Although this is nice and tidy and ensures the picture won't get lost, it doesn't provide a very high-quality photographic image. It also means that you need to carry an expensive laptop computer (which you may not own) and lug some fairly heavy gear around with you.

The best choice for people who need to make prints in the field appears to be one of the tiny photo printers available from Canon and HP. These small devices fit in a camera bag and can quickly make 4 x 6 prints directly from the camera (Canon) or memory card (HP). Several other companies also make small, portable printers.

If you choose this option, be sure it works with your camera. Canon's models, although tiny, must be connected directly to the camera. Although it will work with other brands, the brand must be Pictbridge-compatible. Pictbridge is a new worldwide industry standard for ensuring compatibility between equipment from different vendors. If your camera is Pictbridge-compliant, it should work with any Pictbridge-compliant printer.

HP's offerings can function without a direct camera-to-printer connection. You simply insert your memory card (and these printers accept most of the standard media, including CompactFlash, SmartMedia, Memory Stick, and others) and make your prints. The downside is that you're limited to 4 x 6 prints, although for most people that isn't a problem (see Figure 22-1).

Figure 22-1: With a small printer powered off your car's battery (via an inexpensive power inverter), you have the makings of a portable photo lab.
© 2004 Dan Simon

Don't forget, you can see each figure in full color on this book's web site at www.wiley.com/compbooks/simon.

Powering your portable printer

Power supplies for these portable printers vary. Some run off battery power, whereas others either plug into a wall socket or require a separate car adapter. I personally find that an inexpensive auto power inverter (about $25) works just fine. The inverter gives me a device I can use for my laptop computer, cell phone charger, portable printer power supply, and lots of other uses. Just keep in mind that an inverter can draw only so much power from your car's cigarette lighter. For heavier uses, you have to connect it directly to the car battery.

Remember that if you connect an inverter directly to your car's battery and run your gear too long, you can completely drain the battery. Depending on your gear's needs and your battery's capacity, draining your battery can take as little as 30 minutes.

Finding emergency printing solutions

If you find yourself with a need for quick prints, and your printer isn't working or isn't available, don't forget the self-service kiosks that are becoming more and more prevalent. Although prints from these machines are probably too expensive to use on a normal basis, they do serve quite well for emergencies. An alternative is to take your memory card to a department store, such as Walmart or Target, that offers one-hour printing services straight from your memory card.

Dealing with Lighting Issues

Lighting can be a real challenge for insurance photography in the field. Seldom if ever do you have any control over lighting conditions, and you're often dealing with highly reflective surfaces. To make matters worse, you frequently have a lot of contrast to contend with, as shown in Figure 22-2.

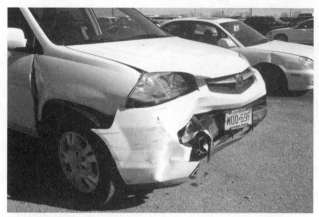

Figure 22-2: High-contrast light and a white car make it difficult to record detail in this photo.
© 2004 Dan Simon

Using your built-in flash

One way to overcome these lighting problems is to turn your camera's flash on and just shoot away. Although this is an inelegant solution for creative photography, it's a better alternative than trusting ambient light alone. Flash can help reduce overall contrast to the damaged area by filling in the shadows, making the photo more legible. Most digital cameras offer a choice between having the camera make the decision whether or not to use flash and another setting that always fires the built-in flash unit. Under these lighting conditions, choose the setting that makes the flash fire for every shot (see Figure 22-3).

Lighting for detail

If possible, you want your main light source to be at a right angle to the damage you're photographing. This position brings out detail and makes the shot more readable.

This positioning can present a bit of a challenge. Odds are, you won't be able to move the damaged property and timing your visit to coincide with the sun being in the right location isn't always practical.

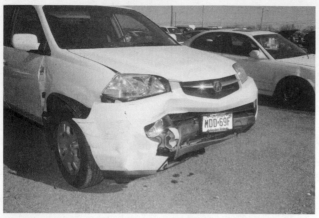

Figure 22-3: I changed positions slightly and used an on-camera flash to even out the lighting for this image.

© 2004 Dan Simon

The easiest way to deal with the problem of positioning your light source is through the use of an off-camera flash unit. These units are usually activated via a cord that connects to the camera's hot shoe (a mount usually found on the top of the camera that the flash would normally slide into). Alternatively, the unit may be connected through a slaved flash activated by your camera's built-in flash firing. Unless you're using a DSLR, the odds are your digital camera will not have a hot shoe, so more than likely, you're going to need the slaved flash option.

 Turn to Chapter 7 for more information about slaved flashes and hot shoe mounts.

Another solution is to use a type of filter known as a low-contrast filter. Several manufacturers make these filters, including one that calls its line *ultra-contrast*. Low-contrast filters do a pretty good job of reducing contrast in an image. At one time, the biggest challenge in using one of these filters was in finding a way to mount it to a digital camera. Many early point-and-shoot digital cameras offered no way to attach filters and had lens barrels too small for any of the filters currently on the market.

 Visit this book's companion web site (www.wiley.com/compbooks/simon) for more information on low-contrast filters and links to filter manufacturers.

With newer mid-range and high-end point-and-shoot cameras, attaching filters is becoming less of a problem. Many of these digital cameras have larger-sized optics (usually to increase the lens's light-gathering capabilities) and have threads for mounting filters. If your camera doesn't have this capability, using a low-contrast filter may not be an option for you.

Summary

Insurance documentation photography calls for an accurate representation of damaged property, whether the damage occurred to an automobile, a home, or a business.

Getting the light right is the first and perhaps most important step in shooting photos that accurately document damage. Digital cameras don't handle high-contrast lighting very well, and hotspots and glare are a big problem whether you're shooting film or digital. This chapter offered ideas for dealing with light that may detract from your photos and suggested alternative solutions for situations when you're faced with high-contrast lighting.

When you're taking photographs for insurance purposes, you are often on a tight deadline. This chapter also provided information on printers you can use in the field to help you speed up your paperwork.

Digital Photography for Research and Documentation

Research often necessitates producing usable photographic images.

Research photos don't have to be works of art, but they do need to be accurate representations of their subject matter. Accurate color and good detail are often more important than aesthetic interests.

Further complicating matters is that for many researchers, the subject matter may be elusive, or a moving target.

Fortunately, you can create good representational images even in the field, provided you take a step beyond the banal point-and-shoot. For those working mainly in a lab environment, photography is perhaps a bit easier because you can set up a photo station and be ready to create images at a moment's notice. This chapter offers advice on how to conduct field research photography and some techniques to help your photos suit your research needs.

The Special Challenges of Field Photography

If your fieldwork is the type that takes you out on the occasional survey to difficult-to-reach wilderness areas, you should try to have at least two of everything.

Equipment failure might make it impossible for you to photograph a specimen. Duplicates should include a second camera, even if it isn't quite as good as your main picture-taking machine. Even a so-so picture of a rare plant or specimen is better than no photo at all. Plus, you can always enhance your images in the digital darkroom.

If you're chasing moving targets, such as animals, refer to Chapter 10, which covers nature photography. Most wild creatures won't let people get near them, so be prepared to have the longest possible optics, either via telephoto lenses or add-on lens adapters.

Something else to consider when you're in the field is boosting the range of an accessory flash if you have one. Devices like the *Better Beamer* (a Fresnel lens that attaches to your flashhead) can double or triple your flash's effective range.

You can also use photoelectric sensor rigs to trigger a remote camera and flash unit. Flash extenders are fairly common and several different types exist (see this book's companion web site for links to relevant vendors), but finding remote triggers can be more of a problem. Usually your camera needs some kind of remote triggering hookup, which is common in DSLRs and frequently found in higher-end point-and-shoot digital cameras, but not so common in cheaper cameras. The section "Manipulating Light," a little later in this chapter, goes into greater detail about lighting considerations.

 Setting up a remotely triggered camera pits risk against reward. Do you want to buy an expensive digital camera and expensive accessories only to leave them in the perilous wild? You may end up with some great images, but you may also end up with a useless camera. If you find the risk too great, you can buy a used film camera body for far less than its digital counterpart. If you're going to stage a remotely triggered camera for days or even weeks, the immediacy and quick review advantages of digital cameras aren't as important.

Capturing good images isn't as challenging for researchers documenting inactive subjects such as plants, rocks, and fungi. Here, the biggest hassle is producing readable images free from photographic flaws that would otherwise hinder legibility. The following sections tell you more about what to take with you and some techniques you can use to ensure success in the field.

Field Research Photography Checklist

As I've mentioned in the other chapters in Part V of this book, refer to the basic checklists presented in Chapter 18 to ensure that your camera is in working order and that you know how to handle simple camera troubleshooting. Have extra batteries and memory with you; getting caught in the field without power is a problem you can't overcome. This is particularly true if your camera uses a proprietary battery type.

Remember that this checklist and those found throughout Part V of this book are available on this book's companion web site (`www.wiley.com/compbooks/simon`) in both PDF and Microsoft Word formats. Be sure to check out the lists, download the ones that seem most helpful, and change them to fit your needs.

Beyond the basics, here are the essential items you need to take with you into the field:

❑ **Extras:** Extra camera, batteries, and memory.

❑ **Diffuser:** Collapsible diffusers are the easiest to transport. Even simpler, you can tie a white pillowcase or sheet to nearby trees with some twine to serve as a makeshift diffuser.

❑ **Reflector:** You can use a commercial reflector or bring along some extra heavy-duty aluminum foil (a good thing to carry even if you do have a collapsible unit). You can position a reflector to bounce light into shadow areas or serve as a wind block when you're photographing small plants. If you're dealing with very small subjects, a small mirror can also work (not to mention serve as an emergency signal device).

❑ **Twine, string, twist ties, gaffer's tape, and other attachment aides:** I like to carry an assortment of odds and ends that can be used to tie off branches and stems or affix backdrops or windscreens. Besides those items mentioned earlier, you can use strips of fabric when you want to exercise extra care in tying back plant stems (just make sure not to include the cloth in your photograph).

❑ **Wire coat hangers or stiff wire:** A cheaper (and more difficult) alternative to using plant holders (discussed later) is to fashion your own plant holders out of a wire coat hanger or some stiff wire.

❑ **Ground tarp:** Tarps can provide a clean surface for you to kneel on in wet or muddy conditions or serve double duty as a makeshift backdrop. In an emergency you can use a tarp, rocks, and some string to fashion a makeshift lean-to or shelter from the elements.

> **Note** To rig a basic shelter, twist a rock into a section of tarp and then tie a cord around the neck created by the twist. Tie the other end of the cord to a nearby tree. Repeat this for one or two other attachment points and you can rig a basic shelter.

❑ **The 10 essentials:** Backpackers and other wilderness enthusiasts know it's a bad idea to head out into the backcountry without certain emergency supplies, known as the *10 essentials*. These include: a map, a compass, a flashlight, extra food, extra clothes, sunglasses, a first-aid kit, a pocket knife, waterproof matches, and a fire starter. Some people recommend adding some extra items such as a water filter or iodine tablets, a whistle, insect repellent, and sun block. A space blanket (a lightweight emergency blanket designed to retain body heat that is also known as a survival blanket), although not on the list, should also be included. It provides emergency shelter for an unplanned overnight stay and can also be used as a larger reflector.

Manipulating Light

You can do several things to produce quality images without having to invest a fortune in equipment. Working with ambient light and a few inexpensive gadgets, you can achieve the results you want.

✦ **Reflector/diffuser combo:** One of the most useful accessories you can own is the combination reflector/diffuser for improving the quality of your lighting. You can use this handy device to create softer or flatter lighting to better show detail and eliminate hot spots. Reflector/diffuser combinations can also be used to bounce light into shadow areas to reveal more detail. Finally, you can fire your flash through it to lessen glare and reflection. Figure 23-1 shows what reflector/diffuser combos can do.

Figure 23-1: Notice the difference between the two images: the image on the left utilizes available light, whereas the image on the right utilizes diffused light, bringing out detail and creating a more even overall tone.
© 2004 Dan Simon

To refresh your memory on using reflectors and diffusers, turn to Chapter 7.

✦ **Plant holders:** You can use stiff metal plant holders with an eyelet for the plant stem to help steady tall plants from breezes. Many plant photographers also rely on a pliable rod with clamps on each end. One end clamps to your tripod whereas the other end holds the plant steady.

✦ **Polarizing filter:** You can reduce reflections on plant leaves by using a polarizing filter. This handy filter does a good job of reducing glare and can also pump up the contrast in an image.

✦ **Ring light:** One particularly helpful device for plant and close-up photography is a type of flash known as a ring light. Ring lights are actually two small flash units that mount on the end of your lens and bathe your subject in light from both sides and at 45-degree angles. This is the best setup for bringing out detail in your images, reducing glare, and producing flat, even light (see Figure 23-2). Ring lights are terrific for any kind of small detailed photography, not just plants. You can use them for photographing coins, rocks, insects, or any other diminutive subject.

Figure 23-2: Ring light brings out detail on these plant leaves.
© 2004 Dan Simon

When working with a ring light, it's best to mount your camera on a tripod, but handholding is possible provided you can hold yourself steady.

Lighting for detail

Whenever possible, you should use side lighting to bring out the most detail in your subjects. Here are some ways to use lighting to bring out detail.

✦ Compose your shot so your main light source is at a right angle to your subject and then position a reflector on the other side to bounce light back into the shadow side.

✦ Set up a pair of lights, each angled to the side of your subject so that their light rakes across the front of it. This is the same design principle the ring light works on, and it can be adapted for larger projects.

✦ Use a copy stand. These contraptions are nothing new; in fact, your lab may already have one. Copy stands feature multiple lights angled toward a flat panel at the base of the stand. There's a rear column with a mount for your camera and a geared transport mechanism that lets you position the camera higher or lower as needed. These devices usually cost less than $200 and are worthwhile investments if you need to do a lot of detail work in the lab.

The color of light

Not all light is created the same. Although Chapter 7 covers the color of light in greater detail, it's important to understand that different light sources can produce color casts that can affect your subject's colors.

There are several ways to deal with light's many different colors:

✦ **Trust your camera's auto white balance feature:** White balance works reasonably well under most normal lighting conditions. It may not do the trick for unusual types of lighting (sodium vapor lights, for example). It can also be a problem when you have a mix of light sources.

✦ **Use flash:** The light from your flash unit normally overpowers ambient light. Because your camera knows that a flash's light contains a lot of blue, it compensates for that problem, but not always, as shown in Figure 23-3.

Figure 23-3: Though not readily apparent in this image, combining white balance and flash results in a strange bluish cast in the lower left portion of the image.

© 2004 Dan Simon

Caution

Combining white balance and flash can lead to problems. I custom white-balanced my camera for the light in the greenhouse shown in Figure 23-3. When my assistant fired a flash into the shadow area of the scene, the light from the strobe unit photographed much bluer than it normally would because I calibrated the camera for a different colored light. In this case, it would have been better to trust either my camera's white balance or the flash, but not both.

On The Web

Don't forget, full-color versions of all figures are available on this book's companion web site at www.wiley.com/compbooks/simon.

Summary

In this chapter, I covered ways to produce high-quality field research photos, how to use light to your advantage, how to isolate your subject from its natural background, and which items to bring with you to ensure that your trip is the best it can be. It's important to remember that accurate documentation photographs are more important than aesthetically pleasing ones. Images don't need to be pretty; instead, they must render an accurate portrayal of your subject matter.

Digital Photography for Artists and Graphic Artists

I t's not unusual for those in the creative fields, particularly artists and graphic artists, to have some training in photography. It's also not unusual for artists and graphic artists to need the ability to make good photographs.

This chapter is geared toward the creative community. I cover the kinds of photographic challenges artists and graphic artists face and offer ways they can migrate their skills from the analog training many artists received in college to the more technocentric digital world.

Artists, graphic artists, and illustrators all face different challenges, so this chapter breaks things down by profession, beginning with graphic artists.

Artist and Graphic Artist's Photography Checklist

Begin with the basic checklists I provided in Chapter 18 to ensure that your camera is in working order and that you know how to handle simple camera troubleshooting. As always, be sure you have extra batteries and memory—getting caught without power on a shoot can be a hassle, especially if your camera uses a proprietary-type battery.

When you have the basics covered, here are some specific considerations for artists and graphics artists:

❏ Keep your table or work area clean—neatness counts. Make your product shots look their best by placing them on a simple, but clutter-free tabletop. Use a neutral color cloth that won't blend into your subject matter. Be careful to consider potential reflections. The wrong color tablecloth will reflect a distracting color in any glass or metallic surfaces. Stick to basic white or black when in doubt.

❏ Keep your background photography-friendly. If you have a professional-quality backdrop, use it to block distracting backgrounds. If you don't, then try to position your posing table so it's a few feet away from the wall. Because you're focusing on a subject that's close to your lens, the area in sharp focus will be small. An extra foot of separation will help throw the background out of focus and make it less noticeable.

❏ If you're using a multi-light setup, position the lights so that they illuminate each side of your product. The lights should be positioned so that they're at a right angle to your subject.

❏ If possible, set up a tripod so that it positions the camera to shoot downward on the product, although not necessarily straight down (unless you prefer a straight-down view). This will help minimize the background.

❏ Have any props you plan on using organized and available in order to minimize down time. If you have to go searching for a particular prop, that's billable time being wasted.

❏ Have camera-ready artwork of the client's logo or identity material handy.

Tweak this checklist as you need to for specific clients. Maintaining a supply of clean client identity materials to use as props in an image is particularly important. Nothing looks worse than a dirty company plaque or emblem.

Remember that this checklist, and those found throughout Part V of this book, are available on this book's companion web site at www.wiley.com/compbooks/simon in both PDF and Microsoft Word format. Be sure to check out the lists, download the ones that seem most helpful, and change them to fit your needs.

Digital Photography for Graphic Artists

I have a soft spot in my heart for graphic artists; after all, I'm married to one. My associate's degree is in computer graphic arts, and after seeing what it's like dealing with the clients that graphic artists sometimes have to deal with, I have nothing but sympathy for them.

Graphic artists, particularly those who specialize in production work, face all sorts of challenges. When budgets don't allow for professional photography, the resident artist is often pressed into service as a photographer. I mean, all you creative types think alike, right?

The reality is that outside of a mandatory photography course or two, graphic artists sometimes don't get much in the way of professional photographic training. It's true that any art major takes many of the same art history and color theory courses, but unless you're a photography major, you get minimal opportunity to actually put that theory into practice photographically.

Typically, you deal with two issues: taking a decent photograph and converting it into usable form for a catalog, document, advertisement, or web site.

Making usable images

One of the primary photographic and artistic concerns common to the print industry is the need to create clean images that can be easily and effectively silhouetted from their backgrounds and dropped into composite images.

Photoshop's ability to separate a product from its background is legendary. Many graphic artists are much more comfortable working in Photoshop than they are with taking pictures, so the tendency is to snap a quick photo and make things right in the digital darkroom. If this sounds like your approach, give some thought to working the photographic side of the equation a bit harder. Like so many things in the age of the digital darkroom, a few minutes of extra effort in setting up and taking your photograph can save loads of time in front of the computer. When creating photos, keep the following things in mind to make your life in the digital darkroom much easier.

Managing color balance is perhaps the most important thing to consider when taking photos. Some of the tips later in this chapter suggest using off-the-shelf lights for illumination. It's a good, money-saving idea, so long as you keep in mind that each type of light creates its own color cast. Managing color balance is easy with digital photography. You can place either a white or a gray card at the edge of the frame, and then either white balance with your camera when you take the photograph or use the card as a reference point when you adjust the image in the digital darkroom.

 You can find more detailed information about white balancing your camera in Chapter 2, and more detailed information about using Photoshop to set white points in Chapter 15.

If you routinely need to photograph small objects (things small enough to fit on a conference table), you might consider buying some green screen or blue screen material. This can save a lot of work as you can quickly separate the object from the background. You just have to be careful that your product doesn't pick up the color of these materials. Generally, if you're shooting an opaque product with little or no reflectivity, using green or blue screen works fine. If you're photographing something reflective or even slightly transparent, use white or a medium gray seamless paper instead. These types of materials are readily found as rolls of seamless backdrop paper and can be set up fairly easily, particularly if you use a portable stand setup. Total cost of this kind of arrangement is less than $200, depending on how many different types of paper you want to stock.

Got a tightwad boss? (Okay, I know. Silly question.) Then you can make do with a tablecloth and a blank wall as a backdrop. It helps if your wall and tablecloth are markedly different colors than your product's packaging. If they're similar, you need to find a different color tablecloth or switch to a different wall. Arranging your table a few feet away from the wall makes removing the subject from the background easier.

Figure 24-1 employs a technique known as bounce flash, achieved by pointing the head of your flash unit up towards the ceiling so light bounces off the ceiling and down towards your subject. Bounced light (and it can be light of any kind, not just flash) softens and spreads as it travels back from the ceiling, creating a more gentle light than firing your flash directly at your subject. Just be careful, a colored ceiling changes the color of your light and provides a color cast to your image. (This is fixable in Photoshop, especially if you set up a reference white or gray somewhere in the photo. Using a color reference chart is explained later in this chapter.)

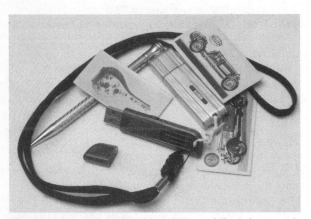

Figure 24-1: A simple white cloth and flash bounced off the ceiling produced this image.
© 2004 Dan Simon

Setting up a mini studio

Assume for a moment that you don't work for the cheapest boss in the world and you have a chance to get some decent equipment. Also assume that your boss needs you to create digital photographs on a regular basis for use in both print and web display. What kind of studio should you set up? Following are my suggestions for building a great studio on a not-so-great budget.

Building a pro-level tabletop studio

Though it may sound fanciful, the idea of having a pro-level studio available for your photographic needs may actually be quite realistic. If your main requirement is to photograph small tabletop items, it shouldn't be hard at all.

Several companies make small lighting tents (often called *domes* or *mini studios*) that you can use to bathe a product in soft even light. They usually cost less than $100. Place your product inside the mini studio (which looks like a small white box), shine your lights into the opaque white material that covers the box, and point your camera through the opening designed for photography. The soft white material provides a diffuse, even lighting that makes your product look its best. Add a small table for the tent to rest on (steal the break room table from your coworkers), buy a light or two, and you're ready to go.

 Visit this book's companion web site at www.wiley.com/compbooks/simon for links to manufacturers of these products.

Another tool for the tabletop studio is a revolving stand that helps you make a 360-degree virtual replica of your product. Mount your product on the stand and photograph it in front of a piece of seamless white paper. You then shoot a series of images as the product is rotated, making sure that you photograph every square inch of the product. The photos are stitched together to create one 360-degree image the viewer can move any way he wants.

This kind of image is popular for web-based catalogues because it lets the visitor move the object around in three virtual dimensions, allowing them to examine the product from all angles.

This kind of imagery is nearly impossible to create from scratch, but relatively simple with the right display stand and the appropriate software. A company called Kaiden makes a wide variety of products designed to help make this kind of photography easier. They can even set up a software/hardware package for your needs.

 Visit this book's companion web site at www.wiley.com/compbooks/simon for a link to the Kaiden web site.

If you routinely need to photograph very small items—such as jewelry or coins—you can be very effective by using black velvet or colored cloth and mounting a ring light on your camera. Ring lights are great for producing quality lighting simply and with minimal fuss. Best of all, ring lights are available for both DSLRs and point-and-shoot digital cameras. Although the versions pros use can run $500 or more, inexpensive ones can be found for less than $200 and sometimes for less than $100.

Here are some other handy gizmos to make your tabletop studio the best in the office:

✦ **Tripod:** Despite your best attempts to remain steady, you can't. Your body always sways back and forth, and tripods eliminate this movement. Normally body sway isn't a big deal, but when you're dealing with close-up shots (and particularly when depth of field is minimal), any movement can affect your image's overall sharpness. Tripods also allow you to move around and perform other tasks (like hide from co-workers who are angry because you stole the break room table) while your camera stays put. When you return, everything's set up, and all you have to do is trip the shutter release.

✦ **Remote control:** Less important, but nice to have, is some form of remote control camera trigger. Remote triggers are more important for slow shutter speeds where the act of pressing the shutter button can cause enough vibration to blur the picture, but even at faster speeds they're still nice to have.

✦ **Bubble level:** It's nice to be sure your camera is level. This saves you the effort needed in Photoshop to straighten the image. (Remember, straightening an image in Photoshop also means cropping it a bit tighter. This can create problems for an already tight composition.) These devices mount in your camera's hot shoe (the bracket where an accessory flash goes) and help you judge level in two dimensions. If your camera doesn't have a hot shoe, for goodness sake, buy one that does! (Just kidding. Just buy a small level at your local hardware store and use that.)

✦ **Posing cloth:** Have some kind of cloth, linen, or velvet material to place over the table to hide any dirt or scratches on the table surface. It's also less distracting than a wood grain finish. Cloth also eliminates the reflections you get from a wood or laminate surface. Have several different color cloths available (usually one light and one dark at least) so you can choose an appropriate one for your product. Place light-colored products on dark cloth, and dark-colored products on light cloth (see Figure 24-2). You can even consider an appropriate shade of blue or green to make silhouetting the product out of the image easier; just remember to think about color reflections.

Figure 24-2: A white linen napkin provides an elegant and effective photographic surface for this picture.
© 2004 Dan Simon

✦ **Posing blocks:** A set of small wooden blocks is useful to support your package or product. Place the blocks under your posing cloth in differing levels, and you can balance an object against them or create a two-tier (or more) platform to show multiple objects.

✦ **Stands or display cases:** Depending on your needs, you may also wish to have jewelry stands and various other display cases and the like that are specific to the kind of items you need to photograph. If small items comprise the bulk of your in-house photography, a *copy stand* may be the solution for you. These devices combine a platform and a geared track (to position the camera and lights and sometimes sold separately) all in one self-contained unit. All you have to do is mount your camera on the stand, turn the lights on and place the object you want to photograph on the platform. Focus the camera; set your exposure settings and you're ready to shoot. After you finish one item, you can pull it away and stick the next one in place. If they're they same size, you probably won't even have to refocus.

Setting up a mini-studio on the cheap

Even if there's next to no room in your budget for photography, there are still some things you can do to create better photos.

The best way to overcome budget shortfalls is to assemble a photo studio in a box. Okay, it's not glamorous, it reeks of low budget, and you probably don't want to pull it out in front of a client, but you can at least have an easy-to-store, helpful little photo kit that fits in a paper box. Here's what should be in it:

✦ **Fabric:** Once again, you need something to position your subject on that looks better than whatever tabletop you're using. With this setup, you can wait until the break room's empty, brush the donut crumbs off the table, and be ready to set up on a moment's notice. A piece of light-colored fabric and a piece of dark-colored fabric would be nice. Add a swatch of neutral gray and you're set.

✦ **Small boxes and pieces of wood:** These create the foundation of your risers and platforms for creating multiple levels underneath your fabric.

✦ **Bogen super clamp:** Okay, at $25 to $30, this one may almost be a budget-buster. It's still cheaper than a decent tripod, and you can clamp it to a table and mount your camera on it. Add a cheap ball head for $10 to $15 more, and you're in good shape. (Cheap ball heads are okay for small point-and-shoot digital cameras. If you're using a DSLR, however, they probably won't be as effective.)

✦ **Pair of bell lamps with spring clamps:** Put the brightest light bulbs you can find in these. For small objects such as pens, paperweights and coins, bell lamps provide enough light to be useful. Being able to light something from two sides is vital for bringing out detail and minimizing hot spots. If you need to photograph glass or aluminum, this capability is huge. (Remember the part about white balancing discussed earlier in this chapter.)

✦ **Stands and cases:** Have some stands or cases for your typical products so you can pose them effectively. This may include gift baskets for soaps and perfumes.

✦ **Props:** Good quality props can help you dress up a shot. Try to have something that's appropriate to the product you're photographing.

Flowers and colored stones would work for jewelry. Money and coins work for pens, pencils, and wallets. Pens and pencils work for wallets and handbags. Heck, you're the creative one, you think of something. A good source for props is eBay, where you can find all sorts of antiques and collectibles. Use old objects to evoke a memory of a slower time, or for contrast against a high-tech gizmo, as shown in Figure 24-3.

Figure 24-3: A piece of jewelry positioned in a cigar box filled with tea and tobacco cards, foreign currency, and other ephemera can evoke a feeling of a more graceful time. Including a high-tech product with these collectibles can grab the eye.
© 2004 Dan Simon

✦ **Reflectors:** Store some heavy-duty aluminum foil in the box to serve as a reflector. This comes in particularly handy if your workspace offers big windows that let sunlight pour in from the outside. Set up your base cloth on the floor or on a tabletop and bathe your product in this natural light. Use a reflector to bounce the light directly onto your subject and to light shadow areas.

You've now assembled a photo studio in a box, which you can store in a safe place. You can even use it as a safe place to store your emergency stash of chocolate. (C'mon. Every graphic artist I know has an emergency stash of chocolate.)

Techniques for eye-catching photos

Sometimes you need to do more than just record what a product looks like. Sometimes you need to evoke a mood or an emotion to help sell that product. Use the props I described earlier to create ambience and catch the viewer's eye. Including props in a picture can make it easier for a customer to picture himself using or owning the item. Carefully choosing your props can also tell the viewer whether an item is upscale or affordable, or if it's for a man or a woman.

If you're designing for a catalog, try to maintain a consistent theme. Most often, products are shown with the items they're used with, such as pens with stationery. Still, there's no reason you can't make oddball combinations of products and props so long as you remain consistent in your approach.

Another reason for adding extraneous items to a product photograph is because they can bring much needed color to an otherwise muted product. By surrounding a black and white pen with colorful flowers or stones, you make the photo more eye-catching.

Using color

One thematic approach that works for a catalog or campaign is the thoughtful use of color. Plan on developing a color scheme for your products, and consider how colors work together when developing a color scheme. Here are some color techniques you can employ in your product shots:

✦ **Complementary colors:** Red/green, blue/orange, purple/yellow catch the eye and improve the chances of the viewer seeing the ad. Just remember that they also have the potential to overpower the product itself.

✦ **Analogous colors:** Colors adjacent to one another on the color wheel are used for the moods they set. Cooler colors (blue, green, purple) provide a more sophisticated feel, whereas warm colors (red, yellow, orange) evoke a sense of passion.

✦ **Sepia tone:** Photographers have known for decades that the faded, brownish look of old photos is powerful and appealing. For many years, Kodak even made a sepia paper so photographers could create that look without having to wait for their pictures to age enough to look that way. (Sheesh! Everybody's in a hurry.) Evoke the image of times gone by through the use of a sepia tone to your image. In the digital darkroom, you can make your product stand out and keep its regular colors: Simply strip the product out of the main layer and place it in its own layer. Alternatively, you can composite the object into a separate sepia-toned image.

 Project: **Creating a sepia-toned shot**

Follow these steps to composite your image into a sepia-toned shot:

1. Open your image in Photoshop.

2. Choose Layer ➪New Adjustment Layer ➪Hue/Saturation to create a hue/saturation adjustment layer.

3. Select the Colorize box.

4. Set Hue to 35 (tweak as desired).

5. Set Saturation to 20 (tweak as desired).

6. Adjust lightness as desired. Making the image lighter gives your product more of an old and faded look. If you're compositing your product into a separate image, this will help it stand out more.

If you're bringing the object into another image, continue with these steps:

1. Silhouette the product out of its background and import the image of your product into your working image.

    If you're not a graphic artist and have just stumbled into this section, you probably need to know more about *silhouetting* or *masking* (same thing) an image. This is covered in Chapter 15.

2. Use Photoshop's Transform command to size your product as needed. Hold down the Shift key to keep your scaling proportional.

3. If you want to adjust skew, distortion, or perspective, choose Edit ➪ Transform, and select either Skew, Distort, or Perspective to help blend your product into the original image.

If you plan to use sepia tone a lot, consider buying some period props. eBay is a good place to find collectible items and other knick knacks. You can find anything from old pens to tobacco cards (an early version of trading cards) and old toys, which all make great, inexpensive props. You can also scour antique shops for other low-cost old stuff for your prop box. Tell your boss that you're building a prop archive, not just antiquing, and you should be fine.

Close-up photography

Working with small items and props calls for skill in close-up photography. This is covered more thoroughly in Chapter 5, but here are some things to keep in mind:

✦ **Shallow depth of field:** When you focus close, the range of sharp focus is very small, even if you work with a small lens opening. Focus on a point about one-third of the way in on the most important area of your product. If you're shooting something with a long dimension and a short dimension (such as a pen), orient the item so that its long end is perpendicular to the camera lens. Keeping the long side on the same plane as the camera sensor keeps the whole length of the pen in focus. You can reverse this orientation for emphasis from time to time. Say your pen manufacturer places its company symbol on the top of the pen. You can orient the pen so you're shooting from the top down the length of the pen, keeping only the manufacturer's symbol in sharp focus. If your client has a recognizable logo or mark, this technique is effective.

✦ **Emphasis:** Getting in close showcases a product well, particularly in an electronic environment. Although it's nice to have an environmental setting (like a photo of the product amongst props), readability is still important. On the web, where images need to be small to keep file sizes manageable, a close-up of just the product may be your most effective option. (You can still use the more ornate prop shot for catalogs and print ads.)

✦ **Light:** The more light you can throw on your product the greater the depth of sharpness you can enjoy. Try to have extra lights for close-up images (extra clamp-on bell lamps will work), especially if you're using a more basic point-and-shoot digital camera.

After you've created your photographs and processed them in Photoshop (or another image-editing program), you're ready to use them however you might need to.

Digital Photography for Artists

Okay, admit it. You were wondering when I would get to you, weren't you? Digital photography can be a very helpful tool for an artist, not necessarily as a primary art form, but as a helpful assistant in committing art.

Digital cameras make great visual note-taking tools. You can photograph a scene and—if your camera has a built-in voice recorder—simultaneously record your thoughts about that scene and how to paint it or draw it in the future.

You can also experiment with some of Photoshop's artistic filters in order to try some ideas. If you find this approach useful, another program, Corel Painter 8 (formerly MetaCreations Painter), may be even more up your alley. Painter provides a nice variety of artistic tools, brushes, and effects and can be used to create a work of art that looks a lot more like a real painting or sketch.

Visit this book's companion web site at `www.wiley.com/compbooks/simon` for a link to the software maker's web site.

Some artists like to use digital cameras for easy note-taking in the field, whereas others find them more useful for making recordings of their own works. A digital camera can be a very useful tool for documenting a painting, especially if you take the trouble to make your photograph as accurate as possible.

One of the most important concerns, of course, is ensuring that the image you photograph shows the same colors in the computer as it does on the canvas. Whereas an image on a computer screen appears via transmitted light, a painting or sketch appears through reflected light. So it's not possible for the colors to be completely identical. It is however, still possible to be accurate.

Photographing a painting

Years ago, to get an accurate color rendition with film, you had to use a neutral light source and include a color chip chart (a paper strip with a defined range of colors on it) in your photos. You would then bring the film to a custom lab and request that the lab technician match the colors in the photo to the colors on the chip chart.

This is still an effective approach. If you include a known, universal standard (such as a Macbeth color checker) in your photograph, custom photo processors can match the colors on the color checker in the photo to the color checker they have on hand. After they get these settings right, they can apply them to a cropped version of your image that just shows your artwork.

One advantage of digital photography over conventional technology is that you no longer have to worry about choosing the right film and light combination when photographing artwork. You do, however, still have to worry about lighting the artwork properly. Too much light on the top of the painting or sketch and not enough on the bottom (or vice versa) results in an unevenly lit image with lost quality at the darker end.

It's best to try to provide a soft, even lighting that brings out the detail of the painting without creating harsh reflections or glare by setting up a couple of lights, one to each side of the artwork. A soft box (for studio lights) or lampshade for lamps helps diffuse the light properly. Remember to white balance the camera before you shoot.

 More detailed information about white balancing a camera is available in Chapter 2.

Make sure the painting and the camera are leveled on the same plane. If one or the other is off axis, some areas of the painting might appear out of focus in the picture. Place the chip chart or Macbeth color checker on the bottom of the picture frame or easel, and then photograph the artwork.

Photographing 3D artwork

Of course, many artists also create three-dimensional art. Accuracy is just as important in photographing these artworks as it is in reproducing paintings. You just have the added complication of working in three dimensions instead of two.

Here are some things to consider if you need to photograph a 3D work of art:

✦ In cases where color accuracy is paramount (such as ceramics), follow the same advice given in the preceding section about photographing paintings and include a standard color reference device. If color accuracy isn't quite so vital (or the image is going to be used in a grayscale document), you can consider skipping this.

✦ Include a scale of some type to mark the size of the object you're photographing. Position slightly to the side of the object (level with its base) so you can crop the scale out of the image later if needed. Ideally, you're going to need multiple scales to show height, depth, and width.

✦ Be sure to position your sculpture, ceramic, or other object on a suitable surface to permit proper photography. Depending on its size, you may decide to use a table or the floor. Place the object on a suitable cloth; be careful to pick a neutral color that won't create distracting reflections. White or black is usually safest.

✦ Have a suitable backdrop for your artwork. Solid black for a light-colored object or solid white for a dark object tends to be easiest and safest.

✦ When you set up your lighting, be sure to first light for detail. This means setting up at least a pair of lights at a right angle to the camera lens and pointing directly at the sides of the artwork. These lights should illuminate each side of the object evenly. (Be sure that each light uses the same wattage bulb.)

 If you are trying to photograph a highly reflective object, such as a glass or metal sculpture, consider pointing your lights straight up and bouncing the light off the ceiling. This works well if you have a white ceiling and can get your lights within a couple of feet of the ceiling (ideally about three feet away.) If you're working with a colored ceiling, you need to incorporate a white card and then white balance the camera for the color cast that results from bouncing lights off a colored ceiling. If you can't get your lights close enough to the ceiling, or if they aren't powerful enough to illuminate the artwork this way, use the lighting suggestion discussed in the preceding bullet (a pair of lights at a right angle to the camera lens and pointed directly at the sides of the artwork). See Chapter 2 for more information about white balancing your camera.

✦ Try to set the camera up on a tripod to allow for a longer exposure, greater depth of field, and increased camera steadiness.

Don't be afraid to move your lights about to improve shadows or reflections. Try different approaches. It's better to spend a few extra minutes trying various techniques than to have to do the shoot all over again because your first approach didn't work.

After you photograph the artwork, you need to find a custom lab willing to match the colors in your image to the colors in your reference chart, and then make a print from the file. Any good lab should be able to do this, but don't expect this service from your typical one-hour photo processor (especially not for enlargements).

Summary

Overworked, underpaid, under-budgeted. Yep, sounds like every graphic artist and artist I know. This chapter offered some budget-priced approaches to creating studio-quality photos. It also offered some basic product information, some handy uses of close-up photography, and some tips on finding and using inexpensive props to help make your products stand out.

Digital Photography for Public Relations Specialists

There's the idea out there that public relations photography is nothing more than getting your client in some outlandish outfit or situation and snapping a photo for the local paper. If you have ever had the need to take a PR photo, you know that's not the case. Getting your boss or client (they're kind of the same thing, aren't they?) recognized by the local media as nothing more than a clown or buffoon won't get you promoted. It could, however, get you fired.

Public relations photography is about taking good, newsworthy pictures. These are the kind of images a newspaper editor expects her own staff to bring back when she sends them out on an assignment. The difference is that as a public relations professional, you have the chance to make sure that photo says everything you want it to say about your client and nothing you don't want to say.

When I first joined the Navy many years ago, the idea of sailors as hard-partying, "a girl in every port" types, was still very strong. But even back then, the Navy knew it had to break away from the image of the drunken sailor. Navy photographers and journalists were trained to never make or use a photo of a sailor with any form of alcohol in the picture, including T-shirts advertising alcohol.

This was but the first step in a long-running and well-managed campaign to reinvent the image of the

American sailor. Although it incorporated many other elements, the example given above shows that if an organization as big and scattered as the U.S. Navy can pull it off, your company can, too.

In this chapter, I discuss the common needs of public affairs photography and point out some pitfalls to avoid. I point out some things for you to consider from the perspective of the PR person taking photographs, as well as for the PR person setting up a photo opp for another photographer.

Staying on Message

One of the first things you need to keep in mind is that every photograph you make should support the basic public relations message you want to get across.

If you want to depict your company or its leadership as energetic and innovative, don't picture them sitting around a conference table in some stuffy office. Instead, get them at a job site or work center checking out a new manufacturing technique or construction project.

On the other hand, if your client is the neighborhood bank that's been servicing your local community for decades, or you want to create the impression that it has, a more conservative look will work. Some ideas would include the "kindly" bank president assisting an elderly client or bank staffers helping out at a community picnic or marching in the local parade.

Whatever you do, stay away from pictures of people doing nothing more than smiling and shaking hands, or smiling and sitting around, or smiling and cutting ribbons, or smiling around leaning on shovels (for ground breaking ceremonies). A number of events fall into this "just standing around" category. One particularly common genre is the beginning or end of a construction project symbolized by ground breaking or ribbon cutting photos. This type of photography is discussed in the following sections.

Ground breaking or ribbon cutting

PR folks are always setting up ribbon cuttings and groundbreaking ceremonies. Although your client or organization probably will insist on such an event, it's tough to get news photographers out for them. Those who do attend will be in a hurry. Maximize your press opportunity by having handout materials for the photographers. When applicable, stress statistics on job creation and the financial benefits to the community—thanks to the construction project that's about to begin.

You still have to stage these events because they're valuable internal relations opportunities. So get some mileage out of them by giving copies of the photos to the people who appear in the pictures, having a commemorative print made to hang in the lobby of the new building when it's done, and going ahead and running the photo in the company newsletter. Just make sure that when you take the picture, you have covered the items on the checklist that follows.

Checklist for taking good groundbreaking and other ceremonial shots

Begin with the basic checklists I provide in Chapter 18 to ensure that your camera is in working order and you know how to handle simple camera troubleshooting. As always, be sure you have extra batteries and memory—getting caught at a groundbreaking ceremony without power can be a hassle, especially if your camera uses a proprietary-type battery.

 Remember that this checklist and those found throughout Part V of this book are available on this book's companion web site (www.wiley .com/compbooks/simon) in both PDF and Microsoft Word formats. Be sure to check out the lists, download the ones that seem the most helpful, and change them to fit your needs.

Here are some specific things to keep in mind when shooting a groundbreaking ceremony:

❑ Line everyone up so they're in the same plane (instead of in a semi-circle). This helps ensure that everyone is in sharp focus. This is because you may be shooting with a wide-open lens and not have much depth of field to play with. (Depth of field refers to the zone of sharpness that extends through the image. This is a variable distance that's dependent on the size of your lens opening. By keeping everyone on the same plane, you minimize the need for great depth of field.)

❑ Use flash. Hard hats produce a shadow that can drop down over the eyes. Turning your camera's flash on will clean this up.

❑ Scope out the area thoroughly. Make sure you're aware of any potential problem spots in the background that you have to plan for. New construction seldom takes place in the middle of nowhere, so it's important to make sure there's no embarrassing or distracting background elements that may show up in your photo.

❑ Look for an interesting camera angle. Generally, the best angle from which to shoot a groundbreaking ceremony is down low with a wide-angle lens. Get close to the shovels and let their shafts lead the eye up to your executives who are looking down toward the lens and smiling. This is a much more interesting composition than a shot made at eye level with a longer focal length where the execs are all looking in different directions. Similar advice works for a ribbon cutting. Use a wide-angle focal length, get level with the ribbon and scissors, and make sure your ribbon cutters are looking either straight into the lens or straight at the ribbon (which should be practically the same thing).

Wearing Two Hats

As a PR person, you should take a moment to consider how a news photographer might look at the scene. If there's a billboard or sign in the background that would provide a humorous contrast to the actual ceremony, there's a good chance they'll include it. Remember, a news photographer's job is to get an interesting photograph, not to make your company look good. So don't automatically assume that the photographer will eliminate an embarrassing background element. It's more likely the element will be included because it makes an otherwise dull photo into an interesting one.

Ideally, you've scoped out the site a day or two ahead of time. This gives you several possible options. First, you can arrange the scene so that the shovel holders are positioned away from the problem background. If this solution isn't possible, arrange to have a large banner, sign, or tent to serve as a backdrop and mask out the problem element.

Awards ceremonies

Another common PR photography challenge is the awards ceremony. You know how it goes. The CEO or department head presents the award with one hand and shakes the recipient's hand with the other. Both people hold that pose and turn their heads to smile for the camera.

Grip 'n' grins, as they're known, are great for the award recipient. They're a nice memento to hang on the wall and provide a special keepsake of the person's moment of triumph. When it comes to staging a photo for a newspaper story or company newsletter, however, why not aim for a photo that truly illustrates why the person is being honored? Arrange for a photo that shows the award recipient demonstrating what it is he did to earn the recognition. Photograph him practicing his skill: working in the lab, consulting with the crew at a construction site, or reading to children in the library—whatever it is that brought him notice and acclaim in the first place. Sure, this requires more work than pulling together a simple grip 'n' grin shot, but it also produces a much more substantive image.

There are a couple of problems with getting the working shot. First, it takes more effort and more skill (see the following checklist for advice on that one). Second, some honorees like seeing their grip 'n' grin picture in the paper, and they'd rather see you release that picture instead of the working photo. If this is your situation, refer to the checklist for shooting grip 'n' grins at the end of this section.

Checklist for creating good working photos of award recipients

Here are some specific things to think about when you want to photograph an award recipient in action:

❑ Arrange to have your subject performing some aspect of her normal job.

❑ Set up some form of interaction between her and another coworker, or her and a piece of equipment she uses. As a rule, interpersonal interaction makes more sense for an office worker than just sitting at a desk pushing paper. If you're photographing someone who performs a skill (someone who makes things or someone who fixes things), show the person performing that skill (see Figure 25-1).

Figure 25-1: Barbara R. McLemore is a successful corporate counsel for a Harrisburg construction company. One reason for her success is her people skills, something I wanted to capture when I photographed her for a magazine assignment.
© 2004 Dan Simon

❑ Make sure the work area is organized and uncluttered even if that isn't the way it normally appears.

❑ Make sure there are no safety or policy violations that show up in the image, and check for politically incorrect materials, as well.

❑ Use flash unless you're really comfortable with something like window lighting as your main light source. If your subject does detail work using a magnifier with its own light source, try a couple of shots with the lights turned down so that the subject's light becomes your main light source. Flash also solves some lighting problems because your camera will white balance properly for the flash. If you work without flash, the in-house light source may produce a color cast that your camera doesn't handle properly.

❑ Create a tight composition showing not much more than from head to waist. Be sure to take at least a few vertical compositions.

Checklist for creating good grip 'n' grin shots

Here are some suggestions for how to set up the typical award + handshake shot during the presentation:

❑ Make sure your equipment is in good working order. Fresh batteries are a must because awards tend to be presented at a brisk pace. If you slow down that pace because you're waiting for your flash to recycle or your camera to catch up to the action, expect some dirty looks at a minimum. There's also nothing worse than having your camera die in the middle of an awards ceremony and finding out you don't have backup batteries with you. Try to have a large enough memory card to cover the entire event. If you have to switch cards mid-way through, it may cost you a shot. This is where digital cameras have a huge advantage over shooting film. At large presentations, you can easily miss several shots because you are changing film.

❑ If possible, meet the award recipients beforehand and make sure they know the procedure. In particular, be sure they know to turn their heads and look at you while still holding the award and the presenter's handshake. Ask them not to stand too far away from the presenter.

❑ Stand nearby but out of the way until the award is presented. Step quickly into position and compose a tight shot from just below the bottom of the hand up to slightly above the people's heads. Make sure they're looking at you (a quick "Look here, please!" helps) and take the shot. As you do, make sure all subjects' eyes are open.

❑ Prepare for the next shot.

Using Symbols in Your Photography

Sometimes the opportunity to add symbolism to your images can help improve the overall content of your photos. Classic examples include positioning an American flag behind the CEO or photographing team members with a company banner in the background.

These efforts provide an extra dimension to your images and, handled properly, can help enhance your message. At bare minimum, it's a good idea to have something with the company name or logo somewhere in the photo, preferably located so that it can't be cropped out of the image by a newspaper photographer.

Figure 25-2 shows one example of how you can incorporate symbolism into a photo. I was on a magazine shoot to showcase the environmental television production company, Greenworks (now Greentreks), when I documented a morning staff meeting. Greenworks/Greentreks has won several Emmy awards, and I wanted to create an image that in some way made the connection between the company and the award. The award was on display near the conference room, so I was able to create a shot that showed both the staff meeting and the award.

Figure 25-2: Emmy award. This wouldn't work as a stand-alone photo, but it did fit the bill as a secondary image for a magazine story on the company.

© 2004 Dan Simon

 Don't forget, full-color versions of all figures are available on this book's companion web site at www.wiley.com/compbooks/simon.

Summary

Public affairs photography aspires to achieve the standards of journalistic photography, but under the control of the public relations professional. There's nothing wrong with this goal. Newspapers can send their own staffers if they want an objective image. Your job is to produce a photo they're willing to use, that also furthers your promotional efforts.

Good composition, interesting action, and a worthwhile photo fulfill that need, even if a company logo also appears in the shot. Newspapers generally aren't interested in pictures of grinning executives posing for the camera; save those for the company publication.

Keep in mind that it may be necessary to take a variety of shots to satisfy the needs of both internal and external communications. Although it is more work to create separate images for these two audiences, it's well worth your effort. The award recipient is quite happy to receive a photo that shows her shaking hands with the CEO as he presents her with a certificate, but the local newspaper is looking for an image with more action and substance. Satisfying both of these functions is an ongoing challenge of PR photography.

Putting Digital Photography to Work

✦　✦　✦　✦

✦　✦　✦　✦

This part covers three topics that didn't quite fit into the other sections of the book. They offer practical and useful advice for some important types of photography.

Digital presentations have replaced the slide show of old, and modern software has made them even more effective. Digital cameras make it possible for many a small business to do its own photography. And, finally, we all hit a point where we need to try something new. Chapter 28 shows you how to open up your photographic horizons.

Creating a Digital Presentation

Ah yes, what would a business meeting or get-together be without a digital slide presentation? Microsoft's PowerPoint software has become so ubiquitous that almost every college business major has already whipped up dozens of presentations before his first frat party.

Sometimes these presentations are succinct and right on target. Other times . . . well, you've been there, haven't you? There's a reason that coffee is always available at these meetings.

One of the most important things you can do is create a company identity for your presentation. All too often, PowerPoint slide shows are made with clip art and royalty-free photos from some CD collection purchased years ago. Although these images have the advantage of being professionally created, they don't bear any resemblance to the people and facilities that make up your company. When practical, it's always better to photograph your own world than show pictures of somebody else's. As you build an inventory of images, it becomes easier still to produce presentations that look like your company.

This chapter looks at the process of creating photographic images for a digital presentation. It also looks at ways of using these photos for best effect, both with and without type. During the next few pages, I show you how to plan your photography so your images work in your favor rather than against you.

Planning a Digital Presentation

The process, as usual, begins with thorough planning. Your slide show needs to follow a logical order, so give plenty of thought to the overall look and feel of the presentation.

Most organizations have a unique personality, and your presentation design should reflect that. If you're working for a legal firm or bank, odds are everyone is most comfortable with conservative slide backgrounds and type. Background music is likely to be more classical and restrained and the use of fancy transitions and effects will be rare.

On the other hand, if you work for a more cutting edge company, jazzier effects and music might be appropriate. The idea is to pick a style that's appropriate for your organization and your message. There are exceptions to this guideline, however. If your presentation is about your company's rollout of a new product or service that's geared to 21st century markets, you may decide to mirror that in a funkier presentation. A lot of this decisionmaking depends on your feel for your company and what is and isn't taboo.

Determining your message

The first question to answer is why are you making the presentation? All too often, the answer to this question is a little vague and unfocused. This isn't necessarily a problem; it's just important to realize that if you're not sure what you're trying to communicate, your presentation is going to reflect that ambiguity.

Try to spend some time articulating what you want the presentation to cover. After you've formulated a specific idea or set of ideas, you can begin the task of creating or gathering images to support your message.

It's important to stay focused on what you want to say. There's nothing worse than a rambling presentation that can't quite seem to stay on target. Lack of focus makes it harder for your audience to receive your information. This doesn't mean you can't cover a variety of topics, it just means that you need to keep things ordered. The good news is that in doing so, you make your life easier. It may even save you some work!

When you know what you want your presentation to cover, create a rough outline. You can either use the outlining feature in your word processing program or just jot ideas down with a pad and pencil. The point here is to put down ideas in an organized manner so that your presentation has a logical flow.

Your outline then becomes a road map and checklist for the images you need and the slides you need to create. Now, rather than going off and randomly taking photos that might work for the presentation, you can go out and make specific images you know will properly illustrate your topic. This forethought and planning will definitely improve the look and reception of your presentation.

Judging the proper length for your presentation

Often when you're preparing a presentation, you know how much time you are being allotted. It then becomes your responsibility to figure out how to fill that time. Sometimes though, you're given some flexibility in the matter.

The best presentation, just like the best television show or movie, is the one that seems like it ended a few minutes too early. This doesn't mean that important information is left out, but rather that the quality of the performance leaves us wanting more.

One way to achieve an optimal presentation length is to resist the temptation to cover every trivial point you can think of in order to be as comprehensive as possible. This isn't really the purpose of a multimedia presentation; that's the function of a written report.

For an analogy, think about the different ways in which newspapers, magazines, radio, and television report the news. A typical TV or radio news story lasts maybe 30 seconds to a minute for a major issue (approximately 100 to 200 words). That same story in your daily paper might receive 750 to 1,000 words of coverage, whereas a weekly news magazine might devote 3,000 to 5,000 words on the topic. The reality is that printed media can—and should—be used to deliver in-depth information. You should use more ephemeral modes of delivery, such as audio and video, in smaller doses.

With printed information, the reader can pause a moment to consider an idea requiring extra thought. He can also stop and reread a point he has trouble understanding. Finally, he can read faster than you can talk, so he may read a much more detailed offering in less time than you can present it.

Visual presentations find their effectiveness in the way they use images and sound to impart extra information. A 750-word newspaper story may not have any artwork accompanying it. Even for a lead story, it's unusual to see more than two images supporting those words. Yet a 30-second TV news story will contain hundreds of actual images (video is delivered at the rate of 30 *frames* or images per second) showing many different vignettes. This video is then reinforced with narration for a one-two assault on the senses that reaches us on a visceral level unobtainable in print.

So under ideal circumstances, you're most effective when you present detailed information in written form and use the multimedia presentation to present an overall view of the most important elements. When done right, your audience will be eager to turn to your literature to learn even more about the topic. This is why so many multimedia presentations are used to introduce reports.

Creating a shot list or storyboard

Chapter 13 provides a good background for anyone thinking about creating a presentation. Because that chapter provides detailed information about planning a picture story and creating shot lists, I just give you a brief review here.

Shot lists and storyboards are tools photographers use to manage their time more efficiently while shooting a project. The idea behind these two documents is to help you plan what you want to accomplish during your shoot and provide a checklist to ensure you don't miss any images.

The shot list

A shot list is merely an inventory or shopping list of images you need to acquire to illustrate your presentation. You can either plan your shot list first, or you can rough out your presentation in a program such as PowerPoint and then create a list of artwork you need to illustrate each slide. I think the latter makes a lot more sense, provided you're in a position to quickly rough out your slides. This is where a good outline is helpful.

The storyboard

This planning tool is made up of rough drawings of the images you want to create. Here's where you would sketch out exactly what's in the image (type of room, furniture, number of people and what they're doing) you want to create. Before you start feeling overwhelmed at the idea of creating detailed drawings for every slide in a long presentation, let me reassure you a bit. Storyboards aren't supposed to be formal presentation documents, they're more like doodles on a napkin that help you think an image through. Formal versions of storyboards are frequently created for high-end projects because they're a lot cheaper and easier to create than the actual presentation. But for your storyboard, very rough sketches will do the trick. Think stick figures.

If you're comfortable with your conceptualization skills or your ability to communicate with whoever is doing the photography, and if you're pressed for time, feel free to skip this part of the process. Likewise, if you already have a huge collection of company images to work from, you can probably live without a storyboard.

Presentation elements

In organizing your presentation, consider the need for certain elements, such as the introduction, body and conclusion. Each one of these is necessary to advance your material. The following sections explain why it's important to include these fundamental elements in your presentation.

The introduction: Why we're here

The introduction tells your audience what the presentation will be about, why it's important, and what they can expect. It doesn't have to be particularly long and shouldn't make up more than 10 to 20 percent of your presentation. (It can be shorter.)

The body

This is the main content of your presentation. Here is where you give your audience the information you came to tell them.

Although the body can be thought of as one distinct element of a presentation, it can be broken down in several smaller parts because it's not unusual for a presentation to cover multiple topics. Consider each separate topic to be a self-contained unit within the body (with a mini-introduction and mini-conclusion).

There are several advantages to working topic by topic:

✦ You're effectively creating a modular presentation that can be re-used and adapted as needed.

✦ You're presenting information in a logical sequence. Remember, your audience can't refer back to a slide you showed earlier unless you repeat that slide. If you can avoid jumping around topics, you make it much easier for them to understand and focus on what you're saying.

✦ Each time you make an introduction and a conclusion, whether your main ones or mini ones inside each module, you have the opportunity to reinforce your message. This is important with presentations that follow the tried-and-true format of "First I'm going to tell you what I'm going to talk about; then I'm going to talk about it; then I'm going to tell you what I talked about."

The conclusion

Here's where you wrap things up. Your conclusion should be brief (10 to 20 percent of the overall presentation length) and should concentrate on reminding your audience of what your presentation was about. If appropriate, it's also an opportunity to make a request for action.

Execution: Creating the Elements

Now that you have a plan, it's time to start creating the materials for your presentation. Photographers shooting for multimedia presentations need to remember the format and limitations of the delivery medium.

Above all, your slides need to be readable. This means images must be understandable for people at the back and sides of the room. In order to accomplish this, try to create photos that present a single dominant subject in easily recognized surroundings. If you make images that have a lot of people off in the distance, they won't be recognizable. The same happens if you need people to focus on a particular object in a scene. If it's a small element (and by small, I mean less than a quarter or fifth of the whole image), it's probably not going to be very readable. These size estimates are based on filling a pull-down projector screen completely with an image. Often, photos are only one part of the graphic you're projecting on the screen, so you have to be really careful that you have a readable image. Figure 26-1 shows an example of an image that's difficult to read. The woman is too small, and she's obscured by shadows. Even if this photo is shown larger, it will still be difficult for your audience to understand the information in the photo. Using text is also challenging because it's easy for letters to disappear into the background. It's best to place text over a colored box so it leaps out at the viewer. If you keep the box small, it won't make the image unreadable.

Figure 26-1: Slides need to be readable from a distance. This one isn't.

© 2004 Dan Simon

 Don't forget, full-color versions of all figures are available on this book's companion web site at www.wiley.com/compbooks/simon.

Making your images understandable

There are several things you can do when you need to show an overall scene and bring attention to one small object or person in the full image.

The first is to treat your full image as an establishing shot. Show the photograph to set the scene and then advance to slides that show closer views of important elements within the scene.

The second approach is to create an inset image that shows the important person or object larger than the person actually appears in the full image. This is also workable, but it doesn't make the important material as noticeable as the first suggestion.

A third and least desirable approach is to simply use a graphic device such as an arrow or circle to point out the significant information or individual. This at least shows people in the back what part of the image they're not getting a good look at.

And finally, you can always use a laser pointer to point out where you want people to look. This has all the inefficiency of the previous idea, with the added problem that someone looking down at his handout for a moment may not see where you're pointing.

Using verticals in a presentation

Projector screens, televisions, and computer monitors are either horizontal or nearly square in format. This would seem to indicate that vertical images aren't a good fit for this medium and, in general, should be used sparingly if at all.

It's possible to use a vertical image in order to leave some space on a slide for text or to pair a couple of verticals for a screen-filling visual, but such effects should be used sparingly. The truth is, the horizontal nature of the medium cries out for horizontal images. Yes, it hurts to say that.

Determining how many pictures you need

There's no set formula for the number of images in a presentation. I do suggest you limit yourself to no more than two images per slide. Although PowerPoint and other programs make it possible to put more photos on a screen, you end up sizing them so small that they become meaningless.

Photos should advance your presentation. Be sure to have a clear-cut reason why the image is being shown to your audience.

Ensuring high-quality photos

Avoid photos with hotspots (overexposed areas); they are distracting and difficult to read. High-contrast images in general are difficult to work with and look amateurish.

Underexposed photos are also a problem because detail is very hard to pick out of a dark slide. To make matters worse, dark images frequently look like they're poorly focused.

Don't try to get away with a photo that's "almost" in focus but not quite. These tend to look their worst when projected on a screen.

Putting It All Together

There's a tendency to overuse the bells and whistles available in programs like PowerPoint. Just like the novice newsletter designer who tries to use every font in the inventory, people go a little nuts with transitions, effects, and sound effects.

It's important to remember that your overall goal when designing a multimedia presentation is to deliver information and not present a catalog of fonts, transitions, effects, and sounds. Instead, you pull these items from your inventory when they help you deliver information.

If I had to sum it up simply (an anathema to someone used to being paid by the word), I'd say *be consistent*. Presentations look amateurish because they go nuts with fonts and effects. They look professional because they have a consistent look and format that is clean and understated.

If possible, provide your audience with a handout that summarizes the main points of your presentation and offers more details than you can provide on a PowerPoint slide. If you don't have a handout, at least plan on telling people where they can find more detailed information if it exists. Trying to present a complex topic solely by multimedia presentation is difficult because you're expecting people to listen, look, and take notes all at the same time.

Using type with photos

I recently sat through some presentations by graduate students at a Philadelphia university. It was distressing to see that every single PowerPoint presentation included text that disappeared into its background (see Figure 26-2). In each case, the students had used a gradient or multi-colored background that allowed the text to blend in and out, reducing legibility. In many cases, too much information per slide also forced tiny type that was far too small to read unless you were sitting just a few feet from the screen.

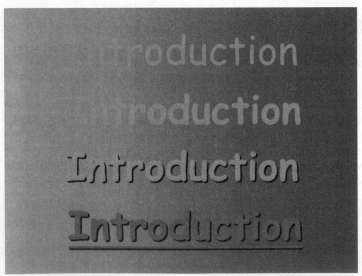

Figure 26-2: Be careful not to let type blend into its background.
© *2004 Dan Simon*

Type use is particularly difficult to plan when you're placing text over photos. It's almost impossible to standardize your font color or even decide whether to work with a bright or dark range of colors. Because of this, it's okay to play around a bit with font colors. Choose an appropriate color to work with each photo. You want something that stands out from the image behind it. Try to limit the total number of colors you use, though. If possible, find one color for dark backgrounds and another for light backgrounds and try to make those two pull as much duty as possible.

Another approach is to create a text box for all your type. This is fine as long as you are consistent. Make all text boxes the same color (PowerPoint takes care of the sizing for you). If you're thinking about using an effect on a text box, either use it all the time or not at all.

I favor bold text for presentations. For written works, bold type is used to make a word stand out from those around it. In slide show presentations (which should use text sparingly), effects such as bold and drop shadows can help make words stand out from the background. Don't be afraid to use these effects to do that, just be consistent.

When in doubt, I like to use a simple textured background as my default background. This provides a visually interesting background that services type well. I can always place a photograph over this background, even sizing it to completely fill the screen.

Using effects

PowerPoint and other presentation programs come with a library of various effects (wipes, dissolves, fades), sounds (both professional and unprofessional sounding), and animations (flying in text, typing in text, dissolving text). These tools can make or break a presentation. Used properly, they help keep interest and provide punctuation to particularly important ideas. Consistency is also important here.

Used improperly, and they turn your efforts into a confused circus of noises, motions, and distractions. It's never good to have your audience wondering what transition you're going to use next or be startled by some weird sound effect. Use these tools judiciously to showcase your thoughts.

Summary

This chapter looked at the process of creating a digital presentation and ways you can make your own presentations more effective. First and foremost is to create a good outline. Don't worry about following outlining procedures meticulously; just make sure you have a sense of what you're trying to say. Then use your outline to create a logical sequence for your slides.

Visual presentations need to be simple, and they need to maintain a logical flow. Your audience will miss your next point if they're still trying to digest your previous one. Save the heavy stuff for the accompanying literature that provides depth to your topic. When possible, provide your audience with a handout so that they don't have to look away from your presentation to take notes.

Finally, resist the temptation to use all the bells and whistles that the presentation program offers. Remember, the software is only a tool to help you deliver information; it's not the show itself. Keep your visual presentation clean, uncluttered, simple, and easy to read—even from a distance.

Photographing Business Subjects

A need often exists for photography in the workplace. If you work for a small company, or if you're working on a project with a limited budget, the money to hire a professional photographer just might not be available.

In recent years, however, the need for business photography has increased with the advent of online marketplaces like eBay. I don't know about you, but I like to see a picture of something I'm considering buying, so it behooves you as an online merchant to take good product photos. Fortunately, it's not that hard even if you don't have much training or experience as a photographer.

This chapter discusses typical photographic tasks that arise in the workplace. I also show you ways to produce effective photos of your products, people, and services without having to become a master photographer.

Product Photography

When photographing products, one of the first things to consider is the necessity of producing *clean* images. By clean, I don't mean PG-rated materials—although that's also an important consideration—but rather photographs that show your product without any clutter or distractions messing up your image.

Your first task is to look for ways to keep your backgrounds clean and simple. How you tackle this challenge depends on the size of your subject.

Keeping Things Simple

Studio pros can sometimes take hours to photograph one scene from a catalog display. I sat in on a session once and watched as the photographers fiddled with lights, adjusted props—first one way and then the other—adjusted lights a little bit more, and finally snapped a Polaroid to check the image. After studying the instant photo for a few minutes, they fiddled with the lights again, adjusted props—first one way and then the other.... This went on for an entire afternoon, and they still hadn't shot any film (other than instant prints) before I had to go.

Obviously, you don't have an entire afternoon to work on getting just one photo. If you did, you wouldn't be reading this chapter.

By setting your sights a little more realistically (just showing your products individually instead of as part of some grand conception), you can eliminate many of the problems that need to be managed in a typical studio setting. Shadows and reflections caused by multiple objects are a real hassle. Every time you shift a light to solve one problem, you create several more. Every time you eliminate one shadow, you create another, so it's back to the drawing board.

Photographing one product at a time is the best way to simplify a product shoot. Since you'll be working with the same lighting setup and product placement for each item, you'll be able to composite multiple products together in the digital darkroom if you need to. If you're shooting for a web catalog, you'll probably be better off with single products that can be displayed and accessed individually.

Working with small products

If you are photographing products of a relatively small size, try placing your product on a table. Then follow these steps to achieve a great product shot:

1. The first thing you need to do is create a background. To create a nice, clean surface and background, hang a large piece of seamless paper from a point a foot or two behind the object and several feet higher, using the end of the paper to cover the table your product sits on.

2. Next, position the product on the table with its most important side facing the camera, positioning it either so it rests against something if it won't stand on its own, or so it lays flat. The idea is to photograph your product so that its main surface is on the same plane as the camera's sensor, which keeps its most important side (and your company's name and logo) in focus. It may be tempting to position the product at a three-quarter angle, but unless you're shooting at a tiny lens opening (to produce great depth of field), such positioning makes for an image where parts of the packaging are softly focused. Positioning also depends on whether your product is being displayed packaged or unpacked. If it's out of the box, the three-quarter view is a better option.

3. Now it's time to light your product. Set up multiple lights (or adjust existing ones) positioned at a 45-degree angle on each side of the

product. Side lighting produces a nice, even lighting that shows detail and minimizes glare and reflections.

4. If possible, always examine the image on a larger monitor before you decide you're done with the shoot. View the image either by copying it to your computer's hard drive, or if your camera has the capability, connecting your camera directly to a television monitor.

See Figure 27-1 to see how all these elements congeal to create an outstanding product shot.

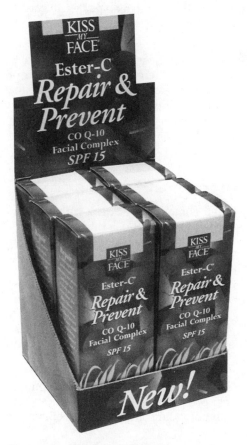

Figure 27-1: A clean tablecloth, an empty background wall, repositioned track lights, and a ping pong table work together to create this product shot.

© 2004 Dan Simon

If your office or shoot site doesn't have adjustable lighting, an alternative light source is small portable flood lamps with spring clips. Insert the brightest incandescent bulbs you can find, and position the lights on each side of the product at a 45-degree angle. Another alternative is to use a set of garage work lights. These lights usually come with telescoping stands and cost less than $100 for a set of three. This can be especially cost-effective if your organization has another use for these items.

When shooting small products, also consider these points.

✦ **Use a tripod:** If you decide to use a tripod, position your camera exactly even and level with your product. If you don't have a tripod or choose not to use one, be sure to keep your camera oriented properly.

✦ **Gauge white balance:** To create a white balance reference, lay a white index card flat on the table in front of the product, anywhere in the shot that gets the same light as your product. Be sure to also place the card in a spot where you can either crop it or clone it out in the digital darkroom.

✦ **Don't include a title card or label:** Resisting these additions is a good thing because they tend to look amateurish. There's no way title cards or labels can compete with the professional packaging design your product displays. Instead, plan on including any labeling information either in the digital darkroom (the best option) or when the photo is used on the web (riskier because it becomes easier for identifying data to get mixed up).

Working with large products

Things become a bit more challenging when it comes time to work with items that are bigger than a breadbox. (Does anybody still use those things by the way?)

Larger sized items are more difficult to separate from their background, and, depending on your lighting resources, more difficult to illuminate properly. There's also the added concern that they may even be too big or heavy for you to move into a better position for photography.

If you have a choice, it's probably a better idea to photograph the item out of its packaging. There are several approaches to tackling this problem:

✦ When possible, try to place some sort of backdrop behind the product. It's important to provide the cleanest possible background for an object. This can help reduce file size for web uploading and also helps eliminate distracting elements.

✦ If moving the object is out of the question, and you can't get a backdrop in place, try overlighting your subject, which allows you to use a very small lens opening. Using a small aperture setting results in a properly lit product and a black background making your product stand out. From here, you can choose between working with the image as it is (with no distracting background elements) or silhouetting the product from the rest of the photo.

 You can find more detailed information about silhouetting under the Masking section in Chapter 15.

✦ Use the background as part of a working scene that showcases your product. For instance, if you're photographing a refrigerator, then documenting it on the display floor as part of a kitchen scene would make an effective image. This is a bit more difficult because you're at the mercy of the display floor or storage area. Your best bet is to create a tight composition that minimizes the background as much as possible. Getting a tight enough composition is easier if you're working with a DSLR because standard lenses tend to have large enough maximum apertures to help blur the background. Point-and-shoot cameras don't quite provide this option, but fortunately, you can achieve a similar effect in PhotoShop or other image editing software.

Remember to take more than one photo of each product, and try a couple shots from different angles and heights. Aim for as tight a composition as you reasonably can, and try to have more light on your product than anything else in the space. If you're photographing the item in a workplace scene, to help your product stand out better, consider using pieces of cardboard to help block some of the light reaching background areas or turn off lights that illuminate the background.

Photographing Your Boss and Other Coworkers

It's frequently necessary to create photographs of your boss or other coworkers, whether for company newsletters, brochures, or an office photo collection. Sometimes these pictures need to be portraits and sometimes they need to be action shots.

You can make such photos even with a modest point-and-shoot digital camera. Just stay with the basics and remember some simple ideas:

Seated portraits

Seated portraits are the simplest and easiest way to create an effective image of the boss. Follow these simple steps and try it for yourself:

1. Seat her at her desk turned slightly toward the camera. (You should be off to one side.) The idea here is to make it look like she just looked up from her desk as you entered the room. In fact, you can have her practice this move a couple of times beforehand.

2. Go for a tight vertical composition (unless you have a specific need for a horizontal image) showing a portion of her desk in the foreground. Leave a bit of headroom at the top of the image, about 10 to 15 percent of the total image area (unless you're trying to be artsy; then it can be a little more).

3. Be sure to check what's behind her body. Vertical blinds or framed pieces of art can be very distracting if they're directly behind your subject.

Conference photos

Conference photos are more complicated, but portray the subject as the person in charge. The idea behind conference photos is to show the person in a conference setting, using other people to provide a frame that emphasizes the subject. When done correctly, the person viewing the shot feels like a part of the conference, with the boss staring straight at the viewer.

Follow these steps to take an effective conference photo:

1. Position your boss on one side of a conference table (but not at the narrow end), and seat two people side by side on the opposite side of the conference table.

2. Drop down to a point level with the boss's eyes and create a vertical composition that shows the subject's face framed by the two people facing him, which draws the viewer's eye directly to the boss's eyes. The boss should be looking directly into the camera lens, making eye contact with the viewer.

3. Think about how to best light the shot. The simplest lighting approach is to use available room light (being careful that windows are screened or shaded to block outside light) and going with your camera's recommended exposure. Another approach is to try to silhouette the people facing your subject to make your subject's face stand out even more. Position your boss with her back to the outside light. Make sure all blinds and shades are wide open to let in as much back light as possible, underexposing the two people framing your subject. Then use an off-camera flash or separate light to illuminate your boss. This is a much more difficult lighting approach because you need a remotely controlled flash or external light. If you do use the external light, use a piece of cardboard to block the light hitting the people on the other side of the table.

4. Look for a reflection of your subject on the table surface (if you have a highly polished table you should get one). If you do have such a reflection, expand the shot to capture everything from the headroom down through the full reflection. From side to side, you only need about half of each person in the picture. This is enough to provide the frame for the boss's face without wasting too much space.

Alternatively, you can actually photograph a meeting in hopes of creating such an image, as shown in Figure 27-2.

Photographing an actual meeting instead of posing the shot is a perfectly reasonable (although less controllable) effort, and if you're patient and take lots of photos, you can achieve some good results. Some advice if you're going to go this route: Try to pick a low-level meeting (or at least one where the boss is meeting with subordinates rather than her bosses). Plan on working without flash because you want to be as little a distraction as you can. Try to use a longer focal length so you can keep some distance, which helps you remain unobtrusive and makes things a little more comfortable for others in the room. There's also an added benefit: longer focal lengths produce more flattering portraits.

Figure 27-2: It takes perseverance and the willingness to make a lot of photos, but you can get a dynamic shot of the boss in a meeting.
© *2004 Dan Simon*

 Chapter 4 presents more detailed information about the benefits of choosing the right focal length.

Now that you've learned how to create interesting photos of your boss, you can turn to photographing your faithful assistant: your computer.

Photographing a Computer Screen or Television Picture

If you've ever tried to take a picture of a television image, you've experienced the problem of the dreaded black horizontal line that travels across the TV screen.

This scanning bar is a result of the television's efforts to redraw the image you're watching. The solution has always been to take the photo at a slower shutter speed. Generally, photographers shoot TV screens at a speed of $\frac{1}{30}$ of a second or slower. The same approach works for photographing computer monitors.

A bigger problem with computer screens is dealing with glare and reflections. You must take great care to prevent these problems from degrading the quality of your photo.

Forget about using your camera's built-in flash for illumination, which just bounces a hard light right back into your lens, ruining the photo. Instead, you need to rig either an off-camera flash or better still, two flashes, positioned above the computer screen and angled in from 45 degrees. This provides even lighting, which brings out detail and prevents hot spots from reflections.

Unfortunately, this option is available to few amateur photographers, particularly those working with point-and-shoot cameras. Instead, let me offer a more practical approach.

Turn down (or turn off) all nearby lights. Set your camera up on a tripod or desktop. With its ISO set to the lowest possible value (usually 100 ISO), focus it on the computer screen and set the self-timer. If your camera lets you set shutter speeds manually, then set yours for $\frac{1}{30}$ or $\frac{1}{15}$ of a second. (If you can't set shutter speeds manually, then hope the low ISO compensates.) A low ISO and a slow shutter speed leads to a properly exposed computer screen, hopefully without the scanning bar. If you still get the horizontal bar, then there's too much light and your camera is picking too high a shutter speed. Try turning down the monitor's brightness setting.

This approach gives you a good picture of the actual monitor screen, but not the external borders of the monitor. Here's where you use your external (house) lights to illuminate the rest of the room. The trick is to block or turn off any of the lights that are in front of your monitor, thus eliminating the glare and hot spots but still providing ambient light.

Photographing Clothing

It's not unusual to have to create images of clothing, particularly things like souvenir T-shirts. A pro photographer usually does this by hiring a handsome model to pose in the particular article of clothing while carefully rigged studio lighting lights the model, the clothing, and the seamless background.

Organizations on a tighter budget look for lower cost alternatives to hiring photographers and usually turn to an employee with a camera and their teen-aged son or daughter as a model. Often, instead of seamless background paper, you get the office parking lot. Instead of carefully rigged studio lighting, you get direct sunlight at noon. The result is a squinting model with a distracting background and a piece of clothing that doesn't show well because part of it has lost detail because of dark shadows and bright highlights. This doesn't have to describe your product shots. As the following sections show, there are better ways to shoot clothing on a tight budget without access to a studio.

Finding the right setting

There are several ways to approach the task of creating good clothing photos without access to a studio or professional models, equipment, and lighting.

First, plan your shoot for somewhere you have control over the lighting. Usually, this means indoors. Try to find a space with blank walls and user controllable lighting.

Once you've found such a space, move enough furniture so your model can stand a couple of feet away from the wall and you have room to photograph her. (For some reason people have a tendency to position themselves near the wall. I don't know if it's some primal fear of a saber-toothed tiger attack or what, but pull them away from the wall for heaven's sake.)

Take a test shot and check the image for blown highlights or blocked up shadows (shadow areas without detail). If you have either problem, dim the lights to reduce blown highlights or turn the light up to fill in too dark shadows. If possible, try to work without using your camera's built-in flash.

Now that the lighting's right, start taking photos.

Employing a model

Sometimes you want to show your clothing on a human being. This is challenging because your budget might not include funds for a professional model, make-up artist, or stylist. Instead, you end up with some friends or relatives who get pressed into service as models and helpers.

There's a reason why experienced models get paid for their time. A good model can make the product she's showing look its best. She can also maximize the photographic opportunities for the shoot.

Few amateur or impromptu models know how to pose. An experienced model can move through a range of poses, pausing a moment at each key body position. In fact, there's a continuous feedback loop going on as the model uses the sound of the camera firing or the visual cue of the studio lights going off to begin her next movement. An experienced model may present the same number of poses in two minutes as an inexperienced model presents in half an hour. Figure 27-3 shows some typical model poses.

If you're working with an inexperienced model, keep your goals reasonable and budget extra time for the shoot. It's frequently helpful to have more than one person available for modeling duty at this kind of shoot. It gives each person a chance to take a break, and more importantly, to watch the other person's efforts and hopefully learn from them.

Figure 27-3: An experienced model presents clothing so it looks its best and gives the photographer a variety of images very quickly.

© 2004 Dan Simon

This lack of experience certainly makes your job harder, because the novice model may not be as helpful as an experienced one. You can help her out by giving her a modest range of movements to concentrate on, asking her to pause briefly at the end of each task. These tasks should be simple things such as turning toward the camera or shifting her body weight from one foot to the other.

Once you're ready to begin photography, your first task is to make sure the clothing fits your model properly. This usually means pinning or taping the garment to fit it to her if need be. Your life is made easier if you can avoid dark black or bright white garments, but if you've followed the advice about lighting in the preceding paragraphs you should still be okay even with these colors.

Make sure you take a variety of photos for each garment. It's best if you have a computer handy to check images while the model changes clothing. This way you can see how the shoot is going and point out ways to improve the model's posing. Remember to always be positive and encouraging with the person who's posing for you. Even experienced models welcome that positive feedback, but it's especially important for someone who's new to posing.

 What do you say to a model? It's important to always strive for professionalism even when both you and your model are amateurs. By all means, compliment your model frequently and enthusiastically, but keep the compliments aimed at performance and not appearance. This can help avoid misunderstandings and make sure no sensitivities are violated.

Going au natural

Another option is to show the clothing sans model. (What did you think I meant?)

This is the easier, and in many ways, more attractive option. All you have to do is lay the garment on a flat surface, smooth out the wrinkles and fire away, right?

Well . . . almost, but not quite. Getting clothing to lie smoothly takes a little bit of work, usually in the form of thumbtacks inside the garment holding it stiff against a flat surface. Once you do that it's a piece of cake right?

Well . . . almost. Your next step is to climb a stepladder so you can shoot straight down on the garment. (This assumes you're positioning it on a table. I suppose you could also use a sheet of plywood on the floor as your flat surface, but depending on the size of the garment, you might still need the ladder.)

You want to shoot as close to straight down as possible because it's important to keep the camera's digital sensor and the garment on the same plane to insure maximum effective sharpness for the length of the garment.

Be careful that your shadow doesn't end up in the picture! Also take several shots using your camera's exposure compensation or manual control settings to *bracket* your exposure. Bracketing is an exposure technique photographers use to make sure they get an accurate exposure. It simply means taking one photo at the proper exposure, a second shot that's overexposed (one half to one full f-stop usually), and a third shot that's underexposed (one half to one full f-stop). If your light meter is off, at least one of the bracketing shots should be okay.

Shooting from a ladder works best if you have one person to do the photography and another person (or two) to ready each garment for shooting. (Or you can all prep the clothes beforehand and then you shoot and your assistant moves garments into place for each shot.)

Summary

In this chapter, I covered ways to produce usable photos in some typical business situations. If you're asked to take business-related photographs, remember to try to keep backgrounds simple and compositions tight. If you're focused in on what's important, you maximize the effectiveness of your image and remove many of the blemishes that make typical novice photographs fail.

Techniques for Unusual Images

CHAPTER

28

Moving water, fireworks, or car lights at night. These are just a few of the special effects that photographers are called on to capture. Each scenario offers its own magic and its own challenges. With some preparation and an understanding of the special techniques discussed in this chapter, you can get stunning photos pretty easily.

Moving water changes its look in an almost Sybil-like dance of personalities as the camera shifts shutter speeds from settings that would blur a snail to those that would freeze an 8-year-old on Halloween sugar. Making it look memorable is what separates magic from banal.

Fireworks have their own magic. We all enjoy watching the colorful displays, but how often can you get really good photos of them? Well, digital cameras make it a lot easier to get good fireworks photos.

Car lights at night—particularly the yellow and red taillights—form colorful ribbons of light when photographed at slow shutter speeds. You can create nifty special effects with this type of photography and all you have to do is hold still.

Then there's the magic of reflections. The phrase "twice as nice" makes sense when you're looking at the image of a lovely scene reflected in a pool of water. Reflective surfaces, whether they are lakes, mirrors, glass windows, or shiny metal, all have their special appeal.

Read on to find out how to make memorable photos using these very special effects.

Moving Water

Water is the essence of life, and it's also a wonderful subject for the camera. This substance, in its many shapes, textures, and forms, can be fodder for all sorts of interesting images.

All too often, people photograph water with a mid-range shutter speed, yet it's the options at the extremes that give you the most interesting results. For instance, you can freeze water droplets with fast shutter speeds for a very different look. Generally, you want to shoot at 1/1000th of a second or faster. This is fast enough to catch individual water droplets moving through the air.

Experiment with your lighting when you photograph water in its various forms. Try side lighting to bring out greater detail, or backlight the water for a glow. Slow to extremely slow shutter speeds blur moving water to create a spun glass effect. These compositions can create an almost mystical look to an otherwise postcard-like cliché.

During a visit to Havasu Canyon at the Western edge of the Grand Canyon, I photographed Havasu Falls, a famous twin waterfall in an area known as "America's Garden of Eden." Although the falls are gorgeous almost any way they are documented, by slowing down my shutter speed to a full two seconds I made a much more interesting shot (see Figure 28-1).

 Be sure to check out this book's companion web site at www.wiley.com/compbooks/simon to see color versions of the photographs shown in this chapter.

One of the things that makes slow-shutter, moving water imagery work is the contrast between the soft spun look of the water and the harder edges of the landscape that aren't moving. It's important to look for such contrasting elements when you create a composition; otherwise it looks like your image is out of focus. In addition, the contrast between the hard edge and blurred water creates a dynamic tension that makes the photo more interesting.

Fall is a wonderful time of year to pursue water images, particularly if you're fortunate enough to have a season where water levels cooperate. One of my favorite places to take fall photos is Ricketts Glen State Park in Northeastern Pennsylvania. The highlight of this park is a five-mile hiking trail filled with waterfalls ranging from just a few feet high to one almost 100 feet tall. Although the hike can be treacherous in places, it also offers dozens of spots to pursue interesting images.

You can safely count on good water levels in the spring, but fall isn't such a sure bet. One year you may see little more than a trickle, while the next you get several weeks of solid flows. I was fortunate to have a wet fall season when I was working on this book. The result was beautiful fall foliage and exciting water, complete with leaves resting on rocks in the creek. As you can see in Figure 28-2, the leaves provided a nice focal point for slow shutter compositions with moving water.

Figure 28-1: Slowing the shutter speed and mounting the camera on a tripod to keep it steady kept the sharp details in focus and created this dreamy flow of water.
© *2004 Dan Simon*

Figure 28-2: Fall foliage and moving water.
© *2004 Dan Simon*

A color version of Figure 28-1 appears in the four-color insert section earlier in the book.

One of the most important tools you can use to capture flowing water is a good, steady tripod. To take the image in Figure 28-2, I used an exposure of 32 seconds to both blur the water and allow a small enough aperture (f32) for maximum depth of field, and I racked my 80-200 zoom out to 135mm.

Making Your Tripod Steadier

Although it may seem like a simple thing to stick a camera on a tripod and get rock-solid exposures, the reality isn't quite so simple. Even though tripods are steadier than humans, when you start planning exposures of more than a second or two, external factors such as wind and people walking on the trail near you can be a problem.

There are a few things you can do to get the most out of your tripod:

✦ **Avoid raising the center column if at all possible.** As a general rule, the less extended the tripod, the steadier it will be, but extending the center column seriously increases the risk of camera shake.

✦ **Weight the tripod down.** One easy method is to drape your camera bag over the tripod so that its weight helps hold the tripod in place (and you thought it was just being lazy!). Any extra weight you can add to your tripod will make it more stable. Some models even have hooks at the end of the center post so that you can hang bags of rocks on for extra weight.

✦ **Lock up your camera's mirror.** If you're using a DSLR, then the movement of the reflex mirror (the mirror that moves out of the way when the shutter trips) can cause enough vibration to soften the image. If your DSLR lets you lock up the mirror, by all means, do so. This step is vital for shutter speeds around 1/15th of a second.

✦ **Trip the shutter with a remote control.** This is another trick to lessen camera shake.

Developing good tripod technique can help you with the type of special effects photography that I discuss next: shooting fireworks. (Not to be confused with shooting off fireworks.)

Photographing Fireworks Displays

Most folks love watching a fireworks display. The color, motion, and variety all serve to hold people mesmerized. Fireworks displays can photograph beautifully, but they can also be a source of frustration to a photographer. It was even tougher back in the days of film; you'd try certain exposure settings and then have to wait to see if you got it right.

Even with a digital camera, photographing fireworks presents some challenges. The dark skies, for example, tend to make camera noise particularly visible. But digital cameras also provide the photographer with the capability to tweak his or her settings for best results.

To get the fireworks and fountains display shown in Figure 28-3, I used a tripod and kept my shutter open for six seconds.

Figure 28-3: Fireworks and fountains display at Southeastern Pennsylvania's Longwood Gardens.
© 2004 Dan Simon

Whether you're using a DSLR or a point-and-shoot, you can make good fireworks photos. The following sections discuss techniques for each type of camera.

Shooting fireworks with a DSLR

The techniques I use for the two types of cameras are very different. When shooting with a DSLR, I find my best results come from keeping the shutter open a long time (usually a second or more) to give multiple fireworks time to register on the image. An aperture of f8 or f11 generally suffices, but experiment for best effects.

Techniques vary among cameras because most DSLRs offer a noise-reduction feature that creates a second exposure with the aperture closed. The camera does this to create a "normal" noise pattern for the conditions. It then compares the noise in the long exposure to its "normal" pattern and tries to eliminate as much noise as possible. The result is that it takes 12 seconds to make a 6-second exposure.

Using noise reduction works fine when you can keep the shutter open long enough to make sure you get a good burst to register on the sensor. If your timing is off, you have to stand there watching all those beautiful fireworks bursting in air while your camera does its noise reduction thing.

I was able to manage these long exposures by mounting my camera on a Bogen superclamp and magic arm rig attached either to my seat or to a railing near where I was sitting. Even though the grounds prohibited tripods (and I had a special dispensation only because I was taking photos for a magazine story), devices such as the superclamp weren't mentioned. No one said a word to me as I set mine up, and I was able to get the longer exposures I needed.

 Many facilities have rules against the use of tripods because space is tight and tripods take up space and block passageways. Frequently, however, you can get away with a monopod or some other device that doesn't take up too much room.

If I'd been forced to take these shots without some form of support, I would have had to try to make myself as stable as possible and work with a shutter speed of 1/15th of a second or so (depending on what lens I was using). The results would likely have been less than stellar.

Shooting fireworks with a point-and-shoot

The first time I visited Longwood's fireworks and fountains display with a digital camera, it was with my Olympus C2000, a 2 mega-pixel unit. I was aware of the no tripods prohibition, and I didn't have a superclamp/magic arm rig at the time. So I was basically stuck holding the camera in my hand.

My first couple of shots were disappointing. I tried a reasonably slow shutter speed (1/25th of a second) and ended up with blurred photos that weren't doing a very good job of capturing the spectacular display.

Part of the problem was that the camera's attempts to provide noise reduction were limiting me to one shot per fireworks burst. In addition, the camera's shutter lag was bad enough to throw off my timing.

The answer was counter-intuitive. I went to a faster shutter speed and set the camera to its burst mode. So instead of trying to time one photo for exactly the right moment, I held down the shutter and let fly until the camera's buffer was full.

It's the last item that made this work. On this particular camera, the buffer usually wasn't used until the camera went into burst mode. Choosing burst mode let me keep making photos during the entire fireworks burst. (For this performance, the fireworks were set to music, so explosives went up in sequence, took a break, and then restarted depending on the music).

Instead of taking one shot and having to wait until the noise reduction process was completed (missing more fireworks than I shot), I was able to blaze away until my buffer filled—usually after 10 or 15 shots. At this point, I'd have to wait until the buffer dumped everything to the memory card; but as soon as that was done, I could start shooting again.

Although this method was somewhat wasteful (lots of rejects), it was still the best answer for this particular circumstance. Because this was an auto-exposure only camera, exposures were usually made with the lens wide open (f2.5) and a shutter speed of about 1/100th of a second.

General fireworks tips

As a general rule, an aperture setting of f8 to f11 tends to work best for fireworks. As illustrated in the preceding point-and-shoot example, however, those settings aren't always practical. Work with what's practical. I prefer to shoot at lower ISO settings, which creates less noise but also makes camera shake more of a problem. I prefer to shoot fireworks with a slow shutter speed, small aperture, and with my camera mounted on a tripod, but if you have to handhold your camera, opt for a wider aperture and faster shutter speed.

If you can set up on a tripod and work with some longer exposures, don't be afraid to experiment. One neat effect, shown in Figure 28-4, occurs when you zoom out with the shutter open.

Figure 28-4: Zooming the lens with the shutter open.

This technique creates a strange, otherworldly effect to the fireworks and makes for an interesting photograph.

Ribbons of Light

Sometimes you can turn the mundane into the sublime by adding some darkness and imagination. What's more banal than a roadway filled with moving vehicles, right? Such a scene is all about getting somewhere rather than representing a final destination. But turn down the lights until darkness falls and reduce your shutter speed to a setting that would blur the slowest of tortoises. Now add that roadway, and you have a recipe for magic.

Automobile lights (particularly the rear lights) turn into beautiful red, white, and yellow ribbons of light when photographed at a slow shutter speed. Try 20 seconds at f5.6 at 400 ISO as a starting point. Then experiment with different ranges of exposure times and ISOs.

Ideally, find a shooting position that's elevated so that you can capture a larger vista. If your circumstances cooperate, you can also experiment with both urban and desolate roads. The first shot gives you the accompaniment of buildings lit up for night, whereas the latter shot is concentrated on the car lights themselves.

Watch out for particularly bright light sources because they can overwhelm the rest of your image. If necessary, try to crop or re-compose to eliminate the trouble spot. A graduated neutral density filter may also help.

Don't forget to try a shot or two made by zooming your lens slowly while the image is being recorded. This creates a strange, surrealistic look.

While you're experimenting, try adding a foreground element to the mix. It can be your own car, an interesting sign, or a human model. To make this technique work most effectively, plan on using flash to illuminate your foreground subject. The best way to do this is to set your flash unit to match your aperture setting while only covering a short distance (far enough to illuminate your foreground subject without spilling too far beyond it). This shouldn't be too hard because you probably want an f-stop of about f5.6 or f8 for this kind of shot. If need be, you can reduce your flash's output by covering the top third of the flash head with a piece of cardboard or dialing down the power settings if the flash unit has that capability.

Other Interesting Nighttime Effects

If you want to create an otherworldly effect on a nighttime shot, use a long shutter speed and have your model shine a flashlight on his or her face. Another fun effect is to have someone move through a scene while you fire your flash at them at different points in the exposure. This one is easier to do if you have a flash that offers reduced power settings. Figure out how many times you want to flash the person during the exposure and then dial down the power setting to a reciprocal of that number (4 times would be 1/4 power). Adjust your aperture or power settings after a test shot, and you should be able to dial your settings right in.

Reflections

Reflections can be a nightmare for photography, but they can also be a blessing. Incorporated properly, reflections can add both depth and contrast to an image, particularly when ripples in water or metal give an impressionistic look (see Figure 28-5).

Figure 28-5: The combination of a tree in sharp focus and its wavy, blurred reflection gives a colorful and impressionistic contrast to this image.
© *2004 Dan Simon*

You can find interesting reflections in puddles, glass buildings, windows, car rear view mirrors, and all sorts of other shiny surfaces.

Keep a couple of things in mind when you're incorporating a reflection into your composition:

✦ Base your exposure readings on your main subject. The reflecting surface is often one to two f-stops darker than your main subject, so if you base your exposure on the reflection, you're likely to overexpose the main area of the photograph.

✦ Reflections tend to be strongest when the sun is lower in the sky.

Use reflections as elements of a composition or even as the reason for shooting an image. The everyday world is filled with mirrors in the form of bodies of water, glass buildings, and other reflective surfaces. Reflections add a nice element to any composition, so I always look for useful reflections when I'm shooting. Incorporating reflections is especially useful when you can't get as close to a subject as you'd like. If you can reflect your small subject, you may be able to double its size and fill the frame.

Summary

In this chapter, I covered some useful tips and techniques that help you get astounding and unique images. Try some of the ideas discussed in this chapter, such as manipulating shutter speeds to capture ribbons of light or moving water and zooming with the shutter open, and see if they lead to more interesting images. My favorite is the moving water/slow shutter speed image. You may be pleasantly surprised at the lovely results.

Digital Photography Definitions

APPENDIX

◆　◆　◆　◆

In This Appendix

Camera terms

Common digital photography terms and phrases

◆　◆　◆　◆

Sometimes it seems like photographers speak a different language. Add in the techno-geek element and all of a sudden it seems like you're trying to master a completely new way of speaking.

This appendix provides definitions for commonly used words and phrases important to photographers.

aperture: The opening created by a series of blades making up the lens diaphragm. These blades combine to form a circular opening whose size is dependent upon the aperture setting selected by the photographer. These settings are known as *f-stops*, and follow a logarithmic progression (f2, f2.8, f4, f5.6, f8, f11, f16, f22, and f32) representing a halving in the amount of light striking the camera's sensor.

ball head: A tripod head that travels via a ball-like mount. Ball heads allow you to quickly reposition your camera in multiple planes because the ball joint can move in any direction.

bokeh: The small out-of-focus highlights you see in a photo. Photographers judge camera lenses for many criteria and Bokeh is one such criterion.

bracket: There are a couple of definitions of bracket as it applies to photography. When used as a verb, bracketing is taking multiple photos of the same basic scene at varying exposures in an attempt to get at least one good exposure. Some cameras even offer an auto-bracketing function in which the camera fires three shots at different exposures. When used as a noun, a bracket is an L-shaped device mounted to the bottom of your camera used to reposition your flash in an attempt to reduce the likelihood of red-eye and eliminate harsh shadows.

depth of field: Describes the area of the photographic image that is in focus from front to back. This can be a short or long distance, depending upon the camera settings used to create the photograph.

diffusion: A method of softening and reducing light or softening an image through filtration. There are several different forms of diffusion used in photography. You can diffuse light by placing diffusion material between your light source and your subject, by mounting a filter on your camera's lens, or by creating diffusion effect in Photoshop. The effect of each of these methods is different. You can't necessarily substitute one for the other.

digital zoom: A method of magnifying the range of the camera's optical (actual) zoom lens. The digital zoom feature magnifies an image by cropping out enough of the outer pixels to create the 2x or 3x zoom effect the user has selected. Most cameras then interpolate (make an educated guess) with the remaining pixels to create the appropriate file size.

DSLR (digital single lens reflex): A single lens reflex camera uses only one lens (as compared to a TLR or twin lens reflex). *reflex* refers to moving a mirror out of the way to allow the image to be projected onto a piece of film or onto a digital sensor. The basic design of a DSLR allows the subject image to travel through the lens and bounce up into a series of mirrors that allow the photographer to view the subject through the camera's pentaprism. Once the shutter is tripped, a mirror that normally projects the image up to the pentaprism moves out of the way and the image is projected onto the film or digital sensor.

dynamic range: Describes the film or digital camera sensor's ability to handle contrast. Current digital camera sensors have a range of five f-stops from the darkest black to the brightest white. If a scene's contrast is more extreme than that, you lose detail in either a highlight or shadow area, or possibly both.

FireWire: Also known as IEEE 1394 or Sony iLink, FireWire is a high-speed connection that transfers images between cameras and computers, between computers and other computers, between computers and devices, or between devices and devices.

firmware: Software operating instructions the camera needs to function. Firmware can frequently be upgraded if necessary, but the method may vary from camera to camera. For some cameras, the user downloads a firmware upgrade to the media the camera uses (or directly to the camera via its connection to the computer) and makes the upgrade himself. Many other models (particularly those aimed at the consumer) may require the user to ship the camera back to the manufacturer for the free upgrade.

focal length: Refers to the optical length of the lens in millimeters (mm). The larger the focal length number, the higher the magnification (or *reach*) of the lens. Generally lenses of 35mm or less are considered wide-angle lens, lenses from 35mm to 75mm are considered to be normal, lenses from 85mm to 200mm are considered short to medium telephoto lenses, and lenses from 300mm and greater are considered long telephoto focal lengths.

four/thirds: The 4/3 system is a new idea from a joint consortium of camera makers. It adopts a 4 to 3 set of proportions and advocates a set of standards for camera development for gear following the format as compared to the 3 to 2 ratio current film and digital cameras follow. Olympus is currently the only camera maker offering a 4/3 camera and lenses, but other members of the consortium are believed to be working on such gear.

f-stop: Individual lens openings are known as *f-stops* and follow a logarithmic progression (f2, f2.8, f4, f5.6, f8, f11, f16, f22, and f32). Each full increase represents a halving in the amount of light striking the camera's sensor.

highlight: Normally the brightest area of a scene. Highlights should contain some detail, if not, then they are described as being *blown out* or overexposed.

interpolation: Efforts by the camera or software program for increasing the resolution of an image by making a scientific guess based on neighboring pixels.

microdrive: A miniature hard drive designed to work as digital film. Microdrives are available in Compact Flash size and work in most digital cameras that accept regular Compact Flash media. Because these devices have moving parts (as compared to Compact Flash, which uses solid state circuitry), they tend to write data more slowly and be more susceptible to damage than Compact Flash. They also tend to be less expensive.

motor drive: A term from film days, motor drives provide automatic film advance making high-speed sequential photography possible. Although today's digital cameras don't have film or motors to advance, many digital cameras offer a sequential shooting capability, and some, such as the Canon EOS 1D, do so at very high speeds (8 frames per second). Alive only in principle, digital photographers use the term motor drive instead of sequential shooting capability.

panning: The act of moving your camera horizontally to follow action. Panning can be done in two ways. You can pan a moving subject before you trip the shutter if you want to capture a stop-action shot, or you can pan your subject while the shutter is open in order to keep your subject in sharp focus while blurring the background to create a sense of motion.

pan/tilt head: A tripod head that is adjustable in both the vertical and horizontal planes.

pentaprism: A part of the camera consisting of a series of mirrors that redirect the image from the camera's sensor to the photographer's eye via a mirror that blocks the sensor. When the photographer "trips" the shutter, this mirror travels upward to allow the image to be made on the sensor. This "reflex" motion is also what causes the momentary blackout that occurs while the shutter is open.

red-eye: Occurs when the flash is mounted too close to the camera lens and describes the reddish color in human eyes that appears when light from the flash bounces off the eyes and reflects back into the lens. (Interestingly, a flash's reflection produces an amber color in the eyes of domesticated animals and a greenish color in the eyes of wild creatures.) The easiest way to avoid red-eye is not to use flash. Other solutions include using an off-camera flash and holding it high and to one side of the lens. You can also use your camera's red-eye reduction mode, which fires a series of pre-flashes, forcing your subject's pupils to constrict and allowing less light to enter.

selective focus: A technique that combines focusing on a specific spot with a wide open lens aperture in order to minimize depth of field. Selective focus helps the photographer direct the viewer's eye to exactly what he or she wants them to see.

sensor: The heart of the digital camera. There are currently three main types of digital camera sensors, although others may be on the way. The most common is the Charged Coupling Device (CCD) sensor. CCD sensors are far and away the most common sensor, and are found in the vast majority of digital cameras. A second type is the CMOS (pronounced see moss). These sensors are found in some DSLRs and some lower end point-and-shoot digital cameras. A third type is the Foveon sensor, currently found in just a couple of DSLRs manufactured by Sigma.

shutter: Once made of cloth (hence the term shutter curtain), now usually made of metal blades, the shutter blocks the film from light until the shutter button is pressed (or shutter tripped in photographer parlance), which causes the shutter curtain (or blades) to move out of the way, exposing the film or digital sensor to light.

shutter speed: A value (usually a fraction of a second) that indicates how long the shutter remains open.

SLR (single lens reflex): A camera uses only one lens as compared to a TLR or twin lens reflex, which uses two. The word *reflex* refers to moving a mirror out of the way to allow the image to be projected onto a piece of film, or in this case, digital sensor. The basic design of an SLR has the subject image traveling through the lens and then being bounced up into a series of mirrors that ultimately allow the photographer to view the subject through the camera's pentaprism. Once the shutter is tripped, a mirror that normally projects the image up to the pentaprism moves out of the way and the image is instead projected onto the film.

Souping: An archaic term old film photographers like to use because most people don't understand it. Souping is the processing of developing film in a conventional darkroom where the film is dunked in the *soup* (chemical developer) in order to convert the latent image into a permanent one. A related phrase *dip and dunk* refers to a method of developing where the reels of film are lifted on hangers from one canister of solution and dunked into the next.

tele-converter: An adapter that multiplies the focal length of a lens. Because tele-converters multiply focal length by inserting another glass element between the camera and lens, there is usually a loss of both light and image quality when you use one. (Top manufacturers' best quality tele-converters may minimize the loss of quality, however.) Tele-converters usually come in a one-stop loss version (with multiplier factor of anywhere from 1.4x to 1.7x), two-stop loss version (2x multiplier), and even a three-stop loss version (3x multiplier).

white balance: Unlike films, which are individually balanced for a specific kind of light, digital camera sensors can work under any kind of lighting, provided that the camera is given some sort of reference point for measuring the existing light. White balance is generally achieved by selecting something in a scene that represents white under particular lighting circumstances. The camera can then use that information to ensure accurate color for the entire scene. Virtually all digital cameras can balance color automatically (and do a good job of it too), but most offer user control of the process as well.

Zone system: A system of evaluating proper exposure pioneered by Ansel Adams. The Zone system is a method of precision exposure that combines image making and film processing to produce the most precise exposure possible for a given scene. The system is more common to large format film photography, but various adaptations have been created in order to apply some of the Zone system's principles to both 35mm film photography and even digital photography. One popular over-simplification of the Zone system is to shoot for the highlights and expose for the shadows, a process that works quite well for digital photography (although is not a true representation of the Zone system).

Digital Photography Techniques

This appendix offers a collection of tips and techniques that seemed to fit best together—as a collection. Some of these are ideas that most casual photographers never try, even though they may have seen them used or read about them in other photo books or magazines.

In some cases, such as using the blur and zoom technique creatively, the application is pretty limited. Although you can make an interesting image by zooming your lens during a long exposure, that kind of thing gets old if you do it all the time. Instead, it's something to try every now and then.

This appendix talks about some techniques photographers use to make images that look different than their typical work. These are the shots you try when you want to step outside your normal shooting habits, or when you just feel like doing something different. They're fun in small doses, but if you did them all the time, they'd get dull in a hurry.

Shooting into the Sun

Here's one your mother warned you about. If mom didn't say anything about taking pictures with your camera pointing into the sun, certainly your camera manual did (you did read the manual, didn't you?). If you didn't (go ahead, admit it) the wrapper the film came in told you not to shoot into the sun, right? (Let me guess. You didn't read that either.) Okay, let's face it, you heard the warning about not looking into a solar eclipse, it hurts when you look at the sun, so you just figured it wasn't a good idea.

In spite of all the warnings, shooting into the sun can produce exciting images—but only if done carefully and at the right time. For example, don't bother trying this technique when the sun is high in the sky and at its brightest. You'll simply waste your time, risk damaging your equipment, and worst of all, risk hurting your eyes.

Shooting into the sun when it is low in the sky provides a lot of advantages. For one, you can actually include it as part of a landscape or use it to create a dramatic silhouette of some distinctive foreground object (see Figure B-1).

Figure B-1: Sunrise over New York. Backlit by the early morning sun, buildings form silhouettes while the sun shows a rich orange glow.

© 2004 Dan Simon

Another benefit of trying this shot early in the morning or late in the day is that's when the sun is most colorful. The mid-day sun tends to be nearly white or pale yellow at best. When it's just above the horizon, it's closer to a rich orange or even a deep red. That's what you're looking for.

Keep in mind, you don't have a lot of time to work with here. The sun is really at its best for only about 15 or 20 minutes for this kind of thing. You're looking to shoot it when it's just above the horizon.

Even when it's low in the sky, you still can't stare at it very long without the light bothering your eyes, particularly if you're using a long focal length. Be prepared to think your shot through. Set things up as much as you can beforehand so you don't have to spend a lot of time staring through the viewfinder as you compose your shot.

Project: **Shooting into the Sun**

Here's a step-by-step approach to creating an image by shooting directly at the sun:

1. Visualize the image. Look at the scene and decide what elements you want to include and what you want to leave out. Decide what your primary foreground element will be.

2. Set your lens to its longest zoom setting and focus on your foreground object. Ideally, the sun won't even be in this composition, so your eyes won't be bothered by it. If it is, lower the lens a bit. All you're trying to do right now is focus on your foreground, so you don't need to see the sun. (You'll either need to focus manually or use your camera's focus lock feature to hold this focus point.)

3. Plan your exposure. Generally you need to underexpose your foreground by two f-stops or more to silhouette a subject. Frequently, the mere act of photographing a scene with the sun in it will cause that much underexposure because its brightness tends to mislead your light meter. If you want precise control, you can set your camera to manual, take a reading off your subject (while zoomed in tight on it) and then deliberately set an exposure two to three stops under the light meter's recommendation. Make sure you have a combination of shutter speed and aperture that will let you make a good photo. (You may need to use your camera's exposure lock feature to hold this reading if you're not shooting manually.)

4. Decide whether you want to make a horizontal or a vertical composition.

5. Take your shot. Now that you've set your exposure and focus, go ahead and back out your zoom until you get the composition you want. Trip the shutter and then turn away from the scene to give your eyes a break.

6. Examine the shot on your LCD screen to see if you got the results you wanted. If you didn't, study the screen to see what you want to do to improve your image.

Bracketing

Bracketing is a technique pros use when they absolutely have to get their exposure right. Simply put, you make one exposure at the recommended settings and then make additional exposures at one f-stop over exposure and one f-stop under exposure. This way if your light meter is off, one of the extra shots should be close enough to make things right.

The big problem with bracketing is that it's wasteful. You generate a couple of bad shots for every good one you make. Back in the days when you had to pay for your own film and processing, this could get pretty expensive, but it's not so much of a problem when you're using a digital camera.

Of course, this method might seem outdated in the digital age. After all, you can just look at your LCD screen, review the image (checking the histogram if necessary), and then make adjustments.

In general, you'd be right, unless you spend so much time evaluating the image on the LCD screen that you miss your next shot. (It happens.) Resorting to exposure bracketing (and many cameras offer a feature that brackets exposure automatically for you) can free you from that particular hassle.

There's a second reason for thinking about bracketing that has more to do with the limitations of the digital sensor than anything else. Say you're dealing with a very high-contrast scene. You know that no matter what you do, you're going to lose detail in either the highlights or the shadows.

If you shoot an image at one f-stop overexposure and one f-stop underexposure, you can merge the two photos together in Photoshop (or another image editing program that uses layers) and combine the highlight detail from the underexposed photo and the shadow detail from the overexposed photo for an image with a good range of tonal values. (Combining photos in this manner only works with subjects that aren't moving because you're taking two separate photos.) There is a more complicated way to combine images of moving subjects, provided that your camera offers the capability to capture images in RAW format. You can convert one image as a regular TIFF file and then convert the same image again as a linear TIFF file. This method gives you one file that shows good shadow detail but has highlights that are too bright and one file that has good highlight detail but shadows that are too dark. From this point on, the two approaches merge and you work the images the same way. The process is generally known as *increasing the dynamic range of a photograph*.

Here's how it works:

1. Open both files in Photoshop. Using the Move tool (found on the Photoshop Tools palette), drag the overexposed image over the darker photo. (Hint: If you hold down the Shift key while dragging the image, Photoshop positions the top image to fit exactly over the bottom image, creating a file with two layers. The darker image will be the bottom layer.

2. Click on the Layer bar to select the top layer. Then click on the Layer mask icon (the small rectangle with the white circle) on the bottom of the Layers palette to create a Layer mask.

3. Click on the Layer mask icon (the white rectangle next to the layer's name) on the top layer to activate the icon.

4. Chose the Gradient tool from Photoshop's Tools palette. (This is the sixth tool down on the right side of Photoshop's Tools palette. It shares space with the Paint Bucket tool.) Once you select the Gradient tool, go the Tool Options bar at the top of your screen and make sure you've picked a Linear gradient. (On the Tool options bar there is a series of five different gradient choices. The Linear gradient is the one on the far left. Click on it to make sure it is active.)

5. Place your cursor at the top of the photo, click, hold and then drag down until you reach a place on the image that isn't overexposed. Release the mouse button. You can now move the Opacity slider to adjust the effect of the Linear Gradient on your image.

Increasing the dynamic range can be a very useful technique for dealing with high-contrast lighting situations. Just be sure to plan your photography out a bit by bracketing your exposures (and using a tripod to keep the shots properly aligned) and it should work beautifully for you.

Creative Blur and Zoom

Sometimes the effort to be creative leads you to try some things that don't at first appear to make sense. That's a good thing. Stretching boundaries is how new forms of artistic expression are created. Because you can easily delete your mistakes, who cares if you try something that doesn't work?

Using blur for creative effect

Using blur to make a more interesting photograph is an example of stretching creative boundaries. Although you usually strive for the sharpest possible image, sometimes that works against you.

Say you want to create a dreamy or romantic image. In such cases too much detail gets in the way. Instead, you want to have enough of a recognizable shape to understand what the image portrays, but lacking the detail necessary to identify its individuality.

Or, perhaps you want to create an explosion of color without showing the specific subject. This is another time when using blur creatively can be helpful.

Finally, suppose you just want to show the speed of an event without documenting the people in it. One example would be to use a slow shutter speed while photographing a cyclist from a moving car. By shooting at a speed below 1/100th of a second while your car is pacing the cyclist, you keep the general impression of someone on a bicycle but blur both the cyclist and his surroundings to be unrecognizable. An advantage to shooting this way is that the only blur that appears is due to the slow shutter speed because the bicycle is moving at relatively the same speed as the car. The background, on the other hand, blurs both from the slow shutter speed and your car's motion. Taken to the next degree (with an even slower shutter speed) you can blur everything until you just recognize what's going on (see Figure B-2).

Zooming with the shutter open

Another way to create an unusual image is to set your camera for a long exposure (several seconds or more) and slowly zoom the camera lens while the shutter is open. This technique works best if your camera is set up on a tripod to keep it as steady as possible.

Figure B-2: A slow shutter speed, a pedaling cyclist, and a chase car combine to create an image of movement. Such photos offer an interesting contrast to typical bicycle pictures.
© 2004 Dan Simon

For best results, try to keep your zooming motion slow, steady, and even. It helps to practice this a couple of times before you actually make the image.

If you want to take a photograph while zooming with the shutter open, some good subject matter includes neon lights in the evening, nighttime light, starscapes, brightly colored flowers, and fireworks. You can also create interesting images this way when photographing people moving toward you.

Zooming with the shutter open works well when your subject has bright colors, which is why many of the subjects listed above work so well with this technique. Keep this option in mind as you look for possible subject matter.

Red-eye Reduction

Red-eye is the reddish color that appears in your subject's eyes when you take a picture using your camera's built in flash. The reason red-eye occurs is because the flash is positioned too closely to the lens. Light from the flash unit reflects back directly into the lens from the eye (human or animal). Reddish pigment in the human eye causes this reflection to be red (animals reflect either yellow or green depending on whether they're wild or domesticated).

The easiest ways to avoid red-eye involves either not using flash at all or mounting your flash higher and at a slight angle (the ways the pros do). These solutions may be impractical for many casual photographers. Besides, what do you do if you already have images you need to fix?

Photoshop simplifies cleaning up red-eye in a digital file.

 Project: **Removing red-eye from a digital photo**

This is a particularly useful technique for the parents of young children. As people get older, their eyes lose pigment, making them less susceptible to red-eye. The eyes of young children, on the other hand, contain lots of pigment. This is why your kids have glowing red eyes in photographs although you and your spouse look just fine (and you thought it was because your kids were possessed didn't you?).

1. Open the photo in Photoshop.

2. Choose Layer ⇨ New Layer to create a new layer.

3. Use the pull-down menu on the Layers palette to change the new layer's Blending Mode to Color.

4. Select the Brush tool from the Photoshop Tools palette. Check the tool options bar at the top of your screen to make sure you have a soft-edged brush selected. Set it to a size slightly smaller than the eyes you want to correct.

5. Set your Foreground Color to black. (The Foreground and Background color icons are located near the bottom of the Photoshop Tools palette). An easy way to set the Foreground Color is simply to type the letter *d*, which sets the Foreground and Background icons to the default colors of black and white, respectively. Make sure black is the upper color of the two. If it isn't, type the letter *x* to reverse them.

6. Paint on the red parts of the eye and the color will be neutralized. You can always use an Eraser (located on the Photoshop Tools palette) to erase parts of your correction if you've gone too far.

 If you have trouble working accurately because your subject's eyes are too small in the picture, then use the Magnifying Glass tool (located on the Photoshop Tools palette) to zoom in on the eyes and see them in better detail.

Digiscoping

Digiscoping is a method of photography that involves mating a point-and-shoot digital camera with a high-quality optical spotting scope to produce a super telephoto lens effect. It's popular with bird-watching enthusiasts, most of whom already own these expensive spotting scopes. By mating their camera and spotting scope to take pictures, they save the considerable expense of a DSLR system and long telephoto lens.

As you might expect, such a jury-rig is tricky and more difficult to use than simply buying the right camera setup in the first place. On the other hand, an equivalent camera setup would run several thousand dollars, so such a jury-rig is frequently worth the trouble.

Digiscoping can work surprisingly well for animal portraits (provided that the animal stays still enough) because getting the focus right can be a bit tricky when shooting animals. Amazingly, some of the best digiscopers have actually been able to make reasonably sharp photos of birds in flight with this technique. It's certainly not easy, though.

Most digiscope practitioners have resorted to creating their own adapters to hold the camera in place next to the spotting scope. Generally the homemade ones use aluminum cut in a T shape. The camera is fixed to the horizontal bar of the T (drill a hole in the bar large enough for a quarter inch screw and then you can mount the camera via its tripod socket). The long end of the T is then maneuvered to position the camera lens right up against the spotting scope eye piece. The scope is focused and then the lens is focused on the scope's view. One problem the adapter must solve is the photographer's need to move the camera away from the spotting scope so he can refocus the scope and then return the camera to its shooting position.

The Scopetronix company offers several different adapters under $200.

I'm not a digiscoping expert, so I'm going to refer you to a set of links at this book's companion web site (`www.wiley.com/compbooks/simon`) for more information on the subject. The digiscoping community is an active and accessible one, and includes a lively and helpful population at Yahoo Groups. If you're seriously considering giving digiscoping a try, visit the links and get to know members of the community.

One other thing, invest in a good tripod. It makes a world of difference in the quality of your photos.

Tools, Solutions, and Emergencies

Ever have one of those days?

You know, the type where everything seems to go wrong.

This appendix tries to help you out when you're having one of those days with your camera. I can't work miracles here, but I do have some advice earned the hard way: through years of taking photographs with all kinds of equipment in all kinds of weather.

First, I look at using your LCD finder to help you check your images out in the field (while there's still time to do something about it) and then I look at things you can try when emergencies happen.

Using Your LCD Screen to Become a Better Photographer

LCD screens are such a handy device for digital cameras that I strongly recommend making sure your camera has one. Some low-cost cameras don't, but this eliminates one of the most useful features a digital camera can offer.

The immediate feedback that LCD screens offer is an incredibly valuable learning tool, one that makes improving your photographic skills a lot easier than it was during the days when photographers relied on a film camera.

In those days, a photographer would try a photographic technique (such as zooming with the shutter open) and then wait a few days for her images to be processed before having a chance to see how her effort worked out. If her photos didn't come out, she would have to try again, then wait a few more days to see how her effort worked out. If it didn't...

Now, you can try a shot, review the LCD screen and have a good idea immediately whether it worked or not. If it didn't, you just try again. This is a hugely important advantage of digital cameras over their film counterparts. (In fact, it may be the biggest advantage of all!)

There's an art to reading your LCD screen, however. These helpful tools have their shortcomings and can't be relied on for everything. Take a look at some of the things they do well and some of the things they don't.

Feedback

Did you get it right? What does your shot look like?

Your LCD screen is the first place you turn after taking a shot so you can see how it turned out (professional photographers call this "chimping"). The LCD can be very helpful for showing things like composition and overall exposure. It can also give you a rough, but somewhat unreliable, guide as to whether your image is in focus or not.

Use your LCD screen to make sure you haven't chopped off anyone's head or inadvertently shifted the camera as you pressed the shutter button. It's also good to check and make sure the camera was held level when you made the exposure.

It's also nice to see a two-dimensional representation of the three-dimensional scene you've just photographed. Still photography is about translating the physical world into a flat image space, and it's difficult to visualize that transition. Often, a spectacular scene doesn't come across nearly as well when reduced to two dimensions. Your LCD screen can let you know when that's the case.

Drawbacks

LCD screens aren't good for letting you know whether or not your image's focus is razor sharp. Often, a photo may look sharp when you view it on the screen, only to be unacceptably soft when you view it on a larger computer monitor.

When in doubt about an image's sharpness, don't rely on the LCD screen, instead take another photo (or two) to try to guarantee the sharpest possible focus. Remember shutter speed concerns and how they affect apparent image sharpness. This is probably a good time to double check your shutter speed to make sure it's fast enough to avoid blur from camera shake.

Another drawback is the tiny size of many LCD screens. This is a particular hassle for those photographers with middle-aged eyes. Sadly, the only advice I can offer here is to invest in a pair of reading glasses to keep in your camera bag.

Using Your LCD Screen for Exposure Evaluation

One of the most useful things your LCD screen can do is help you evaluate just how effective your exposure is. This is a pretty important benefit when you figure that exact exposure is more important when you're shooting with a digital camera than it is when you're shooting with negative film.

Some cameras offer a feature that causes overexposed highlights to flash on the LCD screen, letting you know you've lost highlight detail in those areas. Such a feature is incredibly valuable because it can quickly let you know you've got a problem. Often, this feature needs to be activated before you can use it, so check your camera's manual for how to use this feature. If your camera doesn't offer such a warning, then plan on examining the LCD screen more closely. You should be able to recognize detail even in the white areas of the photograph. If you can't, then it's a good bet your shot is overexposed. Try another photo at a lesser exposure to see if you can pull in detail in the highlight areas. Remember, it's better to underexpose shadow areas than it is to overexpose highlights, so if you have to choose between the two, underexpose a little.

When evaluating images from your LCD screen, sometimes it's necessary to switch from viewing mode to display mode, or to change your display setting (depending on the type of camera you own) to access important features. Some cameras will show highlight problems only from the display mode. If yours is one of these, you'll have to switch back and forth between viewing mode and display mode.

Some cameras offer a histogram feature. This is a graph that shows the distribution of pixels throughout an image's exposure range. If your concentration of pixels is shifted too far one way or another (without running the full length of the graph), your shot is over- or underexposed. Histograms are a valuable tool for objectively judging exposure accuracy.

Using Your LCD Screen as a Viewfinder

Many point-and-shoot digital cameras give you the option of using your LCD screen as a viewfinder (a feature not available in DSLRs). This feature is very handy for close-up photography because it gives you some space between you and your subject (very useful with insects for instance). It's also nice if you're more comfortable composing an image this way (or if more than one person is judging the composition).

Another nice way to use your LCD finder is for high- and low-angle photography because you can reach up or down and still see what you're doing and how your composition is shaping up. This is particularly helpful if your camera has a viewfinder that can move around independent of the direction the camera is pointing. (Several of the Nikon Coolpix and Canon G series offer this feature in one form or another.)

Fixing Your Camera When It Stops Working

Sooner or later it happens. You're cruising along, taking pictures when your camera just stops working. Or, you turn it on after not using it for a while and nothing happens. Your camera's broken. Or is it?

I'm not a camera repairman. I don't even play one on TV. That hasn't stopped me from fixing a lot of cameras over the years.

Often, the problem is something as simple as a dead battery, or a new set of batteries has been installed upside down (this happens a lot).

If your camera stops working, here's a list of quick fixes you can try. If these don't work, then maybe you can start to panic.

✦ Make sure your batteries are installed right side up (this can be harder than you think because the proper orientation isn't always well marked.)

✦ Make sure your batteries are making a good connection with the camera's contacts. Sometimes a thin film of corrosion builds up on battery contacts and interferes with the flow of power from the battery to the camera. Fortunately, this is pretty easy to fix. Take a pencil that has a healthy bit of eraser left and rub on both the battery's contacts and the camera's contacts to clean them off enough to permit a good connection.

✦ Try resetting the camera. Turn it off, pull the batteries and memory card and let the camera sit for a minute. Re-insert the memory card and batteries (making sure they're oriented properly) and try powering up the camera again. (Some cameras even offer a reset button. If yours does, follow the owner's manual on how to use it.)

✦ If you have a DSLR and the problem occurs when you're changing lenses, try using a different lens. Changing lenses can be a real problem if you use third-party optics and/or flash units (lenses or flash units made by a manufacturer other than the one who made your camera). Older lenses may not work with the latest DSLRs, causing the camera to shut down. Go back to a lens you know works on your camera (or remove the flash unit) and reset your camera. If your camera starts working as usual, then you need to return the lens or flash to the company that made it. The original manufacturer will usually re-chip the device (if it's possible) for free (check on this before sending it in). It isn't unusual for third-party optics not to work on all cameras. I have at least one lens and a couple of flash units that work on Lisa's Canon EOS D30 that cause my Canon EOS 1D to shut down and require a reset to get working again. I just don't use those items with my camera.

✦ Panic. Well, take it to the nearest camera store, or, if it's still under warranty, send it back to the manufacturer.

Sometimes the problem is obvious. You've dropped your camera, or even worse, you've dropped your camera into water. At this point you've got a serious problem. What you do next may help you save your photographic gear.

What to do if your camera gets wet

Turn it off! Turn it off! Turn it off! The very worst thing that can happen is for your camera to get wet while it's turned on.

Now that you've shut down power to the camera, the first thing to consider is how wet it got.

If you get caught in a rainstorm and your camera is only lightly sprinkled, just leave it powered down long enough for any moisture that may have gotten inside to evaporate.

For future planning, you can fashion a simple but effective camera raincoat out of a plastic sandwich bag and some artist's or masking tape. Save some packets of desiccant and keep them inside too, so they'll help dry out any moisture that gets inside the raincoat.

Although your camera may be able to withstand a little bit of moisture, irreparable damage may occur if it gets fully immersed (and isn't an underwater camera).

If the unthinkable happens, turn off your camera as soon as you remove it from the water. (Water and power flowing together are not good.) Immediately yank the batteries and media and shake out as much water as you can from these areas.

 If your camera is immersed in salt water, you should immediately place it in a bucket of fresh water before allowing it to dry. If salt water is allowed to dry in the camera, a salt sludge ends up coating and ruining your camera's electronics. It's better to keep the camera immersed than it is to let it dry out if sea water is the culprit.

If you have a hair dryer handy (and don't forget those wall-mounted hand dryers in many public restrooms), blow hot dry air into the camera for a few minutes. (**Only for fresh water.** *Do not do this for salt water!!!* See the preceding Tip about dunking the camera in fresh water before the salt can dry in the camera.)

At this point, it's best to talk to your camera's manufacturer or to take the camera to a repair shop and have them take a look at it. Don't try powering it back up before then. If your camera was turned off when it fell in the water, maybe there's a chance of saving it. If it was turned on, there is little hope of repair. Even if your camera can be fixed, repairs might be costlier than a new camera, and a repaired camera likely wouldn't last as long as a new one.

 If you drop an expensive DSLR into the water, it's certainly worth the effort to have it repaired—especially if it was turned off when it went into the water.

Saving data from a damaged or corrupted memory card

It's frequently possible to retrieve data from a damaged or corrupted memory card. I can't claim to be an expert on this because I've never had a card go bad on me (and I shoot a lot), but it certainly happens.

If you get a corrupted memory message from your camera and need to preserve any images that may be on the card, do not let your camera reformat the memory card. In fact, get it out of the camera immediately.

Once you get home (or wherever you process your images), download a program called Photo Rescue (a link is available at this book's companion web site at www.wiley.com/compbooks/simon). If card problems are a major concern for you, this $29 program is probably your best choice. Photo Rescue has a reputation for being accurate (if it shows you an image, you can expect to recover it) and better at recognizing different photo file formats than other data rescue programs. A data rescue program that's great at normal file recovery may not recognize many photographic file formats and be useless for recovering damaged images.

Summary

Digital cameras offer tools film cameras can't match (unless you add very expensive Polaroid backs) when it comes to their ability to let the photographer review her images. By taking advantage of a digital camera's image reviewing capabilities, you can do much to become a better photographer. Develop the habit of quickly reviewing your images and asking yourself if you could have done anything better (gotten in closer, removed background distractions, used flash for fill). Your LCD screen gives you a second chance to get your image right.

Yet as wonderful as digital cameras are, problems still occur and things do go wrong. Because the expected lifespan of digital cameras is much shorter than their film counterparts, it's not surprising that they may suffer failures earlier than you expect. Don't panic, though. Often, the failure is caused by something as simple as the batteries being put in upside down (you won't believe how often this happens). Do some simple troubleshooting before you give up on your gear and take it to the repair shop.

And remember, water and electronics don't mix. If you dunk your camera only heroic measures may save it. If you're using a modestly priced digital point-and-shoot, you're better off shopping for a replacement than trying to get it fixed. If you've dunked a DSLR, it may be worth the hassle, but try to talk to the camera maker before you decide.

What's New in Photoshop

As the power of digital photography grows, so does the need for more sophisticated tools. It seems like no sooner than the photographic community comes up with a new method of solving a problem using a series of complex steps in Photoshop, the next new version of the program comes out, complete with a simple filter or tool to make that complex solution unnecessary.

A good example are the complicated work-arounds photographers developed to deal with the limitations of editing 16-bit files in earlier versions of the program. Because it was impossible to make selections in a 16-bit file, skilled Photoshop users would have to create a duplicate file, convert it to an 8-bit image and then make the selection in this new file. You could then save the selection, and *voila*, have it available to use in your 16-bit file. It was effective, but not elegant.

In Photoshop CS, Adobe has greatly increased the program's ability to work with 16-bit files, making many established work-arounds unnecessary.

The image-editing powerhouse's very capable little brother—Photoshop Elements—hasn't been left behind either. The inexpensive introduction to the world of image editing has a host of new features designed to make life easier for the budding digital darkroom worker.

In this appendix, I examine some of the changes Adobe has packed into these upgrades and show how they can help you.

Photoshop's New Features

There are several primary audiences for a program such as Photoshop. Digital imaging specialists can be photographers, graphic artists, or digital artists. Each group has its own needs and uses for image editing software.

Because this is a book on digital photography, I'm mainly concerned with how Photoshop CS can help photographers in the picture-making process. New tools that enable you to create photo-impressionistic art or psychedelic buttons for web sites are interesting, but they're not much of a motivation to upgrade.

This new version of the program offers plenty of good reasons to move on up. Adobe has created a nifty package of new tools for digital photographers. If you're serious about digital photography and getting the best out of your images in the digital darkroom, this upgrade is worth the money.

Improved image management

Photoshop CS offers several new tools to make managing your images easier. Whether it's finding a specific image through the improved File Browser, making sure a color theme stays consistent through a series of images, or understanding the effect of changes to an image through a real-time histogram palette, this upgrade boosts your knowledge of an image much faster than its predecessor.

The new File Browser

Adobe first introduced the File Browser in version 7.0 of the program. Although not quite as spiffy as stand alone image management programs such as Extensis Portfolio, or the offerings from iView or ACDsee, the File Browser did make a helpful addition to the program.

Digital cameras are terrific for providing the photographer with unparalleled creative freedom. No longer confined by worries about film and processing costs, digital shooters can explore the photographic possibilities offered by a new scene or model.

The downside to this capability is you generate significantly larger collections of images to weed through once you get back home. It doesn't do you a lot of good to take a great photo and then discover you can't find the shot because it's buried amongst a thousand other pictures.

Fortunately, Photoshop's File Browser has been beefed up considerably in this new upgrade. The first version of the File Browser allowed you to sort images in any of a number of different ways, but if you were looking for a specific image, you were on your own. The new version of the browser makes it possible to search and edit via *metadata* (the information your camera records when you take the image such as shutter speed, aperture and ISO settings, also referred to as *EXIF*, or external information.) and by keywords. Another nice feature inside the new File Browser is the capability to rotate images instead of just their thumbnail representation. Adobe has also linked the File Browser to the program's powerful Batch Processing automations. You can select files via the File Browser and then instruct the program to run a Batch command to process the images. Just some of the things you can do with this feature include producing your own Contact Sheets (sheets of thumbnail images), create Web Photo Galleries, and arrange multiple images for printing on the same sheet of paper.

Match Color command

This new feature is a boon for studio photographers who can use it to quickly match the color scheme of one image to that of another. This is particularly useful when you're working with a series of images that are going to run together in an advertisement or brochure and need the color schemes to match. It won't work miracles, however. You can't necessarily take two images from very different shooting conditions and expect Photoshop to make them look like they were shot at the same place and time. What you can expect is for the Match Color command to do a good job of fixing an image when a sudden shadow from a cloud throws off your color balance or some similar event occurs.

Histogram palette

Unlike the Histogram palette you could access in Photoshop 7.0, this one reacts to the edits you're making while you make them. This dynamic update capability makes it possible to more precisely see the impact of edits on your image file while there's still time to hit the undo key.

Track your editing history

Although this functionality doesn't save your history (which will be a nifty feature whenever Adobe ever manages to include it in Photoshop), it does keep a record of the steps you take in Photoshop.

Ever spend a lot of time tweaking an image to get it just right, then wonder how you would ever re-create the process? (Me too.) Well, this solves that problem. Photoshop can now track every little step you make to get that photo just right. You can also chose just how detailed you want that information to be.

Image editing features

Photoshop CS also improves or adds several important image editing capabilities. Some of these features are tweaks to already existing abilities (such as improvements in the program's ability to process 16-bit image files), whereas others are completely new tools (such as the Shadow/Highlight Correction and Color filters.)

Improved 16-bit editing capability

More, more, more. That's what Photoshop CS lets you do when it comes to processing 16-bit images. CS supports lots more tools including selections, layers, text, and more. For most image editing, it's now possible to process a 16-bit image from start to finish as a 16-bit file, thus preserving as much image information as possible.

Camera RAW file conversion

Adobe now includes its own RAW conversion program (located under the File ⇨ Import ⇨ RAW menu). This addition to Photoshop was introduced after Photoshop 7.0 came out and sold as a $99 plug-in. It's now included in CS at no extra cost and recognizes RAW files from a wide variety of digital cameras. The converter recognizes files from more than 50 different digital cameras made by almost a dozen different manufacturers.

Shadow/Highlight command

This is a completely new tool that improves upon the Fill Flash tool found in Photoshop Elements. You can access the Shadow/Highlight command at File ⇨ Image ⇨ Adjustments ⇨ More Options. It represents an alternative to multi-step editing techniques such as Contrast Masking (see Chapter 15) and others that tweak highlight and shadow values. Although still a destructive edit (you change original pixel values), this tool gives you a lot of control over how it's applied (see Figure D-1).

Figure D-1: The Photoshop CS Shadow/Highlight command benefits most digital camera users because it can help recover highlight and shadow detail from a photo.
© 2004 Dan Simon

Photo Filters

Here Adobe adds the capability to replicate some of the filters (such as warming and cooling filters) photographers used to (and frequently still do) place between the lens and their subject matter (see Figure D-2). Although it's been possible to buy third party (other software makers) offerings, or simulate these effects yourself, Adobe's inclusion into the basic software program is a nice, useful addition. It may not be worth the price of the upgrade alone, but it makes life easier for many photographers. Choose Image ⇨ Adjustments ⇨ Color Filters to find these tools.

Figure D-2: Photo Filters save the Photoshop user from having to recreate these effects manually, giving photographers another useful tool in the new version of the program.
© 2004 Dan Simon

Lens Blur

The capability to simulate lens blur is a boon for photographers using point-and-shoot digital cameras with small maximum apertures. Normally, when a photographer wants to isolate her subject from a distracting background, she chooses a telephoto focal length and large maximum aperture to throw the background as out of focus as possible. Unfortunately, many of today's point-and-shoot digital cameras don't offer such a large aperture at their telephoto ends, resulting in greater depth of field than desirable for such an image.

Photographers finding themselves in such a predicament (having too sharp a background) can turn to the new Lens Blur tool for easy, but decent results.

Select Filter ➪ Blur ➪ Lens Blur to access the Lens Blur tool. Using this tool, you can apply a selective blur to the background without affecting your main subject.

Filter Gallery

The Filter Gallery, found by choosing File ➪ Filters ➪ Filter Gallery, is another nifty new feature in Photoshop CS. It allows you to stack multiple filters and preview the changes on a nice, large preview window. Even better, you can compare different filter effects and tweak the individual filter effects as you create filter stacks. You can also rearrange filters or apply a filter multiple times. All this makes experimenting with filters a lot easier.

What's New in Photoshop Elements 2.0

Although it may get called Photoshop's little brother, Photoshop Elements 2.0 is the only image editing program many hobbyists need. Version 2.0 tweaks an already useful application, making it even better for those who just need to make simple fixes to their images.

Photoshop Elements 2.0 offers a number of improvements to existing features including a spruced up File Browser (which now accepts EXIF data), more presets for existing tools, additional Layer Styles to those already available in the first version, and some new brush presets as well.

Adobe has added almost a dozen new features to Photoshop Elements 2.0, ranging from new tools to an improved help function. Here's a look at a few of the more interesting ones:

✦ **Quick Fix Dialog:** Now you can access a host of image correction tools from just one source. Think of the Quick Fix Dialog as one-stop shopping for image editing purposes. The Quick Fix Dialog gives you access to tools that can make it easy to adjust brightness and contrast, make color corrections, sharpen your images, and more. It gives you a convenient way to handle your basic image processing all from one dialog box.

✦ **Selection Brush:** This new tool allows you to paint selections. Switch to Mask Mode and you can even see a color overlay marking your selection area. Another nice feature of this addition is that you can save and retrieve selections.

✦ **How To palette:** This palette provides tips and quick help to make things easier for beginning users.

Summary

Photoshop CS has a lot to offer the serious photo enthusiast and represents a significant upgrade to Adobe's category-leading program.

Most significant is the program's capability to handle more of the image processing process while your photo is still in16-bit format. For many workflows, it's now possible to stay in 16-bit format from start to finish. You can then make a copy of your file in 8-bit format for printing or web use, and make your final sharpening tweaks and you're done.

The program has added many other helpful capabilities. The new File Browser's capability to search through files for keywords is a big help for many photographers and the added filters and filter gallery provide many new creative possibilities.

Although Photoshop Elements 2.0's improvements aren't quite as significant as those found in Photoshop CS, Adobe has added some nice improvements to its entry-level photo-editing software. Photoshop Elements is a great choice for the hobbyist who doesn't need all of Photoshop CS's power. The program also makes a great stepping stone to Adobe's flagship image editor. When the time comes to move on up, you'll feel like you're already on very familiar ground.

Index

Symbols & Numbers

16-bit file, 299
16-bit images, 256
35mm equivalents, 46
3D artwork photographing steps, 386
8-bit file, 299
8-bit images, 256

A

AA batteries for
    insurance photography, 360
    travel photography, 219
accessory flash for
    field research photography, 368
    sports photography, 143
accessory flash unit, 98
action
    defined, 311
    Photoshop action setting, 311
    Photoshop batch processing action, 313
action capturing in sports photography,
    138
Adjustment layer for JPEG workflow, 292
Adjustment layer mask, 292
adjustment layers, 271
adventure racing photography, 147
aerial photography challenges
    Plexiglass windows, 222
    transportation preparation, 222
    vibration, 222
aerial photography tips, 224
airplane shooting. *See* aerial photography
alkaline AAs, 16
analogous colors, 383
angle of view, 345, 348
aperture
    defined, 20, 23
    setting aspects, 59, 63
aperture priority (AV), 24
aperture priority mode (AV), for exposure setting,
    22
aperture setting for
    fireworks photography, 427
    large product photography, 412
    small product photography, 410
aperture size, determining, 64
aquarium photography considerations
    flash, 201
    ISO settings, 201
    polarizing filter, use of, 201
archery photography, 146
architectural photography using
    DSLR cameras, 8

point-and-shoot cameras, 8
tripod, 29
archival storage
    CDs, 314–315
    DVDs, 314–315
    floppy disks, 314–315
    hard drives, 314
    magnetic tapes, 314–315
archiving methods for
    heavy shooters, 318
    light shooters, 315
    medium shooters, 317
artist and graphic artist's photography checklist,
    375
artist and graphic artist's photography
    considerations
    lighting set up, 376
    mini studio setting, 378
    neatness factor, 376
    photography-friendly background, 376
    props using, 376
artist photography
    lighting considerations, 385
    of 3D artwork, 386
    of painting, 385
auto racing photography of
    hot rod, funny car auto racing event, 149
    NASCAR-style auto racing event, 148
    small track auto racing event, 148
autofocusing in sports photography, 138, 140
automobile lights photography considerations
    ISO settings, 428
    reflection factor, 429
    shutter speed, 428
automobile photography checklist, 345
automobile photography, considerations
    angle of view, 345, 348
    automobile shot, composing of, 348
    depth of field, 345, 349
    focal length, 345, 349
    polarizing filters, use of, 345–346
    reflections and glare, dealing with, 346
    shoot planning, 345
    wide-angle lens, use of, 349
awards ceremonies, photographing
    challenges, 392
    checklist, 392

B

back lighting, 24, 98
backdrop for
    for portrait, 120
    plants and flowers photography, 186

Continued

Continued

Continued

magine everything you want to do with your digital media all in one place. iView MediaPro is an award-winning media management, presentation, editing, publishing, and cataloging application. It offers a rich nd intuitive feature-set essential for creative professionals and digital photographers.

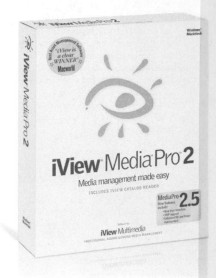

:very iView MediaPro user can import directly rom a digital camera; retouch images; generate veb galleries, movie presentations, contact heets, and high-quality prints; or simply organ-ze, locate, back up, and burn media quickly and :asily.

f you're an advanced user, you can incorporate View MediaPro into your workflow to organize, ag, convert, and repurpose media, and to auto-nate tasks. iView MediaPro also lets you create nultigrid slide shows with background sounds nd global and individual settings.

Here are some of the tasks you can handle quickly and efficiently with iView MediaPro:

Importing
- Over 100 file formats
- Catalog directly from digital cameras, disks, CD-ROM, or the Web
- Keep media up to date with Folder Watching

Organizing
- Create media catalogs
- Batch tag media with text and voice a nnotations for quick search and retrieval
- Sync annotations using industry standards: IPTC, XMP, EXIF, and QuickTime

Editing
- Correct images with professional tools
- Rename, convert, and color-manage media in single or batch mode, with version control

Publishing
- Create multi-grid QuickTime slide shows
- Create customized Web galleries
- Make high-quality PDF composites, contact sheets, and printouts of any size and layout

Archiving
- Store, back up, or burn media and catalogs
- Export catalogs as text, XML, or HTML
- Incorporate into any workflow with full AppleScript support

Free Catalog Reader
- Create royalty-free, cross-platform CD-ROM catalogs
- Distribute and share your iView catalogs with others